Lecture Notes in Computer Science   1565

Edited by G. Goos, J. Hartmanis and J. van Leeuwen

T0217352

Springer

Berlin
Heidelberg
New York
Barcelona
Hong Kong
London
Milan
Paris
Singapore
Tokyo

Peter P. Chen   Jacky Akoka
Hannu Kangassalo   Bernhard Thalheim (Eds.)

Conceptual Modeling

Current Issues and Future Directions

 Springer

Volume Editors

Peter P. Chen
Department of Computer Science, Louisiana State University
298 Coates Hall, Baton Rouge, LA 70803, USA
E-mail: chen@bit.csr.lsu.edu

Jacky Akoka
Ecole Supérieure des Sciences Economiques et Commerciales (ESSEC)
Avenue Bernard Hirsch, BP 105, F-95021 Cergy, France
E-mail: akoka@cnam.fr

Hannu Kangassalo
Department of Computer Science, University of Tampere
P.O. Box 607, FIN-33101 Tampere, Finland
E-mail: hk@cs.uta.fi

Bernhard Thalheim
Department of Computer Science, Brandenburg University of Technology
P.O. Box 10 13 44, D-03013 Cottbus, Germany
E-mail: thalheim@informatik.tu-cottbus.de

Cataloging-in-Publication data applied for

Die Deutsche Bibliothek - CIP-Einheitsaufnahme

Conceptual modeling : current issues and future directions / Peter
Chen ... (ed.). - Berlin ; Heidelberg ; New York ; Barcelona ; Hong
Kong ; London ; Milan ; Paris ; Singapore ; Tokyo : Springer, 1999
 (Lecture notes in computer science ; 1565)
 ISBN 3-540-65926-9

CR Subject Classification (1998): H.2, H.4, F.1.3, F.4.1, I.2.4, H.1, J.1

ISSN 0302-9743
ISBN 3-540-65926-9 Springer-Verlag Berlin Heidelberg New York

© Springer-Verlag Berlin Heidelberg 1999
Printed in Germany

Typesetting: Camera-ready by author
SPIN 10702963   06/3142 – 5 4 3 2 1 0   Printed on acid-free paper

Preface

This volume contains a collection of selected papers presented at the Symposium on Conceptual Modeling, which was held in Los Angeles, California, on December 2, 1997, immediately before the 16th International Conference on Conceptual Modeling (ER'97), which was held at UCLA. A total of eighteen papers were selected for inclusion in this volume. These papers are written by experts in the conceptual modeling area and represent the most current thinking of these experts.

This volume also contains the summaries of three workshops that were held on 6-7 December 1997, immediately after the ER'97 conference at UCLA. The topics of these three workshops are:

- Behavioral Modeling
- Conceptual Modeling in Multimedia Information Seeking
- What Is the Role of Cognition in Conceptual Modeling?

Since these topics are not only very important but also very timely, we think it is appropriate to include the summary of these three workshops in this volume. Those readers interested in further investigating topics related to the three workshops can either look up the individual paper published on the Web or contact the authors directly.

The summary paper by Chen at the beginning of this volume also includes the summary of several interesting speeches at the Symposium.

There are many people to thank in the organization of the Symposium. First, we would like to acknowledge several key members of the organizing committee, who did not have time to participate in the editing of this volume: Ray Liuzzi (US AFRL), Mark Foresti (US AFRL), Mike McNeil (BBN Technologies), Sham Navathe (Georgia Tech), and Leah Wong (US Navy). We also would like to thank the Conference Chair, Wesley Chu (UCLA), and the Program Co-Chairs, Dave Embley (BYU) and Bob Goldstein (UBC) of the ER'97 Conference for their support. Finally, we would like to express our gratitude to Günter Millahn (TU Cottbus), and Leah Wong (again) for their valuable help in preparing this volume.

P. P. Chen,
J. Akoka,
H. Kangassalo,
B. Thalheim

Table of Contents

Summary of Three Workshops

Current Issues of Conceptual Modeling:
A Summary of Selective Active Research Topics

Peter P. Chen

Computer Science Department
Louisiana State University
Baton Rouge, LA 70803, USA

Abstract. This is a summary of the individual papers and workshop summaries collected in this volume ("Current Issues of Conceptual Modeling," edited by P. P. Chen, J. Akoka, H, Kangassalo, and B. Thalheim, Springer-Verlag, 1999, Lecture Notes in Computer Sciences, No. 1565).

Introduction

The first part of this paper is a summary of the individual papers, in alphabetical order of the first author of each paper. The second part of this paper is a summary of three workshops. The third part is a summary of several interesting speeches given at the Symposium. The fourth part is a short discussion of the special paper focusing on the future directions of conceptual modeling.

I. Summary of Papers

The Paper by Dr. Jacob Akoka: "Conceptual Design of Parellel Systems"

Akoka proposes a parallel object-oriented design methodology called POOD, which integrates both object orientation and parallelism. Both the object-orientation and parallelism are discussed from the conceptual modeling point of view. Parallelism is seen as a source of structural simplicity in the conceptual design phase.

He proposes to model a system as objects, their relationships, events, and messages. The underlying model is represented as a collection of concurrently executable objects. The interactions among the components of the parallel system are represented as message transmissions among objects. The messages are divided into three types: current, past, and future messages. In the "past" message, the receiver did not wait for the message. In the "now" message, the sender waits for the receipt of the message.

P.P. Chen et al. (Eds.): Conceptual Modeling, LNCS 1565, pp. IX-XXIV, 1999.

He also discusses the parallelism and cardinalities. He thinks that using integrity constraints is another way to model parallelism into objects instead of using messaging. Therefore, he proposes to use the integrity constraints as another way to build parallelism.

In short, he proposes a design method, claimed to be an adequate formalism in which various concurrent activities, interactions between objects, and inheritance mechanism are expressed naturally. In the paper, several constructs are presented to show how the POOD design method can take into account different types of parallelism.

The Paper by Barry Boehm and Dan Port: "Conceptual Modeling Challenges for Model-Based Architecting and Software Engineering (MBASE)"

Boehm and Port discuss the challenges of conceptual modeling in the Model-based Architecting and Software Engineering (MBASE) approach. They describe the interactions of several models essential in software engineering:

- Cost model
- Schedule model
- Property model
- Product model
- Process model
- Success model.

They think the interactions among these models depend on different situations. In some cases, a cost and schedule property model would be used for the evaluation and analysis of the consistency of the system's product, process, and success models. In other cases, the success model would make a process model or a product model the primary driver for model integration, and so on.

In conclusion, the authors state that the two of the key challenges of the MBASE approach are:

- The choice of the various conceptual models needed to represent and reason about a project's success, product, processes, and property characteristics.
- The integration of these models.

The Paper by Silvana Castano and Valeria De Antonellis: "Deriving Global Conceptual Views from Multiple Information Sources"

Castano and De Antonellis proposes a Schema Analysis Technique to build a semantic dictionary based on three steps:

1. Extraction of information from the source schema.
2. Derivation of global conceptual view.
3. To build a semantic dictionary.

In their paper, they also explain several new terms:

- Thesaurus of Terminological Relationships: SYN (synonym -of) Synonymy definition mainly relies on domain knowledge. The broader terms and narrower terms are extracted from the generalization hierarchies defined in the source schemas.
- Object with affinity: The name affinity of two objects is the measure of the affinity of their names in the thesaurus.

The Paper by Peter P. Chen: "From Ancient Egyptian Language to Future Conceptual Modeling"

Chen continued his pursuit of the relationships between natural languages and conceptual modeling techniques such as ERD technique. He has studied the relationships between English grammar and sentence structures and ERD. He has also studied the relationships between Chinese character construction and the general conceptual modeling principles. In this paper, he changes his focus to ancient Egyptian language. He finds that the construction methods of Egyptian hieroglyphs also follow some of the general conceptual modeling principles although not completely the same as the construction methods of Chinese characters. At the end of his paper, he outlined many possible directions for extensions and application of his research result.

The Paper by Lois Delcambre: "Breaking the Database out of the Box: Models for Superimposed Information"

Delcambre proposes to use the Structure Map (an ERD) as a guide in conceptual modeling. She proposes a new type of entities called "echoes, " which are linked to "conventional" entities. There are also "relationship echoes." The underlying data in these "echoes" entities is not a database, but paper.

She also defines other special terminology and concepts:

- Vertical Information Management (VIM): A facility extracting entities and relationships derived from the underlying data. VIM refers to the problem of trying to move (potentially low-level, detailed) information upwards to decision makers at various levels in an organization. A possible question that can be considered for VIM might be: what is the state dropout level for high school students? VIM extracts relevant information from existing information present in various databases. The extract information is usually much simpler than the original information.
- Structured Maps: A special map based on work in the SGML community to define multi-document glossaries, thesauri, and indices using Topic Navigational Maps. The Structured map allows the situation that each entity type may have one or more facets defined. Each "facet" is like a multi-valued attribute, where the attribute values are references to underlying information elements.

In conclusion, she proposes to superimpose a new model over underlying information sources and to improve the access to underlying information.

The Paper by Antonio Furtado: "Narratives and Temporal Databases: An Interdisciplinary Perspective"

Furtado advocates the use of specification as the executable language. He suggests the following basic principles:
- Database facts as predicates
- Database actions as operations
   - Operations in the application domain: State transition by executing programs
   - Formal specification of operations in terms of predicates involved.
- Temporal databases: state descriptions plus log.

He presents a "plot," which provides several examples of typical operations:
1. Open (client: Beta)
2. Hire (employee, john; client: Beta)
3. Train.

He believes that temporal databases represent narratives. In order to do a good analysis and design of a temporal database, we need to go through an interdisciplinary approach:
a) Computational linguistics
b) Cognitive science
c) Literary theories (narratology).

In addition, he suggests that we use the conduit metaphor in analysis and design: sender -message – reader. Furthermore, we should use these concepts in more details: author, language, text, reader, context, time, critic, vehicle.

He also suggests a sample of points for us to consider:
- Socio-economic contexts, historical circumstance, status, gender, practices, "myths," and deconstruction.
- "language speaks us," two axes; syntagmatic and paradigmatic, denotation and connotations
- Propp's functions, motifs, mental altitude, genre, nuclei and catalysts, closure, inter-textuality.
- authors & characters, many-voiced (hetero-glossia), inconsistencies, goals in conflict or cooperation
- Multiple readings, misreading (misconceptions and mis-constructs), modeling the readers, effect, open text, the (helpful) critic.
- New ways of reading: semi-structured data, full e-texts, links, hypermedia technology, active DB's.

In conclusion, he suggests we look into plots of continuing narratives. He thinks that language analysis is a good way for conceptual modeling. He thinks CASE tools using language analysis will be useful but no tools with this capability are in the commercial market now.

The Paper by Georges Gardarin and Fei Sha: " Using Conceptual Modeling and Intelligent Agents to Integrate Semi-structured Documents in Federal Databases"

Gardarin and Sha discuss the integration of hypermedia documents within a federated database system called IRO-DB. They propose the use of conceptual modeling coupled with intelligent agents to integrate semi-structured files within the query process.

The authors discuss several issues related to the integration of semi-structured data in a federated database:

- Choice of a data model for representing semi-structured data
- Choice of a query language for interrogating semi-structured data
- Storage and query processing strategy for semi-structured data.

In order to integrate various semi-structured documents, the authors describe a conceptual model for documents and how to model the documents using the Mapping Rule Language (MRL). The conceptual schema of documents is then translated into an object database schema for implementation.

The author then go on to describe other relevant work:

- A technique to extract different sections from a web page based on pattern matching.
- Semi-structured wrapper generation
- Query language for the web

The authors are extending their approach to the accessing Intranet databases and files.

The Paper by Terrance Goan: "Supporting the User: Conceptual Modeling & Knowledge Discovery"

Goan points out a weakness of many existing Knowledge Discovery in Databases (KDD) systems: these systems lack the means to actively collaborate with the user over extended periods of time. Goan suggests addressing this problem by tightly coupling the knowledge discovery process with an explicit conceptual model. The user can then use the explicit conceptual model to access different kinds of information.

Goan discusses the knowledge discovery process: the process of identifying valid, novel, interesting, useful, and understandable patterns in data. What is novel? Interesting? Useful? And understandable? How can we better support exploration? How can we move from data to information?

He thinks an explicit conceptual model is necessary and that there is a need to merge several things including database schema.   He then describes the IKODA (Intelligent Knowledge Discovery Assistant) project, which consists of a variety of atomic tools, seamless iteration and recursion, uniform direct manipulation user interface, and intelligent agents.

He describes how sharing a conceptual model can work:
- Use evaluation of IKODA's knowledge
  - Fill in gaps
  - Direct search
  - Form queries
- Recursive/Iterative Discovery
- Automated Data Mining Tool Selection
  - Knowledge maintenance
- Efficiency
  - Utilize use knowledge and high level concept.
- Challenge: Utility problems.

He thinks we should consider the following when we design user interaction:
- Input: Goals, data, existing knowledge, atomic tools, and processes.
- Tasks: tool & process selection, monitoring/refining. Goal processing.

Why do we need conceptual models? Why do we need to share a conceptual model – why not just use the current approach, that is, "isolation"? He points out the need for sharing a good conceptual model.

He then outlines the factors that limited the use of conceptual model because the conceptual schemas could not be used for database access:
- Users, applications must use SQL
- No standard or industry-supported ER query language
- Mismatch between the conceptual model and the database-access languages.

He thinks the object databases can be used as enablers for solving this problem:
- Object formalisms (with non-traumatic additions) can express extended ER
- Languages for conceptual and physical schemas
- Objects in database and programming languages
- Future DBMS will support an object query language (e.g., SQL3, OQL)
- Microsoft repository (UML) will unify the CASE Interface.

He proposes a research agenda for making the conceptual model the center in systems development of KDD systems:
- Multi-tier administration
- Customized behaviors for view update
- Tied to DBMS, Objects, admin interface
- Preserve design work when alter the conceptual or physical schema

- Merge tools could be the key
- Allow all data administration be the main focus.

At the end, he discusses the importance of a multi-hub model to handle a large conceptual model such as the DOD data model, which has 1700 standard data elements:

- Multiple-Hub model at least shows the problem to be solved
- Multiple hubs, redundant and conflicting.

He then outlines the research issues in the multi-hub model as follows:

- Interoperable systems must be created from multiple hubs and interconnections among them
- How can we describe a multi-hub model?

The Paper by Hannu Kangassalo, " Are Global Understanding, Communication, and Information Management in Information System Possible?"

The author is excited about the possibility of forming a global understanding of information, via global communication facilitated by the Internet, and maintained by global information. However, he suggest that we investigate three problems:

- How human concepts are constructed
- How to take into account the point of view
- Applicability of the system of concepts outside the borders of the information system is limited due to the theory of meaning used.

In the paper, the author uses a methodological base approach borrowed from the philosophy of science as well as some principles of meta modeling to attack these issues.

The Paper by Pericles Loucopoulos and Vagelio Kavakli: "Enterprise Knowledge Management and Conceptual Modeling"

Loucopoulos and Kavakli argue that the single most important factor to successful business evolution through the use of information technology is "Enterprise Knowledge Management," which involves many facets of the information systems domain including technical, organizational, social, and teleological considerations. Conceptual modeling plays a central role in that one can capture, reason, represent, use for agreement between many stakeholders and discover new knowledge from legacy systems.

In the paper, the authors discuss several important issues in conceptual modeling:

- Multi-perspective approach to enterprise knowledge modeling: using multiple modeling techniques to produce an integrated, consistent and complete knowledge model of the enterprise.

- Enterprise Knowledge Metamodel: The enterprise knowledge metamodel integrates three complementary views (the enterprise goal view, the enterprise process view, and the information system component view).
- The Enterprise Knowledge Organization and Support Environment: A repository management system is recommended for handing the enterprise knowledge base.

In conclusion, the authors advocate the use of a conceptual modeling paradigm that attempts to support enterprise change by externalizing their objectives, evaluating the impact of changes to their business processes and ascertaining the IT provision necessary for the support of the potential changes.

The Paper by William E. McCarthy: "Sematic Modeling in Accounting Education, Practice, Research: Some Progress and Impediments"

McCarthy describes a series of his papers ranging from applying the ER model to accounting domain to his papers on the REA accounting model. He explores the REA successes in research, practice, and education. More generally, he discusses the difficulties that any new semantic theory must face when it clashes with an existing paradigm of thinking that is based on a different view (oriented toward paper and hand calculation) of the world.

The Paper by John Miller, Amit P. Sheth, and Krys J. Kochut: "Perspectives in Modeling: Simulation, Database, and Workflow"

Miller et al discuss what "workflow modeling" is. The authors think "workflow modeling" is to model the tasks or activities and the flow of control and data between them, while simulation modeling is to model entities (data object).

There are three modeling approaches:
1. Event-scheduling,
2. Activity-scanning,
3. Process-Interaction.

Miller et al then describe the components of the METEOR project:
- Comprehensive workflow design and development,
- map designer,
- data designer,
- task designer,
- web form designer,
- Exception designer.

They also discuss the following research issues:
- Association and disassociation. (For example, the relationship between bus and passengers)
- Data Model in UML including "Composition," "Generalization," and other concepts.

They have developed a Java applet class called FoodCourt.class that simulates 3 different ways of handling the queues.

They also discusses various issues important to the conceptual modeling and simulation:
- Database access
- Type of nodes
- Routing
- Data Transformation
- Timing
- Consistency checking: (a) Outflow, (b) Inflow, (d) at Termination.
- Monitoring/Animation
- Failures
- Mike porter called the "value chain."
- First order
- Generic CASE, Domain-Augmented CASE, and Ontological sense.

In conclusion, they recommend, "Don't throw away the knowledge in building the conceptual schema."

The Paper by Sham Navathe and Andreas M. Kogelnik: "The Challege of Modeling Information for Genome Databases"

Navathe and Kogelnik describe how conceptual modeling can help in analyzing human genome data, in particular, the construction of Human Mitochondrial Map. Currently, only 3 to 4 percent of genome data have been analyzed. The general challenges for Data Management in Biological Applications are:
- Collection of data
- Analysis (Comparing the Desired Properties of Proposed Solutions
- Scalability
- No loss of information between systems
- Constructive approach to data.

The current status of research in this area can be described as follows:
- Lots of genetic info lies in non-electronic form
- Biology is becoming very "data rich"
- Comprehensive data analysis and interpretation is no longer feasible by manual.

The human genome project is a very large research project involving many research teams:
- Began in 1980's
- 3-4 billion nucleotides per genome.

Examples of current Genome databases are:
- GenBank
- Online Mendelian Inheritance in Man
- Swiss-Prot

- Human genome mapping data *GDB
- Locus specific databases
- Miscellaneous cell repositories

The new research work related to computer and information basically focuses on algorithm design and algorithm complexity analysis. For example, the following work is needed:

- Database Modeling
- Database design
- Knowledge system design
- Parallel processing and supercomputing
- Animation
- Virtual environment.

The authors argue that we need to use standardized notations but we should also tailor the notations by defining our own schemas, classes, properties, and functions. Also, we should create an open architecture so that it can be easily extended in the future.

In conclusion, the authors outline the following challenges for database professionals:

- Learning applications
  - Jargon
  - Process model of the environment
  - Complexities, typical scenarios, rules, constraints
- Apply database techniques to help in application.

The Paper by Arnon Rosenthal and Len Seligman: "Trends and Scale-Up for Data Administration"

Rosenthal and Seligman suggest that the conceptual data models should be scaled up to accommodate the object revolution. The authors claim that three "convergences" are occurring in object technology:

1. A unified schema interface formalism
2. The design process for databases and applications are becoming interleaved to form Object-Oriented Analysis and Design (OOA&D)
3. OOA&D will use a common core of representation across vendors and lifecycle stages.

The authors state that there are continuing challenges in the administration of multi-tier schemas even if all models were expressed in a single-object formalism. Some of the remaining difficulties are:

1. Metadata Volume: the burden of data administration will increase greatly if metadata information can not be generated automatically.
2. Change Proportion: When a change is made at one tier, the queries that derive it from related tiers or that derive from it need to be changed.
3. All tiers above the implementation are second class: Many critical services are supported only for the implementation tier.

Rosenthal and Seligman triggered us to think deeply about our role in the ever-changing world.

The Paper by Munindar P. Singh: "Conceptual Modelingfor Multiagent Systems: Applying Interaction-Oriented Programming"

Singh discusses the importance of further extensions to conceptual modeling to include aspects of actions and organizations that will be useful for multiagent systems (MAS). He points out two major directions for research:

- Extensions of the techniques for conceptual modeling of "centralized" information systems to notations (such as ontology and mediation) and techniques (such as process models) useful for modeling of "cooperative" information systems.
- Structured ways to the design of multiagent systems (MAS).

He describes a program called "Interaction-Oriented Programming (IOP)" that develops and studies primitives for the specifications of systems of agents and constraints on their behavior. These primitives include societies, the roles agents may play in them, what capabilities and commitments the roles require, and what authorities they grant. The concepts of coordination in IOP include:

- A coordination model
- Coordination relationships.

At the end, he describes an example in two parts: electronic commerce and virtual enterprises. In conclusion, IOP focuses on some non-traditional conceptual modeling concepts. Specifically,

- Coordination, commitment, collaboration are captured as first-class concepts that can be applied directly.
- The underlying infrastructure is separated, leading to improved portability.

The Paper by Arne Sølvberg: "Data and What They Refer to"

Sølvberg discusses the conceptual modeling of heterogeneous databases. For each database, there is a local view. These local views can be integrated into a "global world view," which must be related to "common sense" (or "databases"). The symbiotic triangle consists of three nodes: "concept," "referent," and "symbols". The basic framework was the one proposed by Plato: there are four corners in the framework: "idea," "matter," "concept," and "image." In the context of conceptual modeling, the four corners become: "program," "data," "concept," and "referent."

Then, he proposes a framework for modeling of symbols and referents. The basic framework supports the view that referents have an existence in their own right, independent of which symbols that denote them. He then proposes a Referent Modeling Language (RML) and claims that there is a one-to-one correspondence between some of the modeling concepts of RML and the ER model.

In conclusion, Sølvberg advocates an approach to information system design that puts more emphasis on conceptual modeling than what is usual in current practice. A major characteristic of his approach is that data and what they refer to are modeled separately. He argues that this separation will provide several advantages.

The Paper by Bernhard Thalheim: "The Strength of ER Modeling"

Bernhard Thalheim argues the strength of ER modeling. In this paper, he proposes the "safe type" extension of ERM.

He defines several new terms:
- Inclusion-based BCNF schema: BCNF, key-based inclusion constraints, hierarchy of types.
- Semantic Extensions: Lookup interpretation versus participation interpretation. The differences between "lookup" and "participation" are described here. An example of lookup interpretation is: a car is owned by 1, 2, 3, or 4 persons. An example for "participation interpretation" is: a person owns at most 4 and at least one car.
- Behavior extensions: Function type system is definable through structural recursion. Structural recursion by insert presentation. Structural recursion by other means.
- Object: There are two objects of interest here: for example, Cierro – as author, historical person; Tully – as friend. It is desirable to handle 1-to-1 association of real world things and objects. Special features of an object include:
  - OID invisible for users.
  - Separation of value/object.
  - Objects have values.
  - Operations (external events) are associated with objects.

He argues what we really want is "value representability," because object identifiers do not have a meaning to the user. An object OID is identifiable iff the orbit is trivial (for the automorphism group). He argues that we also need canonical update operations.

He also thinks consistency is another important issue:
- Classical transaction approach: using rollback.
- RTS: for hierarchical schemata only.
- Rule triggering: it is not powerful enough because of cyclic schemata.

He thinks semantics can not be based on set semantics alone and that we need better translations of semantics. For a given schema, there are exponentially many normalized schemata – but which one to choose from? Tuning is a physical optimization based on behavior, but here we are talking about semantics.

The Paper by Peter Wegner: "Interactive Foundations for Conceptual Modeling"

Wagner points out the fact that "interaction models" are different from other models. He examines how the notion of modeling must change to take into account the irreducibility of interaction to algorithm. He describes a research strategy to develop a comprehensive framework for interactive modeling that combines bottom-up analysis of models of software engineering, artificial intelligence, and virtual reality that abstract from current practice with top-down development conceptual models of interaction.

He thinks that a new modeling framework and new notations of semantics, expressiveness, complexity are needed for interactive models. In conclusion, he thinks that shifting the focus of attention from inner algorithm execution to outward-directed interactive behavior not only allows us to model a richer class of problems but also may help promote social responsibility in serving external clients and creating a technological infrastructure for society.

II. Summary of Three Workshops

There are several workshops held at ER'97. In this volume, we include the summary of three workshops.

Workshop on "Behavioral Modeling", Organized by Stephen W. Liddle, Stephen W. Clyde, and Scott N. Woodfield

The workshop addresses two important topics:
- What constitutes a "good" behavioral model?
- Assuming we have such a "good' behavioral model, what issues related to design transformations we should explore?

For the first question, the discussions focus on:
- What are the essential characteristics of a behavioral model?
- How do we formally compare different behavioral models?

For the second question, the discussions focus on:
- What are the desirable properties of a behavioral model? Are there canonical/normal forms? How do we measure quality?
- What design transformations are desirable? How do we guarantee information preservation in transformations?
- Should behavioral design be independent of the implementation platform? How does the inclusion of behavioral in the conceptual model impact structural aspects of the model?
- How do designers know when a particular design is "done"?

A total of twelve position statement or papers were presented at the workshop, and the workshop proceedings are available in electronic form in the ER97 web site at Brigham Young University (http: //osm7.cs.byu.edu/ER97/workshop4).

Workshop on "Cognition and Conceptual Modeling", Organized by V. Ramesh, Jeffrey Parsons, and Glenn J. Browne

The workshop addresses two important topics:
- How can research on cognition enhance the expressiveness of conceptual models?
- How can research in cognitive psychology help us develop better diagrammatic representations of conceptual models?

Approximately eight papers or position statements were presented at the workshop. The main ideas of these papers and statements can be summarized as follows:
- There is a need for causal relationships.
- A concept can be defined to be an independently identified construct composed of knowledge primitives and other concepts.
- The assumption of inherent classification, though pervasive in conceptual modeling and database design, may be incompatible with recent research in cognition and linguistics.
- Very little consideration has been given to basic cognitive and perceptual guidelines when developing representational schemes for conceptual models.
- The cognitive limitations of analysis may result in flawed application and evaluation of stopping rules, producing premature termination of the information requirements determination process, which in turn will lead to incomplete schemas.
- The process of conceptual schema design can be viewed as a process of achieving a series of goals.

In conclusion, the workshop participants recommend the following:
- There is a need to rethink the way concepts are represented by current conceptual models.
- There is a need to support additional relationship types such as causation.
- There is a need to base the choices of diagrammatic representational schemes on perceptual and cognitive guidelines.

Workshop on "Conceptual Modeling in Multimedia Information Seeking", Organzied by Carlo Meghini and Fabrizio Sebastiani

This workshop focuses on several issues in information seeking:
- Modeling web documents
- Modeling multimedia documents
- Browsing.

In total, approximately 8 papers or positional statements were presented at the workshop. Four of them are related to the first topic: modeling web documents. Several abstract structures of web documents are proposed and debated. Other interesting issues discussed include:

(1) Language constructs for accessing the web
(2) The integration techniques for various types of data from flat files, databases, and the web.

In terms of modeling of multimedia data, a lot of attention is given to the modeling of video data. One speaker discusses how typical content-based queries relate to the four levels of his framework, and discusses the implications of his model for system infrastructure.

In terms of browsing techniques, tools and indexing techniques are discussed. A set of tools is proposed aimed at making browsing the retrieved documents easier and more intuitive. One of these tools is a clustering facility. Another researcher tackle the problem of providing sophisticated facilities for browsing recordings of presentations possibly produced by videoconferencing software. Various indexing and searching techniques are discussed.

In conclusion, as we are moving into the information age, information seeking in the multi-media environment becomes much more important than before. How to extend the conceptual modeling techniques to these new applications is an important research problem.

III. Summary of Talks

There were several very interesting talks at the workshop. However, due to other commitments, the speakers could not provide written papers to be included in this volume. The following is a summary of several such speeches.

The Talk Given by Ephraim McLean (Georgia State University)

Ephraim McLean gave a very inspirational talk on the evolution of information systems and technology (IS&T). Initially, the focus of IS&T in a corporation was for competitive advantage. Then, IS&T was used to promote and enforce total quality Management. Then, in early 90's, the focus was on Business Process re-engineering. Now, the focus is on electronic commerce and on Enterprise software. He suggests that the conceptual modeling field needs to adapt to the changes of focus in each time period in order to be very useful to the corporations.

The Talk by Enrique Ruspini (SRI)

Ruspini gave a talk on Knowledge -Discovery Techniques. He claims that, in certain sense, knowledge discovery is to find the Similarity Relations (similar to "affinity") in data.

He talked in details about several topics in knowledge discovery including:
- Basic primitive concepts
- Fundamental cognitive capability
- Commonly expressed (numerical) measures
- Quantifying probabilistic clustering (C-means visualized)
- Non-point prototype models.

He also proposes that the notions of prototype may be changed to include more general structures.

The Talk by Peter Ng (New Jersey Institute of Technology)

Ng gave a talk on an intelligent browser for document processing system. He described a new network for browsing information and documents by taking the advantage of the dual model of the document processing system. The system he developed provides efficient frame instance access by limiting the searches to those frame instances of a document type within those folders, which appear to be the most similar to the corresponding queries.

IV. The Future

From the above discussions of the contents of papers, workshops, and talks, we can see that the field of conceptual modeling has moved in a very fast speed in the past decade. Some of these papers, talks, and workshop summaries also discuss about future research issues but with a more narrow focus. In order to give a much broader perspective of the field, we include a paper (specifically written for this volume) focusing on the future research directions of the conceptual modeling. We hope that the papers collected in this volume as well as the special "Future Directions" paper will provide a lot of stimulating ideas to researchers around the world so that the field of conceptual modeling can move at an even faster in the next decade than in the past.

Conceptual Design of Parallel Systems

Jacky Akoka

Ecole Supérieure des Sciences Economiques et Commerciales (ESSEC)
Avenue Bernard Hirsch - BP 105
95021 CERGY - France
Tél. : 33.1.34.43.30.77 Fax. : 33.1.34.43.30.01
E-Mail : akoka@cnam.fr

Abstract. The aim of this paper is to present a parallel object-oriented design method which integrates both object orientation and parallelism. The concept of object-orientation has initially emerged from programming. It has evolved to become a conceptual approach. In this paper, object-orientation is seen as a mean of conceptual modelling. Parallelism is seen as a source of structural simplicity in the conceptual design phase. It is the cornerstone of communication between objects. Our approach is characterized by object-orientation and concurrency. It can be summarized by the following points :

- The design method allows us to identify the objects, their relationships, events, and messages.
- Its underlying model is represented as a collection of concurrently executable objects. The latter are the primal agents of the information system and can be entities and/or relationships. The objects can be manipulated by actions which are seen as public or private methods.
- The interactions among the components of the parallel system are represented as message transmissions among objects. The messages are one way to manage parallelism. In this paper, parallelism can also be managed by cardinalities and/or integrity constraints.
- The design method and its underlying model present an adequate formalism in which various concurrent activities, interactions between objects, and inheritance mechanism are expressed naturally.

Several constructs are presented to show how the design method can take into account different types of parallelism problems. These constructs are illustrated by examples. The design method is not specific to databases and can be applied to concurrent systems design.

Keywords: object - message - parallelism - data model - concurrency - design method.

1. Introduction

Parallel systems and parallel database systems have become more than a research curiosity. They are beginning to made their presence felt beyond the research community. The successes of both concurrent object-oriented programming

P.P. Chen et al. (Eds.): Conceptual Modeling, LNCS 1565, pp. 1-23, 1999.
© Springer-Verlag Berlin Heidelberg 1999

languages and highly parallel database commercial products demonstrate the viability of parallel systems. A consensus on parallel database systems seems to emerge, based on *share-nothing* dataflow architecture in which processors communicate with one another by sending messages via an interconnection network.

Despite considerable advances in parallel computing and parallel database systems, over the past decade there has been relatively little attention devoted to the conceptual modelling of such systems. As for traditional database systems, parallel systems conceptual design is the most crucial phase in the development process. If a correct conceptual design is produced, then the remainder of the development task is at least based upon a firm foundation. On the contrary, if an inadequate conceptual design model is produced, a disastrous technical development may result.

In this article, we consider how we might exploit the potential that concurrent programming and object-orientation have for facilitating the conceptual design of parallel systems. Our view is that development in both object-oriented systems and parallel computing have removed some of the practical difficulties facing conceptual modelling of parallel systems. The aim of this paper is to present a parallel object-oriented design method. POOD (an acronym for Parallel Object-Oriented Design) is an attempt to integrate both object-orientation and concurrency to solve the conceptual design problem of parallel systems. The method presented here is a pragmatic synthesis that is consistent with the mainstream development in the field of conceptual modelling. It has been found in practice to yield robust designs. It has been applied to a range of problems characterized by concurrent activities. POOD was motivated by the perceived need for :

- a conceptual design approach built upon a sound framework,
- a comprehensiveness that embraces all design issues, including identification of objects.

POOD is an object-oriented design method capable of supporting parallelism. The method is not about parallel processing in a database sense. Its underlying data model is not specific to databases. Rather, it uses the object-oriented and the concurrency paradigms to solve the conceptual design problem of parallel systems characterized by concurrent activities.

The remainder of this article is organized as follows : the next section presents a state of the art in parallel systems design. It describes the basic concepts and approaches used in parallel systems and parallel database systems. The third section is devoted to the description of the underlying data model used by POOD. The model is represented as a collection of concurrently executable objects manipulated by public and/or private methods The interactions among the components of the model are represented as message transmissions among such objects. The fourth section describes POOD. This conceptual design method embraces issues ranging from the development of an Extended Entity-Relationship model and its mapping to an Events Flow Diagram to the construction of an Events Dependency Graph. It also decomposes the problem into processes. This section describes also an application of POOD. In the last section, we conclude and discuss several areas for further research.

2. Parallel Systems: A State of the Art

From a conceptual design point of view, the description of parallel systems can be divided in two major components. The first one comprises pure parallel computing concerning concurrency and distribution. The second one deals with parallel database systems.

2.1. Parallel Systems

Developments in both object-oriented languages and concurrent programming have removed the main difficulties facing applications of systematic concurrent object-oriented programming. As Briot and Guerraoui point out, three main approaches have been used in concurrency and distribution which are the principal features of parallel systems [Brg96].

The first approach, called an *applicative approach* applies object-oriented concepts to structure parallel and distributed systems through libraries. Parallel systems are developed using an object-oriented methodology combined with an object-oriented language. This approach has been used in the development of Chorus [Roz92], Mach [Acc92] and Choices [Cam93]. Smalltalk [Gol83] and Eiffel [Mey93] can be seen as good examples of this approach related to concurrent object-oriented computation. The second approach aims at combining concepts such as objects, activities, message passing and transactions. This *integrative approach* allows us to define active objects [Yon87, Lie87, Agh86], synchronized objects [Yon90, Ber87, Ame87, Car93], and distributed objects [Gue92, Jul94, Nic93]. The last approach integrates protocol libraries and a programming language. This *reflexive approach* leads to a Meta-Object Protocol [Kic91] and to its components represented by meta-objects [Mae87].

As it can be seen, the applicative approach can be used at a conceptual level. However, it cannot be considered as a design methodology. The integrative approach is useful only at the programming level. Finally, the reflexive approach can be considered as the combination of the integrative and applicative approaches but does not represent a conceptual design method.

2.2. Parallel Database Systems

One explanation of the success of parallel database systems is the widespread adoption of the relational data model. In parallel database systems, relational queries are suited to parallel execution. By partitioning input data among multiple processors, a relational operator can be split into independent operators each working on a part of the input data, giving rise to partitioned parallelism [Deg92]. Several approaches have been proposed to solve the main problems facing parallel database systems:

- *Parallel query optimization* requires query optimizers to consider all the parallel algorithms for each relational operator [Grw89].

- *Application program parallelism* allowes us to structure programs in order to take advantage of parallelism in database parallel systems [Hul91].
- *Physical database design* tools are used to help database administrator to select among physical design options.

However several important issues remain unsolved including on-line parallel database reorganization, algorithms for handling relations with skewed data distribution, and conceptual design methodologies.

As it can be seen, there have been many attempts to provide object-oriented languages with a model of concurrency. Few have dealt with design methodology. POOD permits definition of a parallel object-oriented design as an extension to the method of systematic software construction that addresses the need of concurrent and distributed computing. It uses a semantic model considering a collection of concurrent executable objects. It uses similar graphical representations for object structure and behavior as several object-oriented design methods such as OMT [Rum91], OOSA [Emb92] and OBD [Kas91a].

Some simularities can be found with object life cycles diagrams [Saa94, Scs95, Scs97,Kas91b, Mae92]. Finally, POOD objects synchronization modes can be compared to those used by OOD [Boo91].

3. POOM: The Object-Oriented Underlying Model

POOD's underlying model is a concurrent object-oriented model. The Parallel Object-Oriented Model (POOM) offers the ability to model shared objects with changing local and global states. It provides the property of dynamic reconfigurability and inherent concurrency. POOM advances the state of the art in data modelling by combining both the advantages of object-oriented methodology with those of parallelism. It has been developed to exploit message-passing as a basis for concurrent object-oriented data model. We consider that the parallelism is the **cornerstone** of communication. The object-orientation provides a framework for natural modelling through its flexible modularization capabilities. Parallelism is the source of computational power. The encapsulation guaranteed by the notion of objects enhances the order and safety that are necessary to exploit parallelism. We assume that the object is a complex entity. The basic mode of message passing is asynchronous as an object can send a message whenever it wants, irrespective of the receiver of the message. This expands the degree of parallelism allowed in a system. We assume that an object is able to create new objects dynamically. This capability is necessary in order to model and represent complex open systems. Our model has four principal features : objects, events, communications among objects, and the Inheritance mechanism. These basic constructs are described below [Ako92, Ako94].

3.1 Objects and Events

In our model, the primal agent of the information system is a set of entities and relationships called objects. Each object may correspond to a physical or conceptual abstract "thing" that describes the problem of interest. Each object has its own processing power. An object can be an entity or a relationship. Entities and relationships allow us to represent theoretically any system using a set of associations between concepts. The latter can be in turn represented using the relationships that may exist between other concepts, and so on. This kind of representation leads to the creation of an *associative memory* which allows to navigate from one type of information to the other one, using the relationships that exist between them. An object is defined by :

- a *name*, which designates the role of the object in the Information System,
- a *set of properties* which characterize it,
- a *set of actions*, called methods, which are the reactions of the object to all possible events. Each action defines some *service* that can be delivered by the object. This leads the object to establish a *mutual contract* to deliver the services requested,
- a *set of integrity constraints* related to the evolution of the object-types.

The preceding elements and constraints define what we call the *sensitivity* of the object to a set of events. An event is something that happens at a point in time. It may logically precede or follow another. Two events can be causally unrelated. In this case, the events are said to be concurrent and may have no effect on each other. An event conveys information. In our model an event can be represented by the following features :

- a *state* : this is an encapsulated dynamic characteristic of the object which expresses the evaluation of a Boolean condition. It is obvious that this characteristic does not belong to any semantic domain of the other static attributes,
- a *valuation* : this is a congruence which depends on the system cycle and the tokens necessary to firing of actions.

The behavior of the object can be defined by :

- a *"know-how"*, defined by a set of methods which describe the way the object behaves independently of its environment. Those methods are activated by explicit messages,
- a *"reaction"*, which represents the way the object reacts (given its *sensitivity*) to events, using its methods.

The events can be internal and/or external. An action can have an effect on the objects and its neighbouring. The *global* state of an object at a point in time may depend not only on the proper states of the object, but also on other object-states in its neighbouring.

The objects can be manipulated by actions which are seen as public or private methods among objects. A public method is a method that all objects are aware of its existence. This kind of method can be activated by any form of event (external or internal to the object). A private method is a method that only the object is aware of its existence, and it can be activated only by internal events. This kind of method is generally used by the object to control its self-integrity, or provide some private services. The graphical formalism used to represent an object is as follows (Fig.1).

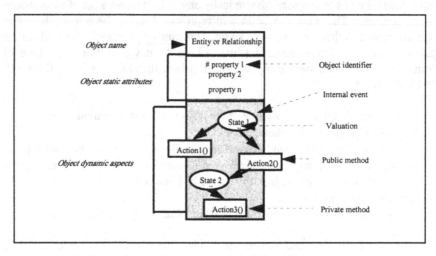

Fig. 1. Graphical formalism of a POOM object

3.2 Messages and Parallelism

We consider parallelism at a conceptual level [Hoa85] and not at a physical level like in parallel computing. We are not interested in parallel architectures but in the parallelism that may exist between objects' behavior. Therefore, an information system can be characterized by a set of autonomous objects which evolve in parallel. The objects commmunicate in asynchronous mode using messages. This may lead to critical situations involving concurrency. Our aim is to model these critical situations [Yon87]. Messages are sent to objects in order to use methods encapsulated in the objects. A message indicates the state of the object at a given moment. It exhibits an event which is the conceptual perception of a fact. It informs the object that some event happened.

The object is requested to react. An object has two piles of messages :

- a static pile when the object is in the dormant mode,
- a dynamic pile when the object is in the active mode.

In our model we distinguish three types of message-passing, considering a temporal aspect :

- **Past-message** : The message is sent without waiting for a response. It corresponds to a situation where one requests someone to do some task and simultaneously proceeds with its own task without waiting for the request to be completed. This type of message increases the potential of concurrency (Fig. 2).

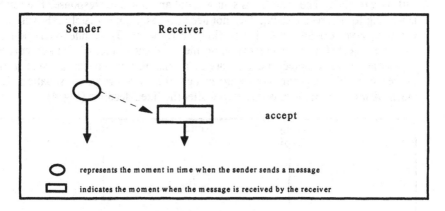

Fig. 2. Past-message

- **Now-message** : The message is sent, and the sender waits for an immediate response from the receiver. *This is similar to a procedure call.* However, it differs in that the receiver's activity does not have to end with sending some information back to the sender. This type of message provides a convenient mean to synchronize activities performed by independent objects (Fig. 3).

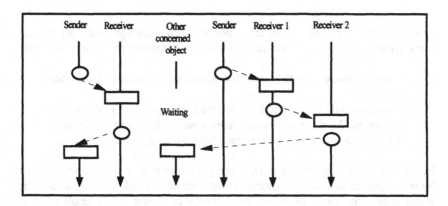

Fig. 3. Now-message

This is similar to ordinary function calls, but it is more general and differs in the following two points :
-   The receiver activation does not have to end with sending the reply to the sender. The receiver may continue its computation after sending the reply.
-   The reply to the request does not necessarily have to be sent back by the receiver. The responsibility of replying can be delegated to other objects concerned by the message. The reply can be sent to an object different from the initial sender.

- **Future-message** : The message is sent without an immediate response. The sender is waiting for the response but does not need the result immediately. Then it gives it a rendez-vous point, when it will find the response. The rendez-vous point is itself an object. It is a queue containing the different responses of the receivers. This object is represented in our model by a relationship between the sender and the receiver objects. A future-message can generate a non-response situation. This means that the set of responses is empty after the fixed deadline (Fig. 4).

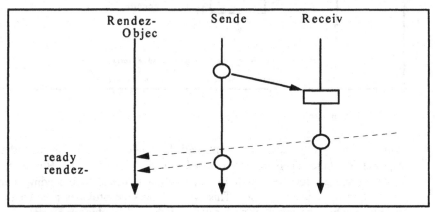

Fig. 4. Future-message

In general if an object R receives two different messages from an object S, the transmission order is preserved. In our model we consider two transmission modes :

- **Normal mode** : in this case the messages are received depending on their priorities.
- **Express mode** : it is a mode where the messages have a higher priority than the normal mode. When a message in express mode is sent to a receiver it can stop the execution of a method activated with a message in a normal mode.

In our model we do not differenciate between the activation of methods by events and by messages. In fact, a communication between objects takes place as an event. The message-passing is considered as the valuation of a state or the result returned by a method.

3.3 Parallelism and Cardinalities

Message passing represents one mean of managing parallelism. Cardinalities represent a second mean. The *associative object* (or relationship) can be seen as a dynamic object. It behaves as a conceptual *pile*. Then the cardinality may be interpreted as a *mutual* state characterizing the couple entity-relationship. The valuation of this state is the value of the cardinality. Any change in the cardinalities can be interpreted as an event describing the creation of a relationship among some objects.

Then the system-configuration is the set of all objects states. This concept is illustrated in the example described in Section 4 (second process). There are cases where the cardinalities can be interpreted as a *non-event*. In fact, the non-realization of a certain event can be interpreted as a particular event. This is equivalent to the case where the resource is equal to 0 in Extended Petri Nets. This extension called, "zero-testing", involves the introduction of arcs from a place to a transition which allows the transition to fire only if the place has zero token. These special arcs are called *inhibitor* arcs.

3.4 Parallelism and Integrity Constraints

Integrity constraint is a special mean to solve concurrency problems. It is the equivalent of "Guard" in parallel programming languages. Let us consider "The dining philosopher's problem" [Hoa85], an example using semaphores. It is a well-known problem of philosophers eating spaghettis :

N philosophers (N>=2) share a common table and N chairs. Each chair is reserved for one philosopher. At the table there is a perennial food dish and there are N forks and N plates. Usually a philosopher's life is one of thinking and eating. A philosopher who feels hungry sits in the correct chair and picks up the two forks on either side of the plate. (We assume that a philosopher needs the two forks to eat). If the philosopher's neighbours have already picked up the two forks, the philosopher cannot eat. If two forks are available the philosopher takes the food from the perennial food dish, eats and places the forks back. The problem is to devise a protocol (a code of conduct) that will allow the philosophers to eat..The protocol must satisfy the following requirements :

1. *Mutual exclusion : no two philosophers fight for the same fork.*
2. *Absence of deadlock : if all the philosophers sit and each one takes the right-hand fork simultaneously then every one is delayed forever and a deadlock results . This should be avoided.*
3. *Absence of starvation : a philosopher who never gets right and left forks starves. This must be allowed. For example, if philosophers 1 and 3 conspire, they can lock out and starve to death philosopher 2.*

This is a case where the global state of the philosopher does not depend only on its local state (i.e. eating or thinking). It depends also on other states of other objects in its neighbouring. These objects are left and right neighbours. More precisely, it depends on the facts that the left and right forks are used or not. The state of the fork depends on the philosopher located at the left or the right of the concerned philosopher. Therefore, the state of the fork depends both on the fork itself and the philosopher. It is a mutual state, represented in our model by a cardinality. For a philosopher to be able to eat, he needs two resources : one fork at the right side and another one at the left side. For N philosophers (with N = 5), the complete configuration is described by 5 x 3 = 15 states. We can therefore derive the following model (Fig. 5).

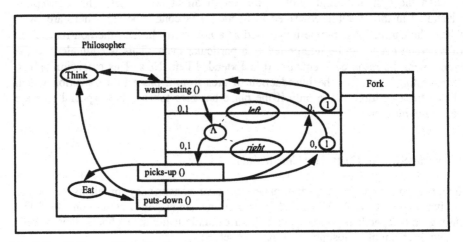

Fig. 5. Parallelism and Integrity Constraints

We can see that we have an object called Philosopher with two states (thinks, eats) and three methods (wants-to-eat, picks-up and puts-down). When the philosopher wants to eat, it is absolutely necessary that the two forks will be free. The state of the fork depends on the fork itself and on the identification of the philosopher who wants to use it. We have two dynamic relationships linked by an integrity constraint. The validity of this constraint, is in this case the valuation that triggers the method picks-up().

3.5 Inheritance and Generalization/Specialization

The inheritance mechanism is an important characteristic of object-oriented approaches. It is a powerful abstraction for sharing similarities between objects. In our model we call inheritance the transmission mechanism of properties from one object-type to another one. The concept of Generalization/Specialization in POOM is based on the relationship "is-a". It means that every occurrence of an object-type is an occurrence of another object-type. We can have :

- Some sets of occurrences representing generic-types,
- other sets representing specialized-types.

For a given set of occurrences two cases are possible :

- Only one generic-type. This is a simple Generalization/Specialization or simple inheritance. On the other hand we can have several specialized-types with set-constraints existing among them,
- Several generic-types. This is a composed Generalization/Specialization.

The multiple inheritance is a kind of composed Generalization/Specialization. Message-passing to a specialized object is typically a good example for delegation.

When a generic-object receives a message, and if this function has been redefined, it will delegate the service to its specialized object. In this case it corresponds to a "conceptual-polymorphism". In some cases the specialized object must be seen as a refinement of the generalized object. Then a state or an action may be replaced by specialized states and actions providing a more detailed description of an object (Fig. 6).

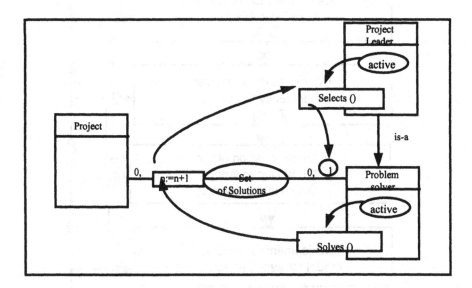

Fig. 6. Inheritance and Generalization/Specialization

4. POOD: The Multi-stage Parallel Design Method and Its Application

The parallel design method presented in this paper corresponds to what the author believes to be a reasonable partitioning of the decisions involved in designing concurrent object-oriented systems. It is a member of the class of multi-stages design approaches involving six stages as shown below (Fig. 7).

Each of these stages are examined below. However, it must be stressed that the Parallel Object-Oriented Design (POOD) method is an iterative process. It is possible to loop back from any stage to previous stages to correct bad choices.

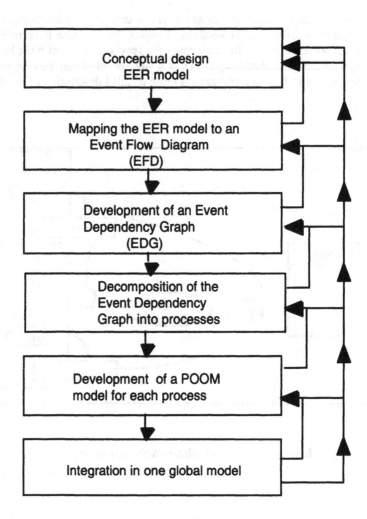

Fig. 7. POOD Stages

4.1 The Conceptual Design Phase

This stage involves formulating the data objects. The input to this stage are the application requirement specifications. The formalism used is the Extended Entity-Relationship model [Che76]. The result is a clear, concise, and comprehensive description of the universe of discourse.

4.2 The Mapping Phase

This stage maps the conceptual model of real world data objects into an event flow diagram representing encapsulated dynamic characteristics of the data objects. The events describe part of the behavior of the parallel system to be modeled. To obtain the EFD, we first develop an Event Interaction Matrix representing the type of interactions taking place between the data objects. We then proceed to the events synchronization, in particular for parallel events. Finally, we derive the events flow diagram which includes the data objects, the events and their synchronization.

4.3 The Event Dependency Graph (EDG)

This stage involves building an event dependency graph which takes into account the scheduling of events according to time. The EDG is derived from the EFD developed during the preceding stage.

4.4 The Decomposition in Processes

A process is an autonomous set of actions having the same finality, running in the same periodicity, and returning as a result an equilibrium general-state (or configuration) of the system. In our case, a process is formalized as a cluster of object-types. This latter can be more or less detailed in a given process. A major reason to model process by process is to alleviate the design task allowing an incremental approach. Therefore, the designer can incorporate additional and more complex characteristics of the system under consideration. A second reason to model the problem process by process is due to the fact that presenting a global model can be difficult to be read and understood. By considering process by process, the designer can reduce the size of the model in order to achieve an easy validation by the user.

4.5 The Development of a POOM Model

Having in the previous stage decomposed in processes the EDG, we next decide upon the conceptual modelling of each process. In order to take into account the concurrency existing between objects, we establish a POOM model for each process.

4.6 The Integration in One Global Model

This stage involves merging several POOM models (or schemas) into one integrated schema. To achieve such a result, the designer may have to resolve integration problems such as type conflicts and constraint conflicts [Boc90, Lel97].

4.7 An Example

Let us illustrate the POOD design method using the following example :

Suppose a manager is requested to create a project team to solve a certain problem within a certain time limit. He first creates a project team comprised of the project leader and multiple problem solvers, each having a different problem solving strategy. The project leader dispatches the same problem to each problem solver. For the sake of simplicity, the problem solvers are assumed to work independently in parallel. When a problem solver has solved the problem, he sends the solution to the project leader immediately. We assume the project leader or some problem solvers, or both, have solved the problem. The project leader selects the best solution and sends the success report to the manager. He also sends a kill or stop message to all the problem solvers. If nobody has solved the problem by the deadline, the project leader sends the failure report to the manager and commits suicide.

POOD design phases are described below :

a) The Extended Entity-Relationship Model

The EER model comprises four entities and two relationships. The special entity *member* allows us to consider the project leader as a member of the project team. Therefore, he can contribute to the set of solutions. As a consequence a functional dependency exists between the entities *project leader* and *project team*.

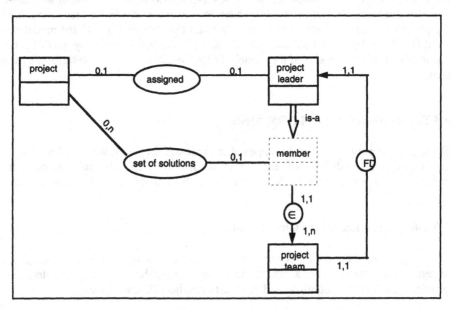

b) The Event Flow Diagram (EFD)

As explained above, the EER model should be mapped to an Event Flow Diagram. To achieve such a result, we need first to derive an event interaction matrix, and events synchronization. This process is described below.

i) Event Interaction Matrix

To obtain the elements of the matrix, we should identify the main actors of the EFD and describe their interaction. Using the fact that an actor of the EFD is an entity of the EER in interaction with another, we derive the following matrix.

↙	Manager	Project	Project Leader	Project Team
Manager			asks for deadline extension proposes solutions	
Project				
Project Leader	assigns the project agrees for deadline extension		commits suicide	proposes solutions
Project Team			dispatches the project	

Although the *Manager* is not an entity of the EER model, we need to consider him as an actor in order to take into account its interaction with the main actors of the model.

ii) Events synchronization

The events described in the event interaction matrix are synchronized according to time.

The events synchronization graph describes the sequences of events undertaken by the actors. As it can be seen in the following example, manager assigns the project to the project leader and decides a deadline. In return, he receives the solutions proposed by the project leader and accepts to extend the deadline.

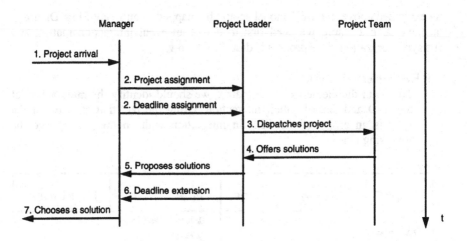

The final event flow diagram is given below :

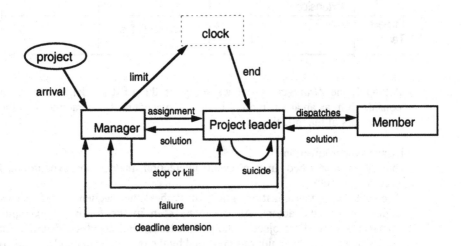

This graph incorporates the actors, their roles and the sequence of events taking place. The *clock* is not an actor but allows the measure of time for the deadline.

c) The Events Dependency Graph.

This graph is deduced from the EFD. It considers only the events described above and presents the dependencies that might exist between them. The final EDG is given below.

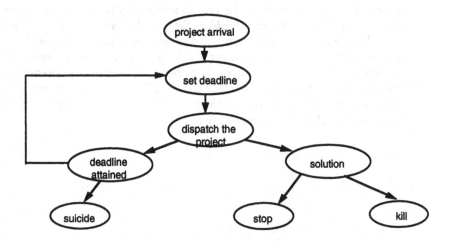

d) Decomposition in processes

Using the definition of processes given in paragraph 4.4, we obtain three different processes :
- the first process is related to the assignment of the project. It includes the arrival of the project to the Manager, the setting of the deadline and the dispatching of the project to the project leader,
- the second process concerns the solutions of the problem to be generated,
- the last process describes the potential failure of the project.

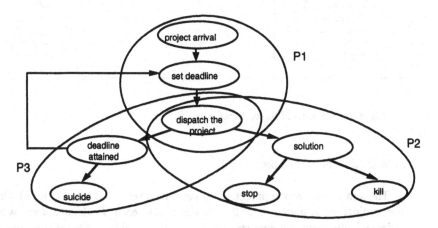

e) Modelling the processes using POOM :

i) Modelling the first process P1

The goal of the first process is to take into account the project and to dispatch it to all the problem-solvers (Fig. 8). When the project arrives, it is in a waiting mode. Then it is assigned to the project-leader who sends a future-message called "dispatching" to the *Problem-Solvers*. In fact, the *Project-leader* dispatches the project to the solvers and continues its activity without waiting for an immediate response. The manager decides a deadline limit and indicates the location where to put the solutions. The object *Manager* is a mono-occurence entity compared to an organizational unit [Zac87]. There is a generalization-specialization between *Project-Leader* and *Problem-Solver*. Finally, the message *Problem-dispatching* is a future message.

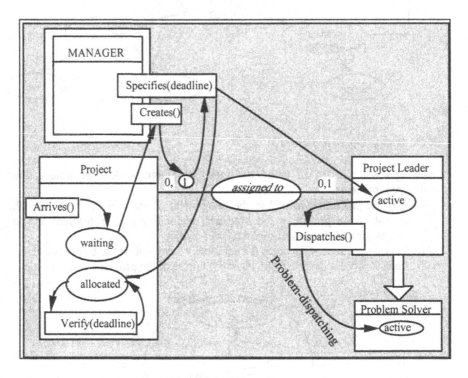

Fig. 8. First process : Project dispatching

ii) Modelling the second process P2

The aim of the second process is to generate a set of solutions (Fig. 9). Once the project is assigned and the deadline set, each *Problem-solver* works independently using his own *strategy* to solve the problem. All the solutions are put in the "rendez-vous-point", called *Set of solutions*. The *Project-Leader* is himself considered as a *Problem-Solver*. Besides, he has to choose one solution among those proposed by the solvers. This solution is therefore sent to the Manager using a now-express message. The *Project-Leader* is waiting for a message indicating that the project has been solved and inviting him to kill the team. The cardinalities are used as a mean to manage parallelism. The *Project-leader* dispatches the problem to all the *solvers* and does not wait for an immediate solution. He gives a rendez-vous using the deadline specified by the Manager. The rendez-vous object is *Set-of-Solutions* which is a relationship between the *Project* and the *Problem-Solver*. The *Problem-Solver* tries to solve the project. If he finds a solution, it will be added to the set of solutions of the project. This changes the valuation of the mutual-state, and the cardinality of the link between *Project* and *Set-of-Solutions* increases from n to n+1. The project leader uses this set to select the solution. When he selects it, the method *Selects ()* changes the cardinality from 0 to 1. The associative object *Set-of-Solutions* can be regarded as a pile shared by the different solvers and the *Project-leader*.

The solvers add their own solutions to the pile allowing the project-leader to make his choice.

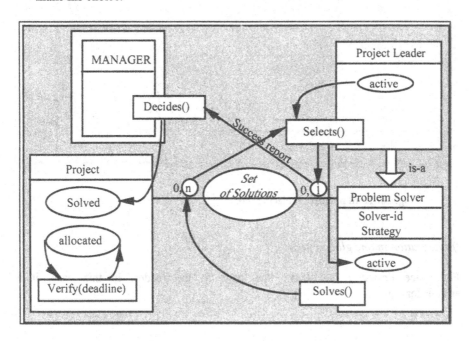

Fig. 9. Second process : Project solving

iii) Modelling the third process P3

The third process allows either to ask for an extension of the deadline or to take into account the failure of the project (Fig. 10). If the manager refuses to grant an extension of the deadline, the project leader will have to "kill" the team. This is the reason for the arc connecting the *Decides* method and the event *killed* of the *Team* object. Finally, note that cardinality values are modified.

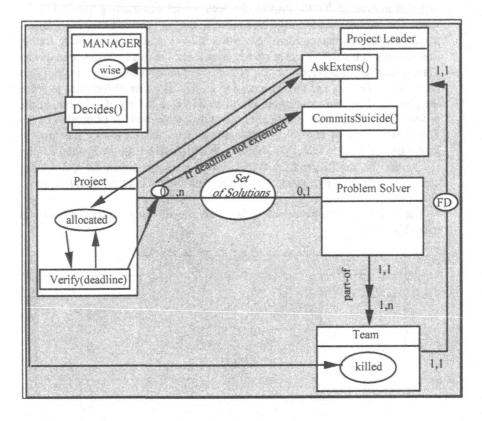

Fig. 10. Third process : Project failure

f) Integration in one global model

For space limitation we leave this stage to the reader. In this case, it is straightforward.

5. Conclusion and Further Research

In this paper, we present a parallel object-oriented design methodology based on a semantic model which integrates data and processes. The model is a collection of concurrent executable objects. It is an encapsulated model which contains data and the associated procedures to operate on the data. It also performs message passing among objects. It takes advantage of the object-oriented methodology and encompasses the computing power of parallelism. The model unifies the notions of objects and processes into a concurrent object. We have developed an adequate formalism in which various concurrent activities and interactions of objects are expressed naturally. Our approach shows how to easily determine at a given high level of abstraction, what kind of objects are necessary and natural to have to solve a given problem. POOM serves as a design model for parallel database systems [Deg92], offering a mean to model parallel applications and systems. The design method embraces issues ranging from the development of an Extended Entity Model and its mapping to an Events Flow Diagram to the construction of an Events Dependency Graph.

In this paper, POOD has been illustrated using a typical object-oriented and parallel problem. POOD has been experimented on various parallel system applications showing its ability to tackle concurrent system examples. Furthermore, POOD decomposes the problem into processes allowing us to perform an incremental design approach.

There are several limitations to POOD. The first limitation is related to the complexity of the design task. Time is needed to integrate all the concepts of the method. A second limitation stems from the graphical formalism used. The models can be seen as difficult to interpret.

Beyond these limitations, there are several interrelated agenda for research in parallel systems design. Items on the technical agenda principally involves an attempt to expand the basic power of POOD to include parallel database design. It involves a need to define the amount of locking mechanism to be implemented to ensure that parallelism does not lead to inconsistent states. At another level there is a functional agenda concerned with the choice of message passing approaches (cardinalities or integrity constraints) appropriate to specific parallel systems.

References

[Acc86]   M. Accetta, R. Baron, W. Bolosky, D. Golub, E. Rashid, A. Tevanian, and M. Young, "Mach : A New Kernel Foundation for Unix Development", Summer Usenix Conference, Atlanta GA, 1986.

[Agh93]   G. Agha, S. Frolund, R. Panwar, D. Sturman, "A Linguistic Framework for Dynamic Composition of Dependability Protocols", Dependable Computing for Critical Applications III (DCCA-3), IFIP Transactions, Elsevier, 1993.

[Ako92]   J. Akoka, R. Oudrhiri, "La Modélisation des Systèmes d'Information Complexes : l'Approche Objet", Brises, n° 17, 1992.

[Ako94]   J. Akoka, "POOM : A Parallel Object-Oriented Model", Computer Science Advanced Research Colloquium, Jerusalem (Israël), 1994.

[Ame87]   P. America, "POOL-T : A Parallel Object-Oriented Language", [Yon87].

[Ber87]   P. Bernstein, V. Hadzilacos, and N. Goodman, Concurrency Control and Recovery in Database Systems, Addison Wesley, 1987.

[Boc90]   M. Bouzeghoub, I. Comyn-Wattiau, "View Integration by Semantic Verification and Transformation of Data Structures", 9th Int. Conf. on Entity-Relationship Approach, Lausanne, 1990.

[Boo91]   G. Booch, Object-Oriented Design with Application, Benjamin Cummings, 1991.

[Brg96]   J.P. Briot, R. Guerraoui, "Objets pour la programmation parallèle et répartie : intérêts, évolutions et tendances", Technique et Science Informatique, Vol. 15, n° 6, 1996.

[Cam93]   R. Campbell, N. Islam, D. Raila, and P. Madany, "Designing and Implementing Choices : An Object-Oriented System in C++", [Mey93].

[Car93]   D. Caromel, "Towards a Method of Object-Oriented Concurrent Programming", [Mey93].

[Che76]   P.P. Chen, "The Entity Relationship Model : Toward a Unified View of Data", ACM Transactions an Database Systems, Volume 1, n° 1, 1976.

[Deg92]   D. Dewitt, J. Gray, "Parallel Database Systems : The Future of High Performance Databases Systems", Communications of the ACM, Vol. 35, n° 6, 1992.

[Emb92]   D.W. Embley, B.D. Kurtz, S.N. Woodfield, Object-Oriented Systems Analysis - A model-Driven Approach, Yourdon Press, 1992.

[Gol83]   A. Goldberg, and D. Robson, Smalltalkll-80 : the Language and its Implementation, Series in Computer Science, Addison Wesley, 1983.

[Grw89]   G. Graefe, K. Ward, "Dynamic Query Evaluation Plans, in Proceedings of the 1989 SIGMOD Conference, Portland Ore. June 1989.

[Gue92]   R. Guerraoui, R. Capobianchi, A. Lanusse, and P. Roux, "Nesting Actions Through Asynchronous Message Passing : the ACS Protocol", European Conference on Object-Oriented Programming (ECOOP'92), Lehrmann Madsen (eds.) LNCS, n° 615, Springer-Verlag, 1992

[Hoa85]   C.A.R. Hoare, Communicating Sequential Processes, Prentice-Hall, 1985.

[Hul91]   K.A. Hua, C. Lee, "Handling Data Skew in Multiprocessor database Computers using partition Tuning", in Proceedings of the Seventeenth International Conference on Very Large Data Bases, Barcelona, Spain, Sept. 1991.

[Jul94]   E. Jul, "Separation of Distribution and Objects", [Gue94].

[Kas91a]   G. Kappel, M. Schrefl, "Using an Object-Oriented Diagram Technique for the Design of Information Systems", in Proceedings of the International Working Conference on Dynamic Modelling of Information Systems, (eds.) H.G. Sol, K.M. Van Hee, 1991.`

[Kas91b]   G. Kappel and M. Schrefl, "Object/Behavior Diagrams", in Proc. 7th Int. Conf. IEEE Data Engineering, 1991.

[Kic94]   G. Kiczales (editor), "Foil For The Workshop On Open Implementation", "http://www.parc.xerox.com/PARC/spl/eca/oi/workshop-94/foil/main.html", 1994.

[Lel97]   M.L. Lee, T.W. Ling, "Resolving Constraint Conflicts in the Integration of Entity-Relationship Schemas", 16th Int. Conf. on Conceptual Modelling, L.A., Ca. 1997. Springer Verlag Lecture Notes in Computer Science, Embley and Goldstein (Eds.).

[Lie87]   H. Lieberman, "Concurrent Object-Oriented Programming in Act 1", [Yon87].

[Mae87]   P. Maes, "Concepts and Experiments in Computational Reflection", ACM Conference on Object-Oriented Programming Systems, Languages and Applications (OOPSLA'87), Special Issue of Sigplan Notices, Vol. 22, n° 12, 1987.

[Mey93]   B. Meyer (editor), Concurrent Object-Oriented Programming : Special Issue, Communications of the ACM (CACM), Vol. 36, n° 9, 1993.

[Mgo92]   J. Martin, J.J. Odell, Object-Oriented Analysis and Design, Prentice Hall, 1992.

[Nic93]   J. Nicol, T. Wilkes, and F. Manola, "Object-Orientation in Heterogeneous Distributed Computing Systems", IEEE Computer, Vol 26, n° 6, 1993.

[Roz92]   M. Rozier, "Chorus", Usenix Symposium on Micro-Kernels and Other Kernel Architectures, 1992.

[Rum91]   J. Rumbaugh, M. Blaha, W. Premerlani, F. Eddy, W. Lorensen, Object-Oriented Modelling and Design, Prentice-Hall, 1991.

[Saa94]   G. Saake, P. Hartel, R. Jungclaus, R. Wieringa, R. Feenstra, "Inheritance Conditions for Object Life Cycle Diagrams", in EMISA Workshop, 1994.

[Scs95]   M. Schrefl and M. Stumptner, "Behavior Consistent Extension of Object Life Cycles", in Proceedings OO-ER 95, Springer LCNS 1021, 1995.

[Scs97]   M. Schrefl, M. Stumptner, "Behavior Consistent Refinement of Object Life Cycle", Institutsbericht, Inst. für Wirtschaftsinformatik, Universität Linz, Austria, 1997.

[Yon87]   A. Yonezawa, and M. Tokoro, Object-Oriented Concurrent Programming, Computer Systems Series, MIT Press, 1987.

[Yon90]   A. Yonezawa, ABCL : an Object-Oriented Concurrent System, Computer System Series, MIT-Press, 1990.

[Zac87]   J.A. Zachman, "A Framework for Information Systems Architecture", IBM Systems Journal 26, n° 3-276-292, 1987.

Conceptual Modeling Challenges for Model-Based Architecting and Software Engineering (MBASE)

Barry Boehm and Dan Port

USC Center for Software Engineering
{boehm, dport}@sunset.usc.edu

1 Summary

The difference between failure and success in developing a software-intensive system can often be traced to the presence or absence of clashes among the models used to define the system's product, process, property, and success characteristics. (Here, we use a simplified version of one of Webster's definitions of "model" a description or analogy used to help visualize something. We include analysis as a form of visualization).

Section 2 of this paper introduces the concept of model clashes, and provides examples of common clashes for each combination of product, process, property, and success models. Section 3 introduces the Model-Based Architecting and Software Engineering (MBASE) approach for endowing a software project with a mutually supportive base of models. Section 4 presents examples of applying the MBASE approach to a family of digital library projects.

Section 5 summarizes the main conceptual modeling challenges involved in the MBASE approach, including integration of multiple product views and integration of various classes of product, process, property, and success models. Section 6 summarizes current conclusions and future prospects.

2 Model Clashes and the Need to Avoid Them

The concept of model clashes among software product models has been addressed in several forms. Examples are structure clashes between a project's input and output structures [Jackson, 1975]; traceability clashes among a product's requirements, design and code [Rosove, 1967]; and architectural style clashes in integrating commercial off-the-shelf (COTS) or other reuseable software components [Garlan et.al., 1995].

There is also an increasing appreciation of the need to avoid clashes between a system's product model and its development process model. A good example is the clash between a COTS-driven product model, in which the available COTS capabilities largely determine the system's "requirements," and the use of a waterfall process model, in which a set of predetermined requirements are supposed to determine the system's capabilities.

P.P. Chen et al. (Eds.): Conceptual Modeling, LNCS 1565, pp. 24-43, 1999.
© Springer-Verlag Berlin Heidelberg 1999

Less well appreciated is the importance of two other classes of models--software-system property models and success models--and the need to apply all four of these classes of models in consistent and integrated ways.

An example of a model clash between a product model and a property model is to use a multiprocessor product model and a throughput property model which assumes that system throughput scales linearly with the number of processors. For most multi-processor applications, data dependencies, control dependencies, or resource contention problems will cause the product strategy, "If we run out of throughput, just add another processor," to actually yield a decrease in throughput beyond a certain number of processors.

The classic New Jersey Department of Motor Vehicles system failure [Babcock, 1985] was a good example of a clash between product model (build the product using a fourth generation language) and a success model involving two properties (low development cost and good throughput). The 4GL system was developed at low cost, but its throughput was so poor that at one point over a million New Jersey automobiles were driving around with unprocessed license renewals.

Unexamined success models can also cause serious clashes. A good example is the Golden Rule, "Do unto others as you would have others do unto you." An expert programmer will frequently interpret this to mean, "I would like people to build me systems with terse, maybe obscure, but powerful commands; and direct access to system files and operating system calls; so that's how I should build systems for others." This can cause many serious problems when the "others" are doctors, airplane pilots, or fire dispatchers, who would be better served by a user-task oriented interface resulting from a stakeholder win-win success model.

Table 1 provides a model-clash matrix showing that serious model clashes can come from any combination of product, process, or success models.

	Product Model	Process Model	Property Model	Success Model
Product Model	• Structure clash • Traceability clash • Architecture style clash	• COTS-driven product vs. Waterfall (requirements-driven) process	• Interdependent multiprocessor product vs. linear performance scalability model	• 4GL-based product vs. low development cost and performance scalability
Process Model		• Multi-increment development process vs. single-increment support tools	• Evolutionary development process vs. Rayleigh-curve cost model	• Waterfall process model vs. "I'll know it when I see it" (IKIWISI) prototyping success model
Property Model			• Minimize cost and schedule vs. maximize quality ("Quality is free")	• Fixed-price contract vs. easy-to-change, volatile requirements
Success Model				• Golden Rule vs. stakeholder win-win

Table 1. Examples of Model Clashes

3   MBASE Overview

Figure 1 summarizes the overall framework used in the MBASE approach to nsure that a project's success, product, process and property models are consistent and well integrated. At the top of Figure 1 are various success models, whose priorities and consistency should be considered first. Thus, if the overriding top-priority success model is to "Demonstrate a competitive agent-based data mining system on the floor of COMDEX in 9 months," this constrains the ambition level of other success models (provably correct code, fully documented as a maintainer win condition). It also determines many aspects of the product model (architected to easily shed lower-priority features if necessary to meet schedule), the process model (design-to-schedule), and various property models (only portable and reliable enough to achieve a successful demonstration).

The achievability of the success model needs to be verified with respect to the other models. In the 9-month demonstration example, a cost-schedule estimation model would relate various product characteristics (sizing of components, reuse, product complexity), process characteristics (staff capabilities and experience, tool support, process maturity), and property characteristics (required reliability, cost constraints) to determine whether the product capabilities achievable in 9 months would be sufficiently competitive for the success models. Thus, as shown at the bottom of Figure 1, a cost and schedule property model would be used for the evaluation and analysis of the consistency of the system's product, process, and success models.

In other cases, the success model would make a process model or a product model the primary driver for model integration. An IKIWISI (I'll know it when I see it) success model would initially establish a prototyping and evolutionary development process model, with most of the product features and property levels left to be determined by the process. A success model focused on developing a product line of similar products would initially focus on product models (domain models, product line architectures), with process models and property models subsequently explored to perform a business-case analysis of the most appropriate breadth of the product line and the timing for introducing individual products.

3.1   Anchor Point Milestones

In each case, property models are invoked to help verify that the project's success models, product models, process models, and property levels or models are acceptably consistent. It has been found advisable to do this especially at two particular "anchor point" life cycle process milestones summarized in Table 2 [Boehm, 1996].

The first milestone is the Life Cycle Objectives (LCO) milestone, at which management verifies the basis for a business commitment to proceed at least through an architecting stage. This involves verifying that there is at least one system architecture and choice of COTS/reuse components which is shown to be feasible to implement within budget and schedule constraints, to satisfy key stakeholder win conditions, and to generate a viable investment business case.

The second milestone is the Life Cycle Architecture (LCA) milestone, at which management verifies the basis for a sound commitment to product development (a particular system architecture with specific COTS and reuse commitments which is shown to be feasible with respect to budget, schedule, requirements, operations concept and business case; identification and commitment of all key life-cycle stakeholders; and elimination of all critical risk items).   The AT&T/Lucent Architecture Review Board technique [Marenzano, 1995] is an excellent management verification approach involving the LCO and LCA milestones. The LCO and LCA have also become key milestones in Rational's Objectory process [Rational, 1997].

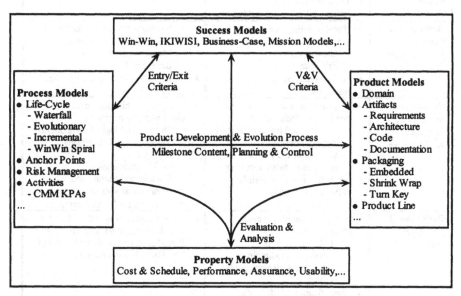

Fig. 1.MBASE Integration Framework

4   Example MBASE Application

4.1   Digital Library Multimedia Archive Projects

Our first opportunity to apply the MBASE approach to a significant number of projects came in the fall of 1996. We arranged with the USC Library to develop the LCO and LCA packages for a set of 12 digital library multimedia applications. The work was done by 15 6-person teams of students in our graduate Software Engineering I class, with each student developing one of the 6 LCO and LCA package artifacts shown in Table 2. Three of the 12 applications were done by two teams each. The best 6 of the LCA packages were then carried to completion in our Spring 1997 Software Engineering II class.

Milestone Element	Life Cycle Objectives (LCO)	Life Cycle Architecture (LCA)

Definition of Operational Concept	• Top-level system objectives and scope
	  - System boundary
	  - Environment parameters and assumptions
	  - Evolution parameters
	• Operational concept
	• Operations and maintenance scenarios and parameters
		• Elaboration of system objectives and scope by increment
		• Elaboration of operational concept by increment

System Prototype(s)	• Organizational life-cycle responsibilities (stakeholders)	

Definition of System Requirements	• Top-level functions, interfaces, quality attribute levels, including:
	  - Growth vectors
	  - Priorities
	• Stakeholders' concurrence on essentials
		• Elaboration of functions, interfaces, quality attributes by increment
		  - Identification of TBDs (to-be-determined items)
		• Stakeholders' concurrence on their priority concerns

Definition of System and Software Architecture	• Top-level definition of at least one feasible architecture
	  - Physical and logical elements and relationships
	  - Choices of COTS and reusable software elements
	• Identification of infeasible architecture options
		• Choice of architecture and elaboration by increment
		  - Physical and logical components, connectors, configurations, constraints
		  - COTS, reuse choices
		  - Domain-architecture and architectural style choices
		• Architecture evolution parameters

Definition of Life-Cycle Plan	• Identification of life-cycle stakeholders
	  - Users, customers, developers, maintainers, interpreters, general public, others
	• Identification of life-cycle process model
	  - Top-level stages, increments
	• Top-level WWWWWHH* by stage
		• Elaboration of WWWWWHH* for Initial Operational Capability (IOC)
		- Partial elaboration, identification of key TBDs for later increments

Feasibility Rationale	• Assurance of consistency among elements above
	  - Via analysis, measurement, prototyping, simulation, etc.
	  - Business case analysis for requirements, feasible architectures
		• Assurance of consistency among elements above
		• All major risks resolved or covered by risk management plan

* WWWWWHH: Why, What, When, Who, Where, How, How Much

Table 2. Contents of LCO and LCA Milestones

The multimedia archives covered such media as photographic images, medieval manuscripts, Web-based business information, student films and videos, video courseware, technical reports, and urban plans. The original Library client problem statements were quite terse, as indicated in Table 3. Our primary challenge was to provide a way for the student teams to work with these clients to go from these terse statements to an LCO package in 7 weeks and an LCA package in 11 weeks.

We enabled the students and clients to do this by providing them with a set of integrated MBASE models focused on the stakeholder win-win success model; the WinWin Spiral Model as process model; the LCO and LCA artifact specifications and a multimedia archive domain model as product models; and a property model focused on the milestones necessary for an 11-week schedule (see Figure 2). Further details are provided in [Boehm et al, 1997].

Problem Set #2: Photographic Materials in Archives
Jean Crampon, Hancock Library of Biology and Oceanography

There is a substantial collection of photographs, slides, and films in some of the Library's archival collections. As an example of the type of materials available, I would like to suggest using the archival collections of the Hancock Library of Biology and Oceanography to see if better access could be designed. Material from this collection is used by both scholars on campus and worldwide. Most of the Hancock materials are still under copyright, but the copyright is owned by USC in most cases.

Problem Set #8: Medieval Manuscripts
Ruth Wallach, Reference Center, Doheny Memorial Library

I am interested in the problem of scanning medieval manuscripts in such a way that a researcher would be able to both read the content, but also study the scribe's hand, special markings, etc. A related issue is that of transmitting such images over the network.

Problem Set #9: Formatting Information
Caroline Sisneros, Crocker Business Library

Increasingly the government is using the WWW as a tool for dissemination of information. Two much-used sites are the Edgar Database of Corporate Information (http://www.sec.gov/edgarhp.htm) and the Bureau of the Census (http://www.census.gov). Part of the problem is that some of the information (particularly that at the EDGAR site) in only available as ASCII files. For information that is textual in nature, while the files can be cleaned up, formatting of statistical tables is often lost in downloading, e-mailing, or transferring to statistical programs. And while this information is useful for the typical library researcher, who usually have a very distinct information need, the investment in what it would take to put this information is a usable format is often too much trouble.

Problem Set #13: Moving Image Archive
Sandra Joy Lee, Moving Image Archive, School of Cinema/TV

The USC Moving Image Archive houses USC student film and video productions dating from the1930s to current productions in the School of Cinema-Television. Moving image materials in multiple formats, specialized viewing equipment, limited storage space, and complex access needs create challenges that may be solved with new computer technologies. Fifteen movie clips (.mov format), each approximately 45 minutes in length, over 100 digital film stills (.gif format), and textual descriptions of the films will be made available to students wishing to explore this project.

Table 3. Example Library Multimedia Problem Statements

Project Objectives

Create the artifacts necessary to establish a successful life cycle architecture and plan for adding a multimedia access capability to the USC Library Information System. These artifacts are:

1. An Operational Concept Definition
2. A System Requirements Definition
3. A System and Software Architecture Definition
4. A Prototype of Key System Features
5. A Life Cycle Plan
6. A Feasibility Rationale, assuring the consistency and feasibility of items 1-5

Team Structure

Each of the six team members will be responsible for developing the LCO and LCA versions of one of the six project artifacts. In addition, the team member responsible for the Feasibility Rationale will serve as Project Manager with the following primary responsibilities:

1. Ensuring consistency among the team members' artifacts (and documenting this in the Rationale).
2. Leading the team's development of plans for achieving the project results, and ensuring that project performance tracks the plans.

Project Approach

Each team will develop the project artifacts concurrently, using the WinWin Spiral approach defined in the paper "Anchoring the Software Process." There will be two critical project milestones: the Life Cycle Objectives (LCO) and Life Cycle Architecture (LCA) milestones summarized in Table 1.

The LCA package should be sufficiently complete to support development of an Initial Operational Capability (IOC) version of the planned multimedia access capability by a CS577b student team during the Spring 1997 semester. The Life Cycle Plan should establish the appropriate size and structure of such a team.

WinWin User Negotiations

Each team will work with a representative of a community of potential users of the multimedia capability (art, cinema, engineering, business, etc.) to determine that community's most significant multimedia access needs, and to reconcile these needs with a feasible implementation architecture and plan. The teams will accomplish this reconciliation by using the USC WinWin groupware support system for requirements negotiation. This system provides facilities for stakeholders to express their Win Conditions for the system; to define Issues dealing with conflicts among Win Conditions; to support Options for resolving the Issues; and to consummate Agreements to adopt mutually satisfactory (win-win) Options.

There will be three stakeholder roles:

- Developer: The Architecture and Prototype team members will represent developer concerns, such as use of familiar packages, stability of requirements, availability of support tools, and technically challenging approaches.
- Customer: The Plan and Rationale team members will represent customer concerns, such as the need to develop an IOC in one semester, limited budgets for support tools, and low-risk technical approaches.
- User: The Operational Concept and Requirements team members will work with their designated user-community

representative to represent user concerns, such as particular multimedia access features, fast response time, friendly user interface, high reliability, and flexibility of requirements.

Major Milestones

September 16	---	All teams formed
October 14	---	WinWin Negotiation Results
October 21,23	---	LCO Reviews
October 28	---	LCO Package Due
November 4	---	Feedback on LCO Package
December 6	---	LCA Package Due, Individual Critique Due

Individual Project Critique

The project critique is to be done by each individual student. It should be about 3-5 pages, and should answer the question, "If we were to do the project over again, how would we do it better - and how does that relate to the software engineering principles in the course?"

Fig. 2. Multimedia Archive Project Guidelines

4.2   MBASE Model Integration for LCO Stage

The integration of these models for the LCO stage is shown in Figure 3. The end point at the bottom of Figure 3 is determined by the anchor point postconditions or exit criteria for the LCO milestone [Boehm, 1996]: having an LCO Rationale description which shows that for at least one architecture option, that a system built to that architecture would include the features in the prototype, support the concept of operation, satisfy the requirements, and be buildable within the budget and schedule in the plan.

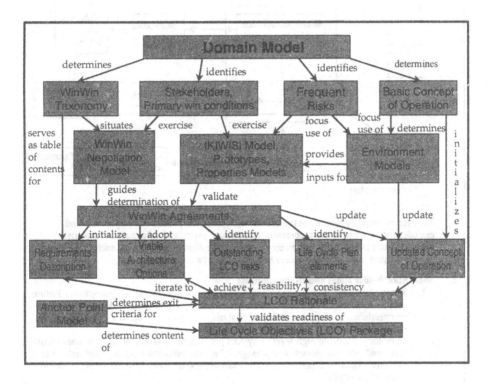

Fig. 3. MBASE Model Integration: LCO Stage

The beginning point at the top of Figure 3 is the multimedia archive extension domain model furnished to the students, illustrated in Figure 4. The parts of the domain model shown in Figure 4 are the system boundary, its major interfaces, and the key stakeholders with their roles and responsibilities. The domain model also established a domain taxonomy used as a checklist and organizing structure for the WinWin requirements negotiation system furnished to the teams. As shown at the left of Figure 3, this taxonomy was also used as the table of contents for the requirements description, ensuring consistency and rapid transition from WinWin negotiation to requirements specification. The domain model also indicated the most frequent risks involved in multimedia archive applications. This was a specialization of the list of 10 most frequent software risks in [Boehm, 1989], including performance risks for image and video distribution systems; and risks that users could not fully describe their win conditions, but would need prototypes (IKIWISI).

1. **System Block Diagram:**
   This diagram shows the usual block diagram for extensions providing access to and administration of multimedia information archive assets from an existing text-based information archive (IA) System:

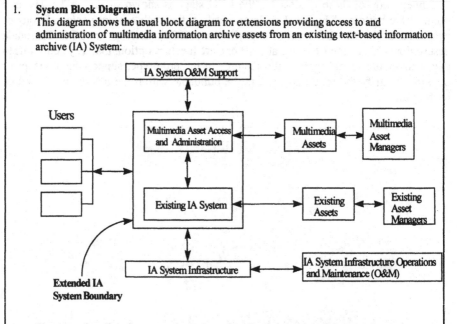

The system boundary focuses on the automated applications portion of the operation, and excludes such entities as users, operators, maintainers, assets, and infrastructure (campus networks, etc.) as part of the system environment. The diagram abstracts out such capabilities as asset catalogues and direct user access to O&M support and asset managers.

2. **Some Stakeholder Roles and Responsibilities**
   2.1. Asset Managers. Furnish and update asset content and catalogue descriptors. Ensure access to assets. Provide accessibility status information. Ensure asset-base recoverability. Support problem analysis, explanation, training, instrumentation, operations analysis.
   2.2. Operators. Maintain high level of system performance and availability. Accommodate asset and services growth and change. Protect stakeholder privacy and intellectual property rights. Support problem analysis, explanation, training, instrumentation, operations analysis.
   2.3. Users. Obtain training. Access system. Query and browse assets. Import and operate on assets. Establish, populate, update, and access asset-related user files. Comply with system policies. Provide feedback on usage.
   2.4. Application Software Maintainer. Perform corrective, adaptive and perfective (tuning, restructuring) maintenance on software. Analyze and support prioritization of proposed changes. Plan, design, develop, and verify selected changes. Support problem analysis, explanation, training, instrumentation, operations analysis.
   2.5. Infrastructure service providers (e.g. network, database, or facilities management services).
   2.6. Similar roles and responsibilities to Asset Managers under 2.1

Fig. 4. Multimedia Archive Extension Domain Model

The sequence of activities between the beginning point and the LCO end point were determined by the WinWin Spiral Model. As illustrated in Figure 5, this model emphasizes stakeholder win-win negotiations to determine system objectives, constraints and alternatives; and early risk identification and resolution via prototypes and other methods [Boehm-Bose, 1994].

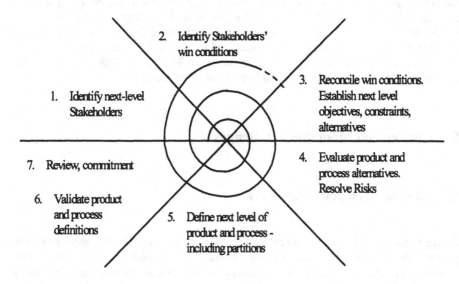

Fig. 5. The WinWin Spiral Model

4.3   Project Results

With the aid of the integrated MBASE models, all 15 of the student teams were able to complete their LCO and LCA packages on time (3 of the applications were done separately by 2 teams). The Library clients were all highly satisfied, often commenting that the solutions went beyond their expectations. Using a similar MBASE and WinWin Spiral Model approach, 6 applications were selected and developed in 11 weeks in the Spring of 1997. Here also, the Library clients were delighted with the results, with one exception: an overambitious attempt to integrate the three photographic-image applications into a single product.

The projects were extensively instrumented, including the preparation of project evaluations by the librarians and the students. These have led to several improvements in the MBASE model provided to the student teams for Fall 1997, in which 16 teams developed LCO and LCA packages for 15 more general digital library applications. For example, in 1996, the WinWin negotiations were done before the LCO milestone, while the prototypes were done after the LCO milestone. This led to considerable breakage in the features and user interface characteristics described in the LCO documents, once the clients exercised the prototypes. As a result, one of the top three items in the course critiques was to schedule the prototypes earlier. This was actually a model clash between a specification-oriented stakeholder win-win success model and the prototype-oriented IKIWISI success model. The 1997 MBASE approach removed this model clash by scheduling the initial prototypes to be done concurrently with the WinWin negotiations.

Another example was to remove several redundancies and overlaps from the document guidelines: as a result, the 1997 LCO packages averaged 103 pages as compared to 160 in 1996. A final example was to strongly couple the roles, responsibilities, and procedures material in the Operational Concept Description with the product transition planning, preparation, and execution activities performed during development. Most of the artifacts from the 1996-97 and 1997-98 project can be accessed via the USC-CSE web site at http://sunset.usc.edu/classes.

5   Conceptual Modeling Challenges

5.1   MBASE Conceptual Framework

Figure 6 provides an overall conceptual framework for the MBASE approach. The primary drivers for any system's (or product-line's) characteristics are its key stakeholders. These generally include the system (taken below to mean "system or product-line") users, customers, developers, and maintainers. Key stakeholders can also include strategic partners, marketers, operators of closely coupled systems, and the general public for such issues as safety, security, privacy, or fairness.

The critical interests of these stakeholders determine the priorities, desired levels, and acceptable levels of various system success criteria. These are reflected in the success models for the system, such as stakeholder win-win business case, operational effectiveness models, or IKIWISI. These in turn determine which portions of an applications domain and its environment are relevant to consider in specifying the system and its development and evolution process. The particular objective is to determine the system boundary, within which the system is to be developed and evolved; and outside of which is the system environment (cf. Figure 4).

The upper loop in Figure 6 shows how the stakeholders use their success models, and associated property models (e.g. cost models and revenue or effeciveness models for the business case analysis) to determine the appropriate operating region for the project. As shown in Figure 7, the operating region consists of operating points, each representative of a choice of system product specification and life-cycle process (including such choices as staffing, methods, and tools). The space of conceptual multimedia archive operating points is shown as an example domain.

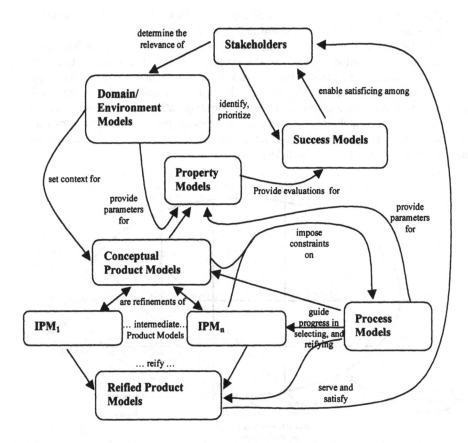

Fig. 6. MBASE Conceptual Framework

Success Models and Metrics

Figure 7 also shows how the stakeholder-determined success models impose metrics on the space of (product, process) operating points, via the use of property models, which enable reasoning about the various success attributes (Figure 6). For example, if a 5 month initial operational capability (IOC) is a critical success condition, a cost-schedule estimation model such as COCOMO, Checkpoint, or PRICE S will determine the estimated schedule for the project as a function of its domain (precedentedness, required reliability, application complexity), product (size, performance, platform characteristics), and process (staffing, methods, and tools) characteristics.

The results of these property-model estimates are shown in conceptual form in figure 7. The "5 month" line divides the space of operating points into systems buildable in more or less than 5 months. Similarly, if other key success conditions include 1-second response-time performance and a set of core product features (e.g.

for a digital image archive) these also determine metrics which divide the space of operating points into satisfactory and unsatisfactory regions.

The intersection of the satisfactory regions for each success condition determines the satisfactory operating region for the project. Often, the initial satisfactory operating region will be empty, and the stakeholders will iterate around the upper loop of Figure 6, adjusting and renegotiating their success models and ambition levels for the domain, product, and process until a feasible operating region is generated. In the context of the stakeholder win-win success model, the satisfactory regions are determined by stakeholder win conditions, and the win-win region is similarly the intersection of these regions [Lee, 1996].

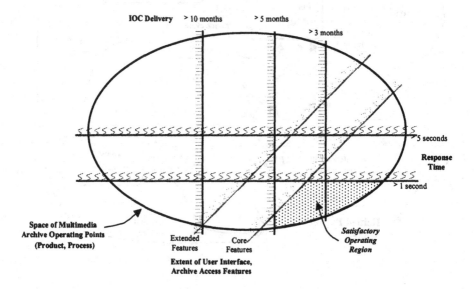

Fig. 7. Success Models Impose Metrics on Space of (Domain, Product, Process) Operating Points

MBASE Product Model Integration

The upper loop in Figure 6 primarily involves top-level conceptual models of the product and process, although these are selectively elaborated in specifics to address critical negotiation issues or to resolve high-risk uncertainty areas. The lower loop in Figure 6 primarily involves elaboration of the conceptual product models through a sequence of intermediate product models until these are reified to the point that a compiler or applications generator can transform them into an executable computer program for a particular platform configuration. This elaboration is guided by the chosen process models, although product choices (COTS components, re-engineered legacy code, hardware choices) may impose constraints on the process models.

Further, these constraints (or new opportunities) may cause a reconsideration of the top-level success models and criteria, and a backtracking process through the upper loop of Figure 6. Finally, the outer loop in Figure 6 involves evaluating how well the reified, executing product actually serves and satisfies the stakeholders, often leading to further traversals of the upper and lower loops as the system evolves through its life cycle.

Intermediate Product Models

The overall MBASE approach draws on, has contributed to, and shares many aspects with Rational's Objectory process [Rational, 1997] and Unified Software Management approach [Royce, 1998]. The particular MBASE object-oriented approach to defining intermediate product models follows the Integrated Systems Development Methodology (ISDM) [Port, 1998].

In the ISDM approach, the conceptual product models in Figure 6 are focused on people-understandable, more general operations-concept and domain entities, attributes, and relationships. The reified product models are automatically translatable into specific-technology, computer-executable computer programs. The transition from general-people oriented representations to specific-technology oriented representations involves sets of specific-people oriented representations (generally associated with requirements or object-oriented analysis) and general-technology oriented representations (generally associated with object-oriented design); see Figure 8. Although the recursive hierarchical nature of why-what-how relationships has been well-known for some time [Ross-Schoman, 1977], within the context of Figure 8 the quadrants can be considered to relatively address the questions of why/where; what; how; and "do."

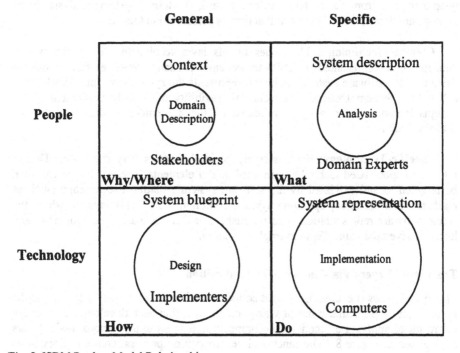

Fig. 8. ISDM Product Model Relationships

The people-technology and general-specific distinctions in Figure 8 are not entirely orthogonal, however they are independent enough to provide natural software development layers in terms of the validators of the model elements (to whom we refer as the audience for the layer) such as stakeholders, domain experts, implementers, and of course computers. The process of translating general-people kinds of abstractions into specific-technology oriented abstractions indicate four development layers that must be concurrently elaborated and continuously reconciled in order to reify a software product. These layers are supported by environments to create model elements using functional decomposition. The layers are:

General-People: Abstractions created here describe parts of the overall domain or environment of the system. This brings the Domain/Environment Models into the Product Model creation process as a natural starting point and relevance tool by setting forth the "why" a project is being done, and "where" it's starting from. As shown in Figure 8, the Domain/Environment Models are validated by the stakeholders. This layer is referred to as the "Domain Description."

Specific-People: Concurrently, a determination must be made for people to understand "what" software product is to be developed in order to realize the system concept. The model elements which describe this are best validated (to reduce risk of unfaithfulness) by domain experts, or people who understand the system concept well and can make decisions on what should or should not be represented in software. This involves careful consideration of particular domain elements and exactly what people require from the system. In this regard, the term "System Analysis" is an appropriate description of the overall activities performed in this layer.

General-Technology: The issues in this layer resolve the "how" the system concept can be represented as a software system. As such, it must describe the overall design of the software system and how it represents the system concept. This layer is called the "System Design;" the technical feasibility of actually implementing the designs it contains can only be validated by the implementers, thus they are the primary audience.

Specific-Technology: For this layer, the implementers reify the System Design into those specialized technology oriented model elements. These software can then be targeted to and validated by the software system's platform technology (such as hardware configuration, operating system, compiler, etc.). This layer is where the actual software representation is accomplished, or the "do" part of development, and hence is given the name "System Implementation."

Traversing Layers Via Functional Decomposition

The model views (i.e. creating related collections of model elements by looking at the system from a particular point of view) contained within each development layer are the result of applying a functional decomposition process to the various model layers as depicted in Figure 8. The functional decomposition process consists of six basic tasks that serve to capture, analyze, and assemble the system concepts into reified model elements (and ultimately software elements). As an example, the process of conceptualizing within System Analysis, that is, describing the top-level specific-people kinds of abstractions, produces the System Requirements view. Moving down a bit into the Design layer, the view that represents identification of general-technology "form" model elements that stem from the System Requirements (which in were identified previously as conceptualizing in Design) is well represented by traditional Object relationship models.

Figure 9 summarizes this functional decomposition process. It is presented in terms of six numbered tasks, indicating the general progression of the process. But the tasks will necessarily have a good deal of risk-driven concurrency, particularly when large-content, high-risk exposure decisions must be made, such as the choice of COTS components. The degree of elaboration of the intermediate representations will be risk-driven as well.

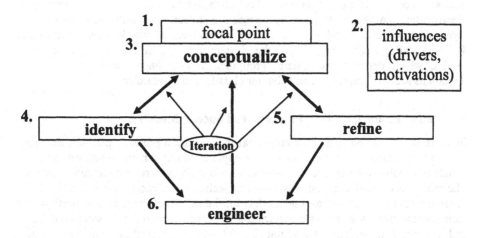

Fig. 9. Functional Decomposition Process

In task 1, a focal point (which serves as a simple an entry point) is chosen which sets the center of context around which this model will be oriented. For example, within the Analysis we seek a specific-people kind focal point which will be called the "Statement of Purpose" for the software system. In task 2, the external influences that may affect the qualities of the abstractions are listed. This often takes the form of goals, as with Product Goals, which come about when describing issues that influence the system with respect to the Analysis but are not strictly part of the system, such as time/cost/quality goals. Note that it is set apart from the process flow indicated in Figure 9. This is to indicate that influences may independently have effects throughout the model. Consider for example, that the Product Goal, "System should be able to handle up to 10,000 new users per year" will very likely effect several of the systems components and behaviors. In task 3, the top-level concepts, such as System Requirements, are generated and used as a reference model to maintain the consistency and soundness of the model elements to follow. This constitutes the top-level "gathering" layer of the process.

We now move to the decomposition (or analysis) layer of the process. In task 4 we identify directly from the concepts derived in task 3, the abstractions that have "form" (i.e. can undergo state transitions), such as System Entities, Components and Objects (when "identification" is applied to Domain Description, System Analysis, and System Design respectively). Concurrently, in task 5, the concepts are decomposed and elaborated on, thereby becoming more specific through refinement. This is often limited to a point appropriate for the particular Product Model being created, for example within System Analysis, a System Requirement may be refined to the point where System Operations are specified, but not so far as to specify the literal functions that carry out the operations. The models created through identification and refinement of the concepts are known as *intermediate product representation* models, as they are never used directly to represent the whole product and are generally not concrete enough to accommodate any such representation. In task 6, the "form" abstractions, along with the concept refinements are merged and reified through engineering operations such as classification, generalization, specialization, factoring, and so forth. This often results in the common technique of classification that is used to formally represent a collection of abstractions related by "type-of" and "kind-of" relationships. Associations were already handled within task 4. Specifically, engineering within the System Analysis results in an Enterprise Model, which describe the general groupings of components within the system domain as sets of component and behavior classification hierarchies.

Integrating Product, Process, Property, and Success Models

In some situations, one can do a great deal to integrate a project's product, process, property, and success models. The best example is domain-driven model integration, which is feasible for families of projects in relatively mature or bounded domains. The multimedia archive domain discussed in Section 4 is a good example. There, the domain model determined baseline models for the stakeholders' roles and portions of their success models; and for the application's concept of operation, system boundary, and environment model. The domain model also determined baseline values and models for properties such as performance, and determined the project's baseline process model within the LCO-LCA-IOC framework.

Similar determinations can be made from domain models in other mature, bounded domains, such as moderate-size financial planning, inventory control, or data acquisition and analysis applications; or from domain models constructed for software product lines, e.g., the XYB banking domain in [Jacobson et al., 1997].

In other situations, compatible models can be determined from previous compatibility analyses. One example is the process model decision table shown in Figure 10 [Boehm, 1989; pp. 436-37]. It shows the results of a risk analysis of various combinations of domain characteristics (size of application, requirements understanding, available COTS components, architecture understanding) and success model characteristics (required robustness; cost or schedule constraint) to determine which process model is the best match to the characteristics. Thus, a pure waterfall model is not a good choice if the requirements or architecture are not well understood. But if the system needs to be very robust to be successful, a process involving initial spiral cycles to determine appropriate requirements and architecture, followed by a waterfall model with strong requirements verification is a good choice.

Objectives, Constraints			Alternatives		Model	Example
Growth Envelope	Under-standing of Rqts.	Robust-ness	Available Techno-logy	Archi-tecture Under-standing		
Limited			COTS		Buy COTS	Simple Inventory Control
Limited			4GL		Transform or Evolutionary Development	Small Business-DP Application
Limited	Low	Low		Low	Evol. Prototype	Advanced Pattern Recognition
Limited to Large	High	High		High	Waterfall	Rebuild of Old System
	Low	High			Risk Reduction Followed by Waterfall	Complex Situation Assessment
		High		Low		High-perfor-mance Avionics
Limited to Medium	Low	Low-Medium		High	Evolutionary Development	New Decision Support System
Limited to Large			Large Reusable Com-ponents	Medium to High	Capabilities-to-Requirements	Electronic Publishing
Very Large					Risk Reduction & Waterfall	Air Traffic Control
Medium to Large	Low	Medium	Partial COTS	Low to Medium	Spiral	Software Support Environ-ment

Conditions for Additional Complementary Process Model Options
-Design-to-cost or schedule: Fixed Budget or Schedule Available
-Incremental Development: Early Capability Needed
(only one condition   Limited Staff or Budget Available
      is sufficient)   Downstream Requirements Poorly Understood
                             High-Risk System Nucleus
                             Large to Very Large Application
                             Required Phasing With System Increments

Fig. 10. Software Process Model Decision Table

Some other examples of model compatibility analyses are the Quality Attribute Requirements Conflict Consultant (QARCC) [Boehm-In, 1996]; the Software Architecture Analysis Method (SAAM) [Kazman et al., 1994]; and Expert COCOMO [Madachy, 1995], which identifies risky combinations of project choices entered as COCOMO cost driver ratings (e.g., proposing to develop an ultra-reliable product with an inexperienced team on a highly compressed schedule).

Beyond this, one can perform some degree of model integration by using model-clash tables such as Table 1 as checklists. We are attempting to elaborate Table 1 into a considerably more comprehensive checklist via analyses of our annual series of digital library projects and other sources of experience. Ultimately, our objective is to develop a knowledge-based toolset to provide advice on avoiding model clashes. Viewed in this way, the MBASE conceptual modeling challenges are a special case of the general knowledge representation challenge for expert systems.

6   Conclusions

Software projects need to make many tactical decisions, and a much smaller number of strategic decisions. It is easy to get so enmeshed in the daily tactical decisions that one makes incompatible strategic decisions involving model clashes. The MBASE approach provides a framework and a number of techniques for avoiding such model clashes.

The MBASE approach is still only partially elaborated. Two of its key challenges are the choice of and the integration of the various conceptual models needed to represent and reason about a project's success, product, process, and property characteristics. Representations such as Figures 1 and 3 begin to capture model integration characteristics, but clearly fall short of representing the full integration of the relevant models. We welcome collaboration with the conceptual modeling community in determining the most effective choices of such models.

References

[Babcock, 1985]. C. Babcock, "New Jersey Motorists in Software Jam," ComputerWorld, September 30, 1985, pp. 1, 6.

[Boehm, 1989]. B. Boehm, Software Risk Management, IEEE-CS Press, 1989.

[Boehm, 1996]. B. Boehm, "Anchoring the Software Process," IEEE Software, July 1996, pp. 73-82.

[Boehm, et al., 1997]. B. Boehm, A. Egyed, J. Kwan, and R. Madachy, "Developing Multimedia Applications with the WinWin Spiral Model," Proceedings, ESEC/ FSE 97, Springer Verlag, 1997.

[Boehm-Bose, 1994]. B. Boehm and P. Bose, "A Collaborative Spiral Process Model Based on Theory W," Proceedings, ICSP3, IEEE, 1994.

[Boehm-In, 1996]. B. Boehm and H. In, "Identifying Quality-Requirement Conflicts," IEEE Software, March 1996, pp. 25-35.

[Garlan et al., 1995]. D. Garlan, R. Allen, and J. Ockerbloom, "Architectural Mismatch: Why Reuse is So Hard," IEEE Software, November 1995, pp. 17-26.

[Jackson, 1975]. M. A. Jackson, Principles of Program Design, Academic Press, 1975.

[Jacobson et al., 1997]. I. Jacobson, M. Griss, and P. Jonsson, Software Reuse, Addison Wesley, 1997.

[Kazman et al; 1994]. R. Kazman, L. Bass, G. Abowd, and M. Webb, "SAAM: A Method for Analyzing the Properties of Software Architectures," Proceedings, ICSE 16, ACM/IEEE, 1994, pp. 81-90.

[Lee, 1996]. M.J. Lee, Formal Modeling of the WinWin Requirements Negotiation System, Ph.D. Thesis, USC Computer Sciences Dept., 1996.

[Madachy, 1995]. R. Madachy, "Knowledge-Based Risk Assessment Using Cost Factors", Automated Software Engineering, 2, 1995.

[Marenzano, 1995]. J. Marenzano, "System Architecture Validation Review Findings," in D. Garlan, ed., ICSE17 Architecture Workshop Proceedings, CMU, Pittsburgh, PA 1995.

[Port, 1998]. D. Port, Integrated Systems Development Methodology, Telos Press, 1998 (to appear).

[Rational, 1997]. Rational Objectory Process, Version 4.1, Rational Software Corp., Santa Clara, CA, 1997.

[Rosove, 1967]. P.E. Rosove, Developing Computer-Based Information Systems, John Wiley and Sons, Inc., 1967.

[Ross-Schoman, 1977]. D.T. Ross and K.E. Schoman, "Structured Analysis for Requirements Definition," IEEE Trans. SW Engr., January 1977, pp. 41-48.

[Royce, 1998]. W.E. Royce, Unified Software Management, Addison Wesley, 1998 (to appear).

Deriving Global Conceptual Views from Multiple Information Sources

Silvana Castano[1] and Valeria De Antonellis[2]

[1] University of Milano
Dip. Scienze della Informazione, via Comelico 39 - 20135 MILANO - ITALY
e-mail: castano@dsi.unimi.it

[2] University of Brescia and Politecnico di Milano
P.za L. da Vinci 32 - 20133 MILANO - ITALY
e-mail: deantone@elet.polimi.it

Abstract. Conceptual modeling plays a relevant role in the development of information systems and software applications. In the last two decades large sets of conceptual schemas have been produced in most private and public organizations, and in recent times the need of analyzing and classifying this large amount of information resources is becoming increasingly important. In the paper, we present a set of methods and tools for the definition of global views of information from multiple and heterogeneous sources, to support querying facilities and navigation among them.

1. Introduction

Conceptual modeling plays a relevant role in the development of information systems and software applications. In the last two decades large sets of conceptual schemas have been produced in most private and public organizations, and in recent times the need of analyzing and classifying this large amount of information resources is becoming increasingly important. Activities of conceptual schema analysis are required in different application contexts: to extract information on schemas of legacy systems in order to migrate them to new architectures by reengineering and restructuring previous systems and information [1, 6, 8] ; to build libraries of reference reusable schemas to be used in building new applications in a given application domain [9, 19, 17]; to enforce interoperability among heterogeneous and distributed dabase systems to support query processing and cooperation [5, 10, 20, 21]. Moreover, the availability of large sets of information in the Web requires to define global views of the information extracted from distributed and heterogeneous sources, to obtain an integrated representation of data relevant to a given application and to constitute a reference model for query processing. Working on conceptual representations of the information stored in a server, as proposed in [7], sites storing related information can be compared, abstracted, and then queried according to this abstract representation.

In the paper, we present a set of methods and tools for the definition of global views of information from multiple and heterogeneous sources, to support querying

P.P. Chen et al. (Eds.): Conceptual Modeling, LNCS 1565, pp. 44-55, 1999.
© Springer-Verlag Berlin Heidelberg 1999

facilities and navigation among heterogeneous sources. To support the definition of global views, an important problem to be addressed is the identification of semantically related pieces of information in the different sources. In particular, techniques to deal with semantic heterogeneity are required. Typically, semantic heterogeneity occurs when the same piece of information is represented in different ways in different database schemas, defined according to the same or different data models, and when the same piece of information has a different meaning, content, or purpose in different databases [18, 21]. Techniques proposed in the multidatabase literature address semantic heterogeneity issues by adopting a terminological perspective or a structural perspective. According to a terminological perspective, the terms used in the schemas of a federation play a central role and are analyzed and re-organized into summary schemas at higher abstraction levels, by mapping them to the concepts of an existing domain taxonomy [5, 16]. According to a structural perspective, the focus is on the attributes and domains of the objects of database schemas and techniques have been proposed for the classification and resolution of the schematic conflicts that can arise between heterogeneous object representations [15, 20].

We propose a comprehensive framework that takes into account both the terminological and the structural perspectives. A basic element of the framework is the concept of *affinity* used to assess the level of semantic relationship between elements of different schemas. The concept of affinity has been firstly introduced by the authors in the domain of reuse, to evaluate the conceptual distance between schema components and identify portions of schemas candidate for reuse. The higher the number of commonalities two components have in different schemas, the higher the affinity between them and the lower their conceptual distance [9].

This concept of affinity is now revised and extended to perform schema analysis in multiple information source environments, by taking into account specific heterogeneity and interoperability requirements. Problems considered in our research work are related to the need of dealing with information which can be found in multiple heterogeneous sources. In this framework, it is necessary to have a global view, that is, a unified representation of shared information in an application domain. Note that, starting from multiple source schemas, the global viewing process is devoted to providing a unified description of elements with affinity in different schemas which mediates among their different representations due to different types (name/type/structure) of conflicts. According to the database view concept, the global view definition includes mapping functions towards the sources schema elements (at the intensional and extensional level). Global views can be structured by identifying "part-of" and "is-a" relationships, or by defining association relationships. The result is a uniform interface, regarding schema elements of interest for querying/browsing activities, that is not required to be the "integrated schema" of the source schemas. In fact, an integrated schema might be too complex in contents and dimension, and not useful for required interaction. We envisage that one possible modern role of conceptual modeling is to support global viewing as much as possible for the following purposes: to facilitate the unification process in cooperation scenarios characterized by different levels of interaction; to improve query processing, by making available global views and related mappings; to support formalization efforts in heterogeneity analysis and resolution.

The paper is organized as follows. In Section 2, affinity-based analysis of sources schemas is described. In Section 3, derivation of global conceptual views is presented, while, in Section 4, their exploitation for query purposes is illustrated. Finally, in Section 5, our concluding remarks are given.

2. Conceptual Schema Analysis

In our approach, a source schema is a collection of elements, $S_i = \{e_{1i}, e_{2i}, ..., e_{mi}\}$. A schema element e_{ji} S_i is defined with a name, a set of structural properties, and a set of dependency properties, $e_{ji} = <n(e_{ji}), SP(e_{ji}), DP(e_{ji})>$, with $SP(e_{ji}) \leftrightarrow DP(e_{ji}) =$ and $SP(e_{ji}) \approx DP(e_{ji}) = P(e_{ji})$. The name of an element is unique within the schema to which the element belongs. Structural properties describe features of an element while dependency properties describe relationships of an element with other elements of the schema.

Each property is defined with a name and a domain of admissible values. Property values can be atomic values (e.g., strings, integers) or object identifiers, depending on the kind of property. Properties can be single-valued or multi-valued. We associate with each property a pair of values (mc, MC), with $mc \bullet MC$, to denote the minimum and maximum cardinality of a property, respectively. Consequently, a property p_k $P(e_{ji})$ is defined as a triple $p_k = <n_{p_k}, d_k, (mc, MC)_k>$, where: i) n_{p_k} is the property name, unique within e_{ji}; ii) d_k is the property domain; and iii) $(mc, MC)_k$ is the property cardinality, with $mc = MC = 1$ if p_k is single-valued, and $MC = n$, with $n > 1$, if p_k is multi-valued. Reasoning in terms of elements and properties allow us to be source independent in the global viewing process, and consider source schemas defined according to different data models (e.g., Entity-Relationship model [4], relational model [2], object-oriented models [13]). For example, in case of Entity-Relationship schemas, elements correspond to entities, structural properties to attributes and dependency properties to relationships to which an entity participates. The goal of conceptual schema analysis is to recognize semantically related elements in different source schemas, based on the concept of affinity. Affinity between elements is evaluated by considering:

-    the name of the elements, using a *Name Affinity coefficient*;
-    the properties of the elements, using a *Structural Affinity coefficient*.

These two kind of affinity are combined by means of a *Global Affinity coefficient* to provide a comprehensive value of affinity, taking into account both terminological and structural aspects of the elements. Affinity-based schema analysis is performed with tool support, limiting manual activities to supervision and validation. Unification is a time-consuming, difficult process, especially if a high number of schemas and elements is involved and a semi-automatic analysis of the schemas is desirable.

2.1   Name Affinity

Name affinity is generally considered the first, heuristic indicator of semantic relationship among elements in different schemas. To compare names in heterogeneous source schemas and determine those that are related, a structured Thesaurus of terminological relationships is employed.

Relevant terminological relationships in the Thesaurus are *synonymy*, denoted by SYN, and *hypernymy*, denoted by BT (Broader Terms). Two names are synonyms if they can be interchangeably used in source schemas, without changes in meaning. For example, we can have the synonymy relationship <Person SYN User>. A name is an hypernym of another one if the first has a broader, more general meaning than the second. For example, we can have the hypernymy relationship <Publication BT Book>. For each BT relationship, its opposite relationship NT (Narrower Terms) is also stored in the Thesaurus.

Terminological relationships are extracted as much as possible from source schemas, by analyzing elements and properties. For example, BT relationships between element names can be extracted from generalization hierarchies in sources schemas. Additional relationships specifying domain-related knowledge not derivable from source schemas directly can be manually supplied.

In populating the Thesaurus, also homonyms have to taken into account, to avoid the evaluation of undesired element affinity subsequently. In our approach, homonym analysis is performed with tool assistance. Discovered homonyms are stored in a separate Thesaurus section for subsequent use in name affinity evaluation.

To make the numerical evaluation of name affinity possible, each terminological relationship $\leftarrow$ is properly strengthened in the Thesaurus. The strength $\sigma_{\leftarrow}$ of a terminological relationship $\leftarrow$ expresses its implication for affinity, with σ_{SYN} • $\sigma_{BT/NT}$. The *Name Affinity coefficient* of two elements e_{ji} and e_{hk}, denoted by $NA(e_{ji}, e_{hk})$, is the measure of the affinity of their names $n(e_{ji})$ and $n(e_{hk})$ (recognized not to be homonyms), evaluated on the basis of the terminological relationships defined between them in the Thesaurus. The existence of a path in the Thesaurus is condition for two names to have affinity. For any pairs of names, $NA()$ $[0,1]$. $NA(e_{ji}, e_{hk})$ is equal to 1 if the names coincide. $NA(e_{ji}, e_{hk})$ coincides with the strength of the shortest path between $n(e_{ji})$ and $n(e_{hk})$ in the Thesaurus, if this strength exceeds a given threshold. $NA(e_{ji}, e_{hk})$ is equal to 0 in remaining cases. The strength of the shortest path between two names is computed by multiplying the strengths of the involved relationships. The longer the path, the lower name affinity. For a given path length, the greater the strength of the involved relationships, the higher the affinity of the considered names.

2.2   Structural Affinity

Name affinity alone is not sufficient to conclude that two elements are semantically related. To this end also structure of schema elements must be analyzed and compared.

To support structure analysis, we introduce the concept of *semantic correspondence* for elements' properties. Semantic correspondences are established between properties of elements with $NA()$ by analyzing their names and domains. First condition in the establishment of a semantic correspondence between two properties is name affinity, to find properties with the same meaning. Second condition in the establishment of a semantic correspondence between two properties is "domain compatibility", to test if their data value representations match each other. Based on this, two kinds of semantic correspondences are introduced for the evaluation of structural affinity of schema elements:

- *weak correspondence*, denoted by $\leftrightarrow^*$, if two properties have name affinity;
- *strong correspondence*, denoted by $\leftrightarrow$, if two properties have both name affinity and domain compatibility.

Conditions to be checked for domain compatibility depend on the kind of domain. For example, compatibility of two pre-defined domains can be due to the internal representation of values. For instance, with reference to SQL domains, examples of compatibility relationships that can be defined for pre-defined domains are the following:

char[n₁]⇔char[n₂], smallint⇔integer, integer⇔float, decimal⇔float, smallint⇔float, where symbol ⇔ denotes compatibility. Moreover, a compatibility relationship is defined between a domain and its restrictions (e.g., integer ⇔[min..max]). In case of reference domains, compatibility is evaluated on the names of the referenced elements, by requiring that they coincide or are synonyms in the Thesaurus. A comprehensive analysis of domain compatibility condition is presented in [12]. The Structural Affinity coefficient of two schema elements e_{ji} and e_{hk}, denoted by $SA(e_{ji},e_{hk})$, measures the level of overlapping between their structure based on the number of properties having a correspondence as follows:

$$SA\left(e_{ji},e_{hk}\right)=\frac{2\cdot|PSEM|}{|P(e_{ji})|+|P(e_{hk})|}$$

where *PSEM* is the set of property correspondences established between e_{ji} and e_{hk}, and notation $|A|$ denotes the cardinality of set A. Also in this case, we have $SA()$ $[0,1]$. The value 0 indicates that no semantic correspondences are defined for properties of e_{ji} and e_{hk}. The value 1 indicates that each property of e_{ji} has a semantic correspondence with at least one property of e_{hk} and vice versa. Intermediate values of $SA()$ are proportional to the number of correpondences established between e_{ji} and e_{hk} properties.

2.3   Global Affinity

To assess the level of affinity of two schema elements e_{ji} and e_{hk} in a comprehensive way, a *Global Affinity coefficient,* denoted by $GA(e_{ji},e_{hk})$, is computed as the linear combination of the Name Affinity and Structural Affinity coefficients, that is,

$$GA\left(e_{ji},e_{hk}\right)=\begin{cases}w_{NA}\cdot NA\left(e_{ji},e_{hk}\right)+w_{SA}\cdot SA\left(e_{ji},e_{hk}\right) & if\ NA\left(e_{ji},e_{hk}\right)\neq0\\0 & otherwise\end{cases}$$

where weights w_{NA} and w_{SA}, with w_{NA},w_{SA} [0,1] and $w_{NA}+w_{SA}=1$, are introduced to assess the relevance of each kind of affinity in computing the global affinity value. We have tested different values for these weights, and we found that an intermediate situation with $w_{NA},w_{SA}=0.5$ gives better results.

2.4   Clusters of Elements with Affinity

Based on $GA()$ coefficients, a hierarchical clustering procedure is employed to group together all schema elements that are semantically related in the considered schemas in an automated way. In brief, the procedure computes $GA()$ coefficients for all possible pairs of elements to be analyzed. An affinity matrix M is constructed of rank K, being K the total number of elements to be analyzed. An entry $M[s,t]$ of the matrix represents the $GA()$ coefficient of corresponding schema elements. Clusters are iteratively constructed, starting from singleton clusters (one for each considered element). At each iteration, the pair of clusters having the greatest $GA()$ value in M is merged. M is updated   at each merging operation by deleting the rows and the columns corresponding to merged clusters, and by inserting a new row and a new column for the newly defined cluster. $GA()$ values between the newly defined cluster and remaining clusters are computed at each iteration as the maximum $GA()$ value between $GA()$ values defined in M for merged clusters and each remaining cluster. The procedure repeats cluster merging until rank of M is greater than 1.

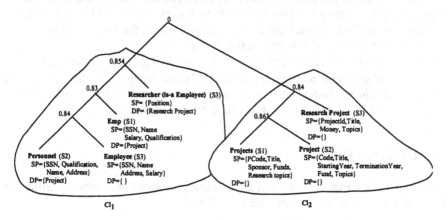

Fig. 1. Example of affinity tree

As the result, an affinity tree is constructed, where schema elements are the leaves and intermediate nodes are $GA()$ values, decreasing from the bottom to the top of the tree. Several element clusters can be identified in the affinity tree, characterized by different values of $GA()$. An example of affinity tree for three simple source schemas (S_1, S_2, and S_3) in the Research&Development domain is shown in Fig.1. Two clusters are formed in this tree grouping all schema elements describing personnel

(Cl_1) and projects (Cl_2), respectively. For the sake of clarity, in the figure we show names for structural and dependency properties of schema elements. $GA()$ values in the tree are computed using formulas previously described, by inheriting properties in generalization hierarchies with $\sigma_{SYN}=1$, $\sigma_{BT/NT}=0.8$, and $w_{NA}=w_{SA}=0.5$.

3. Deriving Global Conceptual Views

A *global conceptual view* is derived from a cluster in the affinity tree, and provides a unified representation of all the elements it contains. Global conceptual views can be virtual or materialized [14], depending on the requirements of the underlying environment.

Clusters candidate for being unified into a global conceptual view are selected within the affinity tree by considering $GA()$ values. One can decide to automatically select as candidate clusters only the ones with very high values of $GA()$ (e.g., by means of a threshold-based mechanism), or, alternatively, the ones having a not null value of $GA()$. The difference is in the number and nature of resulting global views. In the first case, a higher number of global conceptual views is defined unifying highly homogeneous elements. The possibility of re-organizing global views into generalization hierarchies should be evaluated. In the second case, a lower number of global views is defined, unifying more heterogeneous elements. In such a case, the need of generalization hierarchies at the global level is reduced. An automatic criterion for selection of candidate clusters is not definable, in that it depends on how the affinity values in the tree. We found out that candidate clusters can be identified progressively, by starting from the ones with the highest values of $GA()$ (i.e., clusters at the bottom level of the tree) and by moving upwards in the tree, to include other elements until the $GA()$ value is judged significant.

A global conceptual view $V_q=< n(V_q), SP(V_q), DP(V_q), \underline{Cl_q}>$ is defined with a name, a set of structural properties, and a set of dependency properties, and has an associated candidate cluster. Derivation of global conceptual views is a bottom-up process starting from candidate clusters, based on *unification rules*.

3.1 Unification Rules

Unification rules for the derivation of global names and global properties (considering also their domains and cardinality) are defined as follows.

(UR$_1$) Name unification

The global name $\underline{n}$ unification of a pair of names with affinity can coincide with one of them or can be one of their hypernyms or synonyms in the dictionary.

Let p_t and p_q be two properties with $p_t \leftrightarrow p_q$ or $p_t \leftrightarrow^* p_q$. Before introducing the unification rule for properties, we define the rules for unifying domains and cardinalities, respectively.

(UR$_2$) Domain unification

The global domain $\underline{d_{tq}}$ unification of a pair of domains d_t p_t and d_q p_q is automatically defined if the involved properties have a strong semantic correspondence and is user-defined otherwise.

In case of strong correspondences, different solutions are possible depending on the different types of domains. For example, with two pre-defined, compatible $\underline{d_{tq}}$ coincides with the less restrictive domain between them. For example, if d_t=char[n$_1$] and d_q=char[n$_2$], we have $\underline{d_{tq}}$=char[n], with n=max(n$_1$,n$_2$). As another example, if d_t=integer and d_q=smallint, we have $\underline{d_{tq}}$=integer. For properties with a weak correspondence, the corresponding global domain is user-defined, interactively supplied by the analyst. For example, if d_t=char[n$_1$] and d_q=integer, a global domain $\underline{d_{tq}}$ is set equal to one of them only if an isomorphism can be established between the values of d_t and d_q. If no global domains can be specified, $\underline{d_{tq}}$=$\perp$, meaning that the unification is not applicable. All possible cases that can occur in unifying domains of properties with strong correspondence are described in [12].

(UR$_3$) Cardinality unification

The global cardinality $\underline{(mc,MC)}$ unifying two cardinalities of a pair of properties with a semantic correspondence is defined as the less restrictive cardinality between the two, that is, $\underline{mc}$= $min\{mc_t,mc_q\}$ and $\underline{MC}$=$max\{MC_t,MC_q\}$.

(UR$_4$) Property unification

The global property $\underline{p_{tq}}$ unification of two properties p_t and p_q such that $p_t \leftrightarrow p_q$ or $p_t \leftrightarrow^* p_q$ is defined with name and domain obtained by applying corresponding unification rules to the names, and domains of p_t and p_q, respectively, that is,

1. $\underline{n_{p_{tq}}}$= $n_{p_t} \bullet UR_1\ n_{p_q}$
2. $\underline{d_{tq}}$= $d_t \bullet UR_2\ d_q$
3. $\underline{(mc,\ MC)}_{tq}$=$(mc,MC)_t \bullet UR_3\ (mc,MC)_q$

where notation $\bullet\ UR_k$ denotes unification by applying rule (UR$_k$), with k=1,...,3.

3.2   Unification Process

In analogy with the view integration process, we adopt a binary strategy to derive global views from candidate clusters and we distinguish between "unification in the small" and "unification in the large". *Unification in the small* is the basic step to derive a global view from two elements. *Unification in the large* iteratively applies unification in the small to derive a global view from clusters containing more than two schema elements.

Unification in the small. Unification in the small is the derivation of a global conceptual   view V_{jh} from two elements e_{ji} and e_{hk} in candidate cluster $\underline{Cl}_q$. It consists of the following steps:

1. Derivation of the name of V_{jh} by applying (UR$_1$) to the names of e_{ji} and e_{hk}.
2. Derivation of properties of V_{jh} from properties of e_{ji} and e_{hk}. For each semantic correspondence, a unique global property $\underline{p}$ is defined by applying rule (UR$_4$) and is marked as featuring property for V_{jh} . Moreover, each property of e_{ji} or e_{hk} not participating in semantic correspondences is taken "as is" in V_{jh}.

Domain conversions can be required for compatible domains associated with global properties. In analogy with approaches proposed in the literature [20, 21], we introduce "conversion functions" implementing necessary mappings between the values of two compatible domains d_t and d_q. For example, if $\underline{d}$=float is the domain abstracted from compatible domains d_f=integer and d_q=float, a conversion function for $\underline{d}$ converts into a real representation the integer values of d_t.   For candidate clusters $\underline{Cl}_q$ containing only two elements, the global view V_q coincides with the result of the unification in the small. For clusters containing more than two elements, the unification in the large is necessary.

Unification in the large. Unification in the large of candidate clusters containing more than two elements is performed by unifying in the small pairs of elements at a time. Results of the unification in the small are accumulated into intermediate global views V_{jh} which gradually evolve towards the final global view V_q, representative of all elements included in $\underline{Cl}_q$. The order for element comparison is bottom-up, starting from the pair with the highest value of $GA()$ in $\underline{Cl}_q$. For example, the global conceptual view Project data derived from cluster Cl$_2$ of Fig.1 is shown in Fig.2. Project data is characterized by 4 featuring properties (denoted by (f) in the figure) and by two structural properties which are not featuring in that they have a correspondent property only in some element of Cl$_2$.

```
Project data
            ( Code: integer}  (f),
              Title: char[30] (f),
              Topics: char[30]        (f),
              Fund: integer   (f),
              Sponsor: char[50],
              StartingYear: integer,
              Termination Year: integer)
```

Fig. 2. Example of global conceptual view

Schema elements of the affinity tree not appearing in any candidate clusters can become global conceptual views as they are, without being submitted to unification. This decision is left to the analyst, who evaluates their relevance and goodness for being included in the set of global conceptual views, by taking into account interaction and query requirements.

Once global views have been defined, they are analyzed to check their mutual consistency and to compose them by means of semantic relationships. Examples of semantic relationships that can be defined among global views are: i) KIND-OF, to represent the generalization/aggregation relationship; ii) PART-OF, to represent aggregation relationships; iii) ASSOCIATION, to represent other kind of semantic relationships that can be established between global views. Each global view V_q is also connected by means of an INSTANCE-OF relationship with each element of its corresponding cluster Cl_q. Semantic relationships among global views can be defined by analyzing the properties of the views and of the elements in their corresponding clusters. For example, if two global views have a number of common properties, they can be related by means of a KIND-OF relationship, to highlight the generalization/specialization relationship between them. In our example, an ASSOCIATION relationship is defined between global views Project data, shown in Fig.2, and Employee data (derivable from cluster Cl_1 of Fig.1).

4.   Exploiting Global Conceptual Views

Global conceptual views can be exploited for integrated access to distributed information, by mediating between different schema terminologies and representations. In case of virtual global views, "mapping functions" have to be defined to materialize the view with data stored at each source. Mapping functions, denoted by $\rightarrow^M$, are associated with properties of a global conceptual view and specify how to retrieve data at each involved source using its corresponding query language. For example, to retrieve title and topics of projects having funds greater than a specified threshold T, the following query can be posed against Project data,

```
RETRIEVE Fund, Topics
FROM     Project data
WHERE    Fund > T
```

Conversion functions associated with properties in the query are used to evaluate the query and select proper data at each involved source. As an example, mapping function defined for property Topics of Project data (see Fig.2) is the following:

```
Topics  →M
              SELECT Research topics FROM Projects
              SELECT q.Topics FROM q IN Project,
              SELECT p.topics FROM p IN Research Project
```

where SELECT clauses are defined according to the query language of the involved data sources (here we suppose to have both relational and object-oriented data sources). Global conceptual views can also be exploited for browsing, based on semantic relationships established among them. After selecting a global view V_q of interest, the user can explore the view space and find other global views related to V_q. A set of pre-defined functions are available for browsing, which display meta-information associated with global conceptual views, such as (featuring) properties, specialization/generalization views, global views having an association relationship with V_q.

5. Concluding Remarks

In this paper, we have presented an approach to global viewing of heterogeneous information sources. The concept of affinity together with affinity-based clustering and unification techniques are the main features of the global viewing process. The approach has been experimented in the Italian Public Administration domain, on Entity-Relationship conceptual schemas of databases that are required to cooperate and share part of their data for administrative and legal reasons. A support tool environment called ARTEMIS is also available, where affinity-based schema analysis and unification have been implemented on top of a schema repository of Entity-Relationship database schemas in electronic format [11].

Future research work is in the direction of extending the global viewing process to conceptual descriptions of semi-structured information, such as the documents in the Web, in order to provide an integrated conceptual representation of the information in different sites for querying purposes.

References

1. P. Aiken, A. Muntz, R. Richards, "DoD LegacySystems - Reverse engineering data requirements", *Comm. of the ACM*, vol.37, n.5, 1994.
2. P. Atzeni, V. De Antonellis, *Relational Database Theory*, The Benjamin/ Cummings Publishing Company, 1993.
3. Y. Arens, C.Y. Chee, C.N. Hsu, C.A. Knoblock, "Retrieving and Integrating Data from Multiple Information Sources", *Journal of Intelligent and Cooperative Information Systems*, vol.2, n.2, 1993.
4. C. Batini, S. Ceri, S.B. Navathe, *Conceptual Database Design*, The Benjamin Cummings Publishing Company, 1992.
5. M.W. Bright, A.R. Hurson, S. Pakzad, "Automated Resolution of Semantic Heterogeneity in Multidatabases", *ACM Trans. on Database Systems*, vol.19, n.2, June 1994.
6. M.L. Brodie, M. Stonebraker, "DARWIN: On the incremental migration of legacy information systems", *DOM Technical Report, TM 0588-10-92, GTE Labs*, 1992.
7. Special issue on hypermedia design, *Comm. of the ACM*, vol.38, n.8, 1995.

8. S. Castano, V. De Antonellis, "Reference Conceptual Architectures for Re-engineering Information Systems", *Int. Journal of Cooperative Information Systems*, vol.4, nos. 2&3, 1995.

9. S. Castano, V. De Antonellis, "Semantic Dictionary Design for Database Interoperability", in *Proc. of ICDE'97, IEEE Int. Conf. on Data Engineering*, Birmingham, 1997.

10. S. Castano, V. De Antonellis, "Engineering a Library of Reusable Conceptual Components", *Information and Software Technology*, vol.39, 1997.

11. S. Castano, V. De Antonellis, M.G. Fugini, B. Pernici, "Conceptual Schema Analysis: Techniques and Applications", to appear on *ACM Trans. on Database Systems*, 1998.

12. S. Castano, V. De Antonellis, S. De Capitani Di Vimercati, "Global Viewing of Heterogeneous Data Sources", *Technical Report,* Politecnico di Milano, 1998.

13. R. Cattel (ed.), *The Object Database Standard: ODMG-93*, Morgan Kaufmann, 1996.

14. R. Hull, "Managing Semantic Heterogeneity in Databases: A Theoretical Perspective", Tutorial presented to *PODS'97*, 1997.

15. W. Kim, I. Choi, S. Gala, M. Scheevel, "On Resolving Schematic Heterogeneity in Multidatabase Systems", in *Modern Database Systems-The Object Model, Interoperability and Beyond, W. Kim (Editor)*, ACM Press, 1995.

16. P. Fankhauser, M. Kracker, E.J. Neuhold, "Semantic vs. Structural Resemblance of Classes", *SIGMOD RECORD*, vol.20, n.4, December 1991.

17. N.A. Maiden, A.G. Sutcliffe, "Exploiting reusable specifications through analogy", *Comm. of the ACM*, vol. 35, n.4, 1992.

18. Y. Papakostantinou, S. Abiteboul, and H. Garcia-Molina, "Object Fusion in Mediator Systems", in *Proc. of the 22th VLDB Conference*, Mumbai (Bombay), India, 1996.

19. R. Prieto-Diaz, "Systematic reuse: a scientific or engineering method?", *ACM Software Engineering Notes*, 9-10, 1995.

20. M.P. Reddy, B.E. Prasad, P.G. Reddy, A. Gupta, "A Methodology for Integration of Heterogeneous Databases", *IEEE Trans. on Knowledge and Data Engineering*, vol.6, n.6, December 1994.

21. E. Sciore, M. Siegel, A. Rosenthal, "Using Semantic Values to Facilitate Interoperability Among Heterogeneous Information Systems", *ACM Trans. on Database Systems*, vol.19, n.2, June 1994.

From Ancient Egyptian Language
to
Future Conceptual Modeling

Peter P. Chen

Computer Science Department
Louisiana State University
Baton Rouge, LA 70803, USA
chen@bit.csc.lsu.edu

Abstract. This paper discusses the construction principles of ancient Egyptian hieroglyphs from the point of view of conceptual modeling. The paper starts with a summary of author's previous work on the correspondence between the Entity-Relationship diagrammatic (ERD) technique and two natural languages: English and Chinese. In one previous work, the similarity between the English sentence structure/grammar and the construction blocks and rules of ERD was discovered. In another work, the similarity between the Chinese character construction methods and the ER modeling principles was also discovered. In this paper, construction methods of the ancient Egyptian hieroglyph are analyzed with respect to the construction methods of Chinese characters and the conceptual modeling principles. At the end, possible applications and extensions of this research work are discussed.

1   Introduction

One of the most crucial steps in software engineering is to model the user requirements correctly. An accurate model can help not only in developing better quality software system but also in speeding up the software development process, which usually overran in costs and time. More and more systems analysis and design methodologies rely on graphical representations of the user requirements and the software systems. The most frequently used diagrammatic techniques are Data Flow diagrams, Entity-Relationship Diagrams (ERD), Object Diagrams, and State Transition Diagrams. Besides software engineering, ERD and semantic networks are used widely in data and knowledge engineering. Detailed descriptions of these techniques can be found in many software engineering and systems analysis books (for example, [20]) or data/knowledge engineering books.

The Entity-Relationship (ER) diagram technique [2] is a graphical tool for information system designers and users in describing and communicating their understanding of the world. Since its formal introduction in 1976, it has become one of the most widely used techniques in systems analysis and database design projects and the cornerstone of the CASE (computer-aided software engineering) industry [15, 17]. Although the ER diagram technique is primarily used by computer professionals and users, its use has been spreading to other fields such as accounting and music

P.P. Chen et al. (Eds.): Conceptual Modeling, LNCS 1565, pp. 56-64, 1999.

composition. Many recent papers on ER model extensions and applications can be found in [1, 12, 13, 14, 18]. For more theoretical work, the reader can refer to [19, 21].

On the other hand, natural languages are the daily tools for the general public in describing and communicating their understanding of the world. Because both the ER diagram (ERD) techniques and the natural languages satisfy similar human needs, these two "human communication" techniques should have something in common. Furthermore, if we can understand better the correspondence between "ERD" and "natural language," it is very likely that we can use this knowledge to improve our modeling methodologies, techniques, and tools.

In this paper, we will first start with a review of key concepts between "English grammar constructs" and "ER diagram constructs." This section is a summary of the author's previous work on this topic. Then, the next section summarizes the author's previous work on the principles for constructing Chinese characters. Some of these principles are well known by those familiar with the Chinese written language, but we modify the concepts to fit better with conceptual modeling professionals. The rest of the principles either are not well known or are proposed by the author. The fourth section is a short introduction to the history of ancient Egyptian languages. The fifth section tries to organize the construction principles of ancient Egyptian language hieroglyphs into the same framework of modeling principles as the construction of Chinese characters. The final section states the conclusions and the future research/application directions. Throughout this paper, we assume that the reader has some basic understanding of the notations and concepts of the ERD technique.

2 Review of the Correspondence between English Sentence Structures and ERD Constructs

The correspondence between the English sentence structures and the ERD construct was first presented at the 2nd ER Conference in 1981 in Washington, D.C., and later published in [3]. A summary of the basic translation rules is summarized in Table 1.

English Grammar Structure	ERD Structure
Common Noun	Entity Type (a possible candidate)
Proper Noun	Entity (candidate)
Transitive verb	Relationship type (candidate)
Intransitive verb	Attribute type (candidate)
Adjective	Attribute for entity
Adverb	Attribute for relationship
Gerund (a noun converted from a verb)	An entity type converted from a relationship type
Clause	A high-level entity type which hides a detailed ERD

Table 1. Correspondence between English sentence structures and ERD constructs

For example, a "common noun" (such as "desk," "car") in English is a possible candidate for an entity type in an ERD. A "proper noun" (such as "George Washington") is a possible candidate for an entity (an instance of an entity type) in an ERD.

This technique can be used in several ways:

- As an early stage requirement analysis tool: it can help users to identity entity types, relationship types, attributes, and high-level ERD constructs based on the English sentence structures. Recently, researchers in OO (Object-Oriented) Analysis methods also started to advocate the use of English "nouns" as a way to identify possible "objects," and this is the same position we advocated in [3].

- As the basis for (manually or semi-automatically) converting a large amount of requirements specification documents (in English) into ERD-like specifications. Several large consulting firms are practicing this technique. This technique can also be used in reverse direction, that is, to use ERD in assisting users to formulate a more English-like query. In other words, to use it as a basis for building a more English-like interface to database management systems.

In the following section, we will discussions the correspondence between Chinese characters and ERD constructs.

3   The Construction Principles of Chinese Characters

Chinese written language is one of the earliest written languages in the world. The earliest development of Chinese characters was claimed to start as early as 8,000 years ago when a few picture-like characters were carved onto turtleback shells. However, a relatively useful set of approximately 4,500 characters was developed much later (approximately around 2,300 years ago) in the late Shang dynasty.

Most Western language characters (and even some modern Asian language characters) are phonetic-based, while Chinese characters are mostly picture-based. Chinese characters are ideograms; each one represents an idea, a thing, etc. Today, there are tens of thousand Chinese characters in circulation. How can a human brain store and retrieve so many ideograms? Fortunately, there are organized methods for memorizing some basic characters and for constructing new characters from existing ones.

Even though the various methods for constructing Chinese characters have been known for a long time and the genealogy of many Chinese characters have been investigated by researchers (see, for example, [11]), virtually none had looked at the construction methods from the viewpoint of conceptual modeling. In our study [8], we identified the following principles for Chinese character construction, which are also commonly used in conceptual modeling:

- Principle of Physical Resemblance
- Principle of Subset
- Principle of Grouping
- Principle of Composition (Aggregation)
- Principle of Commonality
- Principle of an-instance-of (Something).

We will explain each of these principles in Section 5 when we discuss the construction methods of ancient Egyptian hieroglyphs.

4   History of Ancient Egyptian Written Language

Similar to the Chinese, the Egyptians developed relatively sophisticated written language about four to five thousand years ago. Ancient Egyptian language can be divided into five different phases [9, 10, 16]:
1. Old Egyptian (approximately 2700-2200 BC)
2. Middle Egyptian (approximately 2200-1800 BC)
3. New Egyptian (approximately 1580-700 BC)
4. Demotic (approximately 700 BC-600 AD)
5. Coptic (600 AD - 1,000 AD).

The hieroglyphic script is of a pictorial written form of the Ancient Egyptian language. The earliest documented occurrence dates back to the pre-dynastic period, and the latest occurrence dates back to approximately 400 AD. At the end, the number of hieroglyphs grew to approximately 6,000, which was sufficient to express some complicated thoughts and events during that time.

5   Principles on Constructing an Ancient Egyptian Hieroglyphs

In the following, we will discuss the construction methods of ancient Egyptian hieroglyphs using the same set of conceptual modeling "principles" we derived in analyzing Chinese character construction [8]:

Principle I: Physical Resemblance Principle

"A hieroglyph may depict the physical shape or major visual features of the "thing" it tries to represent."
    For example, Fig. 1 has ten hieroglyphs constructed based on this principle. Fig. 1(a) shows the hieroglyph of the "lower arm," which depicts the lower arm including the elbow and the hand." Fig. 1(b) shows the hieroglyph of a "mouth" of a person or an animal. Fig. 1(c), 1(d), and 1(e) show hieroglyphs for "viper," "owl," and "sieve." Fig. 1(f) and 1(g) shows the hieroglyphs for "man," and "woman."
    Fig. 1(h) shows the hieroglyph for "sun," in which the dot in the middle of the circle may represent the sunspot. It is interesting to note that this ancient Egyptian hieroglyph for sun is the same as an early form of the Chinese character for sun [8]. Fig. 1(i) shows the hieroglyph for "house." Fig. 1(j) shows the hieroglyph for "water," where the hieroglyph depicts the waves at the water surface. This hieroglyph is very similar to the early form of the Chinese character for "water," even though we did not discuss that particular Chinese character in our previous work,
    All these examples show that some hieroglyphs resemble very closely the "things" they try to represent.

Hieroglyph	Meaning		Hieroglyph	Meaning
(a)	lower arm	(f)		man
(b)	mouth	(g)		woman
(c)	viper	(h)		sun
(d)	owl	(i)		house
(e)	sieve	(j)		water

Fig. 1. Hieroglyphs based on the Physical Resemblance Principle

Principle II: The Subset Principle

"Concatenation of a hieroglyph to another hieroglyph may create a new hieroglyph which represents a subset of the things represented by the original hieroglyph."

Fig. 2 (a) shows the hieroglyph for "house." Figure 2 (b) shows the hieroglyph for "wood." When the second hieroglyph is concatenated to the first hieroglyph, these two hieroglyphs together (as shown in Fig. 2(c)) represent a "wooden house." In this case, adding the 2nd hieroglyph may imply that a restriction (or selection criterion) is imposed to the things represented by the first hieroglyph to get a subset of them.

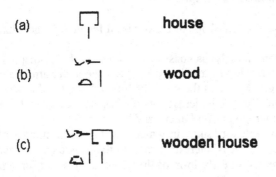

(a)   house

(b)   wood

(c)   wooden house

Fig. 2. Hieroglyphs based on the Subset Principle.

Principle III. Grouping Principle

"Duplication or triplication of the same hieroglyph/character has a new meaning." In ancient Egyptian hieroglyph, the new meaning usually means the "dual" or "plural" of the things of the original hieroglyph. Therefore, we can restate this principle as follows:

"A hieroglyph, which is duplex of an existing hieroglyph, may have the meaning of "dual" of the same thing represented by the original (single) hieroglyph. Along the same line, if a hieroglyph contains the triplex of another hieroglyph, it means the many instances of the things represented by the original single hieroglyph. To reduce the writing effort, the duplication (or triplication) of the whole original hieroglyph can be simplified by just duplication (or triplication) of the ending signs. In many cases, using two or three strokes at the end of the hieroglyph can also represent the duplication or triplication of the whole original hieroglyph.

Fig. 3 (a) illustrates a "god" and many "gods." The "gods" hieroglyph is a triplication of the hieroglyph of the "god" hieroglyph. Figures 3 (b) and 3(c) show two different forms of "two sisters" and "many sisters."

It is worthwhile to note that the use of this grouping principle is significantly different in ancient Egyptian hieroglyphs and in Chinese characters. In Chinese character construction, this principle is used almost solely for the generation of the new meaning of a new character rather than the pure indication of the "dual" and the "plural" concepts. Chinese language uses cardinal number "2" and the word "many" in front of the targeted word (which represents the "things") to represent the concept of "dual" and "plural," respectively. The way that the Chinese language represents the concept of "dual" and "plural" is the same as the English even though the Chinese language does not have nouns in the plural form.

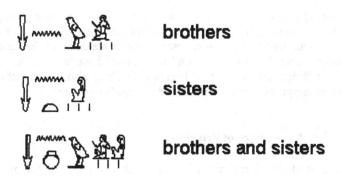

Fig. 3. Hieroglyphs based on the Grouping Principle.

Principle IV: Composition (Aggregation) Principle

"The meaning of a new hieroglyph is the combination of the meaning of its component hieroglyphs." Sometimes, it is not necessary to combine the whole hieroglyphs and only need to combine the parts of the hieroglyphs that are different.

Fig 4 depicts an example of this principle. The hieroglyph "brothers" and the hieroglyph "sisters" combine into a new hieroglyph with the meaning of "brothers and sisters."

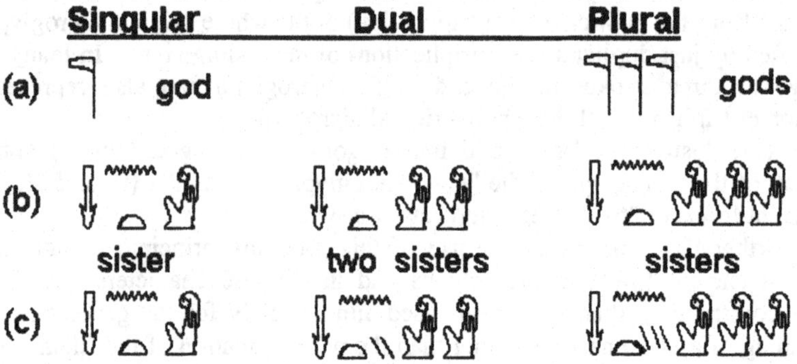

Fig. 4. Hieroglyphs based on the Composition Principle.

Principle V: Commonality Principle

"A new hieroglyph is formed by concatenation of two or more hieroglyphs. Its meaning is the common property of these component hieroglyphs." For example, in Chinese, you can construct a new character by concatenation of the character "sun" and character "moon." What does "sun" and "moon" have in common? The answer is "bright" or "brightness by light." This principle may also be applicable to ancient Egyptian hieroglyph, but we have not found a suitable example yet.

Principles VI: An-Instance-of Principle

"A component of the hieroglyph indicates which entity type it belongs to." This principle is used very often in Chinese character construction and interpretation. Usually, one part (most likely, the left part) of a Chinese character represents the (entity) type, while the other component (the right part) of the character indicates a special instance of this entity type." So far, we have no conclusive evidence that ancient Egyptian hieroglyphs also follow this principle. Further investigation is needed.

6   Conclusions and Future Research Directions

From the three languages we have studied so far, we can see the close mappings between the three languages (English, Chinese, and ancient Egyptian language) and the ER diagram technique, in particular, and the conceptual modeling techniques, in general.

Specifically, the principles used in constructing ancient Egyptian hieroglyphs (and Chinese characters and English grammar sentence structure) and the general principles used in conceptual modeling are very similar.

This is a relatively new research area. There are several ways to extend or apply this research work:

- Another natural language: One direction is to investigate other natural languages to see whether we can find something similar or different than English, Chinese, and ancient Egyptian language. A possible candidate we have in mind is the Mayan hieroglyphs.

- Better modeling and representation techniques: The conceptual modeling people can learn from natural languages (ancient Egyptian language, Chinese, English, etc.) to improve the modeling methodologies and tools.

- Improve natural language understanding and translation techniques. The people who are in the process of learning Chinese/English or building translators from one language to another can utilize some of the conceptual modeling techniques such as ERD to increase the learning speed or to design a better translator. Let us elaborate more on the point of developing new methods of learning natural language characters and statements quickly. In the past, the Chinese characters are always the roadblocks of people trying to learn more about the Chinese written language and culture. Even though some people have advocated the use of genealogy for the learning of Chinese characters, we think there is a very promising direction and much more work is needed.

- Better understanding on how a human thinks: It should be interesting to investigate how human mind works in recognition of the hieroglyph set either with or without the help of the construction principles discussed in this paper.

- Better interfaces between natural language interface and DBMS/repositories: Since ERD is used heavily in DBMS and repositories, the user interface design for these system could take advantage of the correspondence between ERD and natural languages.

- Better Design of GUI Icons: The icons in the graphical user interfaces of many systems or application software packages not correctly designed. As a result, the meaning of the icons confuses a lot of users. It will be nice to use the result of this work as a foundation to build a methodology for icon design.

- Using cognitive type & cultural background to select the "better" conceptual modeler: In a team environment, it is important to put the right person to do the right job. Not everyone is a master of natural languages. Perhaps those who can master natural language usage would be good candidates for the job of conceptual modeling.

- Using "gender" as a one of the factors for selection of "better" data/knowledge modeler: Are women more qualified than men to do conceptual modeling? This is a politically sensitive issue, but it may merit a scientific investigation.

- Adopt modeling methodologies and techniques to local environments: Use cognitive type and cultural background to select the most natural modeling techniques and methodologies for a particular environment.

References

1.   Embley, D. and Goldstein (ed.), *ER '97*, LNCS, Springer, Berlin, 1997.
2.   P. P. Chen, The entity-relationship model: toward a unified view of data, *ACM TODS* 1 (1976) 1-36.
3.   P. P. Chen, English sentence structures and entity-relationship diagrams, *Information Sciences*, (1983) 127-149.
4.   P. P. Chen, The time-dimension in the entity-relationship model, in: H..-J. Kugler ed., *Information Processing* (Amsterdam, 1986) 387-390.
5.   P. P. Chen and A. Zvieli, Entity-relationship modeling of fuzzy data, *Proc. of* 2nd *International Conf. on Data Eng.* (Los Angeles, 1987) 320-327.
6.   P. P. Chen, The denotational semantics of the entity-relationship model, (with N. Chandrasekaran and S.S. Iyengar), *International Journal of Computer Mathematics* (1988) 1-15.
7.   P. P. Chen, ER modeling for multimedia applications on the internet, *Proceedings of 1995 Conference on Applications of Databases, ADB '95*, San Jose, CA, 1995 (keynote speech, abstract only).
8.   Chen, P. P., English, Chinese and ER Diagram, *Data & Knowledge Engineering*, Vol. 23, No. 1 (June 1997), 5-16.
9.   Egyptologica Vlaanderen VZW, *Reading Hieroglyphs: The First Steps, Lessons 1-8, http://hosting.netvision.be/egyptologica /e_home.html, 1998.*
10. Gardiner, Sir Alan H., *Egyptian Grammar*, Griffith Institute, Oxford, 1979.
11. Harbaugh, R.(ed.), *Chinese Characters: A Genealogy and Dictionary*, Zhongwen.com., 1998.
12. Loucopoulos, P. (ed.), *ER '94*, LNCS 881, Springer, Berlin, 1994.
13. Papazoglou, M. P. (ed.), *OOER '95*, LNCS 1021, Springer, Berlin, 1995.
14. Ling, T. W., Ram, S. and Lee, M. L.(eds.), *Conceptual Modeling -- ER '98*, LNCS 1507, Springer, Berlin, 1998.
15. Laplante, P.(ed.), *Great Papers in Computer Science*, West Publishing Co., St. Paul, Minnesota, 1996.
16. Pestman, P.W. (ed.), *Aspects of Demotic Lexicography*, Leiden, 1987.
17. *The Software Challenges*, in the series: Understanding Computers, Time-Life Books, 1993, Third printing.
18. Thalheim, B. (ed.), *ER '96*, LNCS 1157, Springer, Berlin, 1996.
19. Thalheim, B., *Fundamentals of Entity-Relationship Models*, Springer, Berlin, 1997.
20. Whitten, J. L. and Bentley, L. D., *Systems Analysis and Design Methods*, Irwin/McGraw-Hill, 1998, 4th Edition.
21. Yang, A. and P. P. Chen, Efficient data retrieval and manipulation using Boolean entity lattice, *Data & Knowledge Eng.*, Vol. 20, No. 2 (October 1996), 211-226.

Breaking the Database out of the Box:
Models for Superimposed Information
(Position Paper)

Lois M. L. Delcambre

lmd@cse.ogi.edu
(503) 690-1689
Professor, Computer Science and Engineering
Director, Data-Intensive Systems Center
Oregon Graduate Institute
P.O. Box 91000
Portland, Oregon 97291-1000

1   Introduction

A traditional DBMS takes very good care of your data, by using concurrency control algorithms, recovery techniques, integrity constraint enforcement, etc. A DBMS also provides highly flexible access to your data through the use of query languages and views. With the World Wide Web, the Internet, and various intranets, we find ourselves with access to an almost unlimited amount of diverse information. Yet there is an increasing desire to use accessible information to support new, possibly local purposes. In many cases, we have access to information that we do not own. The problem, in such an environment, is that it is not always possible to place all of your data inside a DB. We have applications that would like to use data in all different formats, in all different places, locally managed by all sorts of technologies (including non-DBMS technology). How can we break the database out of the box? How can we take data out of (the very well-managed) jail of a DBMS yet still provide the services of a DBMS?

Our vision is to superimpose database capability over a highly diverse, highly federated universe of underlying information. The goal is to provide the full range of database functions by coordinating the activities of a consortium of information source managers. This vision provides a challenge for all database functions: how do we provide concurrency control, recovery, integrity, query processing, etc. when we must rely on the capabilities of all sorts of information source managers?

We consider, in the research reported here, various models that can be superimposed over an information universe. We focus on: the type of model(s) that can be superimposed, the type of underlying information that can be referenced by the superimposed layer, and the way in which the superimposed technology and the underlying information source manager can work together to provide navigational and query access to the data. Said another way, we are concerned with the modeling of information in an out-of-the-box environment and the kind of access that can be provided, e.g., with queries through the superimposed layer.

P.P. Chen et al. (Eds.): Conceptual Modeling, LNCS 1565, pp. 65-72, 1999.

2   Models for Superimposed Information

We briefly describe three different research projects that focus on models appropriate for the open, out-of-the-box environment described above. In all three projects, new entity-relationship-style models have been introduced over an information universe. The focus of the research reported here is to leverage database models and technology to provide structured access to diverse information sources. We propose to do so in a superimposed layer of technology over an underlying universe, where the layer includes both schema and instance information. The superimposed information can be linked to information elements in the underlying information universe. In these three projects, these links to the underlying information elements are sometimes explicit and sometimes implicit.

We are focusing on applications where we do not own the underlying information. We choose to use the underlying information *in situ*; we access the information using available technology. The superimposed layer allows the introduction of new entity and relationship types and data, as well as the highlighting of existing data. The superimposed layer is analogous to a database view, but with significant differences:

1. It need not be complete; there is no requirement for *all* of the data from the underlying information source to be reflected in the superimposed layer.
2. It is not limited to the data or the structure of the underlying information. The superimposed layer may introduce structure and data that's not present in the underlying information sources.
3. It is not limited to the structure of a single query answer. (Traditional query languages define a single table or collection as a query answer.)   The superimposed layer supports an entity-relationship-style model.
4. It may reference underlying information elements. The superimposed layer may highlight a particular entity or other information element from an underlying information source and may elaborate it with additional attributes or relationships.

Our view of the world, showing the underlying information universe and the superimposed layer is shown in Figure 1. The underlying information sources are managed by individual information sources. They may be of diverse types, as suggested by the different shapes of the IS managers shown in Figure 1. The superimposed layer introduces both schema- and instance-level information, with the possibility of referencing and highlighting underlying information.

In this section, we describe three projects that have introduced structured, superimposed information: Vertical Information Management, Precis-Based Browsing, and Structured Maps. The issues and opportunities presented by superimposed information are discussed in the final section.

2.1   Vertical Information Management

Vertical Information Management (VIM) refers to the problem of trying to move (potentially low-level, detailed) information upwards to decision makers at various levels in an organization. A question considered for VIM might be: what is the state dropout level for high school students? Or what is the volume of nuclear contaminant in the continental US? VIM sets out to exploit existing information present in various databases by extracting relevant information. The extracted information is usually much simpler than the original information.

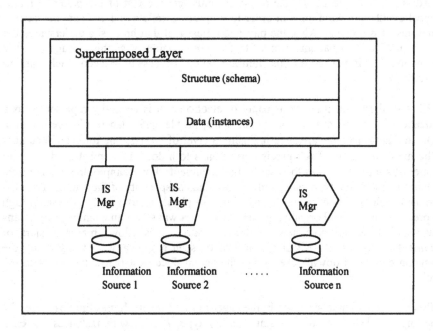

Fig. 1. Introducing Superimposed Information

For VIM, the underlying information sources are databases. (The projects described below relax this assumption.)   The challenges for VIM are: to extract data in a very flexible manner (since the data may be very detailed and complex in the underlying information source yet quite simple in the superimposed layer), to supplement the extracted data with metadata (such as the units of an attribute value), and to fill gaps in the underlying data. As an example of a gap, if we are extracting the high-school dropout rate from the various county school board databases, then it might be that several counties don't have information about dropouts. VIM supports various gap-filling measures such as supplying an estimate.

As a superimposed information layer, VIM can be viewed as a view or a query that produces a database (of entities and relationships) as an answer. Said another way, VIM produces a "database" as the answer to a "query" rather than just a single table or collection. VIM was developed in conjunction with Pacific Northwest National

Laboratory, a Department of Energy National Laboratory, to provide decision makers with high-level information.

2.2   Precis-Based Browsing

In this project, we are collaborating with physicians to work on the problem of familiarization. When a health care provider sees a patient for the first time, he or she must become familiar with the medical record for the patient. Whether the medical record is paper or electronic, the physician must get the gist of the patient's major medical events and conditions in order to properly correlate and evaluate the current symptoms or problems. Also, the physician must feel that he or she understands the "big picture" of this patient in order to feel comfortable prescribing drugs or other treatments. It is important for this "familiarization" process to proceed quickly and to be effective.

Whether the medical record is paper or electronic, it is generally represented as a sequence of documents (e.g., physician notes, problem list, lab result, prescription, etc.). In this project, we are superimposing a layer of *precis,* one for each document in the medical record. Each precis corresponds to a document and it holds a small number of simple attributes to describe the document. For example, the precis might contain the document type, date, author, and medical specialty of the author. To assist with the problem of familiarization, we allow the physician to quickly browse through the precis, selecting and organizing them in various ways. As an example, physicians may wish to see all documents sorted by date. This allows major clusters of documents (and hence medical activity) to be seen graphically. At any point, the physician can "drill down" to examine the actual document that corresponds to the precis.

Precis have a simple structure in the superimposed layer. In the simplest case, the superimposed layer has only a single entity type, *Precis*, with instances for each document in the medical record. In practice, we feel that additional entities and relationships would be beneficial such as an entity type for *Healthcare Provider* with an *author-of* relationship between *Healthcare Provider* and *Precis*.

The basic idea of this project is to superimpose a simple entity-relationship style model over the medical record for use in querying, navigating, and visualization to assist with the familiarization problem. From a database modeling point of view, precis are in one-to-one correspondence with underlying documents (the entities at the information source level). We believe that such "shadows" or "echoes" of underlying entities are potentially useful in any superimposed model.

This project is conducted in collaboration with physicians at the Oregon Health Sciences University, funded by the Department of Energy.

2.3   Structured Maps

The definition of Structured Map is based on work in the SGML community to define multi-document glossaries, thesauri, and indices (analogous to the index that you find at the back of a conventional book) using Topic Navigation Maps. The Structured Map allows entity and relationship types to be introduced in the superimposed layer, populated with entity and relationship instances. The new contribution of the Structured Map model is that each entity type may have one or more facets defined. Each facet is like a multi-valued attribute, where the attribute values are references to underlying information elements. Figure 2 shows an example of a Structured Map with two entity types and one relationship type: Painter, Painting, and painted, respectively. Further the Painter entity type has two facets defined: one to reference information elements that mention the painter and another to reference information elements with biographical information about the painter. The facets are used to reference or highlight selected information elements. The Painting has only a single facet named "mentioned". The Structured Map designer decides which facets should be defined for each entity. The *facet* is the most distinctive feature of a Structured Map. Any entity type may have zero or more facet types defined. A facet states the reason why the references are being made. The references that appear on facets can use any addressing mode supported by the underlying information sources and available for use in the Structured Map. In our first Structured Map prototype, we used SGML IDs to reference information elements. In our second prototype, we placed Structured Maps over HTML and used urls as addresses on facet instances.

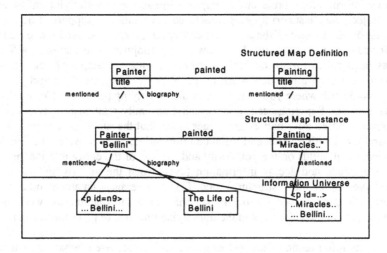

Fig. 2. Example of a Structured Map

In the middle part of Figure 2, we see one instance of Painter with a painter named "Bellini" and one instance of a painting named "Miracles of the Relic of the Cross." And we see that Bellini is connected to the painting through the painted relationship. In the lower part of Figure 2, we see that there are three information sources shown; imagine that they are all books represented in SGML. We see that Bellini is mentioned in the paragraph with an id of n9 in the first book. We see that there is a paragraph in the third book that mentions both Bellini and the Miracles of the Relic of the Cross. Finally, we note that the entire book, The Life of Bellini, provides biographical information about Bellini. Notice that the Structured Map does not disturb the underlying information nor its representation. The paragraphs of the books still appear in their original order, untouched. The Structured Map simply references information elements in the books. Note also that the references can refer to information elements of any granularity supported by the addressing mechanism of the underlying information source. Note also that neither the string "Bellini" nor any explicit mention of Bellini need appear in the underlying information element; if it is deemed to provide biographical information about Bellini, it could be added to the biography facet.

From a conceptual point of view, a Structured Map crosses models at two different levels, with the facet bridging between the two levels. We believe that explicitly modeling this connection between two layers is important. This work is supported by the National Science Foundation and is done in collaboration with Sequent Computer Systems.

3   Discussion

The projects described here are all motivated to superimpose a new model over underlying information sources and to improve the access to underlying information. In each project, we are superimposing structured information to support some purpose beyond the original intent of the underlying information sources. And we are dealing with information sources that we do not own. Superimposed information is a form of what has been called *foreground information*. A simple example of superimposed foreground information is a bookmark on the WWW. They are local and personal: you put a bookmark where you want it. And the underlying pages don't know that the bookmarks exist. Superimposed models, using an entity-relationship-style structure for the superimposed information, go further to say that the superimposed information can be structured with schema and instance information. This provides the following advantages: (1) it builds on the popularity and success of the entity-relationship-style model to organize and access information (even when the underlying information doesn't have an explicit structure) and (2) it leverages database models and technology to support access to the superimposed information as well as the highlighted information elements in the underlying universe (e.g., through facets).

If all of the information of interest were in a single database (perhaps a distributed database), then new applications would likely be supported within the database (e.g., as queries or views). Additional structure and data could be added to the database to support the new application and a superimposed layer might not be necessary. But as investment is made to create foreground information, there is more and more incentive to represent foreground information, including the links to the underlying information, explicitly and to provide useful technology to access it.

Another reason for superimposing a model is to improve performance. A simple "database" at the superimposed layer, with echoes or precis for important entities, might serve as an index to the underlying information source. In fact, the precis project above falls into this category if precis are added to an electronic medical record system. We have not yet explored the performance implications of using a superimposed layer. In general, we believe that: there is a limit to how much data we're willing or able to bring into a single database and there is utility in explicitly creating superimposed information to support new uses of data.

Research questions for this work include:

1. How should superimposed models be defined, particularly when the superimposed model includes echoes from the underlying information sources as well as additional structure and data? Can we take advantage of structure described in the underlying information sources? How much information should be captured in the definition of a facet?
2. How should superimposed models be implemented? In particular, how much can we exploit the technology that manages the underlying information source? What is the minimum capability needed to participate in a superimposed model? (How can we bring DBs out of the box?)
3. What is the query language for superimposed models, particularly when the model includes facets? What is the form of a query answer?
4. How can superimposed models be populated? How do we specify that extracted data is to populate/produce a database (as opposed to a simple query answer)?

Additional information about the three projects can be found as follows.

VIM

"Reuse of High-Level Information Requests: Leveraging the Investment", G. A. Washburn, L.M.L. Delcambre and M. A. Whiting, in *Proceedings of the Eighth International Conference on Scientific and Statistical Database Management.* Edited by Per Svensson and James C. French, IEEE Press, May 1996.

"Queries from Outer Space" by G. Washburn, L. Delcambre, and M. Whiting in *Proceedings of Research Issues in Data Engineering (RIDE) Workshop*, IEEE Press, New Orleans, LA, Feb. 1996.

Precis-Based Browsing

"Precis-Based Navigation for Familiarization", L. Delcambre, P. Gorman, D. Maier, R. Reddy, S. Rehfuss, accepted to *MedInfo '98, The 9th World Conference on Medical Informatics,* poster session. Available as Technical Report No. 97-009, Computer Science and Engineering Department, Oregon Graduate Institute, www.cse.ogi.edu.

Structured Maps

"Structured Maps: Modeling Explicit Semantics over a Universe of Information", L. Delcambre, D. Maier, R. Reddy, and L. Anderson, *Journal of Digital Libraries*, Vol. 1, No. 1, 1997.

"Dynamic Development and Refinement of Hypermedia Documents" by L. Delcambre, C. Hamon, M. Biezunski, R. Reddy, S. Newcomb, in *Proceedings of the Extending Database Technology (EDBT) '96 Conference*, Avignon, France, March 1996.

Narratives and Temporal Databases:
An Interdisciplinary Perspective

Antonio L. Furtado

Departamento de Informatica
Pontifícia Universidade Católica do R.J.
22.453-900 Rio de Janeiro, Brasil
furtado@inf.puc-rio.br

Abstract. A temporal database environment, particularly if equipped with a log of the execution of predefined application-domain operations, can be regarded as a repository of narratives concerning the activities observed in the mini-world of interest. The analysis of these narratives leads to the construction of a library of typical plans, which can be used by Plan-recognition / Plan-generation algorithms to help prediction, decision-making and the adoption of corrective measures with respect to ongoing activities. The formulation of concepts and methods for identifying the typical plans, and, more generally, for discovering meaningful narrative patterns, should be based on Cognitive Science and, especially, on the various contributions of Literary Theories to the interpretation of narratives. The proposed goal-oriented approach emerges as a promising research line to help understanding, and hence better modelling and using, in their many dimensions, today's computer-based information systems.

Keywords: databases, planning, abstract data types, narratives, pragmatic conceptual modelling.

1. Introduction

Originally, database conceptual modelling was applied to *data analysis*. At a second phase, *function analysis* started to be considered, initially receiving relatively less attention, with an emphasis on workflow-based methods [Sh]. In [FCa], we proposed a different method, based on application-domain operations (such as <u>hire</u>, <u>train</u>, <u>assign</u>), within an abstract data type orientation. The method was especially powerful in the presence of a plan-generation tool having access to a *log* recording the executions of operations. We showed that such log, easily implementable as a set of relational tables in correspondence with the pre-defined operations, was a desirable component of temporal database systems. In principle, such tables constituted by themselves a temporal database, since – as we then demonstrated – an inference

P.P. Chen et al. (Eds.): Conceptual Modeling, LNCS 1565, pp. 73-86, 1999.

mechanism was able to answer temporal queries from the records of the operations executed. More recently [FCi], we developed a more advanced tool, combining plan-recognition and plan-generation, able to match the observed behaviour of agents against a library of typical plans, so as to find out as early as possible what each agent is trying to achieve, and propose adjustments whenever convenient. Typical plans are those being used in practice, as one can determine by examining the log.

We then came to realize that any such log of application-domain operations provides a kind of information of great potential value, since its contents can be regarded as a collection of highly interconnected *plots of narratives* about the trajectories of the various entities involved (e.g. employees' careers). We also saw that the analysis of these narratives to detect meaningful patterns offers a promising, albeit non-trivial to undertake, knowledge-discovery opportunity [MC].

The thrust of the present paper is to propose as a research line the development of methods to extract plots of narratives from logs or other temporal database structures, interpret them, and find patterns by suitable clustering and comparison criteria, possibly employing some form of *most specific generalization* [Fu]. Successful methods must start, of course, with the prescription of simple and sound conceptual modelling foundations.

The basic concept of application-domain operations is reviewed in section 2. Section 3 introduces the key notion of plots of narratives, whose goal-oriented aspects are exploited in section 4, in connection with the construction and use of libraries of typical plans, coupled with a Plan-recognition / Plan-generation software device. In section 5 we argue that the additional concepts and interpretation techniques needed for an effective treatment of narratives must be investigated by integrating database technology with other disciplines, including not only Cognitive Science, which incorporates a strong computer-science component, but also Literary Theories, whose scope and relevance to our objectives are briefly and very informally outlined. Section 6 contains concluding remarks.

2. From Facts to Actions

Database *facts* can be conveniently denoted by *predicates*. Given an application domain whose conceptual schema, expressed in terms of the Entity-Relationship model, involves, among others:

    entities: employees, clients
    relationship: serves

the predicates:

  is-employee(E)
  is-client(C)
  serves(E,C)

can be used to express, respectively, that E is an employee, that C is a client, and that employee E is at the service of client C. Specific predicate instances, corresponding to facts of these three types, might be:

is-employee(Mary)
is-employee(Peter)
is-client(Omega)
serves(Peter, Omega)

A database *state* is the set of all predicate instances holding at a given instant. A state provides a *description* of the mini-world underlying the database.

On the other hand, *actions* performed in this mini-world can be denoted, always at the conceptual level, by *operations*. Assume that, among others, one can identify in our example application domain the operations:

hire(E)
replace(E1,E2,C)

in order, respectively, to hire E as an employee, and to replace employee E1 by employee E2 in the service of client C. A specific execution of the second operation is:

replace(Peter, Mary, Omega)

If the set of predicate instances shown before constitutes a state S_i, then executing the above operation achieves a transition from S_i to a new state S_j:

S_i		S_j
is-employee(Mary)		is-employee(Mary)
is-employee(Peter)	===>	is-employee(Peter)
is-client(Omega)		is-client(Omega)
serves(Peter, Omega)		serves(Mary, Omega)

An operation can be specified, in a STRIPS-like formalism [FN], by declaring its pre-conditions and post-conditions, which characterize the states before and after the operation is executed. Pre-conditions establish requirements, positive or negative, which must hold prior to execution whereas post-conditions express effects, consisting in predicate instances being *affirmed* or *negated*. Pre-conditions and post-conditions must be such that all static and transition *integrity constraints* are preserved.

The definition of <u>replace</u> is shown below, in a semi-formal notation:

<u>replace</u>(E1, E2, C):
- pre-conditions: serves(E1, C)
                         is-employee(E2)
                         ~∃ C1 serves(E2, C1)
- post-conditions: ~ serves(E1, C)
                         serves(E2, C)

The pre-conditions make provision for the constraint that an employee cannot serve more than one client. Notice, however, that some other obvious requirements seem to be missing, e.g. it is not indicated that E1 should be an employee. This kind of simplification is justified if a strict *abstract data type* discipline is enforced. Notice also that the effects indicated via post-conditions refer only to what is changed by execution. It is therefore assumed that anything else that held previously will still hold afterwards (so as to cope with the so-called "frame problem").

3. A Key Concept: Plots of Narratives

At a given instant of time, a factual database provides no more than the description of the current state. Temporal databases [Oz] allow to keep descriptions of all states reached, without making explicit, however, what actions caused the transitions; this sort of information becomes available if, in addition, a *log* registering the (time-stamped) executions of operations is maintained [FCa]. We will then say that, besides static descriptions, temporal databases thus enhanced now contain *narratives*, as will be illustrated in the sequel.

Suppose that, after our example database (owned by a corporation called Alpha) has been running for some time, one extracts from the log all operations concerning a given client, say Beta, and the employees assigned to its service, whose execution occurred during a given time interval. Let the obtained sequence, kept ordered by time-stamp, be:

Plot 1

a. open(client: Beta)
b. hire(employee: John)
c. assign(employee: John, client: Beta)
d. complain(client: Beta, employee: John)
e. train(employee: John, course: c135)
f. raise-level(employee: John)

The sequence above, named **Plot 1**, summarizes a narrative, which justifies calling it a *plot* [FCi]. Indeed, it can be read under the expanded form of a natural language text – thus making explicit the underlying full-fledged narrative – such as:

Beta became a client of Alpha. John was hired at the initial level, and then assigned to the Beta account. Later, Beta complained of John's service. John participated in training program c135. No further complaints came from Beta. John's level was raised.

Besides registering past executions of operations, the log can be further used as an agenda. Future executions, either merely possible or firmly scheduled, can be registered in the log, of course subject to later confirmation or cancellation.

4. The Pragmatic View of Narratives

Narratives contained in a database log, far from being fortuitous, exhibit a clear *pragmatic* bent, usually reflecting the *goals* of the several agents who promote the execution of operations [CF]. It is therefore useful to distinguish, among the possibly many effects of an operation, those that correspond to achieving a recognized goal of an agent; intuitively, they are the reason for executing the operation – which justifies calling them the *primary effects* of the operation – in contrast to other minor, seemingly innocuous, ones.

Sometimes a goal corresponds to the combination of the primary effects of more than a single operation. Even when only one operation would seem to be enough, it may happen that its pre-conditions do not currently hold, but might be achieved by the preliminary execution of another operation. In both cases, a partially ordered set of operations is required, whose execution in some sequence leads from an initial state S_0, through an arbitrary number of intermediate states, to a final state S_f where the goal holds. On the other hand, there are cases in which one finds more than one set of (one or more) operations as alternative ways of reaching a given goal.

Such partially ordered sets (posets) constitute *plans*. The complementary processes of automatic plan generation and plan recognition have been extensively studied, and several algorithms have been proposed for each of them. The distinction between plans and operations becomes blurred as we introduce, besides the operations discussed thus far (to be henceforward called *basic*), others called *complex operations*, which are defined either

- by composition - two or more operations (part-of hierarchy)
- by generalization - more than one alternative (is-a hierarchy)

Once complex operations have been introduced, one can build with them a hierarchically structured *library of typical plans*. Plan-recognition algorithms detect what plan an agent is trying to perform, by matching a few observations of the agent's behaviour against the repertoire of plans contained in one such library. As part of our ongoing research project, we have implemented a *Plan-recognition / Plan-generation* tool [FCi], where these two processes alternate. Having recognized that the observed behaviour of an agent indicates that he is trying to execute a library plan, the tool can check whether the plan is executable under the current conditions. If there exist obstacles, the tool can either propose a fix or adaptation (cf. the notion of *reuse* [GH], much in vogue in software engineering) or drop the plan altogether and try to generate another plan capable of successfully achieving the agent's goal. If the original plan of the agent is executable but detrimental to the purposes of the corporation, the tool may denounce it as such.

The plan-recognition part of the tool is based on Kautz's algorithm [Ka]. Plan-generation uses the techniques developed in the Abtweak project [Wo]. Both the plan-recognition and the plan-generation algorithms proved to be powerful enough to handle not only plots of simple database narratives but also of fairly intricate folktales [Pr,Af]. The plan-generation algorithm allows the assignment of costs to operations and, although not guaranteeing optimality, it tends to produce the shortest or the least expensive plans first (alternatives are obtained upon backtracking). The tool is written in a version of Prolog that offers an interface with SQL for database handling. The libraries of typical plans that we have been using (different libraries for different application domains) were constructed manually from previously defined complex operations. The prototype is fully operational, but several important extensions should still be added. We are currently looking at the (semi-) automatic construction of libraries, along the lines indicated in the sequel.

After defining the basic operations and identifying the main goals of the various agents, the plan-generation algorithm itself is an obvious instrument to help finding convenient complex operations, able to achieve the goals. Yet, another attractive strategy is based on the study of plots. Again assuming that the basic operations and main goals were preliminarily characterized, we can let the database be used for some time, allowing the log to grow to a substantial size. Then a number of plots can be extracted and compared, mainly by a most specific generalization criterion [Fu], to find how agents have proceeded in practice towards their goals. From this analysis, the complex operations that will form the library would arise.

Delimiting the meaningful plots to be extracted is in itself a problem. In our example, assume that the identified goals of company Alpha are: obtain clients, keep them happy. With respect to the second goal, a situation where a client has complained is undeniably critical. So, operations related to an unsatisfied client, from the moment when his misgivings became patent to the moment when they ceased, seem to form a relevant sequence. We have shown before:

Plot 1

...

d. complain(client: Beta, employee: John)
e. train(employee: John, course: c135)

...

And now consider another plot, everywhere similar to **Plot 1**, except for the solution adopted:

Plot 2

...

d. complain(client: Delta, employee: Robert)

e. hire(employee: Laura)

f. replace(employee: Robert, employee: Laura, client: Delta)

g. fire(employee: Robert)

...

This reveals two different strategies used by Alpha to placate a client:

in Plot 1 -- <u>train</u>

in Plot 2 -- <u>hire</u> - <u>replace</u> - <u>fire</u>

suggesting the introduction of two complex operations:

- reallocate: composition -- hire, replace, fire
- improve-service: generalization -- train or reallocate

Continuing with this sort of analysis, the library of typical plans may finally take the form shown in the figure below, where double arrows correspond to is-a links and single arrows to part-of links:

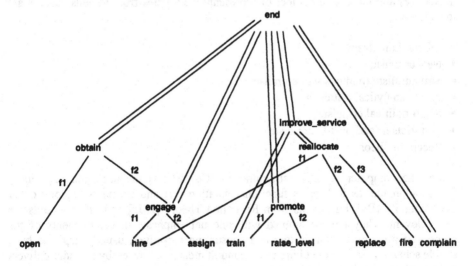

Fig. 1. Library of typical plans

While noting how plots express (or contain) plans of one or more agents, we must bear in mind that such plans are not necessarily optimal, often reflecting policies and practices of the corporation. But, even if for no other reason than becoming aware of these not entirely rational motivations, the detection of typical plans pays off. More generally, the discovery and analysis of narrative patterns appears to be one of the most promising undertakings in temporal database environments. To do it properly, one must look beyond pure database technology, as argued in the next section.

5. Towards an Interdisciplinary Perspective

If temporal databases are repositories of narratives, disciplines studying their aspects deserve attention, such as Computational Linguistics and the broader interdisciplinary area of Cognitive Science, which have results relevant to our research, such as: rhetorical predicates [Mk], text comprehension and generation [GJ], Lakoff's view of metaphoric and metonymic chains [LJ], case-based learning [Ko], semiotics [Ec], Toulmin's extended syllogisms [To], etc. In our search for useful treatments of narratives, we found that Literary Theory (particularly the field of *narratology* [Ge]) should be covered as well.

Narratives found in databases tend, as a rule, to lack "literary value" and yet, even in the simpler cases, they may need to be *interpreted*, so that their meaning, implications and relationships with other narratives be fully understood. We give below a list with some of the most influential literary theories; good surveys are found in [Ea,We] and in [LM] a number of representative articles from various schools are included:

- Liberal humanism
- New criticism
- Structuralism (and post-structuralism)
- Psychoanalytical criticism
- Socio-political criticism
- Historicism (and post-historicism)
- Reception theory

For the computer scientist, structuralism [Cu,Ch] has the attraction of a more formal approach, as in Propp's functional notation [Pr] and Barthes's exploration of intertextuality [Ba], but results from Reception Theory [Is,Ja] and other schools are also relevant. They have examined with unequal emphasis the components of the process of producing, transmitting and consuming narratives, usually depicted by a simple schema based on the ubiquitous "conduit metaphor", whereby a sender delivers a message to a receiver:

AUTHOR — TEXT→ READER

As happens with metaphors in general [La], this schema stresses some components while hiding others. The list below tries a more comprehensive coverage, noting that, especially today, the vehicle or medium carrying the texts, which had slowly evolved from manuscripts to printed volumes, has taken new and still not fully understood forms, thanks to computer and telecommunication technology:

- Context
- Historical circumstance
- Language
- Text
- Author
- Reader
- Critic
- Vehicle

It is outside the scope of the present paper to discuss in detail the contributions of each theory with respect to these components. In what follows, we limit ourselves to a brief sample of points to consider in view of our objectives.

Narratives are produced and later read in an context that evolves in time, as laws and regulations are modified and the socio-economic conjuncture varies. The same narrative may be read differently in different historical circumstances. Status, gender and other similar factors influence how persons perceive their position in organizational structures. And in the behaviour of both persons and organizations one does not expect that rationality will prevail uniformly. Decisions are more often than not based on traditional practices, whose efficacy goes unquestioned. In our example, we saw employees being hired to be used as replacements; in principle, the corporation should first look for employees already hired but currently unassigned. Or it might prefer to transfer to the service of the dissatisfied client an experienced person currently serving another client, which may, occasionally, turn out to be a better strategy despite the need for a second replacement. If the corporation systematically reacts to complaints by no matter which way to improve service, not pausing to consider the possibility that the complaint might be unjustified, this may indicate that it is blindly taking the "market driven" directive as a *myth*. Making explicit the central assumptions which determine how events are understood by the various agents is the objective of *deconstruction*, a vital preliminary step in analyzing narratives.

What we can express, and therefore, to an ample extent, what we are considered to be, is limited by the resources provided by the language that we use. To this effect, the German philosopher Heidegger once remarked that "language speaks us" (cf. [We]). Language allows to produce meaning along the *syntagmatic* and the *paradigmatic* axes [Sa]. The former refers to the formation of sentences and progressively larger text units by concatenating words and phrases; the latter refers to making choices from sets of "similar" alternative words and phrases to fill each position in the text. This is reminiscent of the formation of complex operations by composition and generalization (see section 4). As operations referring to a client are being recorded (in syntagmatic sequence), after complain, either train or reallocate (belonging to the same paradigm) can be added to fill the next position. Both choices *denote* the same purpose of improving the service offered to the client, which coincides with the primary effect of these operations; and yet they have different *connotations* [Ec], inherent in their other effects, since they express a radically different attitude with respect to labour relations.

Our use of operations as linguistic units was largely influenced by the work of the Russian scholar Vladimir Propp. Before him, a common criterion to characterize literary *genres*, such as folktales, was to classify as belonging to the genre any text that consisted of a subset of the *motifs* [Aa] thought to be associated with the genre. Propp objected to that on the grounds of granularity; he argued that motifs (a notion curiously similar to scripts) were composites and therefore should not be taken as basic units. For the folktale genre, on the basis of an empirical analysis over a vast collection compiled by Afanas'ev [Af], he proposed a repertoire of 31 *functions* (e.g. "villainy", "combat", "return"), attributed to 7 *spheres of action* (personages with different roles, such as "hero" and "villain") [Pr,Gr]. A corollary of Propp's thesis is that by changing the repertoire of functions and the roles of personages one can introduce each genre of interest, literary or not (e.g. news, project progress reports, etc.).

An early attempt to adapt Propp's ideas to automatic processing resulted in the "story grammars" formalism [Ru]. As a reaction against this allegedly too syntactical approach, the notion of "points" was proposed [Wi]. Clearly the characterization of genres, as well as other issues such as the poignancy of a narrative, depend on more than one factor. The adopted *mental attitude* [Jo] is crucial to distinguish, for instance, cases (as in law or in business administration) from news or reports. And inside a given text not all passages have the same importance [Ba]; some incidents are "hinge-points" (*nuclei*) and others merely connect the events (*catalysers*) and have little or no impact on the outcome (*closure*).

Narratives belonging or not to the same genre have a tendency to cross and interfere with each other. Roland Barthes observed that "any text is a tissue of past citations" [Ba], a phenomenon known as *intertextuality* [Mo]. The career of an employee may be affected by learning that a colleague was "reallocated" following a client's complaint; thus alerted, the employee may then spontaneously apply for admission in a training program, as a precaution.

The "authors" of database narratives are both those who participate in the design process and, in a different sense, the several classes of agents who can execute (or determine the execution of) some operation. The initiative for the execution of an operation may, in some cases, be granted to more than one agent; the train operation might be executed either through the initiative of the corporation or by the employee involved, as suggested in the preceding paragraph. The plurality of authors (agents) results in the many-voiced (*heteroglossia*) character of these narratives, in which cooperation and competition situations arise, corresponding to complementary or conflicting goals. Besides being authors, agents also play as "characters", in one or more roles. And they are also "readers", whenever they query the database, especially the log, to learn about narratives concerning them or somehow touching a point of their interest.

In general, in addition to being many-voiced, narratives lend themselves to multiple *readings* or versions or views of the same situations, sometimes inconsistent with each other and even wrong (*misreadings*). An agent may suffer from a misconception (false assumption) or misconstrual (false conclusion); as an example of the latter, consider an employee who, having been engaged in a training program in the past, trusts, due to an incomplete knowledge of the corporation's policies, that there is no risk of being fired in the event of a future complaint. Because of this feed-back cycle, whereby agents repeatedly alternate between author and reader activities, their decision about the next operation to execute will largely depend on the observation of what they "read" in the database and how they perceive what they read. So it is important to calculate, in advance, the expected *effect* [Is] of narratives upon such readers.

Still unfinished (hence ongoing) database narratives function as *open texts*. This provides the possibility, therefore, both of predicting their outcome and of trying to change their course whenever problems are detected or seem ready to occur. Such intervention can be much enhanced by technology. Having available automatically accessible models of the agents [Ri], active database features, and a Plan-recognition / Plan-generation tool (as discussed in section 4), one can build a facility to help adjusting narratives found problematic, thus acting as an *online critic*.

As an aside, it is also worthy of mention that the study of plots of narratives may contribute to the treatment of textual databases, both consisting of full electronic texts and of semi-structured data. On the other hand, hypermedia technology [SR], featuring internally multi-layered structures and links to external documents, is inducing new ways of reading which take unprecedented advantage of the intertextuality inherent in literary or business-oriented narratives. Browsing across database narratives would be favoured by the use of these resources, especially if supplemented by two-way translation between plots and natural language texts.

6. Concluding Remarks

Narratives, represented by plots extracted from database logs, tell what is happening in the mini-world of interest to the Corporation owning the database. Taken together, they show what is happening *with* the Corporation as a whole, and point to its possible futures. Past narratives teach lessons. Over ongoing narratives, if observed early, one can interfere to correct or to improve their course.

It is well known how natural language analysis, which has been a continuing source of ideas for Entity-relationship conceptual modelling, passes through different stages – lexical, syntactical, semantic, discourse integration, pragmatic – and there is ample recognition that the contribution of the model has been decisive with respect to semantics. The direction that we are proposing, with its emphasis on goal-oriented behaviour, is towards *pragmatic conceptual modelling*.

In our research project, preliminary results already obtained include the specification of basic and complex application-domain operations, the manual construction of libraries of typical plans, and experience with the Plan-recognition /

Plan-generation tool. We are, at the moment, elaborating methods to compare plots in order to derive typical plans (complex operations) semi-automatically. We are also pursuing the study of literary theories, with the assistance of specialists in the field, with the immediate aim of enhancing our tool's capability to recognize and generate plots obeying more elaborate restrictions.

References

[Aa]   Antti Aarne. *The Types of the Folktale: A Classification and Bibliography*. Translated and enlarged by Stith Thompson, FF Communications, 184. Helsinki: Suomalainen Tiedeakatemia, 1964.

[Af]   A. Afanas'ev. *Russian Fairy Tales*. N. Guterman (trans.). New York: Pantheon Books, 1945.

[Ba]   Roland Barthes. "Theory of the Text", in *Untying the Text*. Robert Young (ed.). London: Routledge, 1981.

[CF]   M. A. Casanova and A. L. Furtado. "An information system environment based on plan generation". in Proc. of the *International Working Conference on Cooperative Knowledge Based Systems*. Univ. Keele, England, 1990.

[Ch]   R. A. Champagne. *French Structuralism*. Boston: Twayne Publishers, 1990.

[Cu]   J. Culler. *Strcturalist Poetics: Structuralism Linguistics and the Study of Literature*. London: Routledge & K. Paul, 1977.

[Ea]   T. Eagleton. *Literary Theory: an Introduction*. Oxford: Basil Blackwell, 1983.

[Ec]   U. Eco. *Semiotics and Philosophy of Language*. Bloomington: Indiana University Press, 1984.

[FCa]   A. L. Furtado and M. A. Casanova. "Plan and schedule generation over temporal databases". in Proc. of the *9th International Conference on the Entity-Relationship Approach*, 1990.

[FCi]   A.L. Furtado and A. E. M. Ciarlini. "Plots of narratives over temporal databases". in *Proc. of the 8th International Workshop on Database and Expert Systems Applications*. R. R. Wagner (ed.). IEEE Computer Society - 1997.

[FN]   R. E. Fikes and N. J. Nilsson. "STRIPS: A new approach to the application of theorem proving to problem solving". *Artificial Intelligence* , 2(3-4), 1971.

[Fu]   A.L. Furtado. "Analogy by generalization and the quest of the grail". *ACM/SIGPLAN Notices*, 27, 1, 1992.

[Ge]   G. Genette. *Narrative Discourse: An Essay in Method*. J. E. Lewin (trans.). Ithaca: Cornell Univ. Press, 1980.

[GH]   E. Gamma, R. Helm, R. Johnson and J. Vlissides. *Design Patterns: Elements of Reusable Object-Oriented Software*. Reading: Addison Wesley Publishing Company, 1995.

[GJ]   B. J. Grosz, K. S. Jones and B. L. Webber (eds.). *Readings in Natural Language Processing*. San Mateo: Morgan Kaufmann, 1986.

[Gr]   A.J. Greimas. S•mantique Structurale. Paris: Librairie Larousse, 1966.

[Is]   W. Iser. "The reading process: a phenomenological approach". inTwentieth Century Literary Theory. V. Lambropoulos and D. N. Miller (eds.). Albany: State of New York Press, 1987.

[Ja]   H. R. Jauss. Toward an Aesthetic of Reception. Brighton: Harvester, 1982.

[Jo]   A. Jolles. Formes Simples.. Paris: ƒditions du Seuil, 1972.

[Ka]   H. A. Kautz. "A formal theory of plan recognition and its implementation", in Reasoning about Plans. J. F. Allen et al (eds.). San Mateo: Morgan Kaufmann, 1991.

[Ko]   J. L. Kolodner. Case-Based Reasoning. San Mateo: Morgan Kaufmann, 1993.

[La]   G. Lakoff. Women, Fire and Dangerous Things: what Categories Reveal about the Mind. Chicago: The University of Chicago Press, 1990.

[LJ]   G. Lakoff and M. Johnson. Metaphors we Live By. Chicago: The University of Chicago Press, 1980.

[LM]   V. Lambropoulos and D. N. Miller (eds.). Twentieth Century Literary Theory. Albany: State University of New York Press, 1987.

[MC]   C.J. Matheus, P.K. Chan. and G. Piatesky-Shapiro. "Systems for knowledge discovery in databases". IEEE Transactions on Knowledge and Data Engineering, 5, 6, 1993.

[Mk]   K.R. McKeown. Text Generation: Using Dscourse Strategies and Focus Constraints to Generate Natural Language Text. Cambridge: Cambridge University Press, 1992.

[Mo]   T.E. Morgan. "Is there an intertext in this text?: literary and interdisciplinary approaches to intertextuality". American Journal of Semiotics, 3, 1985.

[Oz]   G. Ozsoyoglu. and R.T. Snodgrass. "Temporal and real-time databases: a survey". IEEE Transaction on Knowledge and Data Engineering, 7, 4, 1995.

[Pr]   V. Propp. Morphology of the Folktale. Laurence Scott (trans.). Austin: University of Texas Press, 1968.

[Ri]   E. Rich. "Users are individuals: individualizing user models". International Journal of Man-Machine Studies, 18, 1983.

[Ru]   D.E. Rumelhart. "Notes on a schema for stories". in Representation and Understanding - Studies in Cognitive Science. D. G. Bobrow and A. Collins (eds.). New York: Academic Press, 1975.

[Sa]   F. Saussure. Course in General Linguistics. W. Baskin (trans.). New York: McGraw-Hill, 1966.

[Sh]   A. Sheth. "From contemporary workflow process automation to adaptive and dynamic work activity coordination and collaboration". in Proc. of the 8th International Workshop on Database and Expert Systems Applications, September, 1997.

[SR]   D. Schwabe and G. Rossi - "Building hypermedia applications as navigational views of information models". in Proc. of the 28th. Hawaii International Conference on System Sciences, Jan, 1995.

[To]   S. E. Toulmin. *The Uses of Argument*. Cambridge: Cambridge University Press, 1958.

[We] R. Webster. *Studying Literary Theory*. London: Arnold, 1996.

[Wi]   R. Wilensky. "Points: a theory of the structure of stories in memory". in *Readings in Natural Language Processing*. B. J. Grosz, K. S. Jones and B. L. Webber (eds.), San Mateo: Morgan Kaufmann, 1986.

[Wo]   S. G. Woods. *An Implementation and Evaluation of a Hierarchical Non-linear Planner*. Master's thesis. Computer Science Department of the University of Waterloo, 1991.

Using Conceptual Modeling and Intelligent Agents to Integrate Semi-structured Documents in Federated Databases

Georges Gardarin and Fei Sha

PRiSM Laboratory, CNRS
University of Versailles St-Quentin en Yvelines
45 Avenue des Etats-Unis
78035 Versailles, Cedex, France
<Firstname.Lastname>@prism.uvsq.fr

1. Introduction

Object-oriented multidatabase systems (also referred to as federated databases or heterogeneous databases) represents the confluence of various trends in computer science and technology [BGP97], among them object-orientation [CB+97], distributed databases, and interoperability. Recently, the Internet has become the major vehicle in networking industry for information access and dissemination. The Web as a service on top of the Internet focuses on transparent Internet navigation and hypermedia document oriented information access. Thus, today there is a need to integrate the object-oriented multidatabase technology with hypermedia documents. This paper discusses the integration of hypermedia documents within the IRO-DB federated database system [Gar97]. It proposes the use of conceptual modeling coupled with intelligent agents to integrate semi-structured files within the IRO-DB query process.

Documents residing in file systems are the first sources of semi-structured data. These pieces of information are considered unstructured or semi-structured at the database regard. Unlike data managed in conventional database systems, semi-structured data are provided in a variety of formats. These formats can have very weak and irregular internal structures. Furthermore, data structures can evolve in an ever-changing fashion along with the data itself. Due to these characteristics of semi-structured data, several problems need to be solved for an efficient integration with a federated database : (i) Choice of a data model for representing semi-structured data. (ii) Choice of a query language for interrogating semi-structured data. (iii) Storage and query processing strategy for semi-structured data.

Several approaches are currently investigated to integrate semi-structured data within advanced DBMSs. As semi-structured data have heterogeneous and changing structures, one possible choice is to use a schema-less approach [PGMW95, AQMH+97, BDH+96]. Data are then encapsulated in a self-descriptive format, generally built from a labeled graph of component objects. This approach solves the paradox of static schema and changing data structure. Changes of data structures are reflected immediately to the user. Another approach is to build on existing data models, relational [KS97] or object-oriented [ACC+97], to represent semi-structured data. This second approach although limited by the expressive power of existing data models, benefits from the maturity of the techniques implemented in existing database

P.P. Chen et al. (Eds.): Conceptual Modeling, LNCS 1565, pp. 87-99, 1999.
© Springer-Verlag Berlin Heidelberg 1999

systems. In this paper, we explore the object-oriented approach, based on the IRO-DB system.

IRO-DB is an object-oriented federated database system based on the ODMG standard [GFF+94]. A version is currently operational. It interconnects a relational system INGRES, and three object-oriented DBMSs : O2, Matisse and Ontos. We will briefly describe the main system features and some key components. IRO-DB follows an architecture with three layers of schemas, i.e., with *local schemas*, *import/export schemas*, and *interoperable schemas* (also referred to as *integrated views*). A local schema is a local database schema, as usual. An export schema describes in ODMG terms the subset of a data source that a local system allows to be accessed by cooperating systems. IRO-DB does not support a global unique integrated schema, but allows application administrators to define *integrated views*. A view consists of a set of derived classes with relationships ; it is associated with mappings to the underlying export schemas. Queries on integrated views are formulated in OQL. The system efficiently processes complex queries: a query is decomposed in sub-queries, which are sent to and processed by local database adapters on top of each local database. The results are sent back to the client site through an extended remote data access protocol. On the client, results are processed by a main memory object-manager running a synthesis query whose result is delivered to the user. The system also support updates of previously retrieved objects.

The problem is now to extend the system to support semi-structured documents as HTML, SGML or LaTex files, program source codes or multimedia documents including images and sounds. To this goal, we propose first to use conceptual modeling to specify export schemas generated from a set of documents. ODL export schemas will be generated from graphical specifications. The export schemas are given by database administrators or end-users. These schemas will be generated in local dictionaries based on the ODMG model, including type, attribute, key, operation, relationship, and inheritance definitions. The conceptual model will only refer to relevant parts of the document, which we intend to extract for query processing.

Exported views of documents conforming to the conceptual model will then be extracted from local documents through intelligent agents. Through file extensions and content analysis, mappings from existing documents to object models will be established. The mapping process will discover tags and delimiters to extract document parts in conformance to the ODL schemas. It will generate a document format description in the *mapping rule language* (MRL). Using the MRL file, exported features of documents will be extracted and cached in a local object database. The features may also refer to the document through a specific external attribute type. Updating the document features from document updates requires a push model and the integration of active rules to the MRL file. This is a subject of future research.

Based on this approach, a conceptual document modeler and an intelligent extractor are currently being developed for HTML files at PRiSM. We will present the document extraction mechanism, the Mapping Rule Language, and the architecture of the intelligent document wrapper agent. We strongly believe that the future is in cooperative information systems integrating databases and Web technology. Conceptual modeling and intelligent agent could help in solving some of the issues.

This paper is organized as follows. In section 2, we give an overview of the IRO-DB system. In section 3, we describe the approach we have investigated to integrate semi-structured documents within IRO-DB. In section 4, we present the rule language used to map documents to objects. Section 5 analyses some related work, mostly based on semi-structured data models. In conclusion, we summarize the contributions of this paper and introduce some directions of our current research.

2.   Overview of IRO-DB

IRO-DB is an object-oriented federated database system. A version is currently operational. It interconnects a relational system INGRES, and three object-oriented DBMS : O2, Matisse and Ontos. In this section, we briefly describe the main system features and some key components.

2.1   Project Overview

IRO-DB (Interoperable Relational and Object-Oriented DataBases) is an ESPRIT project developed in Europe from 1993 to 1996. The novelty of the IRO-DB architecture is to use the ODMG'93 standard [CB+97] as a common object model supporting the ODL object definition language and the OQL object query language to federate various object-oriented and relational data sources. The IRO-DB architecture is clearly divided into three layers, thus facilitating the cooperative development of the project in several research centers. The local layer adapts local data sources to the ODMG standard ; the communication layer efficiently transfers OQL requests and the resulting collections of objects ; the interoperable layer provides schema integration tools, security management, transaction management, object management, as well as a global query processor.

Accordingly, IRO-DB follows an architecture with three layers of schemas, i.e., with *local schemas, import/export schemas,* and *interoperable schemas* (also referred to as *integrated views*). A local schema is a local database schema, as usual. An export schema describes in ODMG terms the subset of a database that a local system allows to be accessed by cooperating systems. IRO-DB does not support a global unique integrated schema, but allow application administrators to define *integrated views*. It consists of a set of derived classes with relationships together with mappings to the underlying export schemas. Figure 1 gives an overview of the system architecture and of the various schemas. A more complete presentation of IRO-DB can be found in [GFF+94].

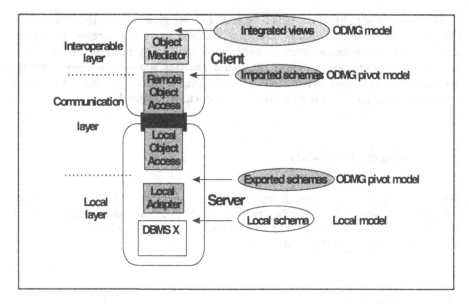

Fig. 1. The IRO-DB system architecture.

Let us point out one interesting feature of IRO-DB, which has not been emphasized in previous papers : Each integrated view behaves exactly as an ODMG database, which can be queried through OQL. Thus, integration can be done recursively, through various levels of IRO-DB systems cooperating. Figure 2 illustrates this somehow recursive architecture. We believe this is important to give capabilities of integrating hierarchically structured or semi-structured data in a complex organization.

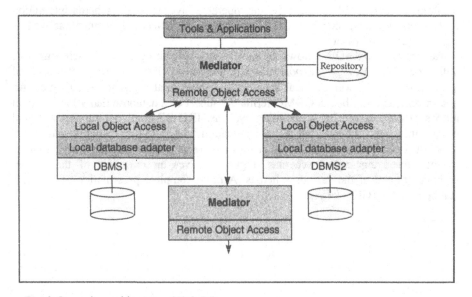

Fig. 2. Recursive architecture of IRO-DB.

The *local layer* is composed of Local Database Adapters (LDA). A local database adapter provides functionality to make a local system able to answer OQL queries. It manages an abstraction of a local schema in term of ODMG concepts, namely the export schema. As an export schema only describes locally implemented types, only locally available functionality are available for querying through OQL. That means for example that methods and access paths cannot be invoked with simple LDA who does not know how to export complex ODMG schemas. In that case, only flat objects without relationships are handled at the local layer for relational systems. Of course, if the local system supports the full ODMG model, all syntactically correct ODMG queries are acceptable.

3.   Integration of Semi-structured Documents

The integration of semi-structured documents within IRO-DB is based on partial extractions of concepts from documents. The extracted concepts are modeled using MRL. From the conceptual model, rules are generated to extract relevant information from the documents. An object database is then created and loaded. This database can participate in federated databases and be queried through integrated views. In other research works, a tendency is the attempt to represent semi-structured data in all its details. This can make the view too complex and confusing to end users due to the diversity of semi-structured data. Moreover, the user view changes as often as the structures of the underlying data changes. Thus, it is difficult to maintain a full view and formulate queries. We believe that partial extraction of directed by a conceptual model is a viable approach, which can be efficient and helpful.

3.1   Steps for Integrating Documents

The integration of a collection of documents within a federated database proceeds in three steps :
1. Conceptual modeling of the documents. Using a graphical tool, a conceptual model of the attributes and relationships to extract from the documents is elaborated. As already pointed out, only document properties relevant for querying are described.
2. Generating the mapping rules. We propose an approach based on intelligent agents to generate mapping rules from a collection of documents to a given object model. The intelligent agent uses the conceptual model, general knowledge about documents, and a library of existing mapping rules to elaborate a mapping. The agent is intelligent in the sense that it can access to an extensible library of known document types.
3. Extracting the relevant features. Using the results of step 2, the document is scanned and relevant components are extracted and copied in a local object database.

We describe these steps in more details below.

3.2   Conceptual Modeling of Documents

At the conceptual level, a set of possibly related semi-structured documents are represented using classes with possible relationships. An individual document may be represented by several classes organized as a tree. Each class corresponds to a concept instanced 0, 1 or N times in the document. The concept can have attribute details. For each document type, an entry point is given, which defines the document root class. Child classes are linked to parent classes through relationships, with cardinalities corresponding to the number of instances of the concept for one given parent instance. Multi-valued relationships in which order is important can be specified through annotations. Only interesting document components have their counterparts in the conceptual model. Different document types can share the same class definition at conceptual level depending on their similarities. Relationships between documents or document components can be added as special relationships between classes. They could be used in the future for generating hyperlinks.

For modeling classes and relationships, we use MRL notations. For illustration, Figure 3 gives a conceptual model of a collection of research papers with description of authors, sections and subsections. The entry point, denoted Entry, is the Article class. Title, keywords (of a special type Search) and date have to be extracted from the document. The document may have several authors, with name, string and age to extract. The document is composed of several sections, themselves composed of several subsections. Note that sections are ordered within documents ; Subsections are ordered within sections. External is a predefined type, which is a black box to support link to the actual external subsection contents. Get is a special method used to get the actual subsection content handled in a transparent way.

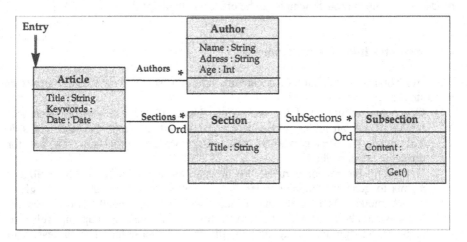

Fig. 3. A conceptual model for a collection of articles and authors.

3.3   Generating the Mapping Rules

Using conceptual level representation has several advantages. The conceptual level view is closer to the user viewpoint thus easier to understand. Also, using uniform view for similar document types makes the view smaller. When there are minor changes in the document structures, only mapping and extraction rules need to be adapted, the conceptual view can stay relatively stable.

The problem is to generate rules to extract components from the documents accordingly to the conceptual specification. To do that, we use intelligent agents. Our intelligent agents are not capable of inferring the grammar of all types of documents. They use an extensible library of predefined document type grammars organized in a class hierarchy. To extract information from semi-structured documents, we use a top-down approach. Instead of trying to discover the grammar of a document, then match it against the existing class hierarchy, we try to find which part of a document can match existing classes. This can be done in several ways.

The extraction rules for known document types can be used to see if they apply to an unknown document. Another possibility is using existing values in the database to discover the similar components within a document. This can be applied to the class members having a small set of values. For example, this technique can be used at the beginning of a document to find out an author list or at the end of a document to infer the reference list. Once the matching value is found, the extraction rule may be guessed by applying known coding style, e.g., the start-end delimiter style. This supposed extraction rule must be verified by parsing more documents or by the local database administrator. We can also collect repeatedly occurring patterns with special characters such as <FOOTER> or /section. These patterns can often be tokens for structural delimiters.

Figure 4 shows an example of how the grammars of documents stored in different formats are organized in a class hierarchy rooted at Grammar. We make first a rough classification of semi-structured documents in two classes : The first contains the documents which structures are derived from the semantics, for example SGML and BibTex documents. The second contains the documents which structure is mostly derived from presentation tags ; HTML and Latex documents fall in this second category. Grammar described by the leaf classes can be HTML, SGML, LaTex, BibTex, or any other type of documents. They have common components such as title, author, abstract, section, etc., which are defined through keywords and tags. The grammars give production rules for these elements. In the future, style sheets or files should also be considered, e.g., for interpreting word documents.

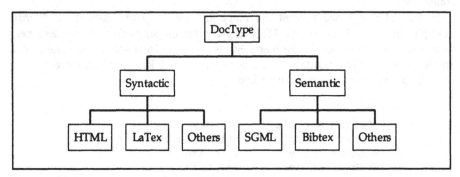

Fig. 4. The hierarchy of document type definitions.

The function of an intelligent agent is first to match given document samples within the given document class hierarchy. Document extensions (e.g., .html, .tex, etc.) can be used first. If no direct match is possible, new subclasses have to be added. When an acceptable grammar is produced for a sample of documents, a new subtype is included in the document type hierarchy. Production rules to extract the conceptual schema elements are then generated using a mapping rule language described in the next section.

3.4   Extracting the Relevant Components

From the conceptual schema, an object database schema is derived. It is directly exported as a classical IRO-DB export schema. On client sites, integrated views will then combine this schema with others for query purpose, as described in section 2. To locally support queries, a local database is created according to this schema. To demonstrate the feasibility of our approach, we use O2. This choice was made because a local adapter for O2 already exists in IRO-DB. Then, based on the mapping rules generated in the previous step, the document is parsed. If a class member does not apply to a document instance, a null value is assigned. Components being considered irrelevant or too specific are simply ignored. The result of the parsing is loaded in the object database. Each component gives rise to an object that refer to it when *external* is specified in the conceptual model. It is in some sense the queryable summary of the component.

4.   Overview of the Mapping Rule Language

Since the conceptual level representation is an abstraction of the internal structure of the underlying documents, each document type must provide a set of mapping rules between its components and the class members. For this purpose, we have defined a *mapping rule language*. Each document type thus has a *mapping rule definition* associated. In the *mapping rule definition* are specified (i) the document type, (ii) the components and their extraction rules, (iii) the mapping rules between the components and the class members, and (iv) the document layout in term of defined components.

In the following, we present the *mapping rule language* through an SGML example. In figure 5, an SGML DTD is given for the simplified *article* document type, a subtype of SGML in the hierarchy of figure 4. To simplify, we assume that articles only have a title, authors and a body from which keywords are extracted. No sections and subsections are distinguished.

```
< !DOCTYPE article [
< !ELEMENT article - - (title, author+, body)>
< !ELEMENT title   - - (#PCDATA)>
< !ELEMENT author  - O (#PCDATA)>
< !ELEMENT body    - - (#PCDATA)>
]>
```

Fig. 5. SGML DTD for article.

This definition tells that a document of type *article* has a title, a list of authors and a body. Figure 6 gives a sample document of article type.

```
<article>
<title>Integrating …</title>
<author>G. Gardarin</author>
<author>F. Sha</author>
<body>
This is a sample document of article type, a
subtype of the SGML document type.
</body>
</article>
```

Fig. 6. A sample document of article type.

Figure 7 gives the mapping rule program for the SGML *article* type. It is composed of a document type definition statement, procedures for extracting the document features, rules for describing how to assemble them into the conceptual classes, and finally the definition of the document layout to determine the sequence of features within the documents.

```
# document type
document_type = sgml.article ;
# components definition and extraction rule
title = start_end("<TITLE>","</TITLE>") ;
author = start_end("<AUTHOR>","</AUTHOR>") ;
body = start_end ("<BODY>", "</BODY>") ;
keywords = index(body) ;
# mapping rule
title -> article.title ;
author -> author.name ;
keywords -> article.keywords ;
# document layout
article ::= title [author]+ body
```

Fig. 7. Format description for SGML article type.

The document_type denotes the name of the document type with which the mapping rule program is associated. In the component definition and extraction rule section, specific methods are used to extract tagged fields, or to compute the most frequently used keywords. The left hand of each statement is the identifier of the component while the right hand of the statement tells that a component can be extracted using a specific function (e.g., start_end, which takes as parameters the *start* and the *end* delimiters). By using extraction functions, the system is easy to extend. New extraction functions can be defined when needed. For example, if a new document type introduced contains components that are delimited by a start tag and a length, then we can define a start_length function to extract such components.

The mapping rule section in the format description establishes correspondence between the components in a documents and the attributes in the conceptual level view. This section also implies what database action should be taken out after the extraction of a component. For instance, the title should be stored as a string in conformance with the type of its conceptual view counterpart, and the body should be full-text indexed as it is represented as keywords at the conceptual level. The final section shows the document layout in a BNF style.

The mapping rule language is easy to read and can be used directly to extend the document type hierarchy. Format descriptions for some common document types can also be obtained by converting their grammar in rules, e.g., the BNF specification of C program sources or DTD of HTML files for instance. As semi-structured documents have variety of formats and some of them are irregular or previously unknown, it is unrealistic to write mapping rule programs for all document types manually. Generating the mapping rules requires an automatic process of structure discovery and data extraction. That is why we propose an intelligent agent as sketched above, which has to be investigated further.

5.   Related Work

Related works on automatic data extraction can be found in recent papers. Different techniques have been proposed for particular data and particular circumstances. Integration of external information into a DBMS for semi-structured data is described in [CGMH+94]. In [AK97], a technique based on pattern matching is used to extract different sections from a web page. [HS96] proposed a configurable extraction process for extracting summary information from files. Another structure inferring technique can be found in [NAM97]. We survey these approaches below and compare them with our.

5.1   Semi-structured Data Extraction

A lot of work has been done recently using a semi-structured data model to model flexible document structures. The most well known model is OEM [PGMW95]. With OEM, documents are organized as a labeled graph of objects. Nodes represent objects and are composed of a label, a type, a value, and an optional object identifier. OEM does not distinguish between the schema and the data instances, which are integrated. This makes the model very flexible, able to cope with any type of irregular data. Our document description is less flexible, but done through an existing and well understood object model. This simplifies the implementation, as it can be implemented directly on top of an object oriented database system, and integrated in IRO-DB, an object-oriented federated database system. The difference is that we cannot handle simply irregular data, e.g., an office that is once a number, another time a building name and a door number. In this case, we can either use a union type in the conceptual schema, or a null value for the building number. We gain in regularity for query processing. As a consequence, we are able to use pure OQL with possibly specific methods.

For mapping documents to the conceptual model, we try to develop an automatic push technique based on intelligent agents. They generate the mapping rules and process them against the documents. With OEM, the dynamic integration of external information is described in [CGMH+94]. This is basically a pull technique, where documents are mapped on demands for answering user queries. Using a pull technique avoids useless mappings, but could give low performance with large queries on keywords for example. In the future, we also plan to explore pull techniques.

5.2   Semi-structured Wrapper Generation

Automatic generation of wrappers for Web sources has been proposed in [AK97]. A wrapper for a Web source accepts database-like queries about information in the pages of the source. Wrappers are generated in three steps : (i) Structuring the source, which involves identifying sections and sub-sections of interest. This step includes discovering tokens of interest and the nesting hierarchy within sections. (ii) Building a parser for the source pages, based on the results of the first step. (iii) Adding communication capabilities between the wrapper and the source.

Our approach has some similarities, but several differences with the [AK97] one. First, we do not discover automatically the source structure. Rather, we ask a data source administrator to build a conceptual model of the only data to extract from the source for query purpose. Thus, the approach is more directed and avoids extracting irrelevant information. Further, we do not add communication capabilities to wrappers. Rather, we extract the conceptually modeled data and copy them in a local object database. This database participates in the federation as a normal exported object database. The object database copy also keeps the address of the source document as an external link attribute. The document can then be directly extracted from a browser if requested.

5.3   Query Language for the Web

Several query systems for Web sites have recently been proposed. Most of them are based on a graph representation of Web sites, similar to the OEM representation. STRUDEL [FFK+97] is a system implemented at AT&T to build web sites. Queries are expressed in StruQL on the hypermedia graph of site and allow the user to derive a new graph. Query expressions are based on path expressions with a regular grammar to traverse the graph site and on Skolem functions to derive new nodes linked by new edges. This is very general, but requires the development of a brand new graph processing DBMS, with new optimization techniques to invent. W3QL [KS95] is another system to query the Web both through the graph derived from the hypertext and through content based queries. Again, it does not capitalize on existing object technology. WebSQL [MMM97] and HyOQL [GY95] are other older query languages for the Web allowing to traverse graph structures. The authors do not give much hints for discovering the underlying structure of documents.

6.   Conclusion

To query collections of unstructured data, of which a Web site is only one example, new technology can be developed based on semi-structured data models. This requires the development of new query languages, new optimization techniques, and probably new distributed DBMSs. In this paper, we rather try to capitalize on new technology, namely object-oriented federated systems. IRO-DB is such a system developed in a European Esprit project. It uses the ODMG data model as the common model, and OQL as query language.

Based on this experience, we try to develop intelligent agents to map semi-structured documents to an open object model. The intelligent agent receives a conceptual object model of the source document as input. Based on an extensible library of extraction functions and document types, it generates a rule mapping program to map the relevant part of the document to an object database, which can then be federated with other using IRO-DB. This technology is quite impressive in power. It is extensible, and efficient as object databases summarizing the documents are extracted off line. Considering this experience, we now start a new Esprit project called MIRO-WEB to develop this approach for accessing Intranet databases and files. MIRO-WEB will be based on an object-relational modeling of documents, which could integrate some semi-structured data types. Thus, it should be an intermediate approach between the "structuring everything" one described in this paper, and the "schema-less" approach of Lore, for example. We believe that structured and semi-structured data models should cooperate to solve real life application problems, as the one tackled in MIRO-WEB (i.e., an hospital and a tourism applications).

References

[Abi97]   S. Abiteboul "Semi-Structured Data", In proceeding of ICDT, p1-18, Delphi, Greece, 1997

[ACC+97]   S. Abiteboul, S. Cluet, V. Christophides, T. Milo, G. Moerkotte and J. Simoen « Querying Document in Object Databases » International Journal of Digital Libraries, p5-19, Vol.1, 1997

[AQMH+97] S. Abiteboul, D. Quass, J. McHugh, J. Widom and J. Wienner « The Lorel Query Language For Semi-Structured Data », International Journal of Digital Libraries, p68-88, Vol.1, 1997

[AK97]   N. Ashish and C. A. Knoblock « Semi-Automatic Wrapper Generation For Internet Information Sources » SIGMOD Record 26(4) p8-15, 1997

[BDH+96]   P. Buneman, S. Davidson, G. Hillebrand and D. Suciu « A Query Language And Optimization Techniques For Unstructured Data » In SIGMOD, San Diego, 1996

[BE95]   O. A. Bukhres, A. K. Elmagarmid Ed. « Object-Oriented MultiBase Systems », Book, Prentice Hall, 1995.

[BGP97]   M. Bouzeghoub, G. Gardarin and P. Valduriez « Object Systems and Methodology », Book, Thomson Press, London, 1997.

[CB+97]   R. Cattell, D. Barry et. al. « Object Database Standard : ODMG 2.0 » book, Morgan Kaufman Pub., 1997.

[CGMH+94] S. Chawathe, H. Garcia-Molina, J. Hammer, K. Ireland, Y. Papakonstantinou, J. Ullman, and J. Widom. « The TSIMMIS Project : Integration of Heterogeneous Information Sources ». In Proceedings of IPSJ Conference, p7-18, Tokyo, Japan, October 1994

[FFK+97]   M. F. Fernandez, D. Florescu, J. Kang, A. Y. Levy and D. Suciu, « STRUDEL: A Web-site Management System ». In proceedings of SIGMOD'97 Conference p549-552, Tucson, Arizona, USA, May 1997

[Gar97]   G. Gardarin « Multimedia Federated Databases on the Web : Extending IRO-DB to Web Technology » DEXA, Springer-Verlag Ed., LNCS, Toulouse, Sept. 1997

[GFF+94]   G. Gardarin, B. Finance, P. Fankhauser and W. Klas « IRO-DB : A Distributed System Federating Object and Relational Databases », In book "Object Oriented Multibase Systems : A Solution for Advanced Applications", Chap. 1, O. Bukhres and A. Elmagarmid Editors, 1994

[GY95]   G. Gardarin and S. Yoon « Object-Oriented Modeling and Querying of Hypermedia Documents ». In proceeding of Database Systems for Advanced Applications, p441-448, Singapore, 1995

[HS96]   D. R. Hardy and M. F. Schwartz « Customized Information Extraction As A Basis For Resource Discovery » TOCS 14(2) p171-199, 1996

[KR97]   V. Kashyap and M. Rusinkiewicz « Modeling and Querying Textual Data Using E-R Models and SQL » 1997

[KS95]   D. Konopnicki and O. Shmueli « W3QS: A Query System for the World-Wide Web » In proceedings of the 21st International Conference on Very Large Data Bases, p54-65, Zurich, Switzerland, September, 1995

[MMM97]   A. O. Mendelzon, G. A. Mihaila and T. Milo « Querying the World Wide Web » International Journal on Digital Libraries 1(1), p54-67, 1997

[NAM97]   S. Nestorov, S. Abiteboule and R. Motwani « Inferring Structure In Semi-Structured Data » SIGMOD Record 26(4) p39-43, 1997

[PGMW95]   Y. Papakonstantinou, H. Garcia-Molina and J. Widom « Object Exchange Across Heterogeneous Information Sources », In Data Engineering, Taipei, 1995.

Supporting the User: Conceptual Modeling & Knowledge Discovery

Terrance Goan

Stottler Henke Assoc. Inc.
1660 South Amphlett Blvd. Suite 350
San Mateo, California, 94402
goan@shai-seattle.com

Abstract. Civilian and military organizations are collecting huge amounts of data from a variety of sources. In order to make intelligent use of this data possible, researchers have developed countless data mining (or Knowledge Discovery in Databases (KDD)) systems that seek to aid in the task of extracting valid, novel, and interesting information from these large data repositories. Unfortunately, existing KDD systems have several shortcomings. One broad class of these shortcomings arises from the fact that these systems lack the means to actively collaborate with the user over extended periods of time. This paper describes our effort to address this problem by tightly coupling the knowledge discovery process with an explicit conceptual model. Central to our research is an investigation into the relationship between knowledge and discovery. More specifically, we are examining how a stored dynamic conceptual model can be used to improve KDD goal/query specification, algorithm efficiency, and results reporting.

1 Introduction

The sheer volume and growing complexity of the data resident in many of today's commercial and military data warehouses makes traditional data analysis processes ineffectual. However, over the past decade, researchers have responded by developing tools that can greatly improve the prospects for uncovering interesting and useful patterns from such large data collections [1]. Unfortunately, existing KDD systems fall significantly short in their ability to work cooperatively with users. One substantial reason for this deficiency is the failure of these systems to maintain an explicit conceptual model that can facilitate information discovery. This unnecessary separation of domain knowledge from the discovery process leads to a number of difficulties with: goal/query specification, algorithm efficiency, and results reporting and use. This predicament is only worsened by recent efforts to build extensible *integrated* data mining systems that seek to support the entire knowledge discovery process [1][2], because the complexity of using such systems seems to grow exponentially with the number of tools a user has access to.

In this paper, we examine how to improve the interaction between an integrated knowledge discovery system and the user. In the next section, we discuss the knowledge discovery process and how its very definition begs for the use of an

P.P. Chen et al. (Eds.): Conceptual Modeling, LNCS 1565, pp. 100–104, 1999.

explicit conceptual model. We then discuss how we are implementing our ideas in a KDD system called IKODA (the Intelligent KnOwledge Discovery Assistant). Finally, we end with pointers to future work.

2 Knowledge Discovery

Data Mining, or Knowledge Discovery in Databases (KDD) has been defined as the process of identifying valid, novel, interesting, useful, and understandable patterns in data [1]. A quick review of the latest KDD conference proceedings [3] shows that this definition has been adopted widely. In fact, there doesn't appear to be substantial interest in defining the process more precisely. But, what does it mean for a pattern to be novel, interesting, useful, or understandable? The answers to these questions provide motivation for our work because it is simply impossible to define these terms without making reference to what a user knew prior to engaging with the KDD system or what task the user is currently engaged in.

The other aspect of KDD that is critical to understanding our research, is its interative and/or recursive nature. The steps in the KDD process can include: data selection, preprocessing (i.e., data cleaning), dimensionality reduction, data mining, and results interpretation. Additionally, the user may utilize numerous tools in each step. Clearly, in order for KDD tools to be accessible for any but the most expert user, it will be critical to support the user throughout the process.

3 The Intelligent Knowledge Discovery Assistant

IKODA is an integrated knowledge discovery tool under development at Stottler Henke Assoc. Inc. (SHAI). IKODA includes a number of atomic tools for data selection, preprocessing, and data mining. These tools are accessible through a direct manipulation user interface specifically designed to support the *process* of interactive/recursive and automated knowledge discovery. The driving force behind this interface is a commitment to reduce the complexity of the tool through the use of a simple, intuitive, and pervasive control mechanism.

To support the user in the use of IKODA, we provide three agents: a tool selection agent, a goal processing agent, and a monitoring and refinement agent. These three agents work in the background to reduce the cognitive load on the user by leveraging IKODA's integrated dynamic conceptual model. Additionally, the user can access this internal model directly and use it in data selection and query formation. This is an important feature because, as has been pointed out by a number of other KDD researchers, effective goal/query specification is both critical to the success of data mining and troublesome. By retaining knowledge (e.g., derived models, conceptual labels, and concept hierarchies) over time, IKODA can greatly improve the users ability to uncover novel patterns.

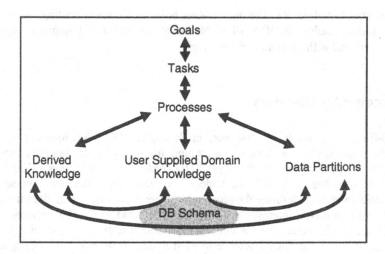

Fig. 1. The user can access IKODA's explicit conceptual model to access a variety of useful information. The user can begin his exploration from a particular *goal* and descend an object oriented framework to access previously discovered *derived knowledge*, *domain knowledge*, and *data partitions*. Likewise, a user can move between different objects in this model through the links shown above that represent previously formed associations

From IKODA's user interface, a user may also engage in a knowledge elicitation process, providing additional *domain knowledge* about the form and contents of the databases. This supplementary data can take a variety of forms including: field value ranges, descriptions of functional dependencies, generalization hierarchies (e.g., "Joe" is a "Man" is a "Human"), and useful data categories and subcategories (e.g., "morning hours" may be a useful subcategory of an existing field "time of day"). Fortunately, this type of domain knowledge can also be obtained in two other ways also. First, IKODA can incorporate select *derived knowledge* into the knowledge base, thus allowing it to learn about the user's tasks over time. While this approach may seem obvious, most existing KDD systems simply discard their discoveries after reports are made to the user [4][5]. A second way to automatically obtain domain knowledge is to observe users as they process data. Frequently, analysts will tentatively segment database fields during their processing hoping to uncover interesting patterns. By keeping track of the categories users create *during the search process*, IKODA can automatically add this information directly to its knowledge base and allow users to retrieve these new derived values in future queries.

The Tool Selection Agent: IKODA's tool selection agent has three responsibilities. First, this agent guides the selection of algorithm classes (e.g., pruning, clustering , discrimination, dependency analysis etc.) based on the current context (i.e., currently selected data or model). Second, the agent automates the selection of specific algorithms (e.g., SPRINT [6] decision tree learning algorithm) based on user requirements (e.g., efficiency vs. quality) and data characteristics extracted from the shared conceptual model. Finally, the tool agent will dynamically determine which operations are applicable at any one time (e.g., not allowing users to visualize non-spatial data on a map), and will automatically determine how valid operations should be interpreted.

The Monitoring & Refinement Agent: Also included in IKODA is a monitoring and refinement agent. The monitoring agent is utilized in the same manner as other tools in our interface. The purpose of this agent is to monitor changes in the specific derived knowledge stored in the conceptual model. The process starts with the user requesting to be notified if new data significantly changes to a previously extracted model. As fresh data comes into the databases, the mining algorithm is run over this data, and the triggering pattern is searched for. In the event that the trigger is satisfied, the users will be alerted, and an explanation of the alert is given. This agent will be useful in cases where, for example, a derived high confidence association rule used for monitoring marketing efforts has its confidence level drop suddenly [7].

Another example of a monitoring task from a military domain is the monitoring cluster formations. As Devany and Ram [8] point out, army echelon units may appear to move from one spatial cluster to another spatial cluster as they maneuver. It could be that rapid or significant changes in the clustering of ground units is indicative of certain tactics (or unconventional tactics). By monitoring the spatial clusters formed by observed ground units over time, it may be possible to detect coming events.

The *refinement agent* may work as a background process to develop more accurate derived models (e.g., decision trees or clusters). This agent may use different (more time consuming) algorithms, incorporate more training examples, or utilize techniques such as "bagging" that integrate multiple learned models. The agent will determine which technique is applicable based on the type of model desired, the time available, and the level of accuracy desired. It must also consider how the user wants to use the information. For example, if the user wants an accurate description of the data, bagging is a poor choice because its results are not easily understood. Similar to the monitoring agent, the refinement agent will alert the user to significant changes. In this case, the changes will be in the accuracy and complexity of the model, not in how it changes in response to new incoming data.

Goal Processing Agent: The "goal processing" agents form the glue between the data mining tool and the goals of the user. The job of these agents is process the data mining operations associated with a particular goal or task involved in the achieving of a goal. For example, a goal may be to improve sales of widget X, and a task in achieving that goal may be to analyze the consumers in the geographic regions where sales are weak. When presented with a goal such as this, the agent may either have a predefined model (e.g., a spatial cluster model and associated classifier) that can be autonomously verified and monitored, or the agent may simply act to aid the data analyst by collecting the relevant data and suggesting particular tools to utilize (based on previous analysis of this goal).

4   Concluding Remarks

SHAI is still in the relatively early stages of developing IKODA, but it is clear from our early implementation that the use of an explicit conceptual model within a knowledge discovery system is extremely important. Our objective is to develop

IKODA into a tool that does not require users to be experts in the areas of machine learning or databases. By leveraging a stored model that is utilized and modified by the user and IKODA we can allow users to focus their cognitive abilities on the truly challenging tasks of goal definition and result understanding.

Looking forward, our single greatest challenge will be scaling our approach to conceptual modeling. We must be careful to refine our modeling approach to allow users to access the information they require without being overwhelmed by the complexity of the model.

Acknowledgments

Ray Liuzzi has provided valuable guidance throughout the execution of this project. This work was supported by the United States Air Force under the Small Business Innovative Research program under Contract Number F30602-97-C-0158 .

References

1. Fayyad, U.; Piatetsky-Shapiro, G.; and Smyth, P. 1996. From data mining to knowledge discovery: An Overview. In *Advances in Knowledge Discovery and Data Mining*. Cambridge, USA: AAAI/MIT Press.
2. Wrobel et al., 1996. "Extensibility in Data Mining Systems," The Second International Conference on Knowledge Discovery and Data Mining.
3. Simoudis et al. Editors, 1997. The Third International Conference on Knowledge Discovery and Data Mining, 1997.
4. Kaufman et al. 1991. "Mining for Knowledge in Databases: Goals and General Description of the INLEN System," *Knowledge Discovery in Databases*, G. Piatetsky-Shapiro and W. Frawley, eds. Cambridge MA; AAAI/MIT.
5. Terveen et al. 1993. "Interface Support for Data Archeology," CIKM 1993. Proceedings of the 2nd International Conference on Information and Knowledge Management.
6. Shafer et al., 1996. "Sprint: A scaleable Parallel Classifier for Data Mining," Proceedings of the Conference on VLDB.
7. Agrawal and Psaila, 1995. ""Active Data Mining," The First International Conference on Knowledge Discovery and Data Mining.
8. Devany & Ram, 1997. "Situation development in a complex real-world domain," ICML-97 Workshop.

Are Global Understanding, Communication, and Information Management in Information Systems Possible?

A Conceptual Modelling View - Problems and Proposals for Solutions

Hannu Kangassalo

University of Tampere, Department of Computer Science
P.O. Box 607, FIN-33101 Tampere, Finland
Internet: hk@cs.uta.fi

Abstract. A recent trend in thinking about information systems and data bases is the idea that shared knowledge forms a globally understood phenomenon, based on global communication facilitated by the Internet and maintained by the global information management. The idea sounds good, but difficult ontological, epistemological, logical, and methodological problems are penetrating out. One is based on the way how human concepts are created. Another problem is that the point of view is not usually taken into account properly. The third one is that a system of concepts on which the information system is built seems to form an unique entirety, limiting the applicability of constructs of the system of concepts outside the borders of the information system. We study the idea and analyse some of the problems that seem to be revealed. The answer to the question in the title seems to be negative, but many improvements to information systems can be made. Systematic studies of concepts, systems of concepts and their descriptions are regarded as necessary. Information systems should be defined on the basis of their conceptual content, not on the basis of the data flow and linguistic representations of occurrences, as it is done today.

1 Introduction

Traditionally, databases were used to storage data needed for producing more advanced and refined information. Later they evolved to various types of distributed repositories of actual data that geographically may reside in the world wide computer network. Increase in size and complexity of the content of data has forced us to develop another collection of data, called a metadata repository. It describes properties of data at several levels of abstraction: at the physical level, the linguistic level, and the level of concepts. A special kind of meta-data at the conceptual level is a conceptual schema, which describes the possibilities and necessities of a domain only, i.e. the types and rules recognised in the domain, as well as those of information systems based on that domain [25].

P.P. Chen et al. (Eds.): Conceptual Modeling, LNCS 1565, pp. 105-122, 1999.

A recent trend of thinking about information systems is the idea that shared knowledge forms a globally understood phenomenon, based on global communication facilitated by the Internet, and maintained by the global information management. Shared knowledge could form a global data base. The idea sounds good, but some difficult problems start to penetrate out. The purpose in this work is to study the idea and analyse some of the problems which seem to be revealed. We also study briefly information systems design on the conceptual level. We shall use approaches borrowed from the philosophy of science, as well as some principles of meta-modelling.

Databases and metadata repositories, together with the software needed to manipulate them, are technical implementations of information systems. A fundamental asset in these systems is knowledge, carried by data, and described by the conceptual schema corresponding to 1) the Universe of Discourse (UoD) and 2) the data base [25]. Information is the knowledge increment brought about by a receiving action in a message transfer, i.e. it is the difference between the conceptions interpreted from a received message and the knowledge before the receiving action [25]. Knowledge is a relatively stable and sufficiently consistent set of conceptions possessed by single human actors [25]. Both information and knowledge are based on human conceptions resulting from an action whereby a human actor aims at in-terpreting a perception in his mind, possibly in a specificaction context, or from an action whereby a human actor aims at constructing a conception in his mind [25]. The term 'data' denotes any set of representations of knowledge expressed in a language [25].

We analyse the notions of information, conceptualisation, communication, and information management. Then we introduce the notion of conceptual information requirements specification. It provides us with the framework in which the understanding of the system of knowledge can be studied. Then problems of global information systems are analysed.

2   Communication, Understanding, and Information Management

2.1   Basic Notions: Information, Concept, and Conceptualisation

Nauta presents a rather detailed account of the notion and role of information in a semiotic process [17], i.e. in the process where something is a sign to some organism. He recognises seven levels of cognition, and at each level a different notion of information with the corresponding theory. The type of information changes and the degree of organisation of knowledge increases when one moves from a lower level to a higher level. The levels are based on this degree of organisation of knowledge. In this level structure, only at three highest levels a language is assumed. A language is a non-empty set of permissible symbolic constructs [25]. He does not take human concepts in this semiotic study into account.

Conceptualisation, i.e. human concept formation, is a process in which individual's knowledge about something is formed and gets organised (see e.g. [13]). In the area of formal ontology, conceptualisation is regarded as an intensional knowledge structure which encodes the implicit rules constraining the structure of a piece of reality (cf. [5]). The results of conceptualisation are concepts or more weakly organised conceptions. Conceptualisation process seems to be mainly located on below the level of the grammar in Nauta's levels of cognition. We will not study here relationships between conceptualisation and language.

A concept is regarded to be an independently identifiable structured construct composed of knowledge: either knowledge primitives and/or other concepts [7]. Concepts are not classified e.g. into entities, attributes, or relationships because this kind of classification is not an intrinsic feature of knowledge - it is a superimposed abstract scheme into which knowledge is forced, and which depends on our ontological commitments. Different classifications are possible, and each of them is a basis for different ontology, i.e. the rules and principles of how knowledge is composed.

According to the constructivistic personal construct psychology [4, 12], a concept structure in a person develops on the basis of his experiences, including his own observations, communication with other persons, his own reasoning, reading, organised learning, etc. Kelly describes it as follows: Knowledge construction is the result of a person's attempt to use his existing knowledge to make sense of new experiences. This entails the modification of concepts, the reorganisation of knowledge structures, and the acquisition of new knowledge. Since knowledge construction depends on the extent of knowledge in the person, different individuals will come away e.g. from an instructional experience with their own unique understanding, no matter how well the instruction is designed, and no matter how much effort the individuals devote to making sense of what they have seen and heard. This construction of knowledge is a life-long, effortful process requiring significant mental engagement by the person. The knowledge that we already possess affects our ability to learn and organise new knowledge. Knowledge previously constructed by the person will affect the way s/he interprets the knowledge that the teacher is trying to impart. [12].

So far, we have studied human knowledge. For practical work, it must be transferred to the external world, i.e. it must be externalised. Externalisation is an activity that represents human concepts, ideas or problems explicitly, in the form of an external model [19]. An important aspect in externalisation is that knowledge of substantive conditions and the justification principles of externalised knowledge should be externalised, too, if possible.

2.2 Communication

Communication can be studied at any of these seven levels of cognition, with the corresponding notions of information. We shall here use the conceptual (mainly discursive in Nauta's terminology) and semantic levels. Communication takes place if a person S (sender) has knowledge of a topic T, and he wants to send it to some receiver. His knowledge of the topic T is included into his knowledge K_S. It consists of his own conceptions. The sender codes knowledge of T using some language and sends it using a communication channel. A message M may contain facts, concept descriptions, or both.

We are interested in the conceptual content of M. It is a conceptual structure M_S, concerning the topic T. A conceptual structure consists of concepts, relationships between concepts, and possibly of some additional knowledge primitives (see [7]). Concepts consist of knowledge of things, i.e. conceptions about the domain or conceptions developed by the sender. Relationships are special things composed of one or several predicated thing(s), each one associated with one predicator characterising the role of that predicated thing within that relationship, i.e. they are abstractions which connect concepts together, (see [25]). Note that a message is transmitted only in the form of physical signs.

A receiver R receives a message and interprets it using his own conceptions. He recognises the words and applies his own conception to every word. On the basis of these conceptions and some linguistic information, he constructs his own interpretation of the conceptual content of the message. He associates that structure to his own knowledge K_R. The receiver tries to understand the message from his own point of view, and often he also tries to interprete it as much as possible like the message he would make himself in similar circumstances (see a detailed discussion in [20, 21]). It improves possiblities in understanding and achieving a common agreement in communication but does not guarantee that.

He already knows a part of the conceptual content of the message, but some part of it may be new to him. From that part he gets information. That new part may change his knowledge. If the receiver sends a reply to the sender, several things may happen: e.g. the receiver sends knowledge which the sender did not know before. In that case the sender gets new information and his knowledge evolves.

In addition to the amount of new information, the success or failure of a communication act depends on how similar or different the conceptions used by the communicating parties are, how the sender codes his conceptions to the expressions of the language, how the receiver encodes them to his own conceptions, and how well the communicating parties master and share the communication language. Because the conceptions are constructed on the basis of their personal experiences, abstractions, or reasoning, it is likely that they are more or less different.

Differences in conceptions and in the way how the communicating parties are using words of the language in the communication process have the effect that the receiver understands only some fraction of the message in the way the sender thought it should be undersood. There are several methods how the communicating parties may try to improve understanding of the message [20, 21] but complete understanding can hardly be achieved. However, learning and the extensive education systems tend to standardise some of the conceptions, and the use of language, but not all of them. Communication is also in many ways related to understanding.

2.3 Understanding

Communication is not only exchange of data. Data must be understood and located in the knowledge structure of the person. Understanding and relating the knowledge received are processes which are strongly interwoven together.

M. Bunge says that understanding is not an all-or-none operation: it comes in several kinds and degrees. Understanding calls for answering to what is called the six W's of science and technology: what (or how), where, when, whence, whither, and why. In other words, understanding is brought about by description, subsumption, explanation, prediction, and retrodiction. [3].

Neither of these epistemic operations is more important than the others, although many researchers specialize in only some of them. Collectors, classifiers and field workers are more interested in description than in explanation or prediction, theoretical researchers and technologists want to know not only the facts but also why they are so. Subsumption, explanation, prediction and postdiction are typical theoretical operations, i.e. activities performed by means of theories - the better, the richer and the better organized. [3].

2.4 Information Management and Its Role

Human information management consists of several cognitive processes performed by the human mind. They are fundamental for all information processing. Information management function in an organization is, together with users and their cognitive processes, responsible for acquisition and storing new data, for that knowledge available is understandable - possibly by using metadata which describes the conceptual content of data, as well as for modelling knowledge concerning data, systems and the organisation.

In the design of new information systems, more responsibility of the work is given to the users. Problems are expressed by domain-oriented concepts and rules. The conceptual structure of the system, as well as the content of databases, must be defined by using concepts which the user applies in his work. The ultimate edge of this evolution is that the users can work with the information system as if working with concepts of the UoD alone, without being confused by implementation-oriented concepts of the system. [7].

From the user's perspective, we should replace the whole information system with the conceptual schema of the UoD, supported with facilities for [7]:

- accessing, developing, analysing, changing, manipulating and maintaining concepts (rather: concept descriptions) from which the conceptual schema describing the UoD has been constructed, and

- accessing, manipulating and maintaining data corresponding to the conceptual schema. All operations on data should be performed through the conceptual schema. All the technical functions of the system should be hidden from the users.

This paradigm is based on the view that a conceptual schema defines a systematic 'theory' of the UoD and the knowledge based on it. A theory is an attempt to bind together in a systematic fashion the knowledge that one has of some particular (real or hypothetical) aspect of the world of experience [22]. It is a conceptual construct which, depending on the case in analysis or design, can be represented as a more or less systematic set of statements, only, or a hypothetico-deductive system. Concepts are constructed on the basis of purposes, goals and business rules of the user organisation. That approach applies to the Internet-based information systems as well.

We shall describe the situation in which all information needs and requirements specifications can be analysed and specified. The same model can also be applied in a global environment because it is always the person needing information who has to determine from which point of view the information must be received and/or constructed. On the other hand, the person may receive information which is not in concert to the point of view defined by him.

A point of view (of a person) refers to the selection of a certain aspects of the information. It is a collection of concepts, called determinables, which is used to characterise an object. The notion of a point of view contains the idea that only part of all possible concepts are used to characterise the object in a given situation [6].

A user has to recognise the situation in which he is specifying his information requirements. He has to specify the point of view and select what kind of information he wants, as well as formulate the requirements on the basis of the properties of the situation, his own knowledge and needs. He has to evaluate the relevance of information he requires (relevance problem) and to solve the problem of how the information can be produced (production problem), and finally produce the information, and use it in order to reach his goal (see [7, 8]). Information management function in an organisation should take care of facilities needed to make these activities. The situation is described in Figure 1.

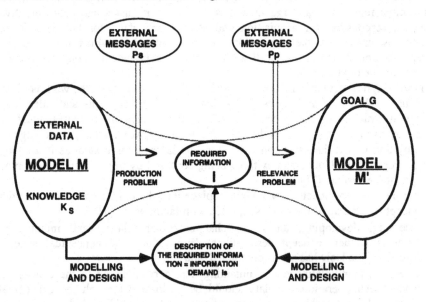

Fig. 1. The situation for satisfying information requirements

Model M and model M' are constructs consisting of all the relevant knowledge and data in the present situation and future situation, respectively. Both of them can be based on one of several different ontologies, they can be based on one of several different structuring principles and are expressed by using some language.

Model M consists of (knowledge of) the current UoD known by the user S. It consists of the user's knowledge K_S and the external data available, relevant for the situation. Knowledge K_S consists of conseptions, concepts and facts, as well as of some procedural and tacit knowledge. Facts are e.g. knowledge about instances based on the model. External data consists of texts, algorithms, pictures, animations, graphs, sounds, etc. Descriptions of the conceptual content (i.e. metadata) of external data should be available, either in the minds of the users, in data description repositories, or in conceptual schemata. Otherwise users cannot understand the meaning of data.

Model M, in its primitive form, is a simplified description of the UoD, constructed by using ordinary or simplified conceptions and concepts of person S, from his point of view. A more advanced model M may contain concepts which belong to some theoretical structure defining the UoD from a certain point of view. In that case, at least part of that theoretical structure must be included into the model, too.

Model M' describes the future situation, which should appear according to the goal G specified by the person S. Recognition of the future situations usually requires knowledge acquisition, concept formulation, conceptual modelling, and possibly analysis of epistemic changes, too. The goal specifies the conditions under which model M' should appear.

The required information I is what is wanted by the user in order to reach his goal. In the beginning, it is a hypothetical construct. It contains e.g. the data with the desired meaning, descriptions of new concepts, (partial) conceptual schemata required to change the present conceptual schema of the user S, and possibly an analysis of consequences of the proposed epistemic changes. Information demand I_S is the description of the required information which the user really works on.

The required information I must be derivable from knowledge in the model M and/or in external messages P_S. Because I is only a hypothetical consctruct in this phase, it should be possible to infer on the basis of an information demand I_S and the model M that the required information can be produced. This is called a requirement of producability (a production problem). In addition, it should be possible to infer on the basis of I_S, the model M', and possibly the model M that the satisfaction of the information demand I_S will help to reach the goal G. This is called a requirement of relevance. A solution of the production problem indicates how the information can be constructed from external data and the users' knowledge K_S in the model M.

It may be that the model M does not contain enough knowledge and data so that required information could be produced from it. External messages P_S and P_P represent additional knowledge which may be needed to solve the problem of missing knowledge. Knowledge in P_S is needed for solving the production problem.

A relevance problem is a problem of: 1) how to recognise that the required information helps in reaching the situation described in the model M' in G, 2) is the required information relevant for reaching the situation in the model M', and 3) how we can find the information relevant for reaching the situation in model M'. Knowledge in P_P may be needed for solving the relevance problem. In the world of the Internet, sources of P_S and P_P are very large, but it may be difficult to recognise the most relevant information from huge sources and derive the justification of it.

The models M and M' are not necessarily constructed by using the same ontological principles, and possibly they do not belong to the same structuring principle class. If they belong to different classes or are based on different ontologies, it may be necessary to search for transformations which make it possible to change concepts, conceptual constructs, and conceptual schemata and data from one structuring principle to another and from one ontology to another, i.e. define a mapping from one model to another. In some cases complete transformations cannot be found. Similar problems are discussed in detail by e.g. Rantala in [20, 21]. It may also require epistemic changes for the users to accomplish.

In the same way, the models M and M' are not necessarily constructed by using the same epistemological principles, i.e. substantive conditions and justification principles of knowledge may be different. Therefore, detailed comparing the models may become difficult, if not impossible.

Models M and M' describe only the concepts and conceptual structures based on conceptualisations from the UoD. Other aspects important for modelling can be described e.g. as in [2].

3 Concept Structures and Information Requirements Specification

3.1 Concept Structures and Information Requirements Specification

Human concepts, human knowledge, and their externalisations, are always based on some, more or less specific point of view, on the basis of which they were constructed, and which must be taken into account to understand them properly. They are related to a set of implicit rules of application, specifying the conditions to which they can be meaningfully applied (cf. [24, e.g. Chapter 14]).

Concepts can form large concept structures. In the description of an organisation there may be several concept structures interlaced. Concepts and concept structures contain knowledge needed to understand the data manipulated in information systems and describing the occurrences. In the following, we shall not separate concepts and concept structures.

An information requirements specification consists of knowledge available for the person making the specification needed to justify the information demand and for constructing the description of it. The information demand description may consist of: 1) one (or more) concept description about which data describing occurrences of that concept is missing, and is therefore required, or 2) approximate, coarse and/or imprecise description of a 'missing' concept in which knowledge of precisely formulated, required concept is missing and is needed, or 3) both cases. Knowledge of 'missing' concepts can be of several different types.

3.2 Environment of Information Requirement Definitions

The person S who defines information requirements has to relate with each other two conceptual models, M and M', which both describe the UoD but in different situations (see Fig. 1).

Models M and M' may in an information requirement specification be related in many different ways [8]. The conceptual and semantic structure of an environment of requirement definitions consists of all (relevant) relations between concepts and facts in M and concepts and facts in M'. The conceptual, logical and semantical characteristics of the structure can be used as a basis for defining structural classes of different cases of the requirement definition.

A systematic classification based on these characteristics provides all semantically different cases which may appear in information requirement environments based on the point of view of the design. The point of view may be combined from several structuring principles. More details can be found in references [8, 9].

3.3 The Problem of Stating Information Requirements

A solution to the problem of stating information requirements is to find and define a conceptual construct C_{MG} which relates models M and M', satisfies the requirement of producability and the requirement of relevance and, too, satisfies requirements stated in the goal. The construct connects the goal and the relevant knowledge available for the person S in the model M. It also specifies how concepts in the model M are ralated to the model M'.

The problem of stating information requirements in multi-perspective settings contains several additional sub-problems. The solution is based on the systematic use of one or more classifications of the concepts, called model concepts, used in the UoD. Model concepts may form abstract structures. Each classification defines a set of points of view, which directs further design.

3.4 Understanding Requirements Specifications

The problem of understanding information requirement specifications may be complicated, especially if the specification contains 'missing' concepts, because in this case the conceptual content of the specification is not yet fixed (case 2, in section 3.1). On the basis of the analysis of understanding, made by Bunge [3, p. 58], we conclude that achieving the solution requires knowing answers to one or more questions concerning our information requirements: what (or how), where, when, whence, whither, and why. We have to know *what* information we want to get, and *why* we want to have it (the relevance problem).

To answer to the latter question may require several levels of answers to be produced. Understanding is related to the growth of knowledge, but any kind of knowledge does not help understanding. Explanatory knowledge is superior to descriptive knowledge, which is in turn superior to mere information [3]. Achieving higher explanatory levels may require constructing new concepts and embedding them into the construct C_{MG} and the corresponding rules, although they may not be needed computationally.

Understanding a thing means knowing (in a deep sense) the position and role of the thing in the environmental epistemic framework into which it is embedded [3], and also knowing the internal structure and behaviour of the thing. The epistemic framework cannot only be an agglomeration of knowledge. It must be a systematic theory based on the concepts and rules of the corresponding discipline. Knowledge must in some systematic way connect concepts needed to contain enough information about the phenomenon to be understood, to make up a theory about the phenomenon. The best result can be achieved by constructing a system of concepts and rules developed by using a scientific methodology and organised by using some systematic structuring principle which helps to understand the theory in which the concept corresponding the thing appears.

In addition to receiving mere information, we are interested in explanations and predictions in a conceptual schema, which provide scientific accounts of some part of our environment, e.g. an application area in the company. In practical information systems design work we cannot make a complete scientific research of the application, but we can systematically apply principles of conceptual modelling and search for a good conceptual solution for the knowledge content of the system. In communication and information management it is not enough to receive or possess some piece of data, without receiving some explanatory information along it.

4 Conceptual Systems for Satistying Information Requirements

4.1 Systems of Concepts

Systems of concepts are becoming important in information systems design and application. Conceptual schemata and technical ontologies are examples of their emerging use. They contain a systematically developed set of concepts, in which the concepts are related to each other by relationships indicating the epistemological connections between concepts. The type of these relationships is important in deciding how we can apply the concepts in forming an information system, and how different information systems can be related to each other.

4.2 Theories Concerning the Models M and M'

We are interested in the ways how models M and M' are constructed on the basis of theories, and how they can be related to each other. We can not analyse here all the alternatives but show some basic ideas, only.

A theory contains (at least) basic concepts and basic rules to be used in a model, possibly including the dynamic rules of the model, i.e. which kind of changes are allowed in the model based on the theory. It can be organised in several ways depending on which features of knowledge the designer wants to emphasise with it.

An ontology is a special theory which gives an explicit, partial account of a conceptualisation (this is only one of several interpretations of the term, see [5]). That notion is quite close to the theory of a modelling principle, e.g. ER-model, OR-model, or some concept description system[1], i.e. some kind of "grammar" of the modelling principle. In the following we shall use the notion of a theory in that sense, but we do not necessarily mean a strictly formalised system because in the concept analysis and design strictly formalised systems do not appear so often.

Figure 2 illustrates the theory T concerning both models M and M'. They have the same ontology, i.e. the same model concepts and general rules of the theory have been used, but the actual concepts and the actual models M and M' do not need to be the same. If the theory is very general, the models may differ considerably. They may contain same and/or different concepts and rules, depending on how detailed level the ontology has been constructed. For example, in the ER model, actual entities can be different, but they obey rules concerning all entities. Because both models are based on the same theory, their essential features are quite similar.

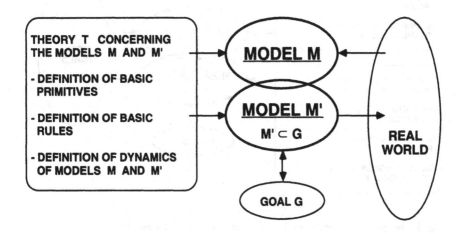

Fig. 2. One theory governs both models M and M'

A more complicated situation appears when the theory T is applied to the model M, but the model M' is constructed by using a different theory T', see Figure 3. In this case, several alternatives exist, e.g. the models M and M' may share some components, or they do not share any components.

It may be possible that both models contain a concept which is represented by the same word but the meaning of the word is not necessarily the same. This is not the case of homonyms common in database integration problems. The whole theory of meaning applied in the model may be different than the one in another model. The theory of meaning studies the sense of an expression, construction, or sentence in a given language, or of a non-linguistic signal or symbol [16].

If we take into account that the conceptual meaning of a descriptive term is constituted by what can be inferred from it in accordance with the logical and extra-logical rules of inference of the language (conceptual frame) to which it belongs (see [23], p. 317]), then the meaning of the term depends on the whole theory in which the word is embedded (semantic or conceptual holism), or depending on the case, only some part of the theory (semantic or conceptual molecularism). If in one model holism is used and in other one e.g. atomism is applied, then the meanings of the same names in models are different. For example, in the original version of the ER model atomism was used in almost complete form, except the case of an existence dependency. It means e.g. that in all cases the name refers to an object, only, and nothing else, except in the case of the dependent entity. In that case, in order to refer to the dependent entity, also the identifier of some other entity, an "owner", is needed.

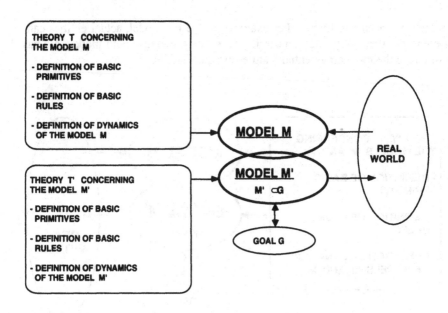

Fig. 3. The models M and M' are based on different theories T and T'

In an information system, as well as in a modelling method, some theory of meaning is always applied, although it may not have been recognised. Different theories may be used in different information systems, and e.g. in the environment of the Internet the systems may be related and co-operate in various ways. The user does not necessarily know which theory he should apply. The problems and correctness of combining different theories of meaning used in different information systems or conceptual schemata are studied very little, as well as the consequences of using them together. In linguistics and AI, there has been quite a lot of discussion about properties of various theories, e.g. holism, molecularism, atomism, and nihilism (see a short description e.g. in [15]). In the following, these terms are not necessarily used exactly in a similar way than in philosohy of language.

Semantic atomists hold that the meaning of any representation (linguistic, mental, or otherwise) is not determined by the meaning of any other representation. Some philosophers in the eighteenth and nineteenth centuries thought that an idea of an X was about X's in virtue of this idea's physically resembling X's. Resemblance theories are no longer thought viable, but a number of contemporary semantic atomists still believe that the basic semantic relation is between a concept and the things to which it applies, and not one among concepts themselves. [15]. On data base and information systems areas atomism is often used, too. In simple systems it may be acceptable, but in developing more advanced systems, e.g. complicated deductive databases or databases based on complex multilevel concept systems that may not be enough.

The holistic view is a thesis about the nature of representations on which the meaning of a symbol is relative to the entire system of representations containing it. Holism has some startling consequences, such as that scientific theories that differ in their basic postulates are "empirically incommensurable" [15]. The development and use of different conceptual schema models or formal ontologies bring the same problem into the area of information systems and databases.

An example of the system based on conceptual holism is described in [7, 10]. In the theory developed by Kauppi, formal concept operations can be applied to manipulate concepts [11], and concept descriptions, too. The content of all derived concepts can be seen as a function of the inferential operations involving them. The conceptual structure of the universe of concepts, based on the intensional containment relation between concepts, is a complete semi-lattice, where every concept defines a Boolean lattice [18]. As a result, the conceptual content of an information system can be seen as a systematic structure, based on the use of intensional containment relation [11, 9, 18]. A conceptual schema is a concept which contains all other concepts needed to describe the UoD corresponding to the schema.

Semantic molecularism alleviates the requirement of holism that the entire theory should be related to the meaning of a symbol. It is sufficient that some sub-theory is relative to the symbol. Several theories may share that relatively small part. In other words, molecularism holds that the meaning of a representation in a language L is determined by its relationships to the meanings of other expressions in L, but, unlike holism, not by its relationship to every other expression in L.[15]. An example of the use of molecularism is e.g. in Extended ER models, where a generalisation/specialisation construct is used. In that case, a reference to the specific entity means that the user must know and understand a larger construct in order to find out what the entity really means, cf. e.g. the case of the existence dependency.

4.3 Connections between Models M and M'

We may have to relate concepts from one model to concepts in the other model. The models may be based on the same theory, or on different theories. We should be able to understand, formulate, and solve the problem of how the construct contained in one model is related to the construct contained in another model. We should find a 'translation' or a 'transformation' from one model to another model, which would connect both models and facilitate our understanding of mapping between models. Different aspects of the corresponding problem in philosophy of science are much discussed since Kuhn [14], see e.g. [3, 20, 21].

Figure 2 illustrates a situation in which both models are based on the same theory. Conceptualisations of the models may be the same, or they may be partly different. In the second case, which is quite common, the models are different. An interesting question for information systems design is as follows: How can we compare the models M and M' if they are based on different conceptualisations of the UoD? There are several alternatives: conceptually, referentially, or on the level of data values. We shall not study these question here.

If the models are based on different theories, the conceptualisations are always different, and therefore the models are different, too. In some cases, it is possible to construct some bridge rules which connect the models, but not in all cases. A bridge is a system of translation rules which facilitates translation and understanding of mapping between theories.

If we can find a sequence of translation steps from one model to another model, we can describe the UoD by using both models, and we can understand the correspondence between them. The new construct can be seen as an extension of both models and theories.

In the next case, the model M and the theory T define one UoD, and the model M' and the theory T' define another UoD, but the models and theories are incommensurable [14], i.e. even though they may not logically contradict one another, they have reference to no common body of data. The concepts in these theories are based on different conceptualisations. The two theories are incommensurable because their constituent terms cannot have a reference to a theory-neutral set of observations, and there is no overlap of observational meaning between the competitor theories and models, respectively. In other words, the UoD is described in the model M' and the theory T' using concepts which simply cannot be expressed in terms of the concepts of the theory T. The UoD's are conceived entirely differently.

The doctrine of incommensurability has been developed in the framework of the philosophy of science. There has been much discussion about its correctness and accuracy. One of the issues has been the question about the existence of those situations in which that phenomenon might appear. Easy examples have not been found within the framework of the philosophy of science. The reason has been e.g. that often the changes between old and new theories do not take place so quickly that they could cause problems in understanding.

In information systems recent applications of formal ontology seem to offer cases, in which one formal ontology is rejected and a new formal ontology is adopted. These cases are quite close to structural alternatives described above. They may happen e.g. in an information system which is modified by changing its conceptual base, i.e. by changing the conceptualisation of some, or all concepts in the conceptual schema. The 'old' system corresponds to the model M, and the 'new' one to the model M'. Another case may appear in a company which is changing its goal structure (i.e. model M') so that the concepts and rules of the theory T' and the model M' must be changed. In both cases, the change may take place in a very short time (at least in principle) because the ontology or conceptual schema can even be bought ready-made and put into use. All these cases are difficult for global communication and understanding, as well as for global information management.

Another family of problems which may turn out to be difficult in this context is based on the holistic view of concepts. A major theme in the recent philosophy of science has been the rejection of the empiricist thesis according to which, with the exception of terms which play a purely formal role, the language of science derives its meaning from some, possibly quite indirect, correlation with experience [1]. This empiricist thinking is applied in information systems design and in database design quite much.

The alternative that has been proposed is that meaning is internal to each conceptual system, that terms derive their meaning from the role they play in a language, and that something akin to "meaning" flows from conceptual framework to experience [1]. The conclusion to be made is that if we adopt holism as the theory of meaning, then data sharing can be made only in very few situations in which the same basic postulates of respective theories hold. If we accept atomism, then a concept is independent of any other concepts. That would be convenient in the Internet world, too. However, we have to take into account that concepts may form hierarchical structures which relate the concept to some other concepts, resulting in at least a molecular concept structure. Therefore, we should adopt at least molecularism as the theory of meaning and accept also that in some cases holism may appear. Users should know which kind of theory of meaning is to be used with data, even in the Internet environment, and they should be able to know and understand also the meaning of molecular concept structures.

4.4   Conceptual Development of Information Systems

The content of all derived concepts is constructed from basic concepts by using one or more sequences of concept operations. The further a concept is from the basic concepts in the sequence, the higher it is on the hierarchy of epistemological abstraction, i.e. the further it is from the immediate experience. As a consequence, the longer chain of concept operations is needed to construct a concept in an information system, the more information is needed to 'know' it in that chain and to understand its content. In other words, information systems seem to grow 'upwards' in the dimension of the levels of epistemological abstraction. If we add a new concept somewhere in the middle to the sequence, epistemological abstraction of the concepts above the added concept is added by one, and the meaning of them is adjusted to include the meaning of the added concept. Conceptual lattice of the resulting system changes, but it grows mainly 'upwards'. If two information systems have a sub-system with exactly the same conceptual properties in both cases, then the systems can be integrated on the basis of this common sub-system. The flow of information goes from lower levels to higher levels, not 'horisontally'.

4.5   New Role of Information Management

The role of information management function is changing drastically. It is not sufficient to describe data, alone. More attention must be paid to the conceptual description of systems, especially to the description of the content of concepts and structures made of concepts. The information systems must be defined on the basis of their conceptual content, (cf. [7]), not on the basis of the data flow and data occurrences, as it is mainly done today. A conceptual description of the system is an abstract structure, in which all relevant concepts and relationships between concepts are taken into account. The concepts must contain as detailed information about the content of them as possible or relevant, not only its name and the form of its representation. Concepts can be multilevel constructs which may also contain some special knowledge primitives which are not meaningful concepts if considered in isolation. For example, an identifying property of an object is not meaningful if considered in isolation.

Information management function must be able to externalise all relevant conceptual descriptions, if needed, and maintain them separately of all implementation aspects. The new information management function should maintain all relevant concepts in concept libraries or repositories from which they should be available for the users who want to use some of them for defining and implementing a new information system, or develop new concepts.

An important role of new information management function is to recognise, describe, analyse, and manipulate concepts and concept descriptions of information systems. Concepts and concept descriptions form a new level of abstraction for information system descriptions. Concept descriptions must be separate from system implementations aspects so that changes in implementations and information technology do not have an effect to concepts and concept descriptions, except as in the form of planned operations. Information system design methodologies should be based on meaningful structured concept descriptions and not only on manipulation of data values.

5 Conclusions

We studied on the conceptual level of information systems the popular idea that shared knowledge forms a globally understood phenomenon, based on global communication facilitated by the Internet, and maintained by the global information management. There are several aspects which force us to suspect that idea. We studied the notions of information, data, knowledge, and use of them in information requirements specification. We noticed that human concept formation is based on a conceptualisation process which leads to the use of personal constructs. Concepts in information systems are always based on some point of view, which makes it difficult to share them without any constraints. The user should always know the point of view from which the concepts of the system are constructed. The contemporary information technology does not support properly the construction, definition, use, and maintenance of meta-knowledge needed to convey the detailed content information of concepts, together with the words on which the surface information is carried. In general, information technology supports quite badly the use of meta-knowledge.

In communication, the conceptual construct of the sender is usually not identical with the conceptual construct of the receiver. Both are using their own conceptualisations, which are at least partly different. Understanding a thing means knowing the position and role of the thing in the environmental epistemic framework into which it is embedded. The frameworks of different persons are at least partly different.

The situation for satisfying information requirements contains two conceptual models (present and future situation) which are very often different. The difference may in some cases be so severe that they are difficult to compare.

In information systems, each concept is unique and augments uniquely to the content of the highest defined concept, i.e. to the conceptual schema. The structure of a conceptual schema seems to have a property that if new concepts are added to the schema, the schema tends to increase the average epistemological abstraction of the concepts.

Taken together, it seems to be that global understanding, communication, and information management in information systems are in general not possible. The answer to the question presented in the title seems to be negative.

Although most information systems design methodologies and information technology seem to emphasise the flow of information, the conceptual structure of knowledge is always more essential than flow of data. The consequence is that we should emphasise more the conceptual level in the design and use of information systems: we have to develop new principles or theories for defining the conceptual content of information systems and semantics of the systems. We have to develop methods and tools for handling concept descriptions and conceptual schemata.

There are some areas of information systems design in which quite considerable progress can be achieved, e.g. in the manipulation of meta-knowledge and concept descriptions, as well as in conceptual modelling methods. However, the permanent problem for the use of shared knowledge as a globally understood phenomenon, always seems to be the huge amount of meta-knowledge which should be available, recognised, acquired, understood, and maintained.

References

[1]   Brown, H. I., (1986) Sellars, Concepts and Conceptual Change. Synthese 68: 275-307.

[2]   Bubenko, J., Kirikova, M., (1995) "Worlds" in Requirements Aquisition and Modelling. In Kangassalo, H., Jaakkola, H., Ohsuga, S., Wangler, B., (Eds.) Information Modelling and Knowledge Bases VI. IOS Press, Amsterdam, pp. 159-174.

[3]   Bunge, M., (1983) Treatise on Basic Philosophy. Volume 6. Epistemology & Methodology II. D Reidel Publishing Company, Dordrecht, Holland.

[4]   Gaines, B.R., Shaw, M.L.G., (1993) Knowledge Acquisition Tools based on Personal Construct Psychology, Knowledge Engineering Review, 8(1) 49-85.

[5]   Guarino,N., Giaretta,P., (1995) Ontologies and Knowledge Bases: Towards a Terminological Clarification. In Mars, NJI, (Ed), Towards Very Large Knowledge Bases, IOS Press.

[6]   Hautamäki, A., (1986) Points of View and Their Logical Analysis. Acta Philosophica Fennica. Vol. 41, Societas Philosophica Fennica, Ph.D. Dissertation, Helsinki.

[7]   Kangassalo, H., (1992/1993) COMIC - A System and Methodology for Conceptual Modelling and Information Construction. Data & Knowledge Engineering 9, 287-319,

[8]   Kangassalo, H., (1979) Logical and Semantical Properties of Environmental Situations for Stating Information Requirements. In Schneider, H.-J., (Ed.) Formal Models and Practical Tools for Information Systems Design. North-Holland.

[9]   Kangassalo, H., (1978) On the Definition and Satisfaction of Information Requirements. Thesis for the Degree of Licentiate in Philosophy. Department of Mathematical Sciences / Computer Science. University of Tampere, Finland, June 1978. 157 pages. (In Finnish).

[10]   Kangassalo, H., (1996) Conceptual Description for Information Modelling Based on Intensional Containment Relation. In Baader, F., Buchheit, M., Jeusfeld, M. A., Nutt, W. (Eds) Working Notes of the ECAI-96 Workshop on Knowledge Representation Meets Databases (KRDB-96). Budabest, Hungary, August 12-13, 1996. pp. 34-39.

[11]   Kauppi, R., (1967) Einführung in die Theorie der Begriffssysteme. Acta Universitatis Tamperensis, Ser. A, Vol.15, Universität Tampere, Tampere.

[12]   Kelly, G. H., (1955) The Psychology of Personal Constructs. W.W. Norton & Company, New York. Two volumes.

[13] Klausmaier, H.J., (1990.) Conceptualizing. In Jones, B.F., Idol, L. (Eds)., Dimensions of Thinking and Cognitive Instruction. Lawrence Erlbaum, Hillsdale, N.J., pp. 93-138.

[14] Kuhn, T.S., (1962) The Structure of Scientific Revolutions. The University of Chicago Press.

[15] LePore, E., (1996) Semantic holism. In Audi, R. (General Editor). The Cambridge Dictionary of Philosophy. Cambridge University Press, pp. 724-725.

[16] Loar, B., (1996) Meaning. In Audi, R. (General Ed.). The Cambridge Dictionary of Philosophy. Cambridge University Press, pp. 471-476.

[17] Nauta, D., Jr., (1972) The Meaning of Information. Mouton & Co. The Hague.

[18] Palomäki. J., (1994) From Concepts to Concept Theory. Discoveries, Connections, and Results. PhD Dissertation. Acta Universitatis Tamperensis. Ser. A, Vol. 416, University of Tampere, Tampere.

[19] Ohsuga, S., (1998) Multi-Strata Model and Its Applications - Particularly to Automatic Programming. In Charrel, P.-J., Jaakkola, H., Kangassalo, H., Kawaguchi, E., (Eds.). Information Modelling and Knowledge Bases IX. IOS Press, Amsterdam, pp. 83-99.

[20] Rantala, V., (1995) Explanatory Translation and Conceptual Change. In Koskinen, I., Oesch, E., Vaden, T., (Eds.), Proc. of the International Conference on Methods of Reading. University of Tampere, October 6-7, 1994. Tampere.

[21] Rantala, V., (1995) Translation and Scientific Change. In Herfel, W. E., Krajewski, W., Niiniluoto, I., Wojcicki, R. (Eds.), Theories and Models in Scientific Processes. Proc. of AFOS'94 Workshop and IUHPS'94 Conference. Amsterdam–Atlanta, GA: Rodopi.

[22] Ruse, M., (1995) Theory. In Honderich,T.,(Ed.), The Oxford Companion to Philosophy. Oxford University Press.

[23] Sellars, W., (1963) Science, Perception and Reality. Humanities Press, New York.

[24] Stegmüller, W., 1976) The Structure and Dynamics of Theories. Springer-Verlag, Berlin.

[25] The IFIP WG 8.1 Task Group FRISCO, (1996) A Framework of Information System Concepts. December, available at: ftp://ftp.leidenuniv.nl/fri-full.zip.

---

i   Another interpretation of the term is conceptualisation [5]. It is roughly a synonym of the notion of a conceptual schema used in conceptual modelling.

Enterprise Knowledge Management and Conceptual Modelling

Pericles Loucopoulos and Vagelio Kavakli

Department of Computation
UMIST
PO Box 88, Manchester, M60 1QD, U.K.
e-mail: {pl|kavakli}@sna.co.umist.ac.uk

Abstract. Turbulence is in the nature of business environments. Changes brought about because of different requirements such as social, political, technical and economic, exert pressures on organisations to respond in a timely and cost effective way to these challenges. In such an unstable environment information system developers are challenged to develop systems that can meet the requirements of modern organisations.

In this decade organisations also experience the effects of the integration and evolution of Information Technology (IT). While information systems continue to serve traditional business needs such as co-ordination of production and enhancements of services offered, a new and important role has emerged namely the potential of such systems in adopting a more supervisory and strategic support role. These developments offer opportunities for changes to organisational structures and the improvement of business processes.

The traditional approach to information systems development has proved to be too monolithic and lacking facilities for dealing with highly complex, multidimensional, and distributed systems. In the traditional paradigm little attempt is made in understanding how the proposed system relates to other components (some of which may be legacy systems themselves) or the effect that the system will have on the enterprise itself. This paper advances a position, based on research work and the application of this work on many industrial and commercial applications, which states that 'the single most important factor to successful business evolution through the use of information technology is Enterprise Knowledge Management'. Enterprise Knowledge Management involves many facets of the information systems domain including technical (business processes, flow of information etc), organisational and social (policies, structures and work roles etc) and teleological (purposes and reasons) considerations. Conceptual modelling plays a central role in the way that one can capture, reason, represent, use for agreement between many stakeholders and discover new knowledge from legacy systems.

1 Introduction

An organisation's knowledge has always been critical to its competitive success; efficient operations come from shared knowledge of how things work and how they could work; market share grows with better knowledge of customers and how to serve

P.P. Chen et al. (Eds.): Conceptual Modeling, LNCS 1565, pp. 123-143, 1999.

them. Such knowledge is normally implicitly managed; knowledge flows naturally, embedded in the everyday business routines and culture.

Today new business forces are demanding of business enterprises to adopt more formal knowledge management. Rapid organisational change, knowledge- intensity of goods and services, the growth in organisational scope, and information technology have intensified organisational needs for knowledge. In addition virtual organisations that are made up of complementary allied entities place greater demands on knowledge sharing [Ruggles   1997].

The increasing business needs for effective knowledge management is indicated in a management report published by Ernst and Young [Ruggles   1997] where it is forecasted that organisations will continuously increase the money spent on knowledge management consulting services.

Unstructured business knowledge is important for a company's performance, but cannot be systematically used and is not an asset a company can own. Clearly there is a need for support in terms of conceptual frameworks for structuring and managing enterprise knowledge so that it is clearly defined, controlled, and provided in a way that makes sure that it is available and used when needed. To this end, the role of conceptual modelling is critical. This paper will show how conceptual modelling fits in the wider spectrum of enterprise knowledge management by defining the requisite methodological framework.

Allied to enterprise knowledge modelling is the larger issue of *enterprise change management* itself. The use of enterprise knowledge modelling is to facilitate the sharing of pre-existing domain knowledge that will represent *best business practice knowledge*. Best practice knowledge is externalised in terms of generic knowledge patterns that can be re-used in similar settings in different applications.

This paper is organised as follows. Section 2 discusses a number of basic issues in enterprise knowledge management giving an overview of the requirements for enterprise knowledge management support. Section 3 introduces a set of modelling views which in their totality constitute the metamodelling level for developing enterprise specific models. Section 4 discusses the way that enterprise knowledge may be organised in terms of (a) its levels of abstraction and (b) its support repository environment. Section 5 discusses methodological issues in using enterprise knowledge models and demonstrates one such approach with the use of an industrial case study. Finally, section 6 concludes the paper with a set of observation on the utility of enterprise knowledge modelling.

2   Conceptual Modelling for Enterprise and Domain Patterns Descriptions

One of the main objectives of enterprise knowledge management is the communication and sharing of enterprise knowledge between different people. An issue of concern therefore, is how to describe enterprise knowledge so that this sharing can be effective. In practice this question has been answered in terms of two possible alternatives: using *natural language* (for example consultants' reports) or using *conceptual modelling*.

The use of natural language has the advantage of ease of transferability but falls short on formality. Lack of formality makes the use of enterprise knowledge problematic and hampers the development of appropriate tools. The use of conceptual modelling languages overcomes these shortcomings.

Enterprise knowledge modelling (or enterprise modelling) is a generic name that refers to a collection of conceptual modelling techniques for describing the structure and business processes of an enterprise, its missions and objectives together with the way that these objectives may be *operationalised* onto system components.

The majority of enterprise modelling techniques provide concise descriptions of what an enterprise "does" in order to operate. To this end, they usually involve two kinds of sub-models. An entity (or data, or information) model and a process (or functional) model [ICEIMT   1992]. For example IDEF0 diagrams [IDEF0   1993], DFDs [DeMarco   1978] or workflows [Swenson and Irwin   1995] are widely used to describe enterprise processes, while entity relationship based diagrams [Chen 1976] are in common use for enterprise data modelling.

However, these enterprise models ignore important topics like: what is the social, organisational structure of the enterprise, what are the roles of enterprise agents; what are the reasons, objectives, motivations that define the enterprise structure and processes. More recent approaches tend to expand on the earlier results, recognising that it is advantageous to examine an enterprise from multiple perspectives [Dobson 1992; Nellborn, Bubenko, et al   1992; Yu   1994; Yu and Mylopoulos   1994] [Easterbrook and Nuseibeh   1995].

In order to deal with enterprise knowledge complexity we advocate a multiperspective approach. The key aspects of this approach are encapsulated in Figure 1. The task of enterprise knowledge modelling is viewed as a co-operative activity which exploits the contribution of different modelling views, each encompassing a specific type of knowledge. When combined, these perspectives will produce an integrated, consistent and complete knowledge model of the enterprise analysed. Within this multiperspective approach enterprise analysis is based on two mechanisms: reasoning within a perspective; and reasoning across different perspectives in order to allow each individual step in the analysis process to exploit the most appropriate knowledge source.

As can be seen in Figure 1, knowledge regarding enterprises can be logically partitioned into three categories (or views): (a) the 'Goals' view i.e. the enterprise objectives and the ways that these may be realised; (b) the 'Operation' view i.e. the enterprise structures and functioning that realise the objectives; and (c) the 'Rationale' view i.e. justification, explanations and arguments supporting the different objectives and corresponding designs of the operations. Within the knowledge components, there are finer details e.g. definition of goals, actors, roles, etc.; these are further elaborated in section 3.

Figure 1: Enterprise Knowledge Modelling overview

Enterprise knowledge refers to the set of *conceptual models* which collectively constitute the expressions about the phenomena being observed in enterprises. One can differentiate between *enterprise specific* and *enterprise independent* (generic) knowledge. Whilst enterprise specific knowledge pertains to particular enterprise settings, generic knowledge would contain information that may be repeatable in many different situations i.e. models representing invariant knowledge. For example, the concept of "electricity distributor" is something which is universally acceptable and therefore applicable to many different enterprises within the electricity supply industry (ESI) sector. However, for different enterprises, there will be a specific type of "electricity distributor" and even within the same enterprise there may be many different "electricity distributors". This distinction between generic enterprise knowledge and specific enterprise knowledge gives rise to the concept of *enterprise pattern*, that is, invariant components describing accepted ways of working within a domain.

A pattern is more than just a description of some thing in the world. A pattern should also be a 'rule' about when and how to create the thing. It should be both a description of the artefact and a description of the process that will generate the artefact. According to Alexander [Alexander, Ishikawa, et al   1977], but also according to the majority of proponents of the patterns movement (see [Coad   1992] [Beck   1997; Buschmann, Meunier, et al   1996], [Coplien and Schmidt   1995; Gamma, Helm, et al   1995; Vlissides, Coplien, et al   1996], [Hay   1996] [Fowler 1997]), a pattern should be a self contained logical system which is capable of stating (a) that a given problem exists within a stated range of contexts and (b) that in the given context, a given solution solves the given problem.

Therefore, a set of desirable properties for a pattern may be summarised thus:

◊ A pattern should be made explicit and precise so that it can be used time and time again. A pattern is explicit and precise if:

- It defines the *problem* (e.g. 'we want to deregulate a monopoly ESI market') together with the *forces* that influence the problem and that must be resolved (e.g. 'customer needs are similar', 'pension rights for employees must be maintained' etc). Forces refer to any goals and constraints (synergistic or conflicting) that characterise the problem.
- It defines a concrete *solution* (e.g. 'how buying and selling electricity is done'). The solution represents a resolution of all the forces characterising the problem.
- It defines its *context* (e.g. 'the pattern makes sense in a situation that involves the transition from a monopoly to a deregulated market with electricity pool'). A context refers to a recurring set of situations in which the pattern applies.

◊ A pattern should be *visualisable* and should be *identifiable*, so that it can be interpreted equally well by all who might share the pattern. In this sense "visualisation" may take the form of 'statements in natural language', 'drawings' 'conceptual models' and so on.

Figure 1 distinguishes between *product* and *process* patterns. By doing so, it advocates a separation of concerns. Product patterns deal with the appropriate description of a solution to a problem regarding some artefact. Process patterns deal with the choices of the product patterns as well as other development actions in order to progress from some high level intention to its detailed realisation. Both product and process patterns will have to be first discovered and subsequently constructed in such a way so as to be applicable to different enterprises within the chosen domain (e.g., enterprise patterns applicable to ESI sector companies).

3   The Enterprise Knowledge Metamodel

3.1   Overview

Both enterprise specific and enterprise pattern knowledge is described in terms of the enterprise knowledge components. These components form the enterprise knowledge ontology, i.e., the enterprise knowledge metamodel (EKM). This defines the *logical form* of the enterprise knowledge. The metamodel includes information about the semantics of the enterprise knowledge; it identifies the enterprise entities their attributes and explicit relationships between them.

The enterprise knowledge metamodel integrates three complementary views (or submodels), namely: the *enterprise goal* view, the *enterprise process* view and the *information systems* components view.

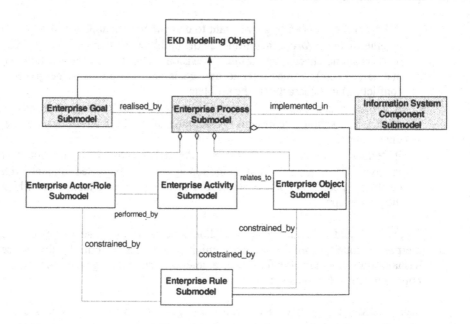

Figure 2: Modelling Views in Enterprise Knowledge Modelling

The enterprise goal submodel uses a 'network' of goals that are used to express the causal structure of an enterprise, in terms of the *goals-means* relations from the "intentional" objectives that control and govern the system operation to the actual "physical" enterprise processes and activities available for achieving these objectives.

The enterprise process submodel represents the organisational and behavioural aspects of an enterprise. The term 'enterprise process' needs some further elaboration at this stage. The traditional view of business process is that of a functional view. A functional view of an enterprise considers business functions related in some hierarchical way, the hierarchy itself being constructed through strict decomposition of business functions. Typically, the linking is done through the successive detailing of functions into sub-functions, sub-sub-functions and so on, until a level of detail has reached according to the wishes and opinion of the analyst. Functions are linked via flows of data. This is not a view adopted in this paper. Instead we consider the concept of an 'enterprise process' as a *composite* of four key enterprise components: (a) the roles that are played by enterprise actors in order to meet the process goals; (b) the activities involved in each role; (c) the objects that are involved together with their evolution from creation to extinction (within the context of the enterprise process); and (d) the rules that determine the process components. In other words, an enterprise process may transcend any functional divisions an in this sense it is truly a dynamic view of the enterprise.

Finally, the information system component submodel focuses on the information systems components that support enterprise processes. At this stage it is worth pointing out that in this paper, we do not advocate yet another information systems development technique; any method may be used, e.g. structured, object-oriented etc. and therefore this part is not elaborated in this document. Given a preferred information systems engineering method, the task is to link the enterprise knowledge model concepts to those of the information systems method. In this way there is a continuous tracing (in both directions) between high level enterprise objectives and detailed support mechanisms in an information system.

The above are summarised in Figure 2 that presents an overview of the enterprise knowledge modelling concepts. A more detailed view of the enterprise goal submodel and the enterprise process submodel is presented in sections 3.2 and 3.3 respectively. These are further illustrated with empirical examples taken from the electricity application case (discussed in section 5).

In using enterprise knowledge one may start at any submodel and move on to other submodels, depending on the situation. For example, if we are unfamiliar of, or there is lack of appropriate documentation about, an enterprise, the most appropriate starting point is at the 'enterprise processes' submodel. Modelling at this level will yield a clear picture of the enterprise processes in terms of the roles that actors play in order to fulfil their obligations in the enterprise; how these roles may interact in co-operatively achieving their goals; what kind of activities they need to engage into in order to meet their obligations; what objects are needed by these activities (physical resources, informational objects etc.); and finally, what rules dictate the enterprise processes. This would be a bottom up approach at the enterprise level.

A more top-down, strategic approach, might necessitate a different approach whereby we may start with the enterprise goals first and then proceed with the modelling of how these goals may be realised in enterprise processes.

3.2   The Enterprise Goal Submodel

The enterprise goal submodel is illustrated in Figure 3. Central to this view is the concept of *enterprise goal*. An enterprise goal is a desired state of affairs that needs to be attained. Typical goals are 'satisfy customer demand for electricity', 'decrease time necessary to fulfil a customer application by 25%', 'increase Distribution competitiveness' or 'transform from monopoly market to a deregulated market with electricity pool', etc.

Goals pertain to stakeholders. A *stakeholder* is defined as someone who has an interest in the system design and usage. Examples of stakeholders are: company managers, company customers, software system designers, system users, regulators etc. A stakeholder may not necessarily be an actor in the enterprise (e.g., 'government regulator').

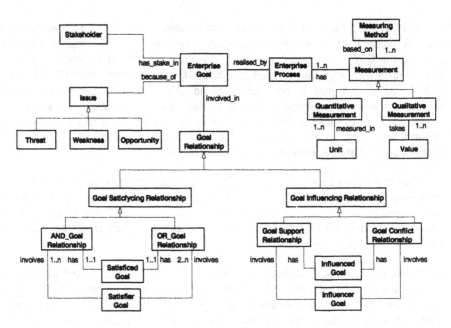

Figure 3: The enterprise goal submodel

Goals are generated because of issues. An *issue* is a statement of a *problem*, *threat*, or *opportunity* that leads to the formation of the goal. For example the goal Issues are shown as arrows entering the bottom left side of the goal. `increase Distribution competitiveness` is formed because of the issue `conform to the European Commission directive regarding the de-regulation of the European electricity market`.

Goals are realised as *enterprise processes*. Though enterprise goals can be stated in a brief they cannot be mapped directly onto business processes. There is a sizeable gap for example between the desire for a more competitive Distribution and the implementable Distribution processes that achieve this goal.

The transition process from intentions to processes encompasses the 'causal transformation' of general goals into one or more subgoals that constitute the means of achieving desired ends. Each step can result in the identification of new goals that are linked to the original one through causal relations thus forming a hierarchy of goals. A directed edge form a goal A to another goal B implies that the achievement of A depends on the achievement of B. This goal transformation is usually referred to as goal *operationalisation*. For each goal more than one alternative operationalisations may be identified, thus leading to different ways of achieving this goal. In addition the same subgoal may contribute to the achievement of two or more goals. Thus, the resulting structure is a goal graph rather than a hierarchy. Relationhips between goals in the goal graph are of the AND/OR type and are defined as such in the metamodel presented in Figure 3.

In addition to AND/OR satisfycing relationships between a goal and its successor goals, the enterprise goal submodel supports two additional goal influencing relation types namely: goal support and goal conflict relationships. A *support relationship* between goals A and B suggests that achievement of goal B assists achievement of goal A; however achievement of goal B is not a necessary condition for achievement of goal A, or else goal B would be a successor goal of goal A. On the other hand, a *conflict relationship* between goals A and B suggests that achievement of goal A hinders achievement of goal B.

Coupled to goal operationalisation is the way of analysing potential 'solutions' at every step of the ends-means process. Due to the very nature of uncertainty and value conflict, the task of defining and agreeing on a set of options that satisfy an enterprise goal may be problematic. Normally, this would be ameliorated by initially setting hypotheses, and subjecting these hypotheses to a process of disconfirmation. This hypothesis setting and evaluation within a goal-directed design paradigm is central to establishing a *rationale* for a particular enterprise design.

Often the choice of a particular solution is determined by the cost attributed to the enterprise process that realises the enterprise goal. This can be measured using some *measuring method*. Two kinds of *measurements* are defined. *Quantitative measurements* are measured in *units* (e.g., kg, meters, gdr/KWh). *Qualitative measurements* can take different *values* (e.g., TRUE, FALSE, HIGH, AVERAGE, LOW). Such measurements can then be subjected to 'what-if' scenarios in order to evaluate alternative designs for the operation of an enterprise.

The identification of the key enterprise process components which can be measured (such as activity duration, actor skills, resource costing etc.) is achieved through the use of the enterprise process modelling concepts, defined in the enterprise process submodel presented in the next section.

3.3   The Enterprise Process Submodel

The enterprise process submodel is concerned with the way that an enterprise process is performed through the involvement of enterprise actors in discharging their responsibilities through their role in a process and the interaction of their role with other roles which collectively bring about the realisation of the enterprise processes. This synergistic view of an enterprise process has a closer alignment to the functioning of real-world rather than using some abstract notion of 'process' that is assumed somehow to be decomposable into smaller components and so on.

An enterprise process is derived through empirical observation of the way that people work in a particular business setting. The enterprise process metamodel considers an enterprise process as a collection of roles whose behaviour determines the satisficing of the process goal. For example the 'electricity supply fulfilment' process, realises the goal 'satisfy customer demand for electricity'.

We describe the enterprise process modelling components in terms of two complementary views: the *actor-role* view and the *role-activity* view. The actor-role view (presented in Figure 4) depicts the actors of the enterprise and the roles that they play. An *actor* is the physical entity (e.g., the `Distribution technician`, or the `Distribution Technical Section`) that plays one or more roles. A *role* expresses a collection of responsibilities (e.g., `service providing`, `service administrative handling`, etc.) and involves a set of *activities*. For example the `service providing` role involves activities such as, `construct customer installation`, `install metering device` and `connect meter to the electricity network`).

An important point to note is the distinction between the *actor*, i.e. the physical enterprise entity, and the *role*, a notion which expresses the responsibility of performing the various activities within the enterprise. Roles are assigned to actors and summarise a set of skills or capabilities necessary to fulfil a task or activity. A role can be acted by a person or a group. A role can be acted by person X on one day and person Y on another day. The role is separate from the actors that play the role. For example, a `managing director` may play multiple roles such as `setting the budget`, `approving expenses`, etc.

This view also describes dependencies that exist between the roles. There are two parties involved in the dependency: the *depender role*, i.e. the one that needs something in order to fulfil its responsibilities, and the *dependee role*, i.e. the one that can provide the missing component. This *dependency relation* can be of various types: (a) *hierarchical dependency* denotes hierarchical dependencies that can exist between roles; the provider role gives authorisation to the requester role, (b) *intentioanl dependency* reflects the fact that the achievement of a goal that the role brings about is dependent on the achievement of a goal of another role, (c) *activity dependency* expresses the need for one role to wait for completion of another role's responsibilities before it can complete its own, and (d) r*esource dependency* illustrates the need for one role to use a resource that can be provided by another role.

Role dependencies take place according to a particular logic (or *rules*); enterprise rules determine the allowable states of enterprise objects and determine the interactions between different roles. An example of a enterprise rule concerning the `installation` object is `WHEN application form submitted IF contract = signed THEN authorise construction of customer installation`.

An additional element represented in this view is the goal (or goals) that the role must satisfy. 'Private' role goals are components of enterprise process goals in the sense that they support the achievement of the enterprise process goals that the role must fulfil.

For each role involved in the process model, information is given about the responsibilities that are assigned to the role in terms of the *activities* that the role carries out and the enterprise *objects* that the role requires in the *role-activity view* illustrated in Figure 5.

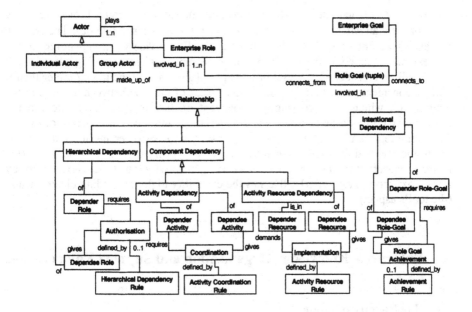

Figure 4: The enterprise process submodel: roles and their activities

This view describes in detail how the role performs each of its responsibilities, in terms of activities undertaken. In addition the model explicitly defines relationships between activities that take place in a role. These are *sequence, concurrency* and *alternative relationships*.

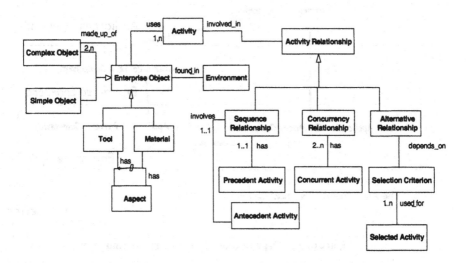

Figure 5: The enterprise process submodel: activities and resources

Activities carried out by different roles use enterprise *resources*. From a resource point of view an *enterprise object* may be either a *tool* or some *material*. The two are not exclusive since a tool may be a material itself and vice versa depending on the context of the activity being performed; for example when recording electricity a meter will be considered as a tool but when replacing a malfunctioning meter then it will be considered as a material. Since the fitness of purpose between a tool and the material on which it is working is dependent on having the appropriate binding between the correct aspects of tools and material, we introduce the concept of *aspect*. For example, if an `electricity meter` at a customer installation is to be electronically read then the meter must be `electronically readable` (the meter's aspect) and the `meter reading` activity must be carried out by a `meter reading tool` that has the capability to do the reading electronically (the tool's aspect).

4   Enterprise Knowledge Organisation and Support Environment

4.1   Logical Organisation

A suitable way for logically organising enterprise knowledge is by using different levels of abstraction as shown in Figure 6.

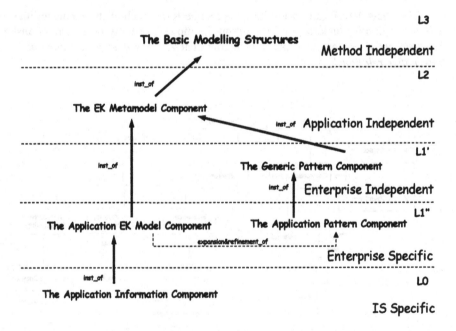

Figure 6: The Organisation of the Enterprise Knowledge

Each level shown in Figure 6 serves a different purpose.

Level L3 defines the 'basic modelling structures' i.e. the concepts being used by whatever language one may choose to implement the knowledge being captured. The use of this level is twofold: first, it defines the allowable modelling structures independent of any implementation system; and second, it determines a unified set of relationships so that all the principal enterprise knowledge concepts conform to the same relationships (specialisation, aggregation etc.).

Level L2 defines both the enterprise knowledge (EK) metamodel. This defines concepts such as enterprise goals, enterprise actors, etc. that constitute the generic enterprise knowledge components and their relationships.

Level L1 represents the application specific descriptions. There are two sub-levels: L1' representing the generic (domain) descriptions and L1'' representing the company descriptions. If generic patterns are not used then descriptions can be found directly at the L1'' level in terms of the 'application EK model'. At L1', the 'generic pattern component' represents a pattern model about some aspect of a domain (e.g. the monopoly model in the ESI sector). Also at L1', the 'domain EK model' is a description of the 'generic pattern' in terms of EK concepts (e.g. the operation model of the generic monopoly model). At L1'', the 'application pattern' is a company specific instance of the generic pattern (e.g. the monopoly model for PPC).

Finally, level L0 represents the 'datalogical' level i.e. instances of company data about processes, objects, actors etc.

4.2   Repository Environment

Meeting enterprise knowledge management needs requires a suitable environment designed to support the process of capture, representing, amplifying and disseminating knowledge from a variety of sources, both internal and external. Typically these tools will provide a repository management system for maintaining enterprise knowledge specifications using some DBMS; editing facilities to insert new information in the knowledge base; browsing functions, etc.

In addition, the particular distributed nature of enterprise knowledge (it is collectively 'owned' by a large number of enterprise stakeholders and is encoded in several enterprise legacy systems), together with the fact that enterprise knowledge should be available and shareable amongst several users, poses additional requirements to EK management tools. Such requirements are expressed in terms of user co-operation, knowledge distribution and platform independence.

A high level architecture of an enterprise management environment is demonstrated in Figure 7. This system uses repository technology to integrate enterprise knowledge and software components over the four levels of abstraction discussed in section 4.1.

The philosophy of this system is driven by the requirement to support users of different profiles, background, and culture, and often drawn from different working environments. The use of SQL Server, Microsoft Repository and Windows operating system allows distributed, network-centric applications. Platform independence is achieved by building on top of the Repository a Java layer (the common services layer) that could interface to other Java components anywhere on a network.

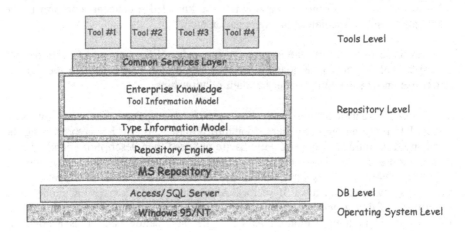

Figure 7: A Repository Based Support Environment

In more detail, the architecture is based on Windows NT. On the bottom sits the DBMS that stores the tool data. This can be either ACCESS or SQL Server. The REPOSITORY ENGINE is the set of classes on which the whole repository relies to perform its functions. The Repository Engine contains the Repository class, used to open, close and manage the repository. The Type Information Model is a set of classes that build upon the fundamental Repository Engine classes. They are used to define new Tool Information Models. A Tool Information Model (TIM) is a metamodel that describes the data a tool can handle. It is again a set of classes, defined using the Type Information Model. The Enterprise Knowledge TIM is also instantiated and stored in the repository. The Common Services layer is a set of components that implement the functionalities that are needed by the upper-level tool layer, like communicating with the repository or drawing diagrams. Finally, any Tool that uses the repository needs to either instantiate a TIM or to read it in order to perform operations related to its semantics.

5   Methodological Aspects of Enterprise Knowledge Modelling

The discussion so far has concentrated on the requirements of a conceptual modelling framework for supporting the management of enterprise knowledge. Orthogonal to this view is the usage perspective and this is the subject matter of this section. To exemplify the use of enterprise knowledge modelling, we choose one example namely "the modelling of business processes in a situation requiring process improvement". Space limitations do not permit us to consider a wider selection of applications in which enterprise knowledge modelling may be equally applicable, such as change management, requirements specification, re-use of domain knowledge etc.

5.1   The Background of the Application

The work presented in this section is part of a big industrial application that concerns de-regulation of a large European electricity company. The company is divided in three operational areas generation, transmission and distribution. Generation is responsible for the production of electrical power. Transmission is responsible for the high voltage transport of electricity. Finally, Distribution is responsible for the medium voltage (M/V) and low voltage (L/V) transport of electricity, its delivery to consumers and the merchandising of electricity services. Currently the company operates in a total monopoly market which means that it is the single operator of all three areas.

In anticipation of the opening of the European electricity market, the company is in the process of re-designing its business structure and planning reforms for the future, in order to increase its competitiveness and retain its market share. This is especially critical in the Distribution area which is the interface of the company with the final customer.

The implications of these external forces on this organisation is that any reform requires, prior to designing new business processes and support information systems, a clear understanding of the current enterprise situation in terms: (a) what are the current enterprise processes; and   (b) what is the purpose that current enterprise processes aim to fulfil. In this section we limit our example to these two activities.

This particular business setting requires a way of working that we may term "bottom up" as illustrated in the diagram of Figure 8.

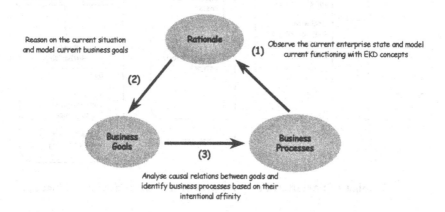

Figure 8: A bottom-up approach applied in Distribution

First, the current functioning is modelled in terms of a process paradigm (in this example the business was in fact organised along traditional functional view which in terms of a process improvement is inappropriate). Second, the process tries to uncover the purpose of the existing processes for if we can define these goals then the new goals for improvement can be compared and contrasted with the current ones thus providing a basis for a reasoned approach for future improvement. Third, the process models are synthesised and rationalised according to the definition of existing goals; the process clustering thus derived gives a definition of the core business processes according to the existing business goals. In the remainder of this section we describe each of the activities illustrated in Figure 8 giving also a brief account of the results.

5.2   Modelling Current Processes

The current structure of Distribution is organised along three functional divisions namely: the district, region and central divisions. Each functional division has distinct responsibilities. In this 'vertical' view of the Distribution operation there is no description of the interrelationships between different functions nor of the way different Distribution divisions co-operate in their effort to satisfy customer requests.

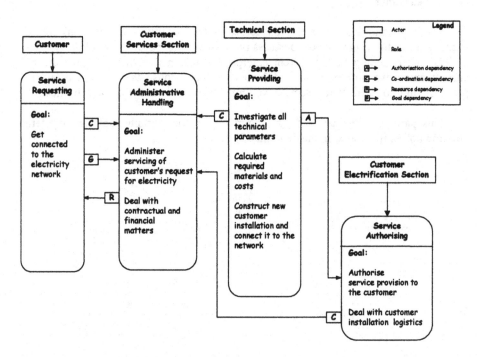

Figure 9: Actors and roles involved in 'Electricity Supply Fulfilment'

In order to understand the interactions between the Distribution functional units we proceeded to modelling the current Distribution behaviour in terms of actor-role diagrams of Distribution activities. An actor-role diagram presents a high-level view of the association between actors and their different roles. An example of an actor-role diagram for the 'Electricity Supply Fulfilment' is illustrated in Figure 9. This diagram describes the actors involved in supplying electricity to an electricity customer. This is a core Distribution activity and is realised through the co-operation of several Distribution actors. The advantage of the actor-role diagram is that it provides a clear view of the interactions across different functional divisions. In this way it becomes apparent that fulfilling a customer application for electricity supply is not solely the responsibility of the Customer Services Section but also depends on the co-operation of the Technical and Customer Electrification Section. Such interactions would appear as inputs/outputs in an activity-oriented view, thus obscuring the fact that 'Electricity Supply Fulfilment' cannot be performed independently of other activities performed by other sections. In addition the ability to include the customer role in the actor-role diagram, is a step towards a process-centred view of the organisation in which each process has a customer.

A more detailed view of these roles was constructed in terms of role-activity diagrams [Ould 1995]. These diagrams show the set of activities that are generally carried out by an individual or group within the context of their role. An example of a role-activity diagram for the 'electricity supply fulfilment' is illustrated in Figure 10. Role-activity modelling encourages the identification of the key operational components which can be measured (activity duration, actor skills, resource costing etc.). In that sense role-activity models provide the context for performing evaluation of process efficiency.

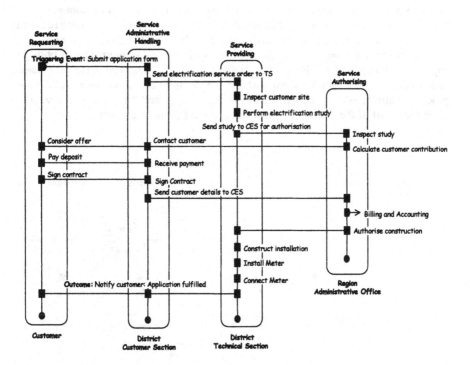

Figure 10: Events, activities and outcomes involved in 'Electricity Supply Fulfilment'

5.3   Constructing Intentions from Roles

In section 5.2 we presented a small example of Distribution micro-processes organised according to the current functional structure of the company. The key question however of "what are the types of processes and how should be logically organised?" still remains unanswered.

We address this question by using the enterprise goals that represent the intentions of processes. Indeed enterprise processes constitute the means to fulfil strategic enterprise goals. An enterprise process is also a purposeful system in itself. Each role involved in the process intends to achieve one or more defined goals. This does not necessarily mean that every role in a process aims to achieve the same enterprise goal rather that satisfaction of the 'private' goals of individual roles supports the achievement of the enterprise goal that is realised by the business process. Therefore, goals related to a enterprise process present a hierarchical structure whereby individual role goals constitute refinements of higher-level goals that ultimately make up the business goal fulfilled by that enterprise process (see Figure 11). In this sense enterprise goals not only define but also shape enterprise processes.

In the example illustrated in see Figure 11, Role1: 'service providing' role achieves goal $G_{i,1}$: 'construct new customer installation and connect it to the electricity network'. On the other hand Role2: 'service administrative handling' role achieves many goals one of which is the goal $G_{i,2}$: 'administer servicing of customer's request for electricity'. Achievement of both goals supports achievement of the overall business goal G_0: 'satisfy customer demand for electricity' which is realised by the 'electricity supply fulfilment' process. Thus 'service administrative handling' and 'service providing' roles form part of the 'electricity supply fulfilment' process.

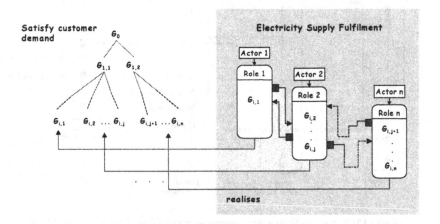

Figure 11: Relation between business goals and business processes

The completed goal graph for the 'electricity supply fulfilment' process is illustrated in Figure 12. The lower-level goals in this diagram are the operational goals presented in the 'body' of each role in Figure 9.

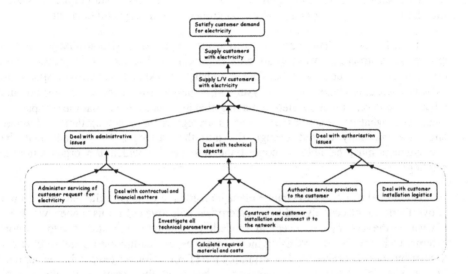

Figure 12: Satisfy customer demand for electricity

5.4   Adopting a Process View, Driven by Discovered Goals

By repeating this process for all Distribution roles a goal hierarchy for all business processes can be constructed that explains what the Distribution is currently trying to achieve. A global view of the Distribution goals and the associated processes is presented in Figure 13.

Business Goal	Business Process
· Supply customer with electricity	· Customer electrification
· Satisfy load increase	· Network reinforcement/extension
· Ensure safe and continuous network operation	· Network operation
· Improve exploitation of company assets	· Exploitation and maintenance of company assets
· Ensure positive profit for services provided to customers	· Customer billing

Figure 13: Distribution processes based on goal affinities

6   Conclusions

Rapid and turbulent changes in many industrial sectors, have led to state of affairs that demands constantly evolving enterprise organisation, processes and culture. It is vital therefore, that the forces of changes are controlled in some appropriate manner.

If the forces of change are to be controlled, it is essential that change itself is analysed in a structured way and not only empirically as is currently the practice. Too often it seems that changes take place for change's sake. Management responds to external pressures without first analysing what the *purpose* of those changes are and what their outcomes will be. Before making changes it is essential that the company is clear about what its objectives are, what its strategy is for achieving them and where and how internally caused change fits into that strategy. This means that the management must be able to control the direction in which the organisation is heading.

Traditional responses to change management have various limitations that do not allow them to effectively address enterprise objectives. In this paper we have advocated the use of a conceptual modelling paradigm that attempts to support enterprise change by externalising their objectives, evaluating the impact of changes to their business processes and ascertaining the IT provision necessary for the support of the potential changes. The approach is based on the premise that the key to successful change is *knowledge* shared by multiple stakeholders about:

- where the enterprise is currently
- where the enterprise wishes to be in the future and
- alternative designs to effectively bringing about transformations about the desired future state.

Within this approach, change management involves the activities of building models of relevant parts of the enterprise, models of legacy and future support systems and testing a number of scenarios for the different situations that satisfy the vision and criteria for change.

References

Alexander, C., Ishikawa, S., Silverstein, M., Jacobson, M., Fiksdahl-King, I. and Angel, S. (1977) A Pattern Language, Oxford University Press, New York, 1977.

Beck, K. (1997) Smalltalk Best Practice Patterns. Volume 1: Coding, Prentice Hall, Englewood Cliffs, NJ, 1997.

Buschmann, F., Meunier, R., Rohnert, H., Sommerland, P. and Stal, M. (1996) Pattern-Oriented Software Architecture - A System of Patterns, John Wiley, 1996.

Chen, P.P. (1976) *The Entity-Relationship Model - Toward a Unified View of Data*, ACM Transactions on Database Systems, Vol. 1, No. 1, 1976, pp. 9-36.

Coad, P. (1992) *Object-Oriented Patterns*, Communications of the ACM, Vol. 35, No. 9, 1992, pp. 152-159.

Coplien, J.O. and Schmidt, D.O. (1995) (ed.) Pattern Languages of Program Design, Addison-Wesley, Reading, MA.

DeMarco, T. (1978) Structured Analysis and System Specification, Yourdon Inc., New York, 1978.

Dobson, J. (1992) *A Methodology for Managing Organisational Requirements*, University of Newcastle upon Tyne, Newcastle NE1 7RU, UK., 1992.

Easterbrook, S. and Nuseibeh, B. (1995) *Managing Inconsistencies in an Evolving Specification*, RE'95, IEEE Computer Society Press, Los Alamitos, California, York, England, 1995, pp. 48-55.

Fowler, M. (1997) Analysis Patterns: Reusable Object Models, Addison-Wesley, 1997.

Gamma, E., Helm, R., Johnson, R. and Vlissides, J. (1995) Design Patterns: Elements of Reusable Object-Oriented Software, Addison-Wesley, Reading, MA, 1995.

Hay, D. (1996) Data Model Patterns: Conventions of Thought, Dorset House, New York, 1996.

ICEIMT (1992) *Enterprise Modeling*, International Conference on Enterprise Integration Modeling Technology (ICEIMT), Technical Report, http://tools.org/EI/ICEIMT/archive/, 1992.

IDEF0 (1993) *Integration Definition for Function Modeling (IDEF0)*, Computer Systems Laboratory, National Institute of Standards and Technology, FIPS Pub 183, December 21, 1993.

Nellborn, C., Bubenko, J. and Gustafsson, M. (1992) *Enterprise Modelling - the Key to Capturing Requirements for Information Systems*, SISU, F3 Project Internal Report, 1992.

Ould, M. (1995) Business Processes: Modelling and Analysis for Re-engineering and Improvement., John Wiley & Sons, Chichester, 1995.

Ruggles, R. (1997) *Why Knowledge? Why Now?*, Perspectives on Business Innovation, Centre for Business Innovation, Ernst and Young I.I.P., No. 1, 1997.

Swenson, K.D. and Irwin, K. (1995) *Workflow Technology : tradeoffs for Business Processes Re-engineering*, Conference on Organisational Computing Systems COOCS 95, CA, 1995.

Vlissides, J.M., Coplien, J.O. and Kerth, N.L. (1996) (ed.) Pattern Languages of Program Design 2, Addison-Wesley.

Yu, E. (1994) Modelling Strategic Relationships for Process Reengineering, Ph.D., University of Toronto, 1994.

Yu, E. and Mylopoulos, J. (1994) *Understanding 'Why" in Software Process Modeling, Analysis and Design*, 16th International Conference on Software Engineering, Sorrento, Italy, 1994, pp. 159-168.

Semantic Modeling in Accounting Education, Practice, and Research: Some Progress and Impediments[1]

William E. McCarthy

Arthur Andersen Alumni Professor,
Department of Accounting,
Michigan State University,
mccarth4@pilot.msu.edu

1   Introduction

In late 1979, the first Entity-Relationship (E-R) Conference was held at UCLA in December, and the first semantic modeling paper in the financial systems domain was published in *The Accounting Review* in October.   Those two papers by McCarthy (1979; 1980) were actually based on his doctoral dissertation work completed in 1977 at the University of Massachusetts where a computer science professor -- David Stemple -- had introduced him to the groundbreaking E-R paper of Peter Chen (1976) that was published the prior year in the initial issue of *ACM Transactions on Database Systems*. An important additional component of that same thesis work was the development of a normative accounting data modeling framework, something which needed more theoretical development at the time of the first E-R Conference. By 1982 however, McCarthy had completed that additional work, and he followed the first E-R paper and conference presentation with a more general semantic theory of economic phenomena in business organizations – the REA accounting model (McCarthy, 1982).

The first and most basic form of the REA semantic framework is portrayed in Figure 1. This basic pattern has been extended both up to the more abstract level of enterprise value chains and down to the more specific level of workflow tasks in more recent work by Geerts and McCarthy (1997). However, its conceptual core remains the template portrayed here, and it is those components that will be the subject of this paper.   Readers may see that the model has three types of primitive entities (economic resources, economic events, and economic agents with economic units being a subset of agents) and four types of primitive relationships (stock-flow, duality, control, and responsibility). The ternary control relationship is often split into

---

[1] This paper is an expansion of a speech given to the *1997 Conference on Entity-Relationship Modeling* at UCLA where Peter Chen arranged a special session for some of those researchers who were presenters at the first conference (also at UCLA) in 1979. All of the judgments of past, ongoing, and future research projects and of the ultimate viability of Entity-Relationship and REA commercial implementations in accounting represent the informed conclusions of the author alone.

P.P. Chen et al. (Eds.): Conceptual Modeling, LNCS 1565, pp. 144-153, 1999.

two binary associations for simplicity sake. The acronym REA derives from the left-to-right economic entity constellation of **resources-events-agents**.

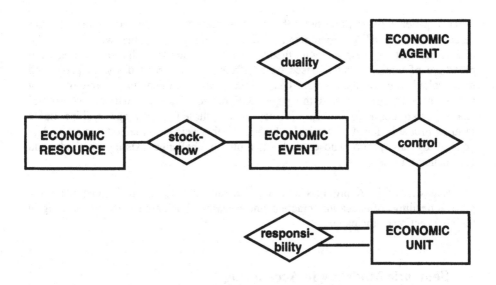

Fig. 1. The Basic REA Model   Source: McCarthy (1982, p. 564)

In the 16 years since 1982, REA theory has expanded considerably in accounting research, practice, and education (Dunn and McCarthy, 1997), and the original paper was honored by the Information Systems Section of the American Accounting Association with its bestowal of the first *Seminal Contribution to the Accounting Information Systems Literature Award* in 1996. However, the rate of this progress and the assimilation of REA work into the mainstream ideas of accounting have not been without problems and impediments. This is probably true of most theoretical and practical changes that an overtly semantic approach (like E-R modeling) causes, but these problems have been especially prominent in the very traditional discipline of accounting. This is a field whose practitioners are noted for their emphasis on conservatism, whose researchers are dismayingly preoccupied with experimentally rigorous evaluation of present methods to the exclusion of relevance and new ideas, and whose students are noted for their affectation with precision and numerical accuracy. A semantic re-orientation of bookkeeping ideas and a more conceptually-relative (and hence imprecise) universe of computerized accounting systems patterned on unfamiliar models are not changes welcomed with open arms by accounting educators, practitioners, or theoreticians. The REA accounting model has had to battle these challenges, and its progress has certainly suffered as a result. However, the recent emergence of certain trends in accounting education and practice (such as holistic curriculum changes in education and widespread acceptance of re-engineered and enterprise-wide accounting systems in practice) has made measurable progress possible again in the late 1990s. Additionally, as acknowledged early on by REA advocates, technological progressions like faster processing and cheaper storage, and conceptual innovations like systems whose semantics are embedded within their basic constructs (like objects) had to become widely available before REA-based implementations could become realistic goals.

This paper will explore both the REA successes in education, practice, and research and the REA impediments. More generally, the paper will discuss the difficulties that any new semantic theory must face when it clashes with an existing paradigm of thinking that is based on a different view (oriented toward paper and hand calculation) of the world. Challenging that traditional view directly is not always a good strategy, and the paper will discuss instances where such frontal challenges are bound to fail. In a greater context, these are challenges and inevitable failures probably faced in particular by many other semantic methodologists and in general by any group whose work attempts to challenge existing methods and entrenched mindsets.

Discussion of REA progress and impediments will be grouped under the three general headings of education, practice, and research. Each area is given a heading in the next section of the paper.

2   Semantic Modeling in Accounting

2.1   Semantic Modeling in Accounting Education

Although REA-oriented development of accounting systems was taught as early as 1979 at Michigan State University (MSU), its general use did not grow beyond the 10-15 schools affected by direct interaction with MSU faculty or doctoral students until the publication in 1995 of the first Accounting Information Systems (AIS) textbook to use REA as an integral foundation (Hollander et al., 1995). Other AIS books (such as Romney et al., 1997) soon followed suit with the result that more than 100 schools nationally now take at least part of this approach to AIS teaching. However, far more schools still cling to manually-oriented bookkeeping methods of teaching systems, and it appears also that at least some new adopters use REA only as a non-integrated topic among many to be covered instead of as a new fundamental way of conceptualizing accounting systems. Some possible reasons for this state of affairs follow.

Until recently, undergraduate accounting curricula across the USA were startlingly similar: two sophomore introductory courses, followed by two junior-level intermediate courses and a cost accounting course, followed by senior-level courses in taxation and auditing. These often were augmented by advanced and governmental accounting courses plus a few electives, but basically this set was the accepted core of the curriculum. Additionally, these courses all had somewhat standardized content nationwide -- a fact attributable in no small measure to the CPA exam and to the presence of well-accepted authoritative books like the Charles Horngren cost text or the Arens/Loebbecke auditing text. Such curriculum standardization is not uncommon across many other university departments of course; one only has to envision freshman composition, sophomore economics (with Samuelson of course), junior organic chemistry, or senior-level Shakespeare. In accounting however, the standardization seemed even more confining, at least until a national commission -- the Accounting Education Change Commission (AECC) -- was convened in the early 1990s to encourage innovation.

In this well-defined curricular environment, accounting information systems (AIS) courses have never fit well. Their content has varied widely from school to school, and the only efforts at national standardization simply resulted in impossibly long laundry lists of possible topics in computerized information system design and use that could be covered in any particular order or fashion. AIS course objectives often still include such diversities as completion of manual bookkeeping practice sets, instruction in spreadsheet fundamentals and web-site design, and coverage of auditing control checklists. Elementary AIS never had a central theme that was accepted at even a small percentage of accounting departments until conceptual modeling and REA came along. Now, books like Hollander et al. (1995) and a tentative recognition by the Information Systems Section of the AAA that a „conceptual database" approach should be a principle component of AIS instruction make increasing acceptance of REA approaches much more likely in business schools across the country. This conceptual database initiative by the IS section is actually in tune with other fields occupied with adaptation to the world of electronic commerce and the concomitant need to develop domain-specific ontologies (Gruber, 1993).

It must be mentioned however that full acceptance of conceptual modeling ideas in AIS still faces many hurdles. The learning curves for REA instruction are very steep, as it most often seems to take more than a year and multiple passes through the AIS course before the normal accounting faculty member feels familiar enough with the material to use it in a completely integrated fashion. Such a time commitment is difficult for many in AIS, especially those who must also cover courses in the traditional parts of the curriculum. Additionally, it is clear that the *Debit-Credit-Account* (DCA) method is more than simply the core of manual bookkeeping systems to most accounting faculty; it is *THE WAY* to teach accounting principles, especially financial accounting principles. Any AIS course that hints at even partial abandonment of these bookkeeping artifacts in the practice of building systems is certain to draw at least some opposition from conservative quarters of a normal accounting faculty. Along this same line, it is interesting to note that there has been some preliminary mention among semantic theorists in accounting of pushing REA-type thinking down into the introductory principles (sophomore-level) of accounting courses. This of course is bound to draw even stronger opposition from traditional faculty.

In theory, conceptual or semantic modeling (like the E-R approach) of any practice domain should yield construct taxonomies and schemas (also called *ontologies*) which in turn could be useful as a basis for instructional development. This is what is happening with E-R modeling of REA process patterns in accounting system courses. It would be interesting to see if a survey of E-R use in other domain-specific courses such as supply chain or manufacturing management (as opposed to generic knowledge representation courses such as information systems or computer science) would reveal the development of other schematic and taxonomic structures like REA.

If such educational infrastructures do exist in other areas, teachers intent on using them might certainly benefit from a review of the difficulties experienced in accounting departments before they attempt such curriculum innovation. A preliminary guess would be that the older methods in these other fields would not be quite as entrenched as accounting (which after all relies on the double-entry equation first promulgated by Pacioli in the late 15th century). If true, these more supple fields would find the acceptance of conceptually-based domain taxonomies much easier.

2.2 Semantic Modeling in Accounting Practice

When the REA accounting model was first published in 1982, it was proposed not only as a theoretical accounting archetype, but as a practical framework for building large-scale enterprise information systems whose databases required view modeling and view integration across accounting and non-accounting users (this dual purpose by the way differentiates REA from other expansionist-accounting proposals such as multidimensional bookkeeping which are conceptual toys with no implementation vision). The theoretical reconciliation between REA primitives and accounting concepts such as claims, matching, and immediate expensing of services came in the latter half of the 1982 paper, and they could be perceived to be as much as an argument for the robust utility of the database integration pattern than as an enumeration of all of the theoretical ramifications of the model. REA was born of practical use, and its seminal exposition even begins with an enumeration of weaknesses in double-entry systems that an REA orientation is intended to overcome in actual practice. This implementation imperative was reflected in many of the early REA papers (Gal and McCarthy, 1983; 1986; Denna and McCarthy, 1987) and even in some of the more recent ones (Geerts and McCarthy, 1992) where „proofs of concept" were demonstrated in different types of database and knowledge-base environments. In all of these systems, however, the Lilliputian scale of the transaction base was fully acknowledged, and the eventual problems with „scaling up" to realistic transaction volumes was discussed as an implementation barrier.

The database design methodology for which REA was proposed has four steps: (1) requirements analysis, (2) conceptual design, (3) implementation design, and (4) physical design. Initial REA use was concentrated in conceptual design, although later research has pushed it both forward into requirements analysis (Geerts and McCarthy, 1992) and backward into implementation design (McCarthy and Rockwell, 1989). To date, there has been no extensive research work on the physical design problems of REA-patterned systems, and it is here in physical design where „scaling up" problems make implementation of *Full-REA* systems still a future dream. This was a impediment acknowledged by McCarthy in 1982 (p. 572), and although present processing speeds have increased dramatically and present storage costs decreased dramatically as well, implementation compromise at the physical level is still theoretically necessary because no enterprise can afford to keep all of its events as part of the active database and to materialize certain conclusions from them only upon demand. Some preliminary work on loosening this constraint with design patterns has been started at the University of Illinois by students of Ralph Johnson (Nakamura and Johnson, 1998).

To date, there have been a number of „directed-REA" implementations in actual businesses. *Directed-REA* means simply that use of the original REA model was an explicit part of the system building process, usually as a chosen alternative to a traditional accounting approach. The first of these cases was documented by Cherrington et al. (1996), and the continued use of REA in the GENEVA practice of Price-Waterhouse Consulting is described in a recent *Management Accounting* paper by Walker and Denna (1997). In all of these cases, REA use was concentrated in requirements analysis and conceptual design of the implemented information systems, and its use was explicitly rationalized as a cure for past problems involved with integration of bookkeeping artifacts within a larger enterprise system. At the physical design level, necessary implementation compromises were made to full-REA structures, although in some cases these compromises were not as severe as one might have predicted. This is especially true in the *GENEVA* systems where Price-Waterhouse has developed a proprietary algorithm to alleviate storage and processing problems.

Completely customized implementation of a new enterprise information system is not a common occurrence, and most installations rely heavily on packaged solutions. To date, there are no directed-REA enterprise packages. In at least one case of a proposed client-server suite several years ago, a developer did consider REA-based implementation. However, that vendor backed away because of the perceived risk in not using the traditional double-entry framework that manually-trained accountants are accustomed to.

There is presently an REA-based industrial system for value chain planning being prototyped by a company led by Haugen (1998). However, that system is still some time from fruition.

In the absence of an established base of directed-REA information systems implementations, David (1995) decided to test the issue of REA vs. DCA systems empirically. She hypothesized that most actual enterprise implementations were hybrids of these two models when one considers accounting systems on a spectrum with DCA anchored at one end and REA at the other. Furthermore, she hypothesized that certain types of advantages would accrue to companies with systems that tended more toward the REA end. In a limited sample of eight companies in the paper and pulp industry, she found evidence of advantages in administrative efficiency and gains in productivity associated with systems more strongly associated with REA. Her preliminary work here has led McCarthy, David, and Sommer (1996) to consider this entire issue of migration of systems toward a more enterprise-wide and more semantic perspective in the context of an evolutionary model based on *Economic Darwinism*. In the very simplest of terms, this theory of enterprise information systems evolution posits that such systems evolve toward an advanced archetype (like full-REA) with more semantics, more integration, and more inter-enterprise orientation as the result of changes in packages that the market responds positively to and which then become the basis for even more advanced information architectures. Both double-entry bookkeeping and REA are seen in this theory as branches in an overall hierarchical classification of information systems in much the same manner that fish, dinosaurs, birds, and mammals are seen as branches of the animal kingdom. Like animal classification, the information system taxonomy has some innate notion of progress toward more complex forms, and some accounting system advances achieved since 1982 (like activity-based costing, value-chain accounting, and more full accounting for human resource use) would actually have been predicted by such a progression toward full-REA. However, also like the animal system, the system evolution framework would predict cases or niches where the less advanced (admittedly, a value judgment) forms would prosper. This type of reasoning could explain for example firms where a bookkeeping system would be better than full-REA in much the same manner that a shark would have a „survival advantage" over a human in a bay of water.

It seems logical that accounting education would usually drive accounting practice, that is that the most advanced ideas would normally be introduced in university settings and carried from there by eager students to be implemented in actual businesses. Such is not the case for the most part in accounting today, and in fact, there is an interesting trend where quite the opposite is true. This is where practice drives educational change in the installation and integrated curriculum use of ERP (enterprise resource planning) packages. An increasing number of accounting departments have installed these packages in the last two years for across-the-curriculum use and then found that the traditional accounting frameworks do not describe well what they are demonstrating. In at least some cases, the solution to this conceptual mismatch has been achieved by moving the instructional models away from DCA frameworks and more toward conceptual frameworks like E-R models with REA patterns.

2.3   Semantic Modeling in Accounting Research

Social science models for generating and evaluating research projects create a less-than-hospitable environment for researchers who are trying to create new constructs, methods, and tools for building better information systems, and there is no place where this is more true than in academic accounting. The mainstream financial and managerial accounting research establishment has for the last 30 years been trying (with increasing degrees of success) to exclude work whose specific purpose has been to develop „better ways of doing accounting," a focus which this establishment pejoratively labels „normative" or „engineering-oriented." This creates a situation that is quite surprising to most computer scientists where accounting researchers are most acutely aware of and responsive to the effect of their ideas on the corpus of present research papers while seemingly being almost indifferent to the effect that their endeavors have on actual practice. This ivory-towered attitude is unexpected in an applied field like accounting, but there is no disputing its inhibitive effect on the ability of the semantic modeling community within accounting to establish a beachhead in the mainstream literature. For example, even if they had significant accounting or economic content, the seminal database papers of both Codd (1970) and Chen (1976) would have been returned to the authors without review as „normative essays" if they were submitted to accounting journals today.

As a result of this narrowing attitude in accounting research, most conceptual or E-R oriented research has been concentrated either in „systems accounting" journals or in journals outside of accounting. This is both a positive and a negative. It is good because it keeps the semantic modeling community in accounting from falling into the irrelevancy trap of the mainstream and because it keeps them acutely aware of how advances in their field interact with advances in the larger computer science or information systems community.   It is bad in the sense that it keeps important conceptual work like the development of accounting ontologies or the development of advanced accounting systems concepts out of the mainstream literature where their influence could accelerate change. An unfortunate side effect of this exclusion is that badly-applied conceptual modeling or ontological efforts are allowed to succeed in the mainstream because they are not subject to review either by the practical world or by the systems accounting community. A good example of such an effort is the paper on taxonomic and schematic knowledge structures by Frederick (1991). This was a cursory and incorrect exposition of basic conceptual modeling ideas that would have been informed greatly by a person familiar with the aggregation and generalization work of Smith and Smith (1977) or by a person who had faced the challenge of building actual systems with implemented taxonomic/schematic structures.

A summary of the effect of E-R modeling on accounting systems was published in the *Journal of Information Systems* by Dunn and McCarthy (1997) who reviewed all the major database work done in this field since the 1960s (with some conceptual work dating back to the 1930s). For those authors, the advent of conceptual database work like Chen's was a watershed because it enabled for the first time realistic assessment of alternative foundations (like REA) for implementing better accounting systems.

At the end of their paper, Dunn and McCarthy use a conceptual framework proposed by March and Smith (1995) to outline future research directions for conceptual modeling work of both a normative (design science) and positive (natural science) nature. Those conceptual directions were augmented and examined more closely in more recent work by David, Dunn, Poston, and McCarthy (1998). To date, the most active ongoing forum for discussion of such research projects has been the annual *Semantic Modeling of Accounting Phenomena (SMAP) Workshop* which started meeting in 1995 and which is next scheduled for August 1999 in San Diego.

3   Summary

The use of Entity-Relationship modeling in particular and of semantic modeling in general has had very noticeable effects in accounting over the last 20 years. The most pronounced impact has certainly been on accounting education where REA models of the type first proposed by McCarthy (1979; 1982) and later extended by Geerts and McCarthy (1994) have permeated the undergraduate and graduate curriculum. REA conceptual modeling of various business processes (or cycles as they are called by accountants) provides a taxonomy of conceptual objects and structures for use in describing and teaching the accounting information architecture of typical business enterprises. These conceptual structures are now embedded in AIS textbooks and used nationwide.

The effect of REA on accounting practice has been less pronounced, partially because the technological impediments to REA implementations are just now starting to be removed. Some progress is being made with prototype directed implementations in actual practice, and additional research insights are being uncovered with empirical investigations that posit evolutionary movement in the enterprise software marketplace toward full-REA conceptualization.

Progress in research on semantic modeling of accounting phenomena is difficult to characterize exactly. Several design science projects intended to extend REA principles both declaratively and procedurally are ongoing at present. However, the achievement of a critical mass of researchers in this field has been hampered by high learning curves and by the inadaptability of mainstream accounting journals who view the outcomes of such projects as more development than research. More promising for the long term of REA research is work on the empirical end where the needed research skills are already possessed by most accounting academics and where the outcomes of the research projects will be more acceptable to traditional publication outlets.

References

Andros, D.P., J.O. Cherrington, and E.L. Denna. 1992. „Reengineer Your Accounting, the IBM Way." *Financial Executive* (July/August), pp. 28-31.

Chen, P.P. 1976. „The Entity-Relationship Model--Toward A Unified View of Data." *ACM Transactions on Database Systems* (March): 9-36.

Cherrington, J.O., E.L. Denna, and D.P. Andros. 1996. „Developing an Event-Based Business Solution: The Case of IBM's National Employee Disbursement System." *Journal of Information Systems* 10 (1): 51-69.

Codd, E.F. 1970. „A Relational Model of Data for Large Shared Data Banks." *Communications of the ACM* (June): 377-387.

David, J. S. 1995. „An Empirical Analysis of REA Accounting Systems, Productivity, And Perceptions of Competitive Advantage." Working Paper, Arizona State University.

David, J. S., C.L. Dunn, R.S. Poston, and W.E. McCarthy. 1998. „The Research Pyramid: A Framework for Accounting Information Systems Research." Working Paper, Michigan State University.

Denna, E.L. and W.E. McCarthy. 1987. „An Events Accounting Foundation for DSS Implementation." in *Decision Support Systems: Theory and Application.* C.W. Holsapple and A.B. Whinston (eds.). Berlin: Springer-Verlag: 239-63.

Dunn, C.L. and W.E. McCarthy. 1997. „The REA Accounting Model: Intellectual Heritage and Prospects for Progress." *Journal of Information Systems.* 11 (Spring): 31-51.

Frederick, D.M. 1991 „Auditors' Representation and Retrieval of Internal Control Knowledge" *The Accounting Review* (April 1991): 240-58.

Gal, G. and W.E. McCarthy. 1983. „Declarative and Procedural Features of a CODASYL Accounting System," in *Entity-Relationship Approach to Information Modeling and Analysis*, P. Chen (ed.), North-Holland, pp. 197-213.

Gal, G. and W.E. McCarthy. 1986. „Operation of a Relational Accounting System." *Advances in Accounting* (3): 83-112.

Geerts, G.L. and W.E. McCarthy. 1992. „The Extended Use of Intensional Reasoning and Epistemologically Adequate Representations in Knowledge-Based Accounting Systems." *Proceedings of the Twelfth International Workshop on Expert Systems and Their Applications*, Avignon, France (June): 321-32.

Geerts, G.L. and W.E. McCarthy. 1994. „The Economic and Strategic Structure of REA Accounting Systems." Paper presented to the *300th Anniversary Program, Martin Luther University*, Halle-Wittenberg, Germany, September.

Geerts, G.L. and W.E. McCarthy. 1997. Using Object Templates from the REA Accounting Model to Engineer Business Processes and Tasks. Paper presented to the *20th Congress of the European Accounting Association*, Graz, Austria, April.

Gruber, T. 1993. „A Translational Approach to Portable Ontologies," *Knowledge Acquisition*, Vol. 5, No.2, 199-220.

Haugen, R. 1998 „Which Business Objects?" in *Proceedings of OOPSLA'98 Business Object Workshop IV*, J. Sutherland (ed.), 1998, Vancouver.

Hollander, A.S., E.L. Denna, and J.O.Cherrington. 1995. *Accounting, Information Technology and Business Solutions*, Richard D. Irwin, Chicago, IL.

March, S.T. and G.F. Smith. 1995. „Design and Natural Science Research on Information Technology." *Decision Support Systems* 15 (4): 251-267.

McCarthy, W.E. 1979. „An Entity-Relationship View of Accounting Models." *The Accounting Review* (October 1979): 667-86.

McCarthy, W.E. 1980. „Construction and Use of Integrated Accounting Systems with Entity-Relationship Modeling." In P. Chen, ed. *Entity-Relationship Approach to Systems Analysis and Design*. Amsterdam: North-Holland, 1980, 625-37.

McCarthy, W.E. 1982. „The REA Accounting Model: A Generalized Framework for Accounting Systems in a Shared Data Environment." *The Accounting Review* (July 1982): 554-578.

McCarthy, W.E., J. S. David, and B. S. Sommer. 1996. „The Evolution of Enterprise Information Systems -- From Sticks and Jars Past Journals and Ledgers Toward Interorganizational Webs of Business Objects and Beyond," in *Proceedings of the OOPSLA'96 Workshop on Business Object Design and Implementation*, J. Sutherland (ed.), San Jose, October.

McCarthy, W.E., and S. R. Rockwell. 1989. „The Integrated Use of First-Order Theories, Reconstructive Expertise, and Implementation Heuristics in an Accounting Information System Design Tool." *Proceedings of the Ninth International Workshop on Expert Systems and Their Applications*. Avignon, France, EC2: 537-548.

Nakamura, H. and R.E. Johnson. 1998. „Adaptive Framework for the REA Accounting Model," in *Proceedings of OOPSLA'98 Business Object Workshop IV*, J. Sutherland (ed.), 1998, Vancouver.

Romney, M.B., P.J. Steinbart, and B.C. Cushing. 1997. *Accounting Information Systems*. AddisonWesley, Reading, MA.

Smith, J.M. and D.C.P. Smith. 1977. „Database Abstractions: Aggregation and Generalization." *ACM Transactions on Database Systems* (June): 105-133.

Walker, K. B. and E. L. Denna. 1997. "Arrivederci, Pacioli? A New Accounting System Is Emerging" *Management Accounting* (July): 22-30.

Perspectives in Modeling:
Simulation, Database, and Workflow

John A. Miller, Amit P. Sheth, and Krys J. Kochut

Large Scale Distributed Information Systems Lab (LSDIS)
Department of Computer Science
The University of Georgia
Athens, GA 30602-7404
<jam,amit,kochut>@cs.uga.edu
http://LSDIS.cs.uga.edu/

Abstract. Development of today's advanced applications is increasingly being accomplished using multi-faceted modeling. For example, the areas of simulation and workflow modeling generally need data modeling as a foundational capability. In addition, simulation modeling and workflow modeling can be used together, synergistically. Based on the experience of the LSDIS group in developing systems and models, we have found that establishing rich linkages between disparate models works better than having one comprehensive unified model. In addition, we agree with the consensus that two dimensional models are generally considered to be easier to create and understand than one dimensional models. Furthermore, just as richly linked text is referred to as hyper-text, richly linked diagrams may be referred to as hyper-diagrams. Two modeling toolkits, METEOR Designer and the JSIM Modeling Toolkit, illustrate the advantages of using such approaches.

1   Introduction

The route to rapid application development is increasingly becoming model oriented. To develop complex applications, facets can be described visually at a high-level using models. Many years ago models were hand translated into code or schema specifications. How tedious. Later, tools and systems were developed that utilized the artifacts of the modeling process to automatically produce part of the application. Today, there is a proliferation of modeling techniques in use. A grand unification into a single notation is probably not useful, since models need to focus on salient features of reality from different perspectives (e.g., data, process, events, usage, authorization, etc.). Still, efforts such as the one producing the Unified Modeling Language (UML) [Sof97] are useful to reduce the learning curve required to use a new modeling technique and to provide common foundations and interrelationships between disparate models. Models are used in nearly all areas of science, engineering and business. This paper examines modeling from three distinct perspectives, Simulation, Database and Workflow, based on our experience developing systems and models in these three areas.

P.P. Chen et al. (Eds.): Conceptual Modeling, LNCS 1565, pp. 154–167, 1999.
© Springer-Verlag Berlin Heidelberg 1999

2 Types of Models

Given a system S(t) evolving over time, a model is simply an approximation M(t) of S(t). Commonly, models are classified according to how they deal with time (*Static vs. Dynamic*), state (*Discrete vs. Continuous*) and randomness (*Deterministic vs. Stochastic*). Two additional criteria are mentioned below that may be used to help assess what constitutes a good model.

– *Abstractness vs. Similarity*. Abstractness measures the level of repression of detail. This is useful for two distinct reasons: First, real systems have too many details to be fully understood in any timely fashion, if at all. Second, abstraction leads to generality. An abstract model may be used to design/analyze several systems simply by adjusting its parameters. Abstractness is fine, but needs to be counterbalanced by another desirable property of models, namely similarity. Similarity (also referred to as fidelity) means that the model should reflect the characteristics of the real system (e.g., similar shapes and interconnections for objects, proportionate scaling as well as analogous performance, behavior, etc.). One should avoid models with low abstraction and low similarity. Obviously, models with high abstraction and high similarity would be ideal. Unfortunately, this is not possible as illustrated in figure 1. There is a tradeoff between abstraction and similarity. Depending on the goals of the modeling effort, good arguments can be made for choosing different points along the modeling frontier.
– *Dimensionality of Models*. Another useful way to distinguish modeling techniques is according to the dimensionality of their representations.
  1. <1D>. Most commonly, one dimensional models are expressed as *text*. Both formal and informal languages can be used.
  2. <1.5D>. A useful improvement on plain text is *hyper-text*, allowing rapid navigation from general concepts to detailed information.
  3. <2D>. Since humans are visually oriented, moving to higher dimensions usually makes the models easier for humans to create and understand. A general term for such two dimensional models is *diagram*. Of course, diagrams can be annotated (on screen or with a pop up window) with text or hypertext.
  4. <2.5D>. As mentioned earlier, it is useful to have multiple types of models as well as multiple instances of the same type of model. It is also useful, if these diagrams are linked to support navigation from one related diagram to the next. This facilitates rapid changes of perspective. One can quickly move from a global view to a detailed view (e.g., by clicking on a compound task icon to display its subworkflow). Alternatively, one could change from a functional view (map design) to a data view (data design) by clicking on an arc connecting two task icons to see the data that flows between them. Analogously to converting text into hyper-text, this converts diagrams into *hyper-diagrams*.
  5. <3D>. To increase the realism of models, creating three dimensional representations is helpful. The advent of cheap fast processors with large memories and accelerated graphics makes this feasible. For example, Taylor II supports the development and animation of three dimensional simulation models. [1] One

---

[1] See *http://www.taylorii.com/scrnsht.htm* for a gallery of screenshots.

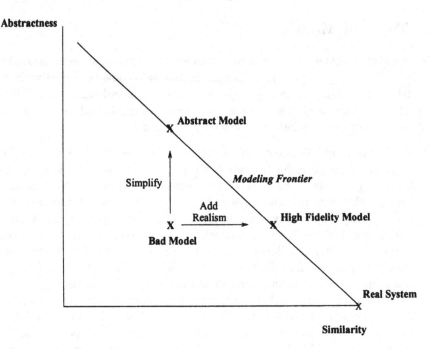

Fig. 1. Abstractness vs. Similarity

could term the process of producing a three dimensional representation as creating a *scene*.

6. <3.5D>. If scenes are linked to support navigation from one scene to another, one could term this a *hyper-scene*. The emergence of virtual reality on the Web is an example of this.

Note, half dimensions are used here in an intuitive as opposed to mathematically rigorous sense. This paper concentrates on the current state-of-the-practice, two dimensional modeling, as well as the current state-of-the-art, two and half dimensional modeling. For these type of models, the most popular modeling techniques for simulation and database are briefly described. For workflow, one possible taxonomy is mentioned.

3   Simulation Modeling

Of the numerous types of modeling, simulation usually stresses similarity. Although abstract simulations are useful, they are often used as a stepping stone to building a higher fidelity model. Simulation models as a representation of an existing or proposed system, strive to capture performance characteristics as closely as possible. Some of them also endeavor to mimic the behavior of real systems. This is particularly important if animation is supported.

There are two broad types of simulation modeling: continuous simulation and discrete-event simulation. The distinction is based on whether the state can change continuously (water level in a reservoir) or at discrete points in time (number of customers in a bank). Discrete-event simulation models are very popular for modeling many types of real-world systems such as banks, hospitals and transportations systems, so we will focus our attention on them.

For discrete-event simulation modeling there are three main world views (simulation modeling paradigms) that can be used: event-scheduling, activity-scanning and process-interaction. Although state-transition diagrams (e.g., finite-state automata or Markov chains) can be used for simulation modeling, they are less common because the state spaces involved are typically very large.

Most of the diagrammatic simulation modeling techniques implicitly or explicitly depict entities (e.g., bank customers) flowing through a system. The classification below mentions five of the most popular general simulation modeling techniques partitioned according to their principal world view. Note, space limitations prevent the display of example diagrams, however, an expanded version of this paper is available on the Web which includes these diagrams. [2]

3.1 Event-Scheduling

These models focus on the events that can occur in a system. An event instantaneously transforms the state of the system and schedules future events.

- *Event Graphs (EG)*. In an event graph, nodes represent events, while directed edges represent causality (one event causing another) [Sch83]. Edges can be annotated with time delays and conditions.

3.2 Activity-Scanning

These models focus on activities and their preconditions (triggers). An activity consists of an event-pair (a start event and an end event). Activities are scheduled when their preconditions becomes true.

- *Activity Cycle Diagrams (ACD)*. These diagrams (graphs) depict the life-cycles of interacting entities flowing through a system. The nodes in the graphs represent either activities or wait states (e.g., a queue) [Pid92]. These models can be used to generate simulations following either the activity-scanning or process-interaction world views.

3.3 Process-Interaction

These models focus on processes and their interaction with resources. A process captures the behavior of an entity. Using an object-oriented approach, entities may be treated as active objects (e.g., in JSIM [NMZ96] this is done by deriving them from Thread and implementing the run () method).

---

[2] See *http://lsdis.cs.uga.edu/publications/model.ps*.

- *Activity Diagrams (AD)*. Activity diagrams are graphs consisting of a well defined set of functional nodes such as start, terminate, delay, engage resource and release resource [Bir79], [PH91]. The graph shows the flow of entities through the system.
- *Network Diagrams (ND)*. Network (or block) diagrams are used by many popular commercial simulation packages (e.g., GPSS [Sch74], SLAM [Pri79] and SIMAN [PSS90]). These network diagrams are similar to activity diagrams but have more type of nodes corresponding to the underlying primitives supported in their simulation languages. The models are very useful, but have been criticized for being ad hoc and having too many types of nodes. JSIM models fall under this category, but have a smaller number of node types to choose from.
- *Petri Nets (PN)*. Petri nets are graphs with two types of nodes, places and transitions [Pet77]. A place is a storage area for tokens (entities), while a transition takes input token(s) to produce output token(s). A transition will fire if there is a token at each of its input places. In Timed Petri Nets, transitions have delays associated with them. In Colored Petri Nets, tokens can have attributes.

4   Data Modeling

These techniques model data objects (their attributes and possibly methods) and relationships between data objects. Data modeling has traditionally been a static approach. With the advent of active databases and multimedia databases as well as the need for workflow models to include sophisticated data models, modeling of activity or behavior is becoming more important. The popular types of diagrammatic data modeling techniques are listed below.

- *Entity Relationship Models (ERM)*. Entities are interconnected by relationships to form an easy to read graphical structure [Che76]. Relationships have cardinality and participation constraints that are very useful. This model has been used extensively in practice and has been extended in numerous ways.
- *Functional Data Models (FDM)*. In this modeling technique, binary relationships are treated as functions [KP76].
- *Semantic Data Models (SDM)*. The semantic data model added the concepts of generalization and aggregation into a convenient graphical form [HM81].
- *Object Modeling Technique (OMT)*. This modeling technique evolved from ERM, converting entities into objects, allowing methods in addition to attributes to be specified [R+91]. It also includes generalization, aggregation and association.
- *Unified Modeling Language (UML)*. UML represents a unification of three popular modeling techniques (OMT, Booch and OOSE) [Sof97].

Note, OMT and UML are themselves multi-faceted making them also usable in many other areas besides data modeling.

5   Workflow Modeling

Workflow models focus on the tasks (or activities) and the flow of control/data between them. Unlike the more mature areas of simulation and database, workflow has yet to establish any widely accepted taxonomy of workflow models. However, several fundamental models of computations, especially distributed computation have provided a basis or framework for developing workflow process models. Principle among these are Temporal Logics such as CTL, Petri Nets, State and Activity Charts and Speech-Act Theory (see [S+97] for further discussion). A comprehensive workflow process model, besides modeling the process (also called workflow map or coordination of activities) may also have secondary models to support modeling of data objects involved in workflow processes, error handling, etc.

6   Interactions between Models

As mentioned earlier, complex systems should be modeled using multiple modeling techniques. Using hyper-diagrams to establish rich and useful connections between the component models provides as great an advantage over ordinary diagrams as hyper-text does over text.

In the rest of this section, useful interactions between simulation, database and workflow models are considered. Then, two concrete examples, the METEOR Designer and the JSIM modeling toolkit, of hyper-diagrammatic modeling toolkits are examined.

- **Simulation Modeling.** Simulations can be used to refine Workflow Models.
- **Data Modeling.** Data objects can be used in both Simulation and Workflow Models.
- **Workflow Modeling.** Statistics from workflow executions can be used to calibrate and later validate Simulation Models.

The group in the LSDIS Lab is currently in the process integrating or establishing interoperability between a simulation system/environment, JSIM, and a workflow management system, METEOR2. The JSIM simulation environment includes a simulation and database component, while METEOR2 includes the development of advanced workflow models and systems. A genealogy, figure 2, of these systems will be useful in subsequent discussions. For a brief description of each of these systems, see the appendix.

The systems at the top of figure 2 relied upon textual models for specifying application elements. Declarative specification languages are certainly a big improvement over programming. The Active KDL language elements as well as METEOR's specification languages, WFSL and TSL, are both sophisticated and straightforward to use. Still, humans are very visually oriented. Consequently, all of the newer systems (at the bottom of figure 2) rely on diagrammatic models.

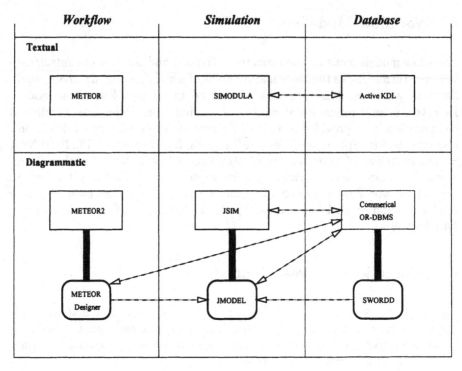

Fig. 2. Genealogy of Systems

6.1   METEOR Designer

The METEOR Designer [K+97] is a good example of a hyper-diagrammatic modeling toolkit supporting several modeling perspectives with a rich set of links between them for convenient navigation and browsing. The METEOR Designer [Zhe97], [K+97] models five distinct facets of workflows:

1. *Map Designer.* This designer is used to specify the control/data flow from one task/activity to another.
2. *Data Designer.* This designer specifies the structure of and relationships between the data that flows between the tasks.
3. *Task Designer.* This designer specifies the interfaces to actual programs (possibly even legacy systems) which carry out the details of a task's execution.
4. *Interface Designer.* This designer produces a simple default appearance for each user task and then launches the user's favorite HTML editor for page customization.
5. *Exception Designer.* This designer produces a simple default mapping of errors and failures to actions to deal with the problem. The designer facilitates changing/extending this default mapping.

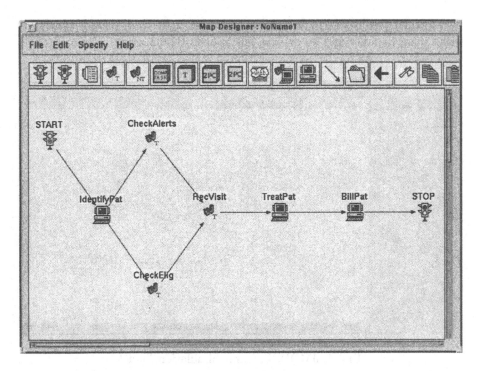

Fig. 3. METEOR Designer: Clinic Workflow Model

6.2   JSIM Modeling Toolkit

The JSIM modeling toolkit consists of two designers: JMODEL and SWORDD.

JMODEL [Zha97] is a graphical designer used to model process-oriented simulations where entities flow in a network of facilities. It provides an easy-to-use, widely accessible graphical model design environment as the front-end for the JSIM software package. For wide accessibility, JMODEL is implemented using the Java programming language (as a Java applet) utilizing the Abstract Windowing Toolkit (AWT). For ease of use, it supplies simulationists with a direct, intuitive means to design a simulation model, check and verify the design, and modify and reconstruct the design. The graphical designer provides database connectivity to allow users to be able to store their designed simulation models in a database and browse existing simulation models in the database. A code generator is also implemented, which resides as a back-end to retrieve simulation model from the database upon a user's request, and to generate Java source code based on the designed model to make the model come alive.

JMODEL designs are more general than METEOR designs in the following sense. JMODEL can model applications like the clinic (see the figure showing the clinic simulation model) which are workflow oriented or model systems that do not necessarily have anything to do with workflow (see the figure showing the bus simulation model). Conversely, less information is available from a JMODEL design for implementing a workflow application or prototype. Each have their own distinct purpose and are useful in their own right. Still, there is synergy in using them together and we explore this later in the paper.

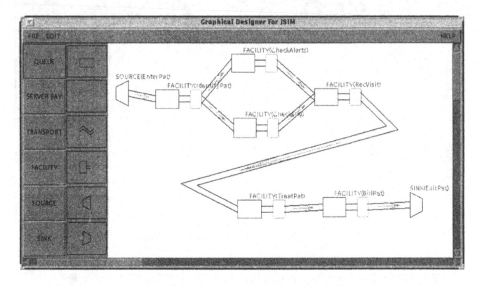

Fig. 4. JMODEL: Clinic Simulation Model

An enhancement that is currently being added to JMODEL is support for (De)Composition nodes in the simulation model graph. A Decomposition node decomposes a data object into component parts and send them along parallel transports.

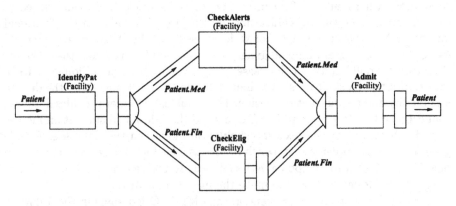

Fig. 5. (De)Composition Nodes

In figure 5, the patient data object is decomposed into medical and financial subobjects which are sent in different directions. At a later stage, the patient data is put back together in by a Composition node. This approach has the advantage that it avoids the lost update problem and merge problem inherent with parallel branching.

These types of nodes are based on the data modeling concept of Aggregation. Composition in UML corresponds to strong aggregation. A weaker connection between data objects (or entities) is an Association. Corresponding to this are Association and Disassociation nodes. These are illustrated in the bus model shown in figure 6.

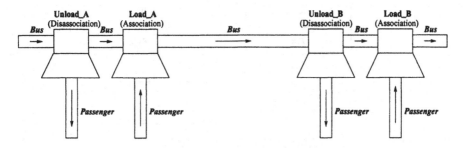

Fig. 6. (Dis)Association Nodes

SWORDD [LeC97] is a graphical designer used to create data models for modern Object-Relational DBMSs such as Oracle 8 or Informix Universal Server. It provides two distinct advantages over forthcoming commercial products such as the Oracle Database Designer for Oracle 8. First, it is Java-based so it provides wider availability, and second, hooks placed in the Java source code facilitate its interoperability with JMODEL, thus supporting the hyper-diagrammatic capabilities of the overall JSIM modeling toolkit.

SWORDD is used to design several types data models for JSIM: scenario (input parameter) definitions, simulation result (output parameter) definitions, model definitions (design graph) and data objects (data flowing along transports).

The data design in figure 7 illustrates an interesting interaction between a JMODEL simulation model and SWORDD data model. When the bus arrives at the loading zone of the bus stop, an association between passengers and the bus will be established. Because of the cardinality constraint on the association given in the data model, unless there are at least 10 passengers waiting, the bus will wait. Similarly, if more than 30 passengers are waiting only 30 will be taken.

6.3   Synergy between METEOR and JSIM

METEOR2 and JSIM provide synergy in two directions: (1) After a workflow has been designed, a simulation model can be created for it. Studying the performance profiles of the workflow design using simulations will provide feedback to the design process for improving the workflow design before developing or

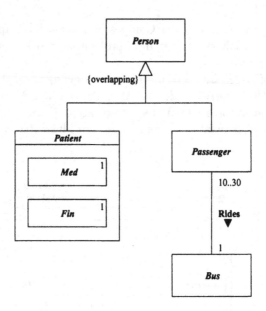

Fig. 7. Data Design in UML

deploying the workflow. (2) Once a workflow is deployed, performance data can be collected to refine or validate the simulation model. A validated simulation model will be very useful for future adaptations of the workflow [MSK+95].

There are similarities between the METEOR map designer and JMODEL. Both conceptualize entities flowing through a network of nodes. Workflow is concerned with scheduling and transformations that take place in tasks, while simulation is mainly concerned with system performance. Similarly, SWORDD and the METEOR data designer have commonality. SWORDD is used to model schema for today's Object-Relational DBMSs, while the METEOR data designer is used to model data objects sent between tasks.

7   Summary

Simulation, database and workflow modeling are distinct areas which overlap and provide synergy when combined together. While simulation and workflow modeling are more dynamic, database modeling has traditionally been more static. Simulation models focus on performance and behavior, while workflow models focus more on use and high-level implementation aspects. Time is essential in simulation although it is a simulated time, while time may be absent in workflow models or used in soft real-time scheduling constraints. Often simulation and workflow models are represented as directed graphs and the nodes in both types of graphs may fall into correspondence, however, the types of nodes are usually different (e.g., Queue, Server and Facility for simulation versus HumanComputer, Transactional and NonTransactional Tasks for workflow).

Finally, this paper has given two examples, METEOR Designer and JSIM Modeling Toolkit, of how hyper-diagrams can be used to link these multiple modeling aspects.

Appendix

- Simulation: *SIMODULA* [MW89]. SIMODULA is a simple simulation system based on the process-interaction simulation world view. A simulation environment was developed to enhance the processes of developing and running models. Because of the complex nature of simulation data and model specifications, relational databases were not ideal, so a toy database system, called OBJECTR, was developed. This was a relational database system with simple object-oriented extensions. It was later replaced with a more sophisticated database system, Active KDL.
- Database: *Active KDL* [PT88], [PTE89], [MPKW90], [MKP+91], [MPK+91], [PBMK92]. Active KDL is an Object-Oriented Database Management System providing methods, constraints and triggers as well as active objects. All schema elements are specified using a high-level functional style. Active KDL has both a query language (QL) and a database programming language (DBPL). The DBPL is sophisticated enough to even express simple simulation models entirely within the language. Active KDL evolved from the Knowledge Data Model (KDM) which is a hyper-semantic data model [PT88].
- Workflow: *METEOR* [SR93], [GHS95], [JNRS93], [KS95], [RS95]. The METEOR Workflow Management System (WfMS) includes a centralized workflow enactment service developed to control task execution from specifications given in the Workflow Specification Language (WFSL) and Task Specification Language (TSL).
- Simulation: *JSIM* [NMZ96], [MNZZ97]. JSIM is a redevelopment of SIMODULA providing higher-level facilities as well as animation. It also has the advantage that JSIM models can run over the Web. At this time, quality object-relational database systems are commercially available and suitable for the job of storing simulation data and models (e.g., Oracle 8 and Informix Universal Server). *JMODEL* makes it substantially easier to produce simulation models.
- Database: *Commercial ORDBMS*. Modern Object-Relational DBMSs provide a comprehensive set of useful capabilities, fully adequate for both JSIM and METEOR. Graphical designers such as Oracle Database Designer for Oracle 8 or *SWORDD* simply schema production.
- Workflow: *METEOR2 (WebWork and OrbWork)* [SKM+96], [MSKW96], [MPS+97], [K+97]. The METEOR2 project in the LSDIS Lab is focused on developing state-of-the-art workflow models (*METEOR Designer*) and enactment systems (WebWork and OrbWork). WebWork is a purely Web-based enactment service featuring ease of development and deployment as well as transactional and recovery capabilities. OrbWork is a CORBA-based

cousin of WebWork which supports advanced transactional and dynamic capabilities. Both WebWork and OrbWork utilize the outputs of the METEOR Designer for generating workflow applications.

References

[Bir79] G.M. Birtwistle. *Discrete Event Modeling in SIMULA*. MacMillian, London, England, 1979.

[Che76] P. Chen. The Entity-Relationship Model - Toward a Unified View of Data. *ACM Transactions on Database Systems*, 1(1), 1976.

[GHS95] D. Georgakopoulos, M. Hornick, and A. Sheth. An Overview of Workflow Management: From Process Modeling to Workflow Automation Infrastructure. *Distributed and Parallel Databases*, 3(2):119–154, April 1995.

[HM81] M. Hammer and D. McLeod. Database Description with SDM: A Semantic Data Model. *ACM Transactions on Database Systems*, 6(3), September 1981.

[JNRS93] W. Jin, L. Ness, M. Rusinkiewicz, and A. Sheth. Concurrency Control and Recovery of Multidatabase Work Flows in Telecommunication Applications. In *Proc. of ACM SIGMOD Conference*, May 1993.

[K+97] K.J. Kochut et al. OrbWork: A Distributed, Dynamic Workflow Enactment Service for METEOR$_2$. Technical report, LSDIS Lab, University of Georgia, 1997. URL: http://lsdis.cs.uga.edu.

[KP76] L. Kerschberg and J. Pacheco. A Functional Data Base Model. Technical report, Portificia Univ. Catolica do Rio De Janeiro, February 1976.

[KS95] N. Krishnakumar and A. Sheth. Managing Heterogeneous Multi-system Tasks to Support Enterprise-wide Operations. *Distributed and Parallel Databases*, 3(2):155–186, April 1995.

[LeC97] L. LeConte. SWORDD: A Simple Widely-Available Object-Relational Database Design-Tool. Master's thesis, University of Georgia, Athens, GA, June 1997.

[MKP+91] J.A. Miller, K.J. Kochut, W.D. Potter, E. Ucar, and A. Keskin. Query-Driven Simulation Using Active KDL: A Functional Object-Oriented Database System. *Int. Journal in Computer Simulation*, 1(1):1–30, 1991.

[MNZZ97] J.A. Miller, R. Nair, Z. Zhang, and H. Zhao. JSIM: A Java-Based Simulation and Animation Environment. In *Proceedings of the 30th Annual Simulation Symposium*, pages 786–793, Atlanta, Georgia, April 1997.

[MPK+91] J.A. Miller, W.D. Potter, K.J. Kochut, A. Keskin, and E. Ucar. The Active KDL Object-Oriented Database System and Its Application to Simulation Support. *Journal of Object-Oriented Programming, Special Issue on Databases*, 4(4):30–45, July-August 1991.

[MPKW90] J.A. Miller, W.D. Potter, K.J. Kochut, and O.R. Weyrich. "Model Instantiation for Query Driven Simulation in Active KDL". In *Proceedings of the 23rd Annual Simulation Symposium*, pages 15–32, Nashville, Tennessee, April 1990.

[MPS+97] J.A. Miller, D. Palaniswami, A.P. Sheth, K.J. Kochut, and H. Singh. Web-Work: METEOR$_2$'s Web-Based Workflow Management System. *Journal of Intelligent Information Systems*, 1997. (to appear).

[MSK+95] J.A. Miller, A.P. Sheth, K.J. Kochut, X. Wang, and A. Murugan. Simulation Modeling Within Workflow Technology. In *Proc. of the 1995 Winter Simulation Conference*, Arlington, VA, December 1995.

[MSKW96] J. A. Miller, A. P. Sheth, K. J. Kochut, and X. Wang. CORBA-based Run-Time Architectures for Workflow Management Systems. *Journal of Database Management*, 7(1):16–27, Winter 1996.

[MW89] J.A. Miller and O.R. Weyrich. Query Driven Simulation Using SIMODULA. In *Proceedings of the 22nd Annual Simulation Symposium*, pages 167–181, Tampa, Florida, March 1989.

[NMZ96] R. Nair, J.A. Miller, and Z. Zhang. A Java-Based Query Driven Simulation Environment. In *Proceedings of the 1996 Winter Simulation Conference*, pages 786–793, Coronado, California, December 1996.

[PBMK92] W.D. Potter, T.A. Byrd, J.A. Miller, and K.J. Kochut. Extending Decision Support Systems: The Integration of Data, Knowledge, and Model Management. *Annals of Operations Research, Special Issue on Model Management*, 38:501–527, 1992.

[Pet77] J.L. Peterson. Petri nets. *ACM Computing Surveys*, 9:223–252, 1977.

[PH91] R.J. Pooley and P.M. Hughes. Towards a Standard for Hierarchical Process Oriented Discrete Event Simulation Diagrams. *Transactions of the Society for Computer Simulation*, 8:1–20, 1991.

[Pid92] M. Pidd. *Computer Simulation in Management Science*. Wiley, Chichester, England, 3rd edition, 1992.

[Pri79] A.A.B. Pritsker. *Introduction to Simulation with SLAM*. Wiley, New York, NY, 1979.

[PSS90] C.D. Pegden, R.E. Shannon, and R.P. Sadowski. *Introduction to Simulation Using SIMAN*. McGraw-Hill, NY, 1990.

[PT88] W.D. Potter and R.P. Trueblood. Traditional, Semantic and Hyper-Semantic Approaches to Data Modeling. *IEEE Computer*, 21(6), June 1988.

[PTE89] W.D. Potter, R.P. Trueblood, and C.M. Eastman. Hyper-Semantic Data Modeling. *Data and Knowledge Engineering*, 4(1), July 1989.

[R+91] J. Rumbaugh et al. *Object-Oriented Modeling and Design*. Prentice-Hall, Englewood Cliffs, NJ, 1991.

[RS95] M. Rusinkiewicz and A. Sheth. Specification and Execution of Transactional Workflows. In W. Kim, editor, *Modern Database Systems: The Object Model, Interoperability and Beyond*. ACM Press, New York, NY, 1995.

[S+97] Sheth et al. A Taxonomy of Workflow Management Systems. Technical report, LSDIS, University of Georgia, 1997.

[Sch74] T.J. Schriber. *Simulation Using GPSS*. Wiley, NY, 1974.

[Sch83] L. Schruben. Simulation Modeling with Event Graphs. *Communications of the ACM*, 26:957–963, 1983.

[SKM+96] A.P. Sheth, K.J. Kochut, J.A. Miller, D. Worah, S. Das, C. Lin, D. Palaniswami, J. Lynch, and I. Shevchenko. Supporting State-Wide Immunization Tracking using Multi-Paradigm Workflow Technology. In *Proc. of the 22nd. Intnl. Conference on Very Large Data Bases*, Bombay, India, September 1996.

[Sof97] Rational Software. UML Notation Guide, version 1.1. Technical report, Rational Software, September 1997.

[SR93] A. Sheth and M. Rusinkiewicz. On Transactional Workflows. *IEEE Computer*, June 1993.

[Zha97] H. Zhao. A Graphical Designer for JSIM. Master's thesis, University of Georgia, Athens, GA, September 1997.

[Zhe97] K. Zheng. Development of the METEOR$_2$ Designer. Master's thesis, University of Georgia, Athens, GA, June 1997.

The Challenges of Modeling Biological Information for Genome Databases

Shamkant B. Navathe[1] and Andreas M. Kogelnik[1,2]

[1]Bioengineering Program & Database Group, College of Computing,
Georgia Institute of Technology, Atlanta, Georgia, USA

[2]Center for Molecular Medicine,
Emory University School of Medicine, Atlanta, Georgia, USA

Abstract. A gene can be defined as a basic unit of heredity and genetics as the study of genes and their properties. In a broad sense, genetics can be thought of as the construction of models based on information about genes and populations and the seeking of relationships between pieces of information. Information science can be applied here to collect and manage the data, model it, and mine it for relationships. This paper will focus primarily on the former two aspects. As a field of study, genetics can be divided into three branches: Mendelian genetics, molecular genetics, and population genetics. Mendelian or "classical" genetics is the study of the transmission of traits between generations. Molecular genetics is the study of the chemical structure of genes and their mechanism of function from a molecular perspective. Population genetics is the study of the variation in genetic information across populations of organisms. This paper discusses domain specific issues in modeling biological and genomic data and their importance in information system implementations. In particular, it focuses on the use of the mitochondrial genome as a model genomic system for the development of human genome databases. At the outset it is worthwhile reviewing the scope and aims of the Human Genome Project

The Human Genome Project

The term genome refers to a complete set of genetic information about an entity. The human genome, for example, generally refers to the complete set of genes required to create a human being. This set is estimated to be between 100,000 and 300,000 genes spread over 23 pairs of chromosomes, with an estimated 3-4 billion nucleotides. The goal of the Human Genome Project (HGP) is to obtain the complete sequence (the ordering of the bases) of those 3-4 billion nucleotides. At present only 8,000 genes are known and less than 10% of the Genome has been sequenced, however, the entire sequence is expected to be completed by the year 2006. By itself, the DNA sequence of humans is not particularly useful. This sequence can however, when combined with other data, be used as a powerful tool to address questions in genetics, biochemistry, medicine, anthropology, and agriculture. In the existing genome databases, the focus has been on "curating" (or collecting with some initial scrutiny

P.P. Chen et al. (Eds.): Conceptual Modeling, LNCS 1565, pp. 168-182, 1999.
© Springer-Verlag Berlin Heidelberg 1999

and quality check) and classifying information about genome sequence data. Other than the human genome, numerous organisms such as *E. coli, Drosophila,* and *C. elegans* have been investigated. We will briefly discuss some of the existing database systems which are supporting or have grown out of Human Genome Project research.

Genome Data Modeling

The Human Genome Project and the related information surrounding it present a number of challenges to the informatics and database communities. The challenges include: complex data modeling and representation; curating, storing, and manipulating such data; and analyzing and visualizing these data sets. The term curation with respect to biological databases carries with it not only a sense of oversight of the data and system but also meticulous research to align and add new data, correct existing data and maintain a consistent knowledge structure throughout the database. The task of curation is a common one for biological databases and stems from the fact that presently the maintainers of the knowledge and the maintainers of the database system are generally not the same individuals. Thus, curation raises issues of data accuracy, scientific validity, and source of data. From a computer science perspective, these challenges can be viewed as a complex domain-specific application of more general problems in data modeling, database system design and implementation; and algorithms and visualization. However, the biological domain does present novel challenges not evident in other application domains.

The information produced by the HGP together with other related sets of information represent a broad spectrum of highly complex, highly variable, rapidly changing, and often poorly-structured information. This information represents a multitude of theories, general knowledge, and commonly accepted relationships in biomedical science. Biology as a science is unique in that it has an enormous body of data, which is rapidly growing, whose structure is continually modified, whose theories and thus data elements and their structures evolve over time, whose individual data elements are written and updated by only a limited number of users but are read and queried by many, and whose information must be shared across a large diverse community. Much of the structure of data produced by the HGP has been rigidly set due to the limitations in the models which technologies could support at the time. Numerous systems have been developed for handling a varied segment of these data. Each was designed to handle a particular type (or types) of data from a particular data set. Table 1 compares the database structures, underlying technologies, and data types of each system. While each system originated to fill a need for curation of a particular data set, they share a number of commonalities with respect to data modeling. Each one of their data models is static - i.e. periodically a new "version" of the database is released - from a technical standpoint often this means that a new set of schemas is adopted and all data is migrated to these new schemas. GDB, Genbank, and OMIM are based on relational DBMSs, while EcoCyc uses an object-oriented system.

Database name	Major content	Initial technology	Current technology	DB problem areas	Primary data types
Genbank	DNA/RNA sequence, protein	text files	~flat-file/ASN.1	schema browsing, schema evolution, linking to other dbs	text, numeric, some complex types
OMIM	disease phenotypes and genotypes, etc.	index cards/ text files	~flat-file/ASN.1	free text entries are unstructured, linking to other dbs	text
GDB	genetic map linkage data	flat file	relational	schema expansion/ evolution, complex objects, linking to other dbs	text, numeric
ACEDB	genetic map linkage data, sequence data (non-human)	OO	OO	schema expansion/ evolution, linking to other dbs	text, numeric
HGMDB	sequence and sequence variants	flat file - application specific	flat-file - application specific	schema expansion/ evolution, linking to other dbs	text
EcoCyc	biochemical reactions and pathways	OO	OO	locked into class hierarchy, schema evolution	complex types, text, numeric

Table 1. Summary of the major genome related databases

One of the primary benefits of having the complete human genome sequence is that it will provide a framework in which to integrate a wide spectrum of human data on gene structure, variation, and disease. While the accumulation of information on human biology and health is a primary motivation for the human genome initiative, little attention has been paid to how such information will be organized or functionally related to the genomic sequence. There are numerous reasons for this. First, genetic data is complex and multi-layered. Medical genetic information ranges from structural to functional to population-based to clinically-based to gene-gene interaction data. Within these groupings of information are a huge variety of data types. Data describing DNA structure is composed of elements including: DNA sequence/nucleotide bases; nucleotide position; chromosomal assignment; gene locus organization - e.g. coding regions/polypeptides, messenger RNA, transfer RNA, ribosomal RNA; map positions; and known allelic positions for genetic loci. Each one of these elements in turn can be broken down into yet another set of complex, variable data types. Functional information describes the type of gene, gene expression, tissue expression, biochemical 3-D structure, biochemical activity, mutational studies, as well as biochemical pathways, reaction rates and other information. Information on DNA variability includes data encoding on point mutations, insertion mutations, deletions, complex rearrangements, frequencies of mutations in patient cohorts versus controls, and frequencies of mutations in different racial/ethnic groups. In addition to this, population data can be included in this category with information on ethnic specific populations, genetic markers for populations, geographic distributions, gene flow, and evolution. Clinical data encompasses classical medical disease presentations and classifications, family studies - genealogical trees, patient and normal phenotypes and genotypes; genotype/phenotype correlations; multifactorial/polygenic predispositions; genetic and other therapy protocols and results, and general patient data. Although presently little data is available in the area of gene-gene interactions, it promises enormous quantities of data describing complex interactions at the protein, RNA, and DNA level, including: nuclear versus mitochondrial interactions, mRNA versus tRNA interactions, and the actions of repressors, activators, gene operons, and transposable elements. Thus, the variety and magnitude of biomedical genome data has only recently pushed the limits of information management systems.

A second reason for lack of attention to the organization of genome data is that until recently, no portion of the human nuclear genome yet sequenced had been studied extensively enough to generate the variety and magnitude of data that would necessitate the development of an integrated genetic information system. In the biomedical sciences, much of the clinical and laboratory data currently collected is poorly utilized due to its enormous volume and the lack of tools required to efficiently and effectively understand, integrate, and manipulate data either in the clinic or the laboratory setting. This is especially true for human diseases such as hypertension, diabetes, Parkinson's disease, Alzheimer's disease, schizophrenia and some forms of deafness and blindness. Such diseases are not only extremely common and economically important, but have complex and heterogeneous genetic etiologies.

The genetic complexities of such diseases are rapidly becoming elucidated due to global initiatives such as the Human Genome Project, but the massive amounts of information this effort produces requires new systems for data storage, integration and analysis. The need to integrate these data sets is clear, as this would provide an extremely effective tool for analyzing disease and biomedical science and discovering new knowledge from previously unknown correlations in these separate data sets. However, without common unifying data which has relationships between data sets, integration of previously separate data sets is difficult. Our project presents one method for accomplishing this sort of integration. The key to accomplishing this integration was the use of the DNA sequence as the central unifying factor in the initial development of the overall database model. The use of information at the nucleotide base level as a key to other information reflects a common point of the fields of molecular medicine, molecular anthropology, biochemistry, and genetics. Other such common points may be identified in the future and could be used in a similar fashion to link other data sets together.

Currently Existing Biomedical Databases

Genbank

Genbank is today the preeminent DNA sequence database in the world. Maintained by the National Center for Biotechnology Information (NCBI) of the National Library of Medicine (NLM), it was established in 1978 as a central repository for DNA sequence data [Benson, et al., 1996]. Since then it has expanded somewhat in scope to include EST data, protein sequence data, 3-D protein structure, taxonomy, and links to the biomedical literature (MEDLINE). Its latest release contains over 602,000,000 nucleotide bases from over 920,000 sequences from over 16,000 species with roughly ten new organisms being added per day. The database size has doubled approximately every eighteen months for five years.

While it is a complex, comprehensive database, the scope of its coverage is narrowly focused on human sequences and links to the literature. Other limited data sources, 3-D structure, OMIM, have been added recently by reformatting the existing OMIM and PDB databases and redesigning The structure of the Genbank system to accommodate these new data sets.

The system is maintained as a combination of flat files, relational databases and files containing ASN.1 structures. Each entry is assigned a unique identifier. Updated entities are assigned a new identifier with the identifier of the original entity remaining unchanged for archival purposes so that older references to an entity do not inadvertently indicate a new and possibly inappropriate value. The most current concepts also receive a second set of unique identifiers (UIDs), which mark the most up-to-date form of a concept while allowing older versions to be accessed via their original identifier. For example, if the complete mitochondrial sequence in Genbank was to be altered, the new data might receive a new UID along with the most current mtDNA UID as a marker, but the old sequence (which previously had the most current mtDNA UID) would still be available under the its old primary UID.

The average user of the database is not able to access the structure of the data directly for querying or other functions, although complete snapshots of the database are available as exported ASN.1 files. The query mechanism provided is via the Entrez application (or its World Wide Web version), which allows keyword, sequence, and Genbank UID searching through a static interface. The ASN. 1 data structures are used to generate static, hard-coded C-structures to be compiled into applications such as Entrez. Data structure browsing is not permitted. The interface is periodically modified to accommodate changes to the database structure or add new types of queries.

Revisions to the database come as re-releases of the public version of the database. When novel structures are added, for example to handle the recent addition of expressed sequence tags to Genbank, often an entirely novel database structure is established and the database and its access software are updated, re-released, and redistributed. The existing search engines are useful for finding related DNA sequences as well as browsing MEDLINE articles which are related to the results of a search.

The Genome Database (GDB)

Created in 1989, the Genome Database is a catalog of human gene mapping data [Cuticchia, et al., 1993]. Gene mapping data is data which associates a piece of information with a particular location on the human genome. The degree of precision of this location on the map depends upon the source of the data, but is usually not at the level of individual nucleotide bases. GDB data includes data describing primarily map information (distance and confidence limits), and PCR probe data (experimental conditions, PCR primers and reagents used). More recently efforts have been made to add data on mutations linked to genetic loci, cell lines used in experiments, DNA probe libraries, and some limited polymorphism and population data.

GDB was built using Sybase - a commercial RDBMS and its data are modeled using standard ER techniques [Chen, 1976]. The implementors of GDB have noted difficulties in using this model to capture more than simply map and probe data. In order to improve data integrity and to simplify the programming for application writers, GDB distributes a Database Access Toolkit. However, most users use a WWW interface to search the ten interlinked data managers. Each manager keeps track of the links (relationships) for one of the ten tables within the GDB system. As with Genbank, users are given only a very high level view of the data at the time of searching and thus cannot make use of any knowledge gleaned from the structure of the GDB tables. Search methods are most useful when users are simply looking for an index into map or probe data. In other words, exploratory ad hoc searching of the database is not encouraged by present interfaces. Links between GDB and OMIM were never fully established.

Online Mendelian Inheritance in Man (OMIM)

Online Mendelian Inheritance in Man (OMIM) is an electronic compendium of information on the genetic basis of human disease [Pearson, et al, 1994]. Begun in hardcopy form by Victor McCusick in 1966 with over 1,500 entries, it was converted to a full-text electronic form in 1987-9 by the GDB. More recently, in 1991, its administration was transferred from JHU to the NCBI and the entire database was converted to NCBI's ASN. 1 flat file/relational format. Today it contains over 7,000 entries.

OMIM covers material on five disease areas based loosely on organs and systems: endocrine / hematology / immunology, connective tissue / skin and appendages / crainiofacial / ear, psychological / neurological / muscular, cardiac / gastrointestinal / pulmonary / renal / genital, and inborn errors of metabolism; as well as seven areas which cross organ and system boundaries: Clinical synopses, Chromosome disorders, Dysmorphology, Mitochondria, Malignancy, MiniMIM, Genes I, and Genes II. OMIM entries consist of descriptions of phenotypes, combined phenotype / genotype entries, or entries describing genes alone. The structure of the phenotype and genotype entries contains textual data loosely structured as general descriptions, nomenclature, modes of inheritance, variations, gene structure, mapping, and numerous lesser categories. In its initial full-text form, this information was not easily accessible via search engines, and limited links between mapping and disease data were available.

The full-text entries were converted to a static ASN. I structured format when OMIM was transferred to the NCBI. This greatly improved the ability to link OMIM data to other databases as well as give a rigorous structure to the data. However, the basic form of the database remained difficult to modify.

EcoCyc

The Encyclopedia of Escherichia coli Genes and Metabolism (EcoCyc) is a recent experiment in combining information about the genome and the metabolism of E. coli K-12 [Karp, 1994]. The database was created in 1996 as a collaboration between Stanford Research Institute and the Marine Biological Laboratory. It catalogs and describes the known genes of E. coli, the enzymes encoded by those genes, the biochemical reactions catalyzed by each enzyme and their organization into metabolic pathways. In so doing, EcoCyc spans the sequence and function domains of genomic information. It contains 1283 compounds with 965 structures as well as lists of bonds and atoms, molecular weights, and empirical formulas. It contains 3038 reactions in 269 classes.

The system was implemented using an object-oriented data model. The data are stored using Ocelot, a frame knowledge representation system. EcoCyc data is arranged within hierarchical object classes. The hierarchy was designed based on the observations that 1) the properties of a reaction are independent of the enzyme that catalyzes it, and 2) an enzyme has a number of properties that are "logically distinct" from its reactions. The hierarchical class structure used by EcoCyc is shown in Fig xxx. While this hierarchy is useful, because it is a hierarchy, it represents a structure imposed by the author/system and not necessarily a knowledge structure found in the real-world. In defining this hierarchy for all classes, relationships between classes are introduced which do not necessarily exist. This becomes more of a problem as more classes are added. Since EcoCyc deals with a relatively small range of data classes in a limited way, this problem can be ignored, however, it severely restricts any large-scale general application for EcoCyc.

EcoCyc provides two methods of querying: direct - via predefined queries - and indirect via hypertext navigation. Direct queries are performed using menus and dialogs. These menus and dialogs can initiate a large, but finite set of predefined queries. The navigational queries are accomplished by traversing existing links and documents. No navigation of the actual data structures is supported.

All of these systems have been well received since they fill a need for information in their domain. Each one gives access to data but not necessarily to the underlying structure of the model. A select few database administrators are relied upon for the creation and maintenance of the data model and the database. Browsing and manipulating the data model usually requires special permission, effort, and knowledge. This makes it extremely difficult for anyone but the curators (administrators) of a database to integrate information in any two databases, particularly on a large scale. In addition, the burden of data curation lies not with those who generated the data, but with a select few editors. In these cases, the databases as a whole are useful because they provide access albeit limited to much needed data. The utility stems primarily from the fact that the data which they contain is important as a collection and has been gathered from many sources and deposited in one place. However, they remain isolated in the sense that data in one database cannot be queried in conjunction with another database and neither existing nor novel correlations between data in disparate databases can be pulled out of existing systems. Thus, the systems as a whole remain far below their potential to provide answers to the user community. It is through the integration of numerous data sets where useful novel information and relationships will be found. The examination of biological information at the molecular level allows such integration to take place.

While all systems mentioned above integrate data, no system is able to do so on a scale encompassing sequence, population, clinical, functional and gene-gene interaction data. All of the systems require enormous effort to restructure in order to accommodate new data types or changes to existing types. Information systems can successfully integrate human DNA sequence data with other types of information such as population variation data, clinical data, functional genomic data, and gene-gene interaction data. Such systems can allow meaningful scientific questions to be asked across large distributed heterogeneous data sets. This work describes a system which enables users to cope with extremely complex, heterogeneous, large data sets. Flexibility, extensibility, and scalability are extremely important features of a biomedical information management system and of biomedical data models given the dynamic, evolving nature of biomedical information. Integration of data from multiple heterogeneous sources demands accessibility to a variety of data and a uniform language of exchange for these data. The separation of data and relationships from defined methods and rigid system formats is essential in accurately and simply storing and managing complex biomedical information.

Mitochondrial Genome as a Model System

In order to begin to address the challenges presented by genome data, a prototype model system was developed. Due to a number of unique characteristics as well as a large number of similarities with other DNA, the human mitochondrial genome was selected as an ideal model genomic system to be used in the development of this prototype.

The human mitochondrial DNA (mtDNA) offered an opportunity to attempt to model and integrate a number of varied data sets. The mitochondrial chromosome was the first human "chromosome" to have its DNA completely sequenced. Since this was accomplished in 1981 [Anderson, et al.], the mtDNA has been subjected to intense study. The result has been that there is now an extensive array of mtDNA functional and comparative genetic information, population variation data, and disease mutations. Analysis of these mitochondrial data sets has repeatedly revealed the interrelationship between the various types of genetic data. For example, functional constraints on the sequences relate to the severity of disease mutations; "neutral sequence polymorphisms must be distinguished from "disease" mutations; and certain mtDNA haplotypes can be correlated with increased penetrance and severity of, or predisposition to, disease.

An integrated, multi-purpose genome informatics system has been developed, using the human mitochondrial genome as a model system. The mitochondrial genome is well-suited for this purpose as it has been completely sequenced; the gene organization is known; it contains 37 genes essential for life; it is highly polymorphic; and it contains a large number of both somatic and inherited mutations which cause human diseases ranging from lethal pediatric disorders to late-onset neurodegenerative diseases [Wallace, 1995]. The human mitochondrial genome is 16,569 nucleotide pairs (np) long and encodes all three major classes of genes (13 polypeptides, two rRNAs, and 22 tRNAs) as well as replication, transcription, and RNA processing signals. The mtDNAs of multiple organisms have been sequenced, permitting the comparison of both genome organization and gene conservation among a wide variety of organisms. The mtDNA has a very high mutation rate, 10-20 times higher than that of nuclear genes. Hence, the human population has an extensive array of ethnic-specific sequence polymorphisms, many of which are inherited in groups associated with specific haplotypes. A wide variety of mtDNA mutations have also been associated with human diseases. The spectrum of deleterious DNA changes includes point mutations, large and small-scale rearrangements, and expanding repeat mutations, thus paralleling genetic defects found in nuclear genes. Some mitochondrial diseases such as the MERRF (myoclonic epilepsy and ragged-red fiber) and MELAS (mitochondrial encephalomyopathy, lactic acidosis and stroke-like episodes) syndromes are associated with single gene mutations, while others like LHON (Leber's hereditary optic neuropathy) can also be multifactorial, involving multiple mtDNA mutations as well as epigenetic factors. Mitochondrial diseases, like nuclear diseases, also show clinical heterogeneity, incomplete penetrance, and variable age of onset. See Figure 1.

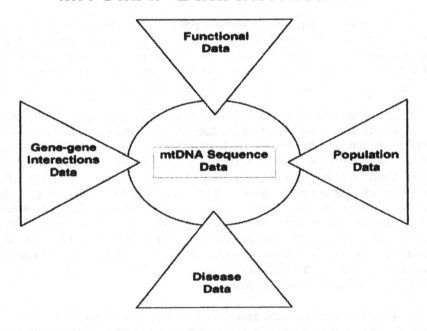

Fig. 1. MITOMAP Data Interactions

Most of these features are only now being realized for the nuclear-encoded chromosomes. Thus, the human mitochondrial genome encompasses the complete spectrum of human genetic data, making it an ideal model system for developing a sequence-based information system for the integration and analysis of genetic, anthropologic, and clinical data.

MITOMAP: A Human Mitochondrial Genome Database

Modeling Mitochondrial Data and Database Design

To demonstrate the utility of a multifaceted, comprehensive database, a database which encompasses all known aspects of human mitochondrial genetics and the associated clinical correlations was designed and then implemented using a variety of techniques. This collection of data is known as MITOMAP [Kogelnik, *et al*, 1997]. Using the DNA sequence as the primary unifying element, the overall design of the MITOMAP database called for a number of partially overlapping sub-databases (see Figure 2): the functional database which contains the available structural and functional data on all known mitochondrial genes; the mtDNA population variation database which documents the nature and extent of sequence variation in various human populations; the mtDNA diseases database which catalogues mtDNA-based diseases and their cognate nucleotide changes; and the gene-gene interaction database which harbors gene expression data for both mitochondrial-encoded and nuclear-encoded bioenergetic genes. All sub-databases are related and integrated through the master mtDNA sequence of 16,569 nucleotides, using the published Cambridge sequence as the master reference sequence.

The mitochondrial genome structure and function database includes the map locations for all genes and functional and regulating elements. When available it will also contain the DNA sequences of other known mitochondrial genomes and gene products encoded in them. This permits the assessment of evolutionary constraints which act on mitochondrial proteins and genes. Functional information comes in many forms: genetic locus names; reaction rates; chromosome designations; and more complex types describing 3-D structure of proteins or the organization of a gene. While the simpler types can be dealt with in a straightforward manner by most models, the complex ones are often simplified by relational models at the expense of a loss of detail, context, or structure.

The mtDNA sequence variation database encompasses all known polymorphic restriction sites and sequence variants, the population frequencies of each variant, and the haplotype and phylogenetic relationships between these variants. Currently, there are hundreds of polymorphic restriction sites but a more limited amount of sequence variation information. In the future, this will be corrected by direct sequencing of mtDNAs from a broad spectrum of ethnic groups and populations. The data in this set comes in numerous varieties, including: population names and sizes, linguistic groupings, the presence or absence of enzyme restriction sites and their respective enzymes, and individual nucleotide changes. These data are obtained from anthropological and laboratory analysis and frequently contain exceptions and missing values for data not collected or uninterpretable data.

The mtDNA disease database includes the nucleotide locations and sequence changes for all known mtDNA disease mutations. It also houses a comprehensive list of mtDNA associated diseases, the clinical characteristics and relevant biochemical and somatic cell genetic data. Clinical data adds to the data types present by often including images or video footage as well as requiring a need for indicating possible known relationships between concepts such as symptoms, diseases or mutations and disease. Another complex type often represented in this data set is the geneaological family tree.

The MITOMAP gene-gene interaction database is designed to contain all available information on the expression of both mitochondrial and nuclear-encoded genes of cellular energy production. This includes data on gene transcription, translation, RNA turnover and mtDNA replication. Information for both mitochondrial disease patients and healthy controls was included since expression rates are different in these two cohorts.

Thus, the overall design of the database demands the ability to represent a complex data structure and relationships between data in a robust, reproducible manner, while the scientific theory behind the data demand a flexibility to change data and relationships and their structure, and the biological basis of the data demand that the data model allow for the variability and unpredictability of biology. Given these criteria, in order to find an optimal solution to this data modeling and management problem, numerous system implementations were attempted.

MITOMAP Implementations - Relational

The first prototype of the MITOMAP database was constructed using the relational database model. The standard entity-relationship (ER) model was used to develop a model for MITOMAP data. During the conceptual design, a normalized implementation of an ER model was used, where each tuple (or row in the relational table) represents a collection of related values which cannot be broken down into simpler sets. This serves to eliminate the problems of data duplication, multiple update issues, and the generation of spurious tuples from join operations [Batini, et al, 1992]. However, the commonly occuring null values increase the decomposition of biological data into smaller tables. In addition under the relational model, frequent exceptions to the structure of a relational tuple forces increased atomization of tables. Given the relatively large size of biological databases, the degree of atomization and quantity of tables rapidly becomes unmanageable and incomprehensible from the standpoint of a curator. Null values also present problems for querying in a relational system (relational joins cannot be performed across null fields). Thus, while increasing atomization of the database makes individual data items simpler to comprehend in isolation, a new difficulty arises in the comprehension and maintenance of the data structure as a whole from a domain knowledge perspective. This is largely due to the fact that the underlying system limits the way that relationships can be defined within a table and thus the way that entities can be structured at the level of the model. For example, an entity might be created for a genetic locus and a mucation. The genetic locus entity might have attributes such as name - a unique identifier, start position, end position, etc. The mutation might be modeled as consisting of a unqiue identifier, a mutation type identifier (e.g. point mutation, insertion, deletion, etc.) and then attributes specific to each mutation type. Under the relational model, this table could be normalized by forming a "mutation" table and a table for each mutation type, splitting the information between them. Thus, each biological object would then be modeled over two or more database tables each having its own primary and foreign keys, making what was an obvious biological relationship less clear in its implementation. The definition of relationships in the ER model is ideal for representing well-defined binary relationships. However, biological data again does not always fit in these categories given its variability - e.g. one could argue that the data is poorly modeled, resulting in these sorts of anomalies. However, given that the nature of since is to continually improve models of the real world, more flexibility for representing the poorly-defined relationships is needed.

Formulating queries under this model required intimate knowledge of the detailed structure of the model, limiting the kinds of questions that would be asked and discouraging exploration/navigation of the data - i.e. only expert database users could properly ask questions of the database, however, these users are not normally the ones with expert knowledge of the biological domain. This reemphasizes the importance of ensuring that the data model as well as the information system is understandable by the users of the data.

The benefits of this model included the fact that when in normal form, normalization theory based on functional dependencies guarantees the lack of anomalies in the database. The relational implementation also provided extremely rapid query responses and a degree of uniformity to the database such that programming the database was simpler. In contrast, however, the validity of normalization becomes irrelevant if the tuple cannot completely represent the data in question, and speed is not an issue if the desired question cannot be asked of the system. In addition, under the normalized relational model, the biological meaning of the data and relationships becomes blurred as the variability and lack of complete data sets increase the number of entities required in a model to represent the data. In addition the model did not easily allow for the variability in biological data types (e.g. multiple data types for a given value are not permitted under the relational model but frequently can occur in nature).

In summary, the entities and relational tables mapped poorly to the initial biomedical data, making comprehension and subsequent updates and changes to the structure of the data as a whole difficult. Such changes could only be performed with a complete understanding of the structure of the resulting relational data model, not necessarily the overall biological or genetic relationships or data. Finally, the ER model or the general relational models and their implementations, do not provide any method for simply sharing schemas and data across systems - tables must be created anew on each system and periodically updated, and data on a system cannot be directly linked to data on another.

With the inability to comprehensively model all of the data types, the primary objective of the data model (representing the data) was not achieved and additional prototypes were necessary.

MITOMAP Implementations - Object-Oriented

The second prototype system developed for MITOMAP utilized the object-oriented (OO) model to build a model based on objects, classes, and inheritance which could encompass all types of biological data relevant to the human mitochondrial genome.

The OO model maintains individual objects with methods or functions with a natural mapping into generalization/specialization arrangements of classes, thereby modeling real-world objects. This is of great benefit to biological model builders, as unlike with the relational model, this allows for a more direct mapping of complex, real-word concepts to a structure in a data model. The designer of the object, rather than the rules of the system, can be allowed to determine the degree to which an object /entity is simplified/normalized. The result is a model which more closely resembles the designer's mental model of the information, not one which has forced information into pre-structured boxes. Thus, because data objects more closely resemble real-world objects, the end user receives the benefit of the knowledge given by the structure of the object. The model also provides collection-based methods and structures for modeling, maintaining, and querying data.

Although OO database management systems available at the time of the study were still immature, there were numerous notable drawbacks. One of the two primary benefits of OO models, the collection types, were not navigable in a manner flexible enough to support the complex unpredictable nature of biological queries and data exploration. While the increased flexibility offered by the use of pointers to objects allowed for more realistic and complete data models, because much of the models required hard-coded methods, alterations in the schema usually required significant reprogramming. Pointers and unique identifiers used in representing the data after it was modeled were not necessarily indicative of any biologically relevant uniqueness (i.e. biological relevance did not necessarily match implementation relevance). On occasion this would make it difficult to reference the data in a manner meaningful to the user. Finally, biological "inheritance" of data types/values did not match well with OO inheritance, i.e. class inheritance did not provide for the types of data, relations and information sharing that was desired in biological inheritance. Biological schema structures represent a broad variety of classes. These classes are often quite unrelated and thus do not derive any benefit from inheriting attributes from other objects classes - i.e. a set of biological data modeled using traditional OO modeling would have a large degree of branching at the top level of its class hierarchy and little below. Biological classes would benefit more from the ability to adjust the class over time. Because biological theories are constantly being augmented and altered, biological databases must be able to evolve their data structures in order to consistently represent the state of biological knowledge over time.

Thus OO modeling was quite complete in representing complex real-world objects and it provided additional collection types for aggregate groupings, further extending paradigms common to biological information. In this regard OO models were more useful for representing biological data then relational data models, however, there were still numerous deficiencies in OO modeling with respect to biological variability.

MITOMAP Implementation - Flat-File

In addition to relational and object-oriented models, a simple flat-file based prototype was also developed where the data model was built directly into the application. The objective here was the provision of an information system which maintained a set of data and was able to perform specific query operations on them. This data model was static and hard-coded in the system.

The benefits of this model and its implementation were that both were tailored specifically to meet the needs of an application, and thus directly delivered the required functionality. For example, irregularities in the collection of data can be accounted for in populational analyses - previously we developed a system which was programmed to exclude individual sample data objects with specific missing data points in order to perform a maximum likelihood analysis. While this gave us the desired data set for our analysis, the application needed to be reprogrammed whenever the slightest change was made to the data model. Unfortunately, this method results in all structure to the data (i.e. the data model) being inherent in programs accessing data files and thus is not readily accessible or modifiable. Even slight changes would require significant reprogramming and thus significant expert knowledge of the database rather than the application domain. This method scaled poorly and did not provide any of the rigor of relational calculus or the flexibility of the object-oriented model. In addition, many of the features of more developed systems such as transaction rollback and recovery are absent.

From the lessons learned in developing these various data models, a more generic system for modeling and handling complex biological data in a distributed environment has been undertaken. We have begun the development of GENOME - a generalized database system for managing human genome project data [Kogelnik, Navathe, Wallace, 1997]

Bibliography

Anderson, S; Bankier, AT; Barrell, BG; deBruijn, MHL; Coulson, AR; Drouin, J; Eperon, IC; Nierlich, DP; Rose, BA; Sanger, F; Schreier, PH, Smith, AJH; Staden, R; Young, IG, "Sequence and organization of the human mitochondrial genome." *Nature* 290:457-465, 1981.

Benson DA, Boguski M, Lipman DJ, and Ostell J, *GenBank.* Nucleic Acids Research 24(1):1-5, 1996.

Chen, P.P. "The Entity-Relationship Model - Toward a Unified View of Data," *ACM Trans. on Database Systems*, 1, 1 (March 1976), 9-36.

Cuticchia, A.J.; Fasman, K.H.; Kingsbury, D.T.; Robbins, R.J.; and Pearson, P.L., "The GDB human genome database anno 1993". *Nucleic Acids Research* 21(13):3003-3006, 1993.

Frenkel, K.A., "The Human Genome Project and Bioinformatics." *CACM.* 34(11) Nov. 1991.

Kogelnik A.M., Lott M.T., Brown M.D., Navathe S.B., Wallace D.C. MITOMAP: an update on the human mitochondrial genome database. Nucleic Acids Research. 25(1), 1997.

Kogelnik, AM; Navathe, SB; Wallace, DC; "GENOME: a system for managing Human Genome Project data." *Genome Informatics '97.*

Pearson, P.; Francomano, C.; Foster, P.; Bocchini, C; Li P.; and McKusick, V., *The status of online Mendelian inheritance in man (OMIM) medio 1994.* Nucleic Acids Research 22 (17):3470-3473.

Robbins, R.J. "Genome Informatics: Requirements and Challenges", The Second International Conference on Bioinformatics, Supercomputing and Complex Genome Analysis. World Scientific Publishing, 1993.

Wallace, D.C. 1995. "1994 William Allan Award Address: Mitochondrial DNA Variation in Human Evolution, Degenerative Disease, and Aging." Am J Human Genet 57:201-223.

Trends and Scale-Up for Data Administration

Arnon Rosenthal[1] and Len Seligman[2]

The MITRE Corporation
[1]202 Burlington Rd., Bedford, MA 01730, USA
[2]1820 Dolley Madison Blvd., McLean, VA 22102, USA
{arnie, seligman}@mitre.org

Abstract. The application development lifecycle is undergoing several grand unifications that, together, will rescue conceptual modeling from the wilderness. At the same time, advances in data warehouses and middleware are removing some of the software barriers to large, multi-organizational databases, creating new data administration challenges. The increasing scale and complexity of our systems identify new "grand challenges" to data administration research; we discuss two of these, in some detail: the administration of multi-tier schema, and exploiting legacy or "foreign" data during the development of new application schemas. We illustrate these issues with examples taken from the United States Department of Defense (DOD).

1 Introduction

Conceptual data models are used in system design, but rarely in operational systems. The application development lifecycle is undergoing several grand unifications that, together, will rescue conceptual modeling from the wilderness. This papers examines likely scenarios as data administration scales upward and accommodates the object revolution.

Section 2 describes three convergences that are occurring in object technology and examines their effects on data administration. These unifications are:

1. A unified schema interface formalism across levels of abstraction
2. The design processes for databases and applications are becoming interleaved, to form Objects Oriented Analysis and Design (OOA&D).
3. OOA&D will use a common core of representations across vendors and lifecycle stages.

In this new world, "scale" will be a critical difficulty for data administration. Middleware products and data warehouses are reducing the amount of "glue" code developers need to write in order to access data from multiple sources. But as the cost of accessing multiple sources goes down, there is an increasing need for another kind of glue: declarative specifications of systems and their interrelationships. The result will be a greater emphasis on data administration.

One scale-related requirement is the need to serve multiple communities, whose world views differ. The solution will involve maintaining multiple schemas, with connections among them, as discussed in Section 3 This task seems to involve a rich

P.P. Chen et al. (Eds.): Conceptual Modeling, LNCS 1565, pp. 183-194, 1999.

variety of theoretical and architectural problems, and seems an appropriate "grand challenge" for database researchers and vendors:

- *Administration of multi-tier databases and schemas* (e.g., a warehouse). Data architectures will include several tiers, where a tier supports an application community, or else describes implementation objects. In addition, one can separate orthogonal issues by defining additional tiers (e.g., to resolve one form of heterogeneity, such as use of different modeling formalisms, or different means of object identification).

A second major problem is the accommodation of legacy information, within the new paradigm, as discussed in Section 4:

- *How do we best exploit legacy or "foreign" data during the development of new (object-oriented) application schemas?*

Our scope is restricted to "classic" data administration, i.e., to facilitate development and evolution of applications over structured data of the sort that traditionally has been stored in a DBMS. Since each structural description typically has many instances, it is worth investing effort in modeling the problem domain, and organizing these descriptions as types. Such data administration aims to provide declarative information to application-development or GUI-development tools, and to facilitate interoperability.[1]

1.1 Terminology

Terminology is a continuing headache in our field. Unless otherwise noted, we use the following terms as described below:

- *Model* will mean a description of some aspect of an application; if it is an interface description, we call it a *schema*. It will be called an *object model* if it includes methods; otherwise, a *data model*.
- We use *formalism* to mean meta-model, such as relational, ER, CORBA objects, etc. (The meta-model is itself a data model, whose domain is general purpose constructs of interest to DBMS experts. However, conventional wisdom states that each use of "meta" reduces the audience 50%, so we use a different term.)
- An *application schema* describes the concepts of an application. An application schema can be either *concrete* (with attributes over implemented data types) or *abstract* (i.e., representation independent), with attributes over domains like Time, Velocity but not bound to a particular representation. An abstract schema is a fine basis for interoperability. However, one then needs a mediator to shield applications from differences in representation.
- *Conceptual* schema will be used almost synonymously with application schema, but with the connotation that it describes a community viewpoint across multiple applications, rather than that of a single group.
- An *implementation* schema consists of objects that represent convenient physical units, which need not be natural application concepts.

---

[1] Classical data administration techniques were not intended for managing diverse sets of documents. We believe that they *do* apply to sets of document templates (e.g., SGML or XML DTDs), and to metadata specifications (such as the Dublin Core or the WWW Consortium's RDF); however, these are outside this paper's scope.

As described in Section 3, there can be multiple tiers of schemas, each derived from the ones below.

2 Effects of Grand Unifications in Object Technology

Object technology (together with componentware [CACM97]) seems likely to be the foundation of application development in the next decade. The benefits of object technology for general purpose software are well known (encapsulation of both data and function, inheritance, identity and relationships, etc.), and will not be reviewed here. Instead, we focus on several long-awaited unifications (here called *convergences*) that will amplify the power of conceptual modeling. A fuller discussion of these convergences appears in [Rose98]

Convergence 1: A unified formalism across levels of abstraction.
- The same object schema formalism will express application, conceptual, and implementation schemas, in many organizations. An object query language provides a declarative mechanism for expressing derivations among them.
- Given the use of an object formalism, application schemas will describe system interfaces that applications can use. (This is not the case with entity-relationship schemas).
- It will be easier to give each community a schema customized to its needs, because a multi-tier schema architecture will be able to relate schemas within one formalism.

It has long been recognized that schemas at different levels of abstraction (conceptual, implementation, or external view) play different roles in data management. An object formalism can appropriately express schemas at these different levels of abstraction, express derivations among them, and provide both navigational and query interfaces. Section 3 discusses the opportunities and challenges presented by a unified formalism across abstraction levels.

Convergence 2: The design processes for databases and applications are interleaved, to form Object Oriented Analysis and Design (OOA&D).
- Object modeling will often be done by developers who are not database experts.
- Applications will be seen as interacting with the object manager, rather than with the DBMS.

The current design process consists of data design plus application design. The future split seems likely to be object design plus implementation design; the implementation then splits into data and code portions. Data administration's goals (including the ability to share and integrate data) still apply, but the techniques will need to be adapted, and object designers will need to be convinced of their value. Techniques currently used within DOD include schemas, dictionaries and ontologies, schema integration, and use of declarative mappings (e.g., SQL) among schemas rather than black-box methods. From this list, only schemas are routinely used in OOA&D.

Convergence 3: OOA&D will use a common core of representations (UML and the Microsoft Repository), across vendors and lifecycle stages.

- Both vendors and user organizations will find it easier to assemble best-of-breed tools from multiple sources.
- Computer-aided Software Engineering (CASE) tool suites should improve rapidly, as market barriers drop, users need less training, and users benefit from tool synergies.

Until very recently, the representations used in software methodologies (and the supporting CASE industry) were hopelessly fragmented and incompatible. But while moving to OO-CASE, the industry has made enormous progress in standardization. Technical inputs came from many directions; the political push came from customers, the Object Management Group (*OMG*), and the Microsoft Repository [Bern97], which (combining concrete form with market power) is being bundled with all Microsoft languages.

The result is that for many types of information involved in OOA&D, we have standard concepts, graphic notations and access interfaces. Leading OO-CASE vendors have agreed to export/import using the Unified Modeling Language (*UML*) [Rati98] and Microsoft's repository interface. UML will provide a standard core (also adopted by OMG) that vendors will interchange easily, as well as standard means of describing vendor-specific extensions. Also, because all UML diagrams are defined over the same metaschema, information can be seen consistently from the perspective of different lifecycle stages, e.g., class diagrams and use cases.

Currently, many DOD database designers use drawing tools (e.g., PowerPoint) for schemas. They reject database CASE systems as not worth the trouble and expense, for now. The future looks better. Standardization should reduce software costs and the learning curve. Improved integration should increase the payback, as the captured information is used for more purposes. As a consequence, there should be less tendency for design information to wither, unmaintained, as a system evolves.

This section has described three important convergences taking place in industry, as a result of the widespread adoption of object technology. The next two sections examine some opportunities presented by these trends, in particular those related to administering multi-tier schemas and bringing legacy or "foreign" data in object-oriented application schemas.

3 Administration of Multi-tier Schemas

We call a structure with two or more schemas, related by derivation, a *multi-tier schema*. Multi-tier schemas, such as the ANSI/SPARC three schema architecture [Tsic77] are a staple of textbook advice, but have rarely met their potential. They are most extensively used in federated databases [Shet90], whose most popular current form is systems that extract data from multiple sources into a data warehouse.

The following subsections discuss the requirements for multi-tier schemas, previous efforts that used multi-tier schemas, how the convergences above help address the shortcomings of these efforts, and some continuing challenges.

3.1 Why We Need To Have (and Manage) Multi-tier Schemas

Two of the guiding principles that motivate the use of multi-tier schemas are:
- One should define resources in a widely supported formalism, rather than hiding their definitions inside, say, a particular vendor's physical design constructs.
- It is better to express derivations in a widely supported declarative language that allows us to reason about them (e.g., SQL, OQL), rather than in black box code. This is essential if one is to build automated tools which span tiers (e.g., for optimizing a query that is specified in terms of an application schema rather than an implementation one.

Given this viewpoint, there are several reasons why multi-tier schemas are needed:
1. *Hide implementation choices:* The need to split, combine, and otherwise mangle conceptual objects for efficiency reasons will not disappear (despite occasional claims to the contrary by OODB vendors). It will still be necessary to create implementation schemas for performance reasons—e.g., to tune, to give important transactions better response, to reduce backup and recovery time (by segregating nonvolatile data), and so forth. However, developers should see a simpler interface (e.g., an application schema), and their code should continue to run when the implementation schema changes.
2. *Be a natural match for an application community:* A large system has many communities, each wanting a different subset of the information, and finding different organizations of the information to be natural. One option is that each request be formulated in terms of the conceptual schema. This is more work for developers, and leaves a lot to maintain when something changes. It is often very worthwhile to give each community an application schema, and map it just once to lower tiers.
3. *Encapsulate legacy systems:* The conceptual schema might be supported by data in multiple legacy systems. It seems cleanest to encapsulate these systems fairly directly, and then find derivations from the encapsulating objects to conceptual schema. (Note that other organizations might wish to derive *their* conceptual schemas from some of the same encapsulations.)
4. *Formalism translations:* A large system might involve multiple formalisms. Rather than encapsulate the legacy system as a black box (item 3), one might want to see some of the objects in it, in terms of a common-denominator model (e.g., with just objects, types, and function calls). A gateway that exploited these similarities might make it possible to provide services like change propagation or configuration control.

Multi-tier schemas have been popular in the literature in two main areas. First, data warehouses and (closely related) federated databases supported by middleware are organized into at least two tiers: component system schemas and an integrated view (i.e., federated schema) [Shet90]. Industrial support for data warehouses and federated databases is growing rapidly, and vendors are quickly bringing out new tools. However, these tools mostly use vendor-specific mechanisms for expressing mappings across tiers, rather than using standard, declarative languages such as SQL or OQL.

Second, even for a database belonging to a single enterprise and designed from scratch, it still can be worthwhile to separate implementation from conceptual schemas, and provide external views (as in ANSI/SPARC). The full potential will be reached when multi-tier becomes the default way to organize any nontrivial database, supported by cheap, easy-to-use tools aimed at a broad market.

3.2 History and Challenges of Supporting Multi-tier Schemas

3.2.1   Barriers That Defeated ANSI-SPARC Multi-tier Schemas

The idea of providing each community with a suitable application schema, and mapping them to an implementation schema, is more than twenty years old. The ANSI/SPARC three schema architecture [Tsic78] is much cited and has influenced CASE vendors to provide conceptual modeling tools. However, implemented systems generally maintain only the implementation schema.

There is a litany of disconnects and disagreements that defeated ANSI/SPARC, up to the present time. Two critical barriers are being removed by the widespread acceptance of object technology:

1. *EER is not queryable.* The conceptual tier (and sometimes the external tiers) were expressed in extended entity relationship formalisms. Once a relational implementation existed, developers ignored the other formulations, since in the end they needed to write queries against the relational implementation. As a result, the EER application schemas were not seen as an important resource that justified maintenance as the database evolved. (A relational representation of a conceptual schema would have been queryable, and hence more interesting to developers. However, without explicit relationships, they do not provide the intuitive picture and structural insight that we need in a conceptual model.

   This problem can be cured by expressing application and conceptual schemas in an OO formalism (SQL3 or ODL) supported by DBMSs—i.e., it is remedied by Convergence #1 described in Section 2.

2. *EER had no standard representation or access interface:* EER standards exist for wall-chart displays (e.g., IDEF1X) but not for interchanging designs between systems. This barrier is being removed by the convergence around UML (i.e., Convergence #3 above).

Objects and object standards go a long way to removing these difficulties. This permits some progress, as described in the following section.

3.2.2   How Do Objects Simplify the Administration of Multi-tier Schemas?

Object formalisms have two big advantages over the earlier mix of relational and entity-relationship formalisms: they are appropriate for all ANSI/SPARC tiers (conceptual, external, and implementation tiers), and they are gaining industrially-supported query languages for deriving the contents of a virtual database. A uniform formalism at all tiers simplifies mappings between them, and an object formalism can encapsulate key aspects of others. Also, while there are multiple standards, there are not dozens.

Ideally, all tiers would be described within a single object formalism; Section 3.2.3 examines the more likely case of a small number of roughly consistent standards.

The mappings would be described declaratively in a standard query language (e.g., SQL3 or OQL). A declarative query language for derivations permits optimizations. More important, if the derivation is simple (e.g., projection, selection), one is better able to generate candidate implementations for generic methods like Update, Error_msg, etc.

We briefly discuss two other advantages to using object formalisms. First, they tend to be more concise (less redundant) than today's relational schemas, for several reasons. User-defined types allow some semantics and structure to be encapsulated and reused. Inheritance reduces the number of separate attribute definitions (as compared with defining attributes repeatedly, and then somehow asserting that they are not really different). Also, methods can provide a way of attaching customized semantics for generic operations.

Second, objects are referenceable by unique identifiers, and they can be any size (especially if the object is not assumed to represent an implementation chunk, to be stored atomically). Hence, we expect that the various forms of consistency management (e.g., [Alon90, Seli97]) across tiers could be more flexibly implemented at the most appropriate level of granularity.

Even with object technology, multi-tier schemas are difficult. Section 3.2.3 examines difficulties because object technology has multiple proposed standards. Section 3.2.4 examines difficulties even when the formalisms are homogeneous.

3.2.3   Difficulties Due to Multiple Formalisms

The same OO formalism *might* be used at all tiers, especially if the system is designed from scratch and all the chosen products support the same formalism. More likely, the OOA&D community's formalism (UML [Rati98]) will retain some differences from the models supported by DBMS vendors (SQL3, OQL) and used for implementation schemas. In addition, it is certain that vendors will provide desirable but proprietary extensions (e.g., for query languages, the "data blades," "data cartridges," and "data extenders" of Informix, Oracle, and IBM respectively).

We thus cannot expect that all models will be "plug compatible"; we do hope they will be "wrench compatible," i.e., able to be connected, using a moderate amount of skilled manual work. The number of competing standards is fairly small, so it may be possible to provide high-quality wrappers (i.e., gateways) that enable information in one formalism to be seen in terms of another. Where heterogeneous formalisms cannot be hidden, they require an organization to have more skills, and (possibly) more people, money, and tools.

Derivations are complicated in a multi-formalism environment. Each standard query language produces results in its own native formalism—i.e., SQL maps tables to tables; OQL maps objects and collections to objects and collections. Despite the maturity of EER modeling, there is no standard language to take relations and produce EER databases.

Dependency-tracking can be difficult when information is managed by different tools, which understand different dependencies. For example, consider a CASE system that understands the gross pattern of schemas being derived from each other. However, one might need knowledge of SQL semantics to determine which attribute definitions are affected by a change to the base tables. It is uncertain how effectively these processes can pass through a gateway between heterogeneous schema formalisms.

A multi-tier system also needs a metamodel for information that relates the tiers. When mapping between schemas in different formalisms, dependency tracking, event notification, and other services should apply end to end. We know of no standards in this area. For example, such a meta-model would describe dependency data, and methods for change propagation. Currently, a UML CASE tool would tend to track dependencies at a coarse level, while only a DBMS might be able to interpret a SQL view definition sufficiently to identify the sources of a view attribute. This complicates configuration management, dependency maintenance, and so forth.

There seem to be at least two relevant tactics. First, one can use gateways between formalisms. At least the basic information then becomes available to dependency tracking, event notification, and other services that should apply end to end. Second, a derivation that maps between two formalisms cannot be analyzed within either formalism. Therefore, when a schema derivation crosses formalisms, the derivation should be split into two parts (inserting an extra tier): one part does the formalism translation but (as far as possible) no other transformation; the other part, expressed in either the source or target formalism, maps the structures.

For example, some middleware products (e.g., UniSQL/M) import relational data into an object model in two steps: translating relations to objects, and then simplifying the object structure (e.g., by exploiting inheritance and nested object types). In the future, the target formalism might instead by UML, used in a CASE tool's models.

3.2.4   Continuing Challenges, Even in a Homogeneous World

Multi-tier schemas would be challenging to administer, even if all models were expressed in a single object formalism that combined the advantages of all the candidate standards. Some of the remaining difficulties are:

1. *Metadata Volume:* The amount of metadata is increased, since administrators must specify multiple tiers, and the derivations that relate them. Unless such information can be generated automatically (exploiting the relationships among the tiers), the burden on data administrators will increase greatly.
2. *Change propagation:* When a change is made at one tier, the queries that derive it from related tiers (and that derive from it) need to be changed. Administrators must understand the related tiers and the derivations, so they need both technical skill and knowledge of the other systems.

    Changes that need to be propagated come in several categories. Some involve traditional issues of schema evolution, when an object class's representation or semantics change (e.g., attributes or methods change, are added, or deleted). Other changes involve ancillary metadata attached to the object, its attributes, or its method signatures (e.g., units, precision, quality, or the source of data).
3. *All tiers above the implementation are second class.* Many critical services including error messages, grant_privilege, and trigger definition currently are supported only for the implementation tier; in some cases, even Update may need to be manually implemented.

As a unifying metaphor, we propose that all interesting information items be appropriately *reflected* at all tiers, in a way that (informally) conforms to the effect of data transformation processes in multi-tier databases. Such reflection is critical to addressing the above challenges. We now briefly discusses reflection and the need for a framework for managing it. (For more detail about reflection in multi-tier databases, with an emphasis on data integrity, see [Rose97].)

Multi-tier databases are defined by derivation processes, both exact (e.g., database views) and approximate (due to time delays and incommensurable representations).

The derived tier is often not precisely a view; instead, we say that the tiers *reflect* each other.

To specify and implement the desired reflection behaviors, developers will need to implement many algorithms (hundreds or more). In addition, administrators will need to select, for each attribute and annotation, which algorithm is appropriate for reflecting each chunk of information (potentially thousands). To keep all this organized and to factor out common features, there is a need for a framework for specifying reflection semantics, and for carrying out reflection requests.

The goal of the framework is to allow the tasks of implementing and administering reflection to be componentized. That is, the framework should allow reflection to be customized, on whatever size data granule is appropriate. At the same time, each customization should be easy to specify and change. Pieces that can be applied repeatedly should be reused, to reduce implementation and administration work. As much as possible, tasks should be automated; for example, the system should semi-automatically compose the reflection semantics for primitive derivation operators to generate reflection semantics for a derivation expression. Finally, the degree to which existing databases manage the annotation information and reflection logic should be adjustable; this could be achieved by managing annotations separate from the underlying database thus minimizing the impact on existing systems.

4 Bringing Legacy or Foreign Data into an OO Application Model

We have argued that future applications will be written in terms of application level concepts (sometimes called "business objects"), rather than in terms of an implementation schema. Some experienced consultants advise strongly against trying to create an application schema for a new system by reverse engineering old structures. Instead, they say one should "identify the natural concepts of the application." This advice seems credible. However, to avoid prohibitive cost and delays, the implementation of the new objects must typically leverage existing code and data. That is, we must connect these existing assets to new application and conceptual schemas. In particular, we need to share the data capture process with other applications; while one can run redundant code, redundant data capture is often far costlier.

Section 4.1 considers the case where the legacy data is described only in terms of implementation constructs. This legacy data (perhaps after wrapping) can act as part of the implementation tier and can support at least the data portion of the new schema. Section 4.2 considers situations where one has an EER conceptual data model, either concrete or abstract. (This is likely to be the case only for systems that have been designed recently, with the use of a CASE tool.)

4.1 Migrating Legacy Systems toward Business Objects

According to the consultants' advice, one should use OOA&D to devise an appropriate application schema, before considering the legacy structures. Next, one faces the task of implementing the new types. In data intensive applications, the source of the data may be an external or legacy system that cannot be changed. We suggest below a gradual approach to doing the migration.

Once the new application schema is defined, it may be best to support the data portion first, by deriving it from the existing sources. Only then would one develop methods for the new business objects. There are several rationales:

1. If part or all of data capture is outside the scope of the reengineering, then the input data *must* come from the existing sources, i.e., the new schema must be a view, not a replacement.
2. Methods cannot work until they have data to work on.
3. A data subset is still a usable artifact, while part of a method is of little use.
4. Data semantics tend to be easier to understand than method semantics. It is often more salvageable, less dependent on context.
5. Data views can be written in a high level query language, with good formal tools.

Of course, if a method is easy to reimplement (e.g., with a GUI toolkit) then it too can be included in the early partial implementation of the business objects.

4.2 Are Conceptual Data Models Suitable as the Data Portion of Conceptual Object Models?

Identifying the natural concepts of the application was also the goal of EER domain analysis, so in principle, an EER conceptual schema should provide a good starting point for an object conceptual schema. However, there may be two concerns:

- *How frequently are good EER conceptual schemas available for existing systems?* We suspect that newly developed systems will sometimes have them; older ones will not. Also, when schemas are deployed in DOD's COE, they are often delivered with an EER model. However, frequently these models use EER to give a cleaner description of the implementation structures (notably, of relationships), rather than to give a real application model.
- *How close is a good EER conceptual data schema[2] to a good OO conceptual schema?* OO type hierarchies will be influenced by the ability to inherit methods (not just attributes), and by detailed changes in inheritance semantics and the semantics of nested structures. We have no experience in whether these omissions from EER make the resulting "natural objects" seriously inappropriate for an OO schema. In the reverse direction, we suspect that the data portion of an OO conceptual schema (with nested attributes turned into separate entities) would be a very reasonable EER conceptual data schema.

5   Conclusions

This paper has described three long-awaited convergences which are taking place as a result of the widespread adoption of object technology. We have explored the likely impacts of these developments on the future of data administration and conceptual modeling. In particular, we have discussed the implications on the administration of

---

[2] I.e., a schema with just attribs, not methods.

multi-tier schemas and on bringing legacy or foreign data into an object-oriented application model.

While these convergences present new opportunities, several open problems remain, including:

- Organizations must choose OO formalism(s) and query language(s) soon, despite uncertainties in the standards competition and middleware market. How should they make these decisions? Given the likely continuing existence of heterogeneous formalisms and tools, how should one cope with that? To what extent can user organizations offload the choices to middleware vendors?

- In a multi-formalism world, to what degree can one formalism encapsulate others? What services can be provided through that encapsulation? For example, what does it mean for end-to-end query optimization, change propagation, etc.?

- How should we implement and exploit dependency tracking and configuration management on objects of arbitrary granularity? Given the presence of multiple such tools, how can they cooperate?

- How can administrative actions and metadata at one tier be "appropriately reflected" to tiers above and below, without increasing the required number and skill of administrators? Many critical services including error messages, grant_privilege, and trigger definition currently are supported only for the implementation tier. Similarly, there is need to reflect ancillary metadata (e.g., data source, quality).

- Some research has been done on appropriate semantics, especially for view update and for triggers (e.g., [Bars91, Hans97]), but more is required. Little has been done for metadata such as precision, certainty, and so forth. For administrative effort to be manageable, reflection semantics must be specified by customizing existing, reusable, defaultable components rather than from scratch. Research on frameworks for reflecting data and generic methods is just beginning [Rose97].

6   References

[Alon90] R. Alonso, D. Barbara, and H. Garcia-Molina, "Data Caching Issues in an Information Retrieval System," *ACM Trans. on Database Systems*, 15(3), 1990.

[Bars91] T. Barsalou, A. Keller, N. Siambela, and G. Wiederhold, "Updating Relational Databases through Object-Based Views," *Proc. of ACM-SIGMOD Int. Conf. on Management of Data*, Denver, CO, 1991.

[CACM97]   "Object-Oriented Application Frameworks", *Communications of the ACM*, special section, Oct. 1997.

[Hans97] E. Hanson and S. Khosla, "An Introduction to the TriggerMan Asynchronous Trigger Processor," *Proc. of Third International Workshop on Rules in Database Systems (RIDS '97)*, Skövde, Sweden, Springer Lecture Notes in Computer Science, June 1997

[Rati98] UML Resource Page, Rational Software, http://www.rational.com/uml/index.html

[Rose97] A. Rosenthal, P. Dell, "Propagating Integrity Information in Multi-Tiered Database Systems", *Workshop on Information Quality*, Cambridge, MA, 1997.

[Rose98] A. Rosenthal, "Where Will Object Technology Drive Data Administration?", *ACM SIGMOD Record*, March 1998.

[Seli97] Seligman, L. and L. Kerschberg, "A Mediator for Approximate Consistency: Supporting 'Good Enough' Materialized Views," *Journal of Intelligent Information Systems*, Kluwer Scientific Publishers, 8(2), June 1997.

[Shet90] A. Sheth, J. Larson, "Federated Databases: Architecture and Integration", *ACM Computing Surveys*, Sept. 1990.

[Tsic77] D. Tsichritzis, F. Lochovsky, *Data Base Management Systems*, Academic Press, 1977.

Conceptual Modeling for Multiagent Systems: Applying Interaction-Oriented Programming*

Munindar P. Singh**

Department of Computer Science
North Carolina State University
Raleigh, NC 27695-7534, USA
singh@ncsu.edu

Abstract. Multiagent systems (MAS) are an important paradigm for building complex systems, especially cooperative information systems. Despite much interest in MAS construction, there has not been sufficient progress on the corresponding conceptual modeling representations and techniques. We believe that further extensions to conceptual modeling to include aspects of actions and organizations will be essential for MAS development. These goals are broader than conceptual modeling is traditionally understood, but are essential to deal with the interactive and dynamic aspects of modern applications. We describe an approach termed *interaction-oriented programming*, which incorporates functionality geared toward coordination, commitment management, and collaboration. This functionality is naturally thought of as providing a conceptual metamodel for describing MAS. We suggest some preliminary methodologies pertaining to the design of coordination and commitment requirements.

1 Introduction

Agents and multiagent systems (MAS) are an emerging paradigm for software development, especially of large-scale information systems that are sometimes known as cooperative information systems (CIS) [8]. CIS occur in several important applications, such as enterprise integration and electronic commerce.

Numerous definitions of agents are known in the literature [5,7,12]. Indeed, the only agreement seems to be that there is a range of definitions! Some of the important properties of agents include (a) autonomy, (b) adaptability, and most importantly (c) interactiveness. In practice, an agent need not have each of the above properties. However, we believe that agents must be capable of interacting with other agents at the social or communicative level. We distinguish social or

---

* I am indebted to Peter Chen and Leah Wong for giving me an opportunity to present these results. I have benefited from discussions with several people, especially Manny Aparicio, Michael Huhns, Anuj Jain, and Peter Wegner. I also benefited from careful comments by an anonymous reviewer.

** Supported by the NCSU College of Engineering, the National Science Foundation under grants IRI-9529179 and IRI-9624425 (Career Award), and IBM corporation.

communicative interactions from incidental interactions that agents may have as a consequence of existing in a shared environment. As we elaborate below, we model agents as participating in mini-societies, and being aware of and following their rules and policies.

Indeed, we would go so far as to claim that the potential for participation in a multiagent system is an essential property of agents. Our motto is that *considering agents without MAS is the waste of a good metaphor!* We defend this view more carefully in [6,7]. In general, we take the view, in sympathy with Peter Wegner, that interaction is a key extension beyond traditional computer science [17]. In broad terms, the goal of this paper is to outline what interaction primitives are suitable for multiagent systems, and how they may be incorporated in designing and implementing them.

1.1   Conceptual Modeling in MAS

Although multiagent systems have been known for a number of years and practical applications of them are spreading, they are still being built in a more or less *ad hoc* manner. There is increasing interest in methodologies for their construction. But sound methodologies presuppose accurate conceptual modeling. Further, just as for information systems, conceptual modeling can enable the structure of multiagent systems to be declaratively captured, analyzed, and reused. Conceptual modeling in MAS can apply in two main ways.

Cooperative Information Systems. Developing a good CIS requires extensions of techniques for conceptual modeling of centralized information systems. Notions such as ontologies and mediation [18] and process models [3] provide some principles for CIS design.

Designing Multiagent Systems. For MAS proper, current approaches are virtually *ad hoc.* Prevailing techniques do not support the fundamental properties that make MAS attractive in the first place. The challenges encountered in CIS will continue to be an obstacle when MAS are considered.

1.2   Interaction-Oriented Programming

Conceptual modeling presupposes the identification of the major dimensions in which the concepts used in a specific model may be expressed. For multiagent systems, the development and refinement of these dimensions—analogous to the famous entity-relationship (ER) metamodel—is a major research direction [2,1].

Accordingly, we have been pursuing a program termed *Interaction-Oriented Programming (IOP)* to develop and study primitives for the specification of systems of agents and constraints on their behavior. These primitives include societies, the roles agents may play in them, what capabilities and commitments the roles require, and what authorities they grant. Agents can autonomously instantiate abstract societies by adopting roles in them. The creation, operation, and dissolution of societies are achieved by agents acting autonomously, but satisfying their commitments. A commitment can be canceled provided the agent then satisfies the metacommitments applying to its cancelation.

The representations for IOP must support several functionalities, which typically exist informally, and are either effected by humans in some unprincipled way, are hard-coded in applications, or are buried in operating procedures and manuals. Information typically exists in data stores, in the environment, or is available interacting entities. Existing approaches do not model the interactive aspects of the above. The IOP contribution is that it

- enhances and formalizes ideas from different disciplines
- separates them out in an explicit conceptual metamodel to use as a basis for programming and for programming methodologies
- makes them programmable.

The present paper is an exposition of some of our recent progress on IOP. Additional results are available elsewhere [9,13,14,15].

1.3 Organization

Section 2 describes the concepts of our coordination approach. Section 3 presents a methodology for inducing agent skeletons and coordination relationships. Section 4 introduces a form of commitments that is suited to multiagent systems. It shows how commitments can be operated on, and used to specify social policies. Section 5 applies these notions to formalize applications in electronic commerce and virtual enterprises. Section 6 concludes with a discussion of future directions.

2   Coordination

We summarize the key concepts of coordination in IOP. Additional details are available in [14].

2.1   Coordination Model

There are two aspects of the autonomy of agents that concern us. One, the agents are designed autonomously, and their internal details may be unavailable. Two, the agents act autonomously, and may unilaterally perform certain actions within their purview. We assume that, in order to coordinate individual agents, the designer of a multiagent system has some limited knowledge of their designs. This knowledge is in terms of their externally visible actions, which are potentially significant for coordination. We call these the significant *events* of the agent. In other words, the only events we speak of are those publicly known—the rest are of no concern to coordination.

Event Classes. Our metamodel considers four classes of events, which have different properties with respect to coordination. Events may be

- *flexible*, which the agent is willing to delay or omit
- *inevitable*, which the agent is willing only to delay
- *immediate*, which the agent performs unilaterally, that is, is willing neither to delay nor to omit
- *triggerable*, which the agent is willing to perform if requested.

The first three classes are mutually exclusive; each can be combined with triggerability. The category where an agent will entertain omitting but not delaying an event is empty, because unless the agent performs the event unilaterally, there must be some delay in receiving a response from the service.

Agent Skeletons. It is useful to view the events as organized into a *skeleton*, which provides a simple model of an agent for coordination purposes. The skeletons are typically finite state automata. However, they can be anything as far as our formal system and implementation are concerned—neither looks at their structure. In particular, the skeletons may be sets of finite state automata, which can be used to model the different threads of a multithreaded agent. The set of events, their properties, and the skeleton of an agent depends on the agent, and is application-specific. Example 1 discusses two common skeletons.

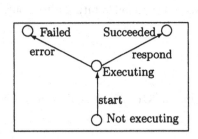
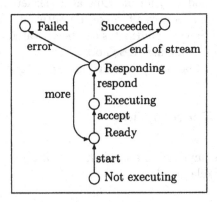

Fig. 1. Example Skeletons: (l) Querying; (r) Information filtering

Example 1. Figure 1 shows two skeletons that arise in information search. The left skeleton is appropriate for agents who perform one-shot queries. Its significant events are *start* (accept an input and begin), *error*, and *respond* (produce an answer and terminate). The right skeleton is appropriate for agents who filter a stream or monitor a database. Its significant events are *start* (accept an input, if necessary, and begin), *error*, *end of stream*, *accept* (accept an input, if necessary), *respond* (produce an answer), *more* (loop back to expecting more input). In both skeletons, the application-specific computation takes place in the node labeled "Executing." We must also specify the categories of the different events. For instance, we may state that *error*, *end of stream*, and *respond* are immediate, and all other events are flexible, and *start* is in addition triggerable.

Although the skeleton is not used explicitly by the coordination service during execution, it can be used to validate specified coordination requirements. More importantly, the skeleton is essential for understanding the public behavior of an agent, and for giving intuitive meaning to its actions.

2.2 Coordination Relationships

Coordinations are specified by expressing appropriate relationships among the events of different agents. Our formal language allows a variety of relationships to be captured. We lack the space to include the formal syntax and semantics here, but please see [14] for details.

	Name	Description	Formal notation
R1	e is·required by f	If f occurs, e must occur before or after f	$e \vee \overline{f}$
R2	e disables f	If e occurs, then f must occur before e	$\overline{e} \vee \overline{f} \vee f \cdot e$
R3	e feeds or enables f	f requires e to occur before	$e \cdot f \vee \overline{f}$
R4	e conditionally feeds f	If e occurs, it feeds f	$\overline{e} \vee e \cdot f \vee \overline{f}$
R5	Guaranteeing e enables f	f can occur only if e has occurred or will occur	$e \wedge f \vee \overline{e} \wedge \overline{f}$
R6	e initiates f	f occurs iff e precedes it	$\overline{e} \wedge \overline{f} \vee e \cdot f$
R7	e and f jointly require g	If e and f occur in any order, then g must also occur (in any order)	$\overline{e} \vee \overline{f} \vee g$
R8	g compensates for e failing f	if e happens and f doesn't, then perform g	$(\overline{e} \vee f \vee g) \wedge (\overline{g} \vee e) \wedge (\overline{g} \vee \overline{f})$

Table 1. Example Relationships

Table 1 presents some common examples. Some of the relationships involve coordinating multiple events. For example, R8 captures requirements such as that if an agent does something (e), but another agent does not match it with something else (f), then a third agent can perform g. This is a typical pattern in applications with data updates, where g corresponds to an action to restore the consistency of the information (potentially) violated by the success of e and the failure of f. Hence the name *compensation*.

3 Designing Coordination

The following example illustrates a methodology for designing the coordination of the agents in a multiagent system. This requires specifying their skeletons and coordination relationships.

3.1 Analyzing Conversations

A *conversation* is a series of communications, possibly terminating in some physical actions. The actions in a conversation are related in various ways. Of the possible relationships among the statements of a conversation, only a few are directly relevant for our purposes. They help structure the conversation in a certain way that is captured in Dooley graphs [4,11]. For simplicity, we consider the communications Solicit (Request or Question) and Assert (Inform, Commit, and Refuse), and the physical actions Ship and Pay [11]. We also consider the following relationships. Here, u_i and u_j refers to different utterances in a conversation. S_i refers to the sender of u_i.

- *Respond.* u_i responds to u_j iff (a) S_i previously received u_j, (b) u_j's impact on S_i caused S_i to send u_i, and (c) u_i is the first utterance of S_i to satisfy (a) and (b).
- *Reply.* u_i replies to u_j iff (a) S_i previously received u_j, (b) u_j's impact on S_i caused S_i to send u_i, and (c) u_i is the first utterance of S_i directed to S_j that satisfies (a) and (b).
- *Resolve.* u_i resolves u_j iff u_i replies u_j and u_i follows the "rules of engagement" defined in u_j.
- *Complete.* u_i completes u_j iff u_j was a Commit and u_i either satisfies or cancels the associated commitment.

Respond, Reply, and Resolve are progressively more restrictive. Complete is mutually exclusive with Resolve—an act cannot both complete an utterance and resolve an utterance (not even a different one).

Example 2. Consider a request for proposals (RFP) from A to B, C, and D. The first act that any of them does that was caused by the RFP is a Response to it. If it is a message back to A, then it is also a Reply. If the Reply is a Commit or a Refuse, then it is also a Resolve.

Example 3. Table 2 shows a conversation from [11]. The #s partially order the utterances from early to late. In this conversation, A announces an RFP for 50 widgets to B, C, and D. B checks with C is C is bidding. C says it is. B then refuses A. C, however, makes a counter offer of 40 widgets. A accepts and C commits. In the meanwhile, D offers to accept the initial RFP, which is more preferable to A. A then declines C, who cancels its commitment. D delivers, but the order is short (45 only). A informs it. When D complies, A pays. Table 2 also shows the discourse relations among the utterances.

#	S	R	Utterance	Respond	Reply	Resolve	Complete
1	A	B,C,D	Request (RFP for 50)				
2	B	C	Question: bidding?	1			
3	C	B	Inform: yes	2	2	2	
4	B	A	Refuse	3	1	1	
5	C	A	Propose (take 40)	1	1		
6	A	C	Request (send 40)	5	5	5	
7	C	A	Commit (deliver 40)	6	6	6	
8	D	A	Commit (deliver 50)	1	1	1	
9	A	C	Assert	7, 8	7		
10	C	A	Refuse	9	9		7
11	D	A	Ship	1	1		8
12	A	D	Assert (short) + Request	11	11		
13	D	A	Ship remainder	12	12	12	
14	A	D	Pay	13	13	13	

Table 2. Example Conversation

A Dooley graph is generated by analyzing a conversation in such a manner that the sets of utterances that are closely related to one another are brought explicitly closer in the representation. Consequently, statements that are temporally separated, but of which one refers to another, are coded as edges from the same vertex, whereas temporally proximate, but unrelated statements are isolated in the graph. The relations among statements are used to induce a set of *characters* from each participant in the conversation. The characters reflect the structure of the conversation, and become the vertices of the graph.

Example 4. Figure 2 gives the Dooley graph for Table 2. The numbered utterances relate the characters that send and receive them.

3.2 Inducing Coordination

We analyze a Dooley graph to identify the causal relationships among utterances. Figure 3 shows the histories derived from the graph of Figure 2. The different characters are highlighted in each history.

Inducing Agent Skeletons Figure 4 shows possible skeletons for B. The first requires the agent to consult C before deciding, and is probably inappropriate (the * indicates an action not in the given conversation). An alternative would require B's decision to depend on C. These would place B's decision-making publicly in the protocol, and are clearly unacceptable. The second skeleton, however, leaves it up to B to decide whether to consult C and how to use its response. This skeleton is preferable, because it captures the intuition about character B_2.

Figure 5 shows a skeleton for C in which C may get a query from B, but this query is structurally independent of how C handles RFPs. Similarly, the

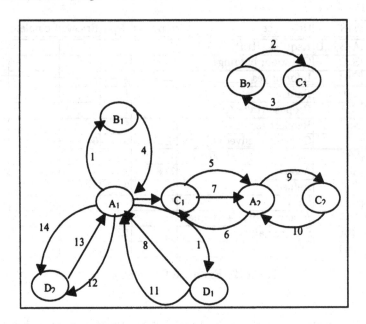

Fig. 2. Example Conversation as a Dooley Graph

B: (A_11B_1); $\boxed{(B_22C_3);(C_33B_2)}$; (B_14A_1)

C: (A_11C_1); $\boxed{(B_22C_3);(C_33B_2)}$; $(C_15A_2);(A_26C_1);(C_17A_2)$; $\boxed{(A_29C_2);(C_210A_2)}$

D: $(A_11D_1);(D_18A_1);(D_111A_1)$; $\boxed{(A_112D_2);(D_213A_1);(A_114D_2)}$

A: $(A_11B_1);(A_11C_1);(A_11D_1);(B_14A_1)$; $\boxed{(C_15A_2);(A_26C_1);(C_17A_2)}$; (D_18A_1);

$\boxed{(A_29C_2);(C_210A_2)}$; $(D_111A_1);(A_112D_2);(D_213A_1);(A_114D_2)$

Fig. 3. The Histories of Agents in a Conversation

counter-proposal is kept as a separate loop but attached to the main flow. This too is a case where a character gets a separate subskeleton, one as a separate thread. (For reasons of space, D is discussed when integrated below.)

Clearly, we must separate what the agents happen to do from what is essential for coordination in the given application. Dooley graphs, by focusing on a specific conversation, are in tension with this process. However, in settings such as our present example, we can derive more information from the graph by recognizing that the same role is instantiated by multiple agents. Here, the multicast by A is a clue that B, C, and D are to be treated alike. In such a case, we can achieve the correct solution by integrating the skeletons. Notice that the integration we propose is much less ambitious than integration of schemas or process models. Integration can be difficult because it is not easy to establish that different components of the objects being integrated are indeed related. In the present

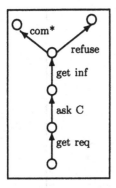

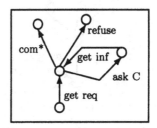

Fig. 4. Possible Skeletons for Agent B

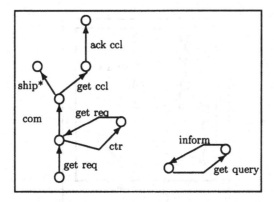

Fig. 5. Possible Skeleton for Agent C

case, our task is greatly simplified because the components being integrated are part of the same family of conversations.

Figure 6 shows a composite skeleton assuming B, C, and D play the role of contractor. By integrating the skeletons, we can construct a single more complete skeleton than any of the agents in the given conversation indicates. The ship and get error loop prior to get paid refers to character D_2 of Figure 2. In this case, giving it a separate loop would have caused the ship action to appear on two different transitions, and would have been less clear.

Figure 7 shows the skeleton for A. The main quirk in this is that A performs a multicast, and effectively keeps a separate thread to deal with each contractor. Note that it is not clear if only one bid can be accepted, because the bids may each be partial. If there were a requirement of uniqueness, it would be captured as a disabling relationship (*a la* R2 in Table 1). For reasons of space, we don't include a discussion of the event classes here.

Inducing Relationships The above example does not involve enough variety of relationships to exercise all of our formal language. There are no important

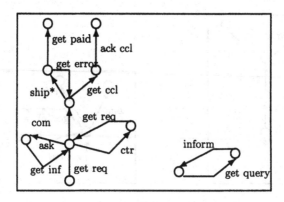

Fig. 6. Integrated Skeleton for All Contractors

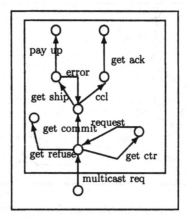

Fig. 7. Skeleton for Agent A

ordering constraints among the events of different agents, except for when triggering is involved. However, the following rules are easily identified—for convenience we refer to Table 1 in the following discussion.

- Every Solicit is Replied to (R1). Replies may or may not be required in every protocol, however.
- The Replies must be enabled by the utterances they Reply to (R3).
- Every Commit is completed (R1).
- Responds is implemented in an application-specific manner. However, input Solicits can enable associated Responds. Sometimes, we may not wish to allow this, e.g., so B can ask C anyway.
- The presence of a non-Reply Respond to an utterance, e.g., $(B_2 2 C_3)$, indicates that the Reply is not required right away. The non-Reply Respond itself is done unilaterally by the agent and must be modeled as immediate.

4   Commitments

We now turn our attention to the next higher layer of IOP, which deals with commitments among agents, especially as the commitments relate to the social and organizational structure of a multiagent system.

The notion of commitments is familiar from database transactions. However, in databases, commitments correspond to a value being declared and are identified with the successful termination of a transaction. When a transaction terminates successfully, it commits, but it is not around any more to modify its commitments. Thus the commitments are rigid and irrevocable. If the data value committed by one transaction must be modified, then a separate, logically independent transaction must be executed to commit the modified value. Traditional commitments presuppose that different computations are fully isolated and that locks can be held long enough that the atomicity of distributed computations can be assured.

Although suitable for traditional data processing, the above reasons cause traditional commitments to be highly undesirable for modern applications such as electronic commerce and virtual enterprises, where autonomous entities must carry out prolonged interactions with one another [13].

Commitments reflect an inherent tension between predictability and flexibility. By having commitments, agents become easier to deal with. Also, the desired commitments serve as a sort of requirements on the construction of the agents who meet those commitments. However, commitments reduce the options available to an agent.

4.1   Commitments Formalized

We propose an alternative characterization of commitments that is better suited to agents and multiagent systems. In our formulation the commitments are directed to specific parties in a specific context. Thus an agent may not offer the same commitments to every other agent. The context is the multiagent system within which the given agents interact. Sometimes, this multiagent system is termed a *sphere of commitment (SoCom)*. Our approach provides a natural mechanism for commitments to be modified dynamically.

The *debtor* refers to the agent who makes a commitment, and the *creditor* to the agent who receives the commitment. Commitments are formed in a *context*, which is given by the enclosing SoCom (or, ultimately, by society at large). Based on the above intuitions, we motivate the following logical form for commitments.

Definition 1. A commitment $C(x, y, p, G)$ relates a debtor x, a creditor y, a context G, and a discharge condition p.

4.2   Operations on Commitments

We define the following operations on commitments.

O1. *Create* instantiates a commitment; it is typically performed as a consequence of an agent adopting a role or by exercising a social policy (explained below).

O2. *Discharge* satisfies the commitment; it is performed by the debtor concurrently with the actions that lead to the given condition being satisfied.

O3. *Cancel* revokes the commitment. It can be performed by the debtor.

O4. *Release* essentially eliminates the commitment. This is distinguished from
both *discharge* and *cancel*, because *release* does not mean success or failure
of the given commitment, although it lets the debtor off the hook. The
release action may be performed by the context or the creditor of the
given commitment.

O5. *Delegate* shifts the role of debtor to another agent within the same context,
and can be performed by the new debtor or the context.

O6. *Assign* transfers a commitment to another creditor within the same context, and can be performed by the present creditor or the context.

For simplicity, we write the above operations also as propositions, indicating
their successful execution. We define some additional operations and propositions
corresponding to important speech acts. These include *notify* and *authorize*.
notify(x, y, q) mean that x notifies y of q, and *authorize*(x, y, p) means that x
authorizes y to allow condition p.

4.3   Policies

Social policies are conditional expressions involving commitments and operations on commitments. Policies have a computational significance, which is
that they can help control the execution of operations on commitments, even
without explicit reference to the context. Agents can commit to social policies just as to other expressions; in this case, the agents' commitments are
higher order, and are termed *metacommitments*. An example metacommitment
is *cancel*$(x, C(x, y, p, G)) \Rightarrow$ *create*$(x, C(x, y, q, G))$, which means that x can cancel his commitment for p if instead he adopts a commitment for q (for suitable
p and q).

4.4   Applying Commitments

We envisage the following way to apply commitments. Initially, abstract SoComs
are defined in terms of their *roles*. Each role is associated with the capabilities it
requires, the commitments it engenders, and the authorities it creates. The capabilities are the tasks the agent can do, the commitments are what the agent must
do, and the authorities are what the agent may do. The commitments, in particular, may be metacommitments. Indeed, they usually are metacommitments,
e.g., that the agent will adopt a base commitment upon receiving a request.

At some point, possibly during execution, an agent may decide to enter into a SoCom as a particular role or roles. To do so, he would have to cause the SoCom to be instantiated from the abstract specification. To adopt a role, the agent must have the necessary capabilities, and accept the associated commitments. In doing so, he also obtains the authorities to properly play the role. The agent must then behave according to the commitments. Agents can join a SoCom when configured by humans or during execution: this requires publishing the definition of the abstract SoCom.

5   Designing Commitments

We consider an example in two parts. The first deals with electronic commerce; the second combines in aspects of virtual enterprises [9]. The commitments are designed based on the corresponding roles in human society.

5.1   Electronic Commerce

We first define an abstract SoCom consisting of two roles: *buyer* and *seller*, which require capabilities and commitments about, e.g., the requests they will honor, and the validity of price quotes. To adopt these roles, agents must have the capabilities and acquire the commitments. Example 5 involves two individual agents who adopt the roles of *Buyer* and *Seller* to carry out a simple deal.

Example 5. Consider a situation involving two agents, *Customer* and *Vendor*, with authority over their respective databases. The SoCom manager has an abstract SoCom for buy-sell deals with the roles of *Buyer* and *Seller*. *Buyer*'s capabilities include asking for a price quote and placing an order. *Seller*'s capabilities include responding to price quotes and accepting orders based on checking the inventory locally. *Buyer*'s commitments include paying the quoted price for anything she orders. *Seller*'s commitments include (a) giving price quotes in response to requests and (b) fulfilling orders that he has accepted.

Customer asks the manager to instantiate a deal between her as *Buyer* and *Vendor* as *Seller*. The manager asks *Vendor* if he would like to join as *Seller*. When *Vendor* agrees, and since both agents have the requisite capabilities, capacities, and resources, the deal is set up.

Customer now wishes to check the price of a valve with a diameter of 21mm. Upon the receipt of the query from *Customer*, *Vendor*—based on its role as *Seller*—offers an appropriate answer.

5.2   Virtual Enterprises

Example 6 considers a more general situation where the role of *Seller* is adopted by an agent who happens to be a Valvano-cum-Hoosier VE—i.e., a SoCom consisting of the hose and valve vendors. Example 7 considers the situation where the Valvano-cum-Hoosier VE detects a problem in the supply of valves for which an order has been placed. The VE automatically meets its commitments by revising the order and notifying the customer.

Now we consider the situation where one or more agents may form a cooperative SoCom or team. For simplicity, we assume that teams have a distinguished agent who handles their external interactions. We refer to this agent as the VE.

Example 6. We now consider two agents with authority over the Valvano and Hoosier databases, respectively. These agents have similar capabilities to the *Seller* of Example 5. They form a VE, called Valvano-cum-Hoosier VE, which can adopt the role of *Seller*. *Buyer* behaves as before and expects *Seller* to behave according to the buy-sell deal. However, *Seller* is implemented differently, with commitments among its members, which we do not elaborate here. The possible commitments of the Valvano-cum-Hoosier VE include the following.

- The VE will give price quotes to anyone who requests them.
- The VE will refund the purchase price if an order with matching valves and hoses cannot be fulfilled. There are still no refunds if an order for matching valves and hoses can be fulfilled.
- If the VE cannot fulfill an order, it will try to find an alternative order that will satisfy *Customer*'s requirements.

Recall that *val* or *hos* would not take refunds individually. Thus a customer might be saddled with valves for which matching hoses could not be found. However, when dealing with the VE, a customer can get a refund in those situations.

In the above examples, the actions are performed by the constituents of the SoCom. Sometimes, however, it is useful to perform actions at a higher level SoCom. Such actions might be necessary when the actions of the member agents need to be atomically performed or undone.

Example 7. Continuing with Example 6, suppose an order for matching valves and hoses is successfully placed. It turns out later that the valve manufacturer discontinued the model that was ordered, but recommends a substitute. The substitute valve fits different diameter hoses than the original choice. The VE knows that the original order could be satisfied using the new valve and a different set of hoses. The VE can handle this replacement itself and, based on its prior commitment, not charge the customer any extra. The customer does not need to know of the internal exchanges among the members of the VE SoCom.

In the above example, the discontinuation of a valve after an order for it was accepted is a kind of failure that arises after the original interaction had ended. By using flexible commitments, our approach can effectively recover from this failure. Traditional approaches would be inapplicable in such a situation.

6   Conclusions and Future Work

We described interaction-oriented programming, and outlined some conceptual modeling issues in it. IOP offers some benefits over previous approaches for building multiagent systems. In the spirit of conceptual modeling, IOP focuses on higher-level concepts than the underlying implementations. These concepts provide a better starting point than the traditional approaches. Specifically,

- coordination, commitment, collaboration are captured as first-class concepts that can be applied directly
- the underlying infrastructure is separated, leading to improved portability.

Fundamentally, conceptual modeling is as good as the methodologies that one may use to build conceptual models. Accordingly, we have been considering methodologies that may be applicable to IOP. In the above, we gave a sampler of some of our preliminary results. These methodologies are presently being applied by hand, although there is some work afoot to build tools to assist in their application.

There are some important directions for future research. Of special interest to conceptual modeling is the development of richer metamodels than we have at present. A potentially important theme is to identify useful patterns corresponding to the "best practices" in key areas, and incorporating them in our metamodels. An example area would be contracting among autonomous entities, which seems to underlie several of the upcoming open applications. Along with richer metamodels, there is need for a corresponding intuitive semantics. We have made some progress along this direction [16]. One of the themes that should be more intensively addressed is the compositionality of conceptual models. For example, one would like to build separate models for electronic commerce and virtual enterprises, and dynamically compose them to produce a model for virtual enterprises engaged as sellers. Lastly, there is great need for expressive formal tools that support the conceptual models and their semantics.

References

1. Carlo Batini, Stefano Ceri, and Shamkant Navathe. *Conceptual Database Design*. Benjamin Cummings, Redwood City, CA, 1992.
2. Peter P. Chen. The entity-relationship model - toward a unified view of data. *ACM Transactions on Database Systems*, 1(1):9–36, 1976.
3. Bill Curtis, Marc I. Kellner, and Jim Over. Process modeling. *Communications of the ACM*, 35(9):75–90, September 1992.
4. R. A. Dooley. Appendix B: Repartee as a graph. In *[10]*, pages 348–358. 1976.
5. Stan Franklin and Art Graesser. Is it an agent or just a program?: A taxonomy for autonomous agents. In *Intelligent Agents III: Agent Theories, Architectures, and Languages*, pages 21–35. Springer-Verlag, 1997.
6. Michael N. Huhns and Munindar P. Singh. The agent test. *IEEE Internet Computing*, 1(5):78–79, October 1997. Instance of the column *Agents on the Web*.
7. Michael N. Huhns and Munindar P. Singh. Agents and multiagent systems: Themes, approaches, and challenges. In *[8]*, chapter 1, pages 1–23. 1998.
8. Michael N. Huhns and Munindar P. Singh, editors. *Readings in Agents*. Morgan Kaufmann, San Francisco, 1998.

9. Anuj K. Jain and Munindar P. Singh. Using spheres of commitment to support virtual enterprises. In *Proceedings of the 4th ISPE International Conference on Concurrent Engineering: Research and Applications (CE)*, pages 469–476. International Society for Productivity Enhancements (ISPE), August 1997.

10. Robert E. Longacre. *An Anatomy of Speech Notions*. Peter de Ridder, Lisse, 1976.

11. H. Van Dyke Parunak. Visualizing agent conversations: Using enhanced Dooley graphs for agent design and analysis. In *Proceedings of the 2nd International Conference on Multiagent Systems*, pages 275–282. AAAI Press, 1996.

12. Charles J. Petrie, Jr. Agent-based engineering, the web, and intelligence. *IEEE Expert*, 11(6):24–29, December 1996.

13. Munindar P. Singh. Commitments among autonomous agents in information-rich environments. In *Proceedings of the 8th European Workshop on Modelling Autonomous Agents in a Multi-Agent World (MAAMAW)*, pages 141–155. Springer-Verlag, May 1997.

14. Munindar P. Singh. A customizable coordination service for autonomous agents. In *Intelligent Agents IV: Proceedings of the 4th International Workshop on Agent Theories, Architectures, and Languages (ATAL-97)*, pages 93–106. Springer-Verlag, 1998.

15. Munindar P. Singh. Developing formal specifications to coordinate heterogeneous autonomous agents. In *Proceedings of the 3rd International Conference on Multiagent Systems (ICMAS)*, pages 261–268. IEEE Computer Society Press, July 1998.

16. Munindar P. Singh. An ontology for commitments in multiagent systems: Toward a unification of normative concepts. *Artificial Intelligence and Law*, 1998. In press.

17. Peter Wegner. Why interaction is more powerful than algorithms. *Communications of the ACM*, 40(5):80–91, May 1997.

18. Gio Wiederhold and Michael Genesereth. The conceptual basis for mediation services. *IEEE Expert*, 12(5):38–47, September 1997.

Data and What They Refer to

Arne Sølvberg

Department of Computer and Information Sciences
The Norwegian University of Science and Technology (NTNU)
Trondheim, Norway
email: asolvber@idi.ntnu.no

Abstract. In data modeling there is an implicit assumption of a one-to-one correspondence between a data model and the world which the data convey information about. Each data item (value) in the data base corresponds to a property of the world. Our view of the data base reflects our view of the world. For simple situations this is enough, e.g., one data record for each person. For complex situations the simple one-to-one correspondence is no longer enough. When the number of worldly phenomena and the number of data names grow, it becomes increasingly difficult to keep track of how the various concepts relate to each other. Many different views of the world may co-exist, each view serving different purpose and/or different people. No view is more correct than another because each view serves a worthy purpose.

Conceptual data models have been proposed as tools for relating the various world views. For many years research has been conducted in the data base field, in artificial intelligence and information systems to find representions of knowledge that may be easily accepted among users as well as among designers of software and data bases. In spite of the many research efforts we find that various dialects of the ER-model still dominate in the practical world.

For a conceptual model to be successful it should relate well to common sense views of the world, and also relate well to commonly known mathematical formalisms. These are necessary preconditions for being widely accepted. We propose a modeling framework which meets these two conditions. We relate to a common sense view of the world which is based on the old distinctions among ideas, concepts, matter, and images. The mathematical form is elementary discrete mathematics, which in its most simple form is common sense knowledge, even known to children in the elementary school. A visual language for data modeling is supported by a tool which at present consists of an editor and an administrative system for supporting concurrent information systems engineering.

Introduction

Techniques for information storage and exchange have changed dramatically over the last 20 years. The information processing machines - the computers - are everywhere. Hybrid systems of humans, computers and physical devices have become commonplace, e.g., in airplanes and in automobiles. How we comprehend the basic relationships among data, machines and humans have nevertheless by and large gone

P.P. Chen et al. (Eds.): Conceptual Modeling, LNCS 1565, pp. 211-226, 1999.
© Springer-Verlag Berlin Heidelberg 1999

unchanged by the computer revolution. The prevailing view is that computers deal in data, and that the data must be interpreted by people in order to convey information. Data is interpreted relative to how the human interpreter perceives the phenomena that the data refer to. More often than not there is no explicit model of the world for the human interpreter to lean to. The usual situation is that world models are conveyed by the names of the various symbols and symbol sets that appear in the computers. The world models are usually implicit to the interpreters.

The relationship between a symbol and what the symbol denotes has always been of concern to philosophers. With the invention of computers this issue is of new importance. Our society has become symbol-oriented to a degree previously unknown. Symbols have been given an extended existence in their own right as objects of manipulation by computers. Symbols that were previously subject only to human interpretation are now interpreted by formal rules. Implicit name-based interpretation schemes are no longer sufficient.

In the sequel we propose a framework for semantic data modelling which is based on the well known distinction between symbols and referents as found in the classical semiotic triangle (1st). The semiotic triangle relates symbols, referents and concepts to each other. A referent is what is referred to by a symbol. The symbol «stands for« the referent. The meaning of the symbol is conveyed by the concept which classifies the referent, and to which the symbol is related.

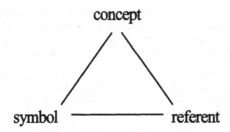

Figure 1 The semiotic triangle

The framework incorporates many of the constructs that have been proposed in previous modeling languages, e.g., the ER-model, the relational model, and binary models like NIAM (Nijssen89). In this paper we discuss the relationships among concepts, information, and data We propose a visual modeling language based on elementary discrete mathematics.

Conventional Data Modeling Needs Enrichment

Contemporary approaches to data modeling, e.g., the ER-model (Chen76) and the relational model of data (Codd70), were proposed in the 1970's in order to support the needs of the data base designers. In those early days most databases were implemented on mainframe computers, and were designed to support single company functions, like payroll or accounting. Each design team was mostly in total control of their data base, and would usually collaborate with representatives of future users in order to forge an agreed way of viewing those parts of the world which were to be represented by data. In most situations the complexity of the task was limited, and the agreed world view could be mapped directly into data structures. The data model was implicitly seen as a model of the world.

This view of a one-to-one correspondence between the model of the data base and the model of the world has been deeply engrained in the data base community ever since. From the beginning it was evident that both the ER-model and the relational model would have to be extended in order to cope with the problems of data base integration, when several data bases employing different world views should be made to co-exist. The relational model was extended with the concept of a universal relation which was to reflect an integrated view of all relevant data bases. The concept of local views of data was proposed, and much effort was given to finding ways of defining the semantics of one local view of data relative to another one (Navathe86). The object oriented model of data represents another effort to the same end. None of these efforts have been completely successful. In spite of that, the original approaches to data modeling are still successful, in the sense that they are widely used, because they solve enough of the modeling problems to still be useful.

In all of the extension efforts the concept of a "super data base designer" - the data base administrator - has been implicit, as a reflection of the view of a one-to-one correspondence between the model of the data base and the model of the world. With the invention of the World Wide Web this view can no longer prevail. All data in the whole world can now be made available to everybody in the world. The problem is that there is no way of finding the desired data, except of by trial and error, and by employing search engines to retrieve data which happen to have a straightforward name. There is no universal data base administrator, and there will never be. All of the world's information is available, but nobody can be sure whether the retrieved data is what they need, or whether what they need is still out there and has not been found. The precision of retrieving is bad, as is the quality of the recall.

One obvious approach to solving the problem is to mimic the librarians taxonomies and classification schemes, by creating large and encompassing meta-data schemes. In that way one enforces a standard world view. This may be seen as instituting a universal data base administrator. It is hard to see that this can be successful if not accompanied by other measures. The world has many facets. It will be impossible to capture enough of the world's variety in a standard vocabulary. It must be possible to work with data bases that reflect on worldly phenomena that have not yet been seen by the "universal data base administrator". To this end we propose, in the sequel, a way of modeling information as a relationship between a model of data and a model of the world that the data refers to.

Conceptual Modeling of Data: The Context

Conceptual models are to be used for communication among those who are involved in the development and operation of information systems. They have different educational backgrounds, ranging from educations that emphasise the students' abstraction skills, to vocational training or primary school alone. In order to serve its purpose as a bridge for communication the modeling framework should relate to a context which is shared by everybody. So we try to relate conceptual modeling to common sense views and concepts.

The basic framework of thinking about nature in the western culture was developed in ancient Greece. Plato used the notions of idea, concept, matter and image (picture, shadow) for discussing the various aspects of the world (2.). These notions were further developed by Aristotle and have been basic to philosophical debate ever since, having been interpreted and reinterpreted over and over again. Different times have seen emphasis put on different aspects of the basic framework, e.g. the ethical/religious aspects (3.), the linguistic aspects (9.). One may even try to place computer science into this broad framework (4.), with its concentration on data (symbol, picture, image) and programs (rules, ideas).

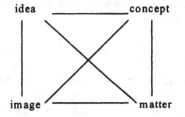

Figure 2 Basic notions of thinking

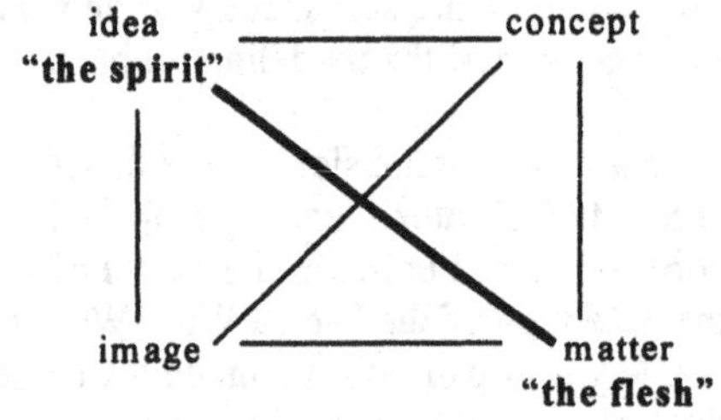

Figure 3 Basic notions for thinking The religious/ethical dimension

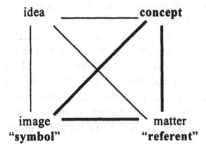

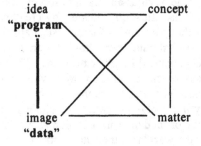

Figure 4 Basic notions for thinking linguistic dimension

Figure 5 Basic notions of thinking The The computer science dimension

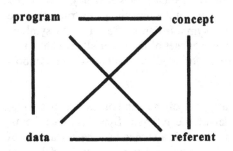

Figure 6 Conceptual modeling: the context

We choose a framework for conceptual modeling where referents substitute matter in the old Greek framework, data substitutes image, and program substitute idea, while the concept of concept is kept in its place in the framework (6.). The different notions are of course reinterpreted relative to the older framework, e.g. referents may be any physical ("matter") or abstract ("idea") entity. A referent is what is referred to. Anything that may be thought of and described may serve as a referent. This means that also data (symbols, pictures, images) may serve as referents, and be referred to by other data.

We may thus view the world as consisting of things, symbols and ideas that all may serve as referents. Everything may be classified in various sets of referents, where each set may be viewed as the extension of a concept, e.g., the extension of the concept of horse is the set of all horses.

The Referent Model of Data: The Framework

In accordance with the distinction between symbol and referent in the semiotic triangle we propose a framework for the modeling of symbols as well as of referents (Figure 7). The basic framework supports the view that referents have an existence in

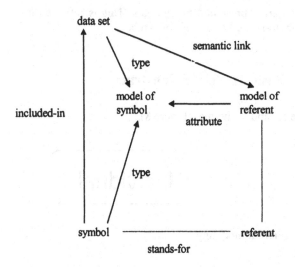

their own right, independent of which symbols that denote them. The symbols may be manipulated by computers - and by human beings- even if the referents may not. The meaning of the symbols is conveyed by their relationship to the referents and to the concepts that classify the referents. The symbol side of the framework supports the modeling of data to be stored in a computer, while the referent side supports the human interpreter's modeling of the worldly phenomena which the symbols "stand" for.

Figure 7 Referent model of data, the basic framework

Because symbols (data) may serve as referents in situations where they are referred to by other symbols (data) it becomes neccessary that the modeling constructs that are applied for referents may also be applied for symbols(data). The set of all symbols (data-elements) are consequently to be seen as a subset of the set of all referents. It is therefore convenient to use similar constructs for modeling referents and symbols (data).

We distinguish between a symbol and a model of the symbol, as we in general distinguish between a referent and a model of the referent. Symbols (data items, values) may be included in collections (data sets). It is assumed that the "meaning" of data may be expressed through "semantic links" between data sets and a model of the referents which the data items carry information about.

In the basic framework of the referent model of data we assume that a data set may be constructed which is in one-to-one correspondence with some referent set. Each data item (symbol, value) in the data set thus "stands" for a referent, and the set of data values is equivalent to a set of referents. Equivalence means that for each item in the data set there is exactly one individual member in a corresponding set of referents, and vice versa.

The framework supports modeling both at the extentional level and at the intentional level. Instances of symbols (data values) and referents (via their abstract models) are viewed as elements of sets. Explicit representation at the instance level is restricted to symbols (data values). It is usually not practical to explicitly handle the worldly instances, e.g., individual horses, when designing information systems that deal with information about horses. This is indicated by the broken lines between the individual referent and its model, and between the individual referent and the symbol that denotes («stands for») the referent.

Referent have properties, which are represented by symbols. This is reflected by letting models of referents be attribute-related to models of symbols.

Conceptual Modeling: The Basic Modeling Constructs

The basic modeling constructs are set and individual (Figure 8).

Figure 8 Sets and individuals in referent modeling

It is furthermore necessary to be able to relate individuals to sets. It is possible to define arbitrary set members, and to define particular members of sets, e.g. let x be a member of the set of Norwegians, and Arne Sølvberg is a particular member of the set of Norwegians, respectively (Figure 9).

Further details of a visual language for referent modeling will be presented in the sequel. First we shall discuss the relationship between referents and symbols, that is in our context, the relationship between referents and data.

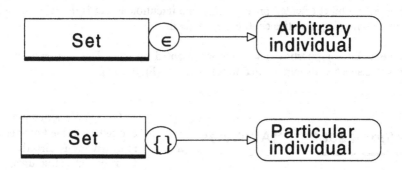

Figure 9 Particular and arbitrary members of sets

We distuinguish between symbol sets (value sets) and data sets. In a data set different data items may hold the same valye, so that one and the same data value may appear several times, as in a data file of the christian names of all Norwegians, where we surely will find a lot of 'Ole' character strings. A value set contains only one instance of each value, e.g. the set of all christian names used by Norwegians, where we will find the 'Ole' character string only once. The visual language symbols are shown in Figure 10.

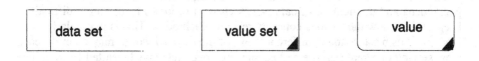

Figure 10 Data set, value set and value

A value set assumes the role of a conceptual model of symbols, in the same way as a referent set serves as a conceptual model of referents. We consequently see from the basic framework in Figure 7 that a value set may serve as a data type as used in programming languages, and a referent set may serve as a referent type.

We want to be able to reason both in extensions and intentions of concepts, so it would be quite useful to let one modeling construct carry both the type aspect and the set aspect of a concept. The set of things (entities) that belong to a concept is called the extension of the concept. There is a distinction between the modeling of the extension of concepts, e.g., a set of horses, and the modeling of the intention of concepts, e.g., what it is to be a horse. The latter has to do with the properties that are characteristic for the things (entities) that belong to the concept. This includes the dynamic properties, and may well be seen as analogue to the "idea" dimension on our framework. In object oriented programming the intention aspect is modeled as object types with dynamic properties captured as methods.

Referents have properties. These are represented by data. This is represented by letting value sets be attribute related to referent sets (Figure 11).

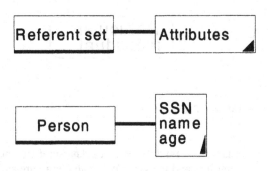

Figure 11 Referent sets have attributes

For simple situations it is enough to define knowledge's representations directly in the form of data structures, e.g., relevant knowledge about persons may be represented as a collection of data for the persons' names, social security numbers, ages, and so on, and may be structured in tuples such as <name, ssn, age, ... > . The tuples (e.g., one tuple for each person) may be stored in a file or a table, or in some other type of repository. For simple situations, when there are few phenomena to keep track of in the external world, such representations are sufficient.

For more complex situations this is not enough. When the number of external phenomena and the number of data names grow, it becomes increasingly difficult to keep track of how the various concepts relate to each other. This is particularly so in large systems because many different views of the external world may co-exist, each view serving different purpose and people, e.g., one view may be suited for suppliers of goods, and another view for the vendors of the same goods (Figure 12).

The world thus becomes subject to various classifications and selections of phenomena, based on judgement of relevance. No view is seen to be more correct than another view, because each view serves a worthy purpose. It becomes important to relate the various views to each other, in such a way that the meaning of data in one view may be preserved when transforming the data into new data structures to be interpreted in another world view. The referent model of data contains constructs for supporting conceptual modeling to this end.

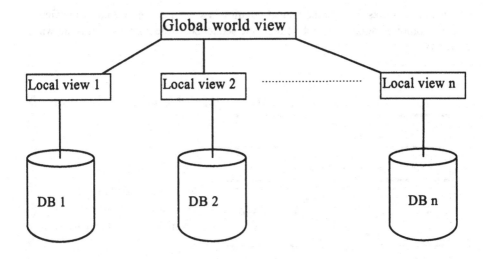

Figure 12 Heterogeneous data bases

The Modeling Language: Basic Constructs for Referent Modeling at the Extensional Level

The modeling language is a visual language which reflects the vocabulary of elementary discrete mathematics. We have shown how we distinguish between set and individual and how data are related to referents through attribute-realationships. In order to relate concepts to each other we use the well known modeling constructs of function, relation, subset, partition, cartesian product and composition. All of these are for modeling at the extensional level.

We choose the visual language to be as close to usual mathematical formalism as possible. Functions are many-to-one relations or one-to-one correspondences. We use the arrow to point from the many to the one, and the double-directed arrow to indicate the one-to-one correspondence (Figure 13). This is in accordance standard mathematical notation. Non-functional relations (many-to-many) are indicated by lines without arrowheads. Coverage is specified by using a filled circle at either end of the functional arrow (the relational line).

In conceptual modeling it is quite commonplace to reason with composite relations, e.g., we use the concepts of father and grandfather in the same sentence, even when we know that the concept of father is enough because grandfather is father's father. Mathematical composition comes in as a handy modeling construct for specifying derived relations. In Figure 14 is depicted an example where students take courses which are lectured at institutes, and where students therefore are related directly to the appropriate lecturing institute by a Takes-course-at relation which is a composition of the two more primitive relations which relate students to courses and courses to institutes. The mathematical notation is shown at the bottom of the figure, while a graphical notation which reflects the sequence of the composition is shown in figure b).

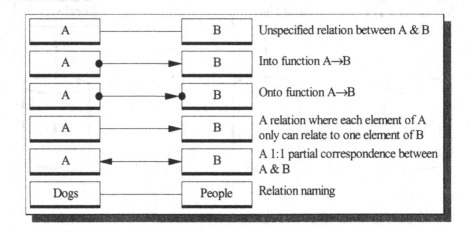

Figure 13 Graphical notations: functions and relations

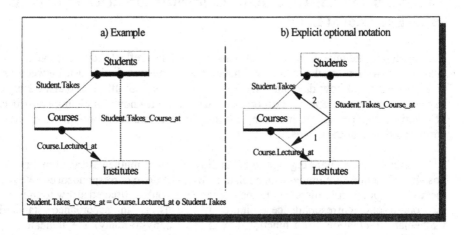

Figure 14 Derived relation (a) with explicit graphical notation (b)

The modeling construct of composition is a very powerful one, because it permits the definition of new concepts in much the same way as we find in a thesaurus, but in a mathematical strict form which prevents misunderstandings. Furthermore, the notion of composition permits us to simultaneously use concepts which refer to different levels of abstraction. This is a very useful feature which reflects common use of language.

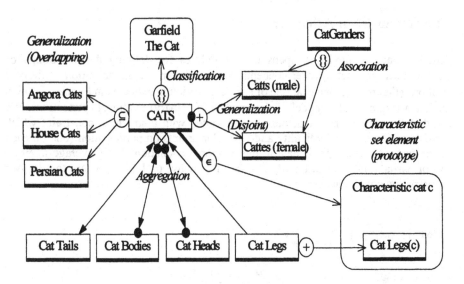

Figure 15 Referent model for the concept of Cats

We also need visual language constructs for the mathematical notions of subset, partition and cartesian product. Together with the membership constructs (Figure 9) these form the constructs that are necessary to express the well-known modeling features of classification, association, generalization and aggregation. As an example a conceptual model of cats is depicted in Figure 15, in its extensional form. We see that the set of CATS have subsets Angora cats, House cats and Persian cats, which are possibly overlapping sets, such that a cat may belong to none, one or more of those sets.

We may also partition the set of CATS in two disjoint subsets Catts and Cattes, so that each cat is either a male catt or a female catte. These two subsets may be viewed as two particular members of the set (of sets) CatGenders (which is a partition of CATS). Furthermore, Garfield The Cat is a particular member of the set of CATS. There is also a possibility for defining the characteristic (stereotype, prototype) cat by using the 'arbitrary member' symbol, a feature which is not explained further here.

By using the crossproduct symbol we define the set of CATS to be a cartesian product in Cat Tails, Cat Bodies, Cat Heads, and Cat Legs. CATS are consequently seen as a mathematical relation. We see that the essential properties of members of the set of CATS are that they must have exactly one body and one head, because of the total one-to-one correspondences. A cat may have exactly one tail, but need not have one (partial one-to-one correspondence), and a cat may have several legs (function into CATS). We also see that there are no spare cat heads or cat bodies, while we open for loose tails and loose legs. This reflects that a cat without a body (or a head) is hardly a cat any more, while cats without tail and/or without one or more legs are still considered to be cats. The cartesian product provides the set-oriented equivalent to the part-of construct found in semantic net based modeling approaches.

The Semantics of Attributes

This approach to modeling opens up possibilities for defining the «meaning» of concepts with respect to other concepts, as was shown for the definition of derived relations (Figure 14). One example of such conversion is indicated in Figure 16 which depicts a fragment of a model of the concept of (binary) relational connections. We see that every relational connection is associated with a structural constraint which consists of Coverage, Cardinality and two Constraints on participation (one on each of the two sets which participate in the relational connction. The Coverage is either full or partial, and the Cardinality is either M (many) or 1 (one), as are the the two participation constraints also.

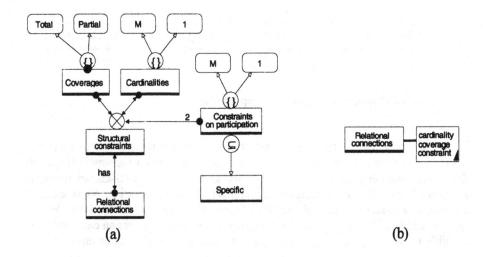

(a)   (b)

Figure 16 Converting from referent set to attribute

The conceptual model of figure a) is converted to the conceptual model of figure b) by applying mathematical composition for defining the attributes coverage, cardinality and constraint. The definition of the coverage attribute is

>   Relational connections $\underline{b}$. coverage =
>   Relational connections $\underline{a}$. has . Structural constraints . Coverages . **id**

which is to be read as follows:

>   The Relational connections coverage-attribute of figure b) is defined by the figure a) path Relational connections . has . Structural constraints . Coverages . **id** where **id** stands for a value set which uniquely selects each of the the elements Full or Partial in the Coverage set of figure a).

While this defines the meaning of the coverage attribute it leaves its representation to be decided, e.g. a boolean, the integer numbers 0 and 1, the character strings 'F' and 'P'.

This example, and the previous examples show that it is possible to keep a model of concepts which are defined relative to each other, which represent different levels of abstractions, and to have a formal expression of the «meaning» of the various concepts.

The Referent Model of Data and the ER-Model

There is a one-to-one correspondence between some of the modelling constructs of the referent model language (RML) and the ER-model, as shown in Figure 17 (Aubert98). The ER-dialect depicted in the figure is representative for the ER-model. We see that the ER-language constructs reflect the RML-constructs for defining sets and relations.

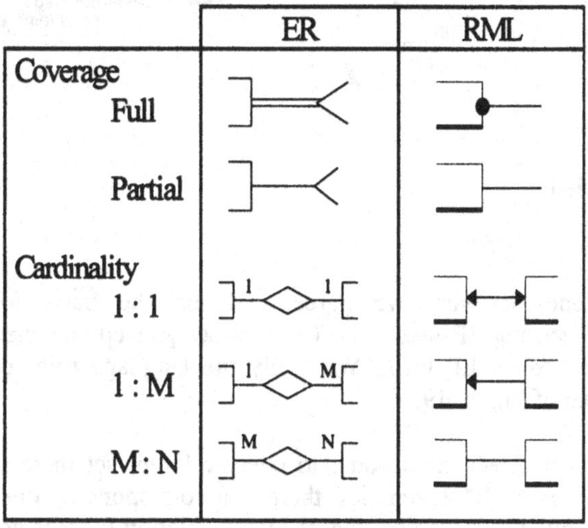

In ER there are no explicit constructs for defining compositions, or for subsetting, partitioning, and so on. All of these may be expressed in various ER-dialects, but in fairly complicated and implicit ways. This is to be expected because the ER-model is first and foremost for data-modeling, not for the modeling of concepts. An ER-model should therefore be seen as a data-model expression of a selection of concepts from a referent model.

Figure 17 Referent model versus ER-model

An Example of Conversion from RML to ER

The following example indicates how one would proceed from conceptual analysis and design of an information system to database design. The example is taken from (Aubert98) and is a modeling of structured storing of ER-diagrams. The example is not complete, due to space considerations. Figure 18 depicts a simplified referent model of the Entity -Relationship model of data. This model is a result of converting the conceptual structures of a previous model to the attribute structure of Figure 18, using the composition technique explained earlier in this paper (see Figure **16**).

The simplified referent model of the ER-model of data contains concepts Datastores, Entities, Attributes, Relationships, and Relational connections, expressed in RML as referent sets. Each of the concepts have their properties described by RML-attributes, and they are related to each other via RML-relations. There is one derived relation R.connects, which represents the path from Entities via Relationships to Relational connections in Figure 18.

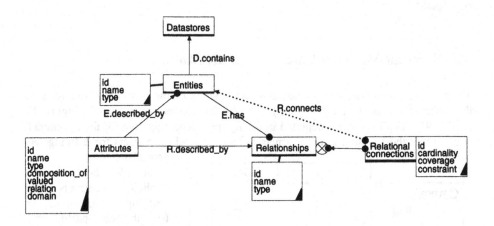

Figure 18 ER-model, simplified

Assume that this RML-model is what we agree shall be the basis for implementation of a database for storing ER-diagrams. The next design step may then be to transform the RML-model to an ER-form. We apply the language rules of Figure 17 and get the ER-diagram of Figure 19.

Most of the transformations are direct one-to-one: to every referent set there is corresponding ER-entity, and to every RML-function there is a corresponding one-many ER-relationship. From the two figures we see that the RML-relation E.has is not represented in the ER-diagram. We have instead decided to represent the concept E.has (the RML-relation between Entities and Relationships of Figure 18) by the ER-equivalents of the derived RML-relation R.connects and the RML-function from Relational connections to Relationships.

From this we see that design decisions are made when going from the conceptual modeling realm of RML to the database realm of the ER-model. In general we lose information through the transformation. ER-models are closer to reflect a one-to-one correspondence to database tables than they are to referent models. It is of course straightforward to set up the database tables that correspond to Figure 19, so we will not do that here.

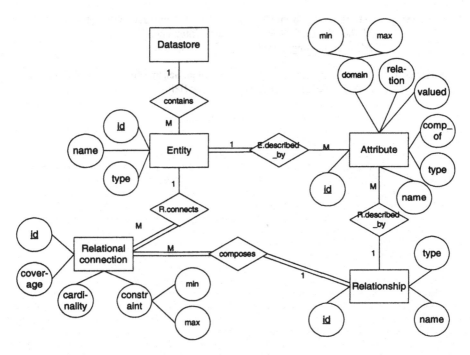

Figure 19 ER-diagram for storing ER-diagrams

Summing Up

We advocate an approach to information systems design which puts more emphasis on conceptual modeling than what is usual. A major characteristic is that data and what they refer to are modelled separately, following NIAMs distinction between lexical and non-lexical objects. The modelling approach is solidly based on elementary mathematical principles. A visual language for conceptual modeling is described. It is shown how the advocated approach relates to the entity-relationship approach to data modeling. Furthermore, it is shown how the «meaning» of data may be formally expressed using elementary mathematical notation.

References

(Aubert98)   Aubert A. B.: Structured Storing of Model Diagrams in the PPP repository. MSc thesis, Dept.Computer and Information Sciences, The Norwegian University of Science and technology, Trondheim, Norway 1998

(Chen76)   Chen P.P.: The Entity-relationship model: Towards a Unified view of Data. ACM Transactions on Database Systems, 1(1):9-36, March 1976

(Codd70)   Codd E.: A relational Model for Large Shared Data Banks. Communications of the ACM 13(6), June 1970

(Navathe86)   Navathe S.B., Batini C., Lenzerini M.: A Comparative Analysis of
                Methodologies for Database Schema Integration.
                ACM Computing Surveys 18(4):323-364, 1986

(Nijssen89)   Nijssen G.M., Halpern T.A.: Conceptual Schema and Relational Database
                Design. ISBN 0-13-167263-0. Prentice Hall.

The Strength of ER Modeling

Bernhard Thalheim

Computer Science Institute, Cottbus Technical University
PostBox 101344, D-03013 Cottbus
thalheim@Informatik.TU-Cottbus.DE

Abstract. The ER model is the most popular model for database modeling. Its popularity is based on simple graphical representations, on graphical extensibility of given design and last but not least on safe constructs. The model strength is its strict hierarchic structure. This basis leads to safe implementations. There has been a large number of different extensions to the ER model both consistent and well-based or intuitive and seldom well-based. In this paper we demonstrate a safe path to extended ER models.

Meanwhile object-oriented model have gained large attention. Most of the object-oriented models are based on very powerful constructs which cannot be safely implemented. Some of the models are based on ER constructs with the extension of methods. We show that this approach is safe and powerful.

1 Introduction

ER'96 celebrated 20 years of the Entity-Relationship Model. The ER model is currently widely used in database, information systems, software engineering. Almost any book which discusses modeling is using some version of the ER model.

Because of its popularity the ER model has been often redefined. Although the first paper by P.P. Chen could be used for standards there are several different definitions of the same construct. The work on the ER model has led to a huge amount of literature. At the same time, some of the most important problems are still open:

Sound framework for all aspects of modeling: Database modelers should be able to represent all aspects of the application in a language which should be easy to use, to understand, to integrate and to represent, which should have an intuitive semantics of constructs. All this should be theoretically well-based.

Modularization and abstraction: In practice database specifications are large and are used for the display of different views on the same application. Thus, we have to integrate zooming, modularization and abstraction into modeling.

Variety of translation techniques: ER schemata can be translated to logical schemata in different fashions. Most of them are implementation dependent.

P.P. Chen et al. (Eds.): Conceptual Modeling, LNCS 1565, pp. 227–242, 1999.

Methods for design which consider the context: Information systems are used to interact in the production etc. process. Organizational, juridical and and general environmental restriction should be integrated.

The sample points for further development of ER modeling clash with the missing standard for ER modeling and confusing notions. An example of the confusing variety for the same notion is the definition of the entity:

- An entity is a specific thing about which an information system collects information[Alt96].
- An entity is an individual and identifiable specimen of a thing, a person or a notion of the real world or imaginations, i.e. it is an object[Bal96].
- An object that represents a useful model of a problem-domain or solution-domain is called entity[Boo93].
- An entity is any distinguishable person, thing, event or concept about which information is kept[Bru92].
- An entity is a thing which can be distinctly identified[Che76].
- An entity is a distinguishable object that is to be represented in the database [Dat86].
- A data entity represents some 'thing' that is to be stored for later reference. The term entity refers to the logical representation of data[Fin89].
- An entity is a person, place, or thing about which information must be kept[LaL97].
- The word entity means anything about which we store information (e.g. customers, supplier, machine tool, employee, utility pole, airline seat, etc.). For each entity type, certain attributes are stored[Mar89].
- Entities are 'things' that exist independently of other entities[MaR92].
- An entity is a thing or concept or object which involve information. It is not a single thing but rather a representation of like or similar things that share characteristics or properties[Rei94].
- Well-distinguishable objects which exist in the real world are called entities [Vos91].

The confusion is almost complete since most of the database and software engineering books do not define at all the notion of the entity. The critics on those definitions is manyfold, e.g. entities are representations and not existing things like persons. Thus, ER modeling is still rather an art than a science. However, ER modeling can be well-based, consistently performed and could be used to consider all application aspects. We will show it in the next section.

Object-oriented database models can be considered to be an extension of ER approaches. In this case, oo models are safe. If the model are extended in order to express universal world formulas then those models are unsafe and inconsistent. We will discuss this in the third section.

This paper summarizes some of our results. The formal definitions can be found in cited papers or in [Tha92, Tha97].

2   Safe Structural Extensions of the ER Model

In this paper we distinguish elements (e.g. entities), classes (e.g. entity classes) and types (e.g. entity types). Often, the three notions are mixed. Types are used to represent structure, methods and semantics of collections like classes. Elements of classes are defined by values for the component of the structure, have methods and obey their local semantics. Classes have also class restrictions. They can be based on other classes.

2.1   Structural and Semantical Extensions of the ER Model

There is a large variety of structural extensions of the ER model. Most of those extensions are based on the notion of type constructors like set, tuple, list, bag constructors. Constructors are used to define complex types based on basic types. Basic types are data types usual in all DBMS like *integer, string, real*.

Components of types can be named. Typical named components are attributes in the definition of entity or relationship types. The type definition can be inductive. This approach allows also the definition of relationship types based on relationship types.

The structural definition of the higher-order entity-relationship model [Tha92, Tha97] is based on the following type definition scheme:

Attributes types are inductively defined by
   atomic attributes types associated with basic data types and
   complex attribute types defined using the given constructors.
Entity types are defined by
   attribute types and
   structural constraints like key constraints, functional dependencies etc.
Relationship types are inductively defined either as
   relationship types of first order with entity types (i.e. types of order 0) and attribute types as components or defined as
   relationship types of order i with relationship component types of order less than i, entity types and attribute types.
Component types can be extended to represent *roles, generalization,* and *specialization*.

Constraints can be added to relationship types or to sets of relationship types. Typical constraints are:

Generalized cardinality constraints defined for relationship types and
Path and graph constraints defined over subschemata like path functional dependencies [Tha92, Tha92'] and graph cardinality constraints.

Classes are defined on the basis of a type. Classes are sets of elements which are structured according to the type and which obey the integrity constraints.

The semantics of types is usually based on set semantics. Sometimes, relationship types are defined using pointer semantics. Pointer semantics can be represented by set semantics. For this reason, we use set semantics. The advantage of this approach is the possibility to define relationship types based on the key values of the component types, i.e. we can inherit the primary (or secondary) key of the component type instead of inheriting the complete component type.

The definition of cardinality constraints can be based on the *lookup* interpretation or on the *participation* interpretation. In Figure 1 different interpretations can be applied:

Lookup: A car is owned by 1, 2, 3 or 4 persons.

Participation: A person owns at most 4 cars and at least 1.

Fig. 1. Lookup/participation cardinality constraints

Furthermore, we can define various meanings for constraint semantics:

Logics approach: A car has 1 or 2 owners or does not have any owner. Whether there are such cars is *unknown*. This approach is the usual one in theory.

Weak semantics: Usually, a car is owned by 1 or 2 persons. This approach is the usual approach in practice.

Strong semantics There are cars owned by nobody and also cars owned by 2 persons. This approach is used sometimes in practice and in theoretical investigations.

It is obvious, that strong semantics implies logical semantics and that logical semantics implies weak semantics. The opposite is not valid.

The HERM is strongly hierarchical. This property has far-reaching consequences. One example is normalization for value-oriented models.
Normalized inclusion-based schemata are HERM-schemata with the following properties:

- Each type is in BCNF.
- All inclusion constraints are key-based inclusion constraints.
- The identification is defined through components.

This notion can be defined for relational schemata as well.
Notice that there are no weak types.
It can be proven[MaR92, Tha92'] that:

- For each HERM schema an equivalent schema in HERM-NF exists.
- Any schema in HERM-NF can be translated to a relational inclusion-based BCNF schema.
- It is decidable whether a HERM schema is in HERM-NF.

2.2   Identification in ER Schemata

The usual approach to identification is based on selection of components of the
type as key components. There have been several trials [AbV95, Gog95, KlR96]
for the definition of identification. We use here the most general approoach in
[BeT95] Extended entity-relationship models have two constructs which could
be used for identification: relationship types and complex types.

Weak entity types, i.e. types whose identification is defined through associations, use the first extension. We can use pathes for the identification. The dot is

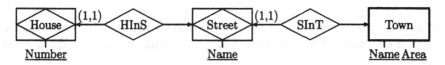

Fig. 2. Address defined by weak entity types

used for component declaration, i.e. moving downwards. The exclamation mark
is used for moving upwards. For example, the attribute *Number* in Figure 2 can
be reached from *Town* using the path

   Town!SInT.Street!HInS.House   and is denoted by
   Town!SInT.Street!HInS.House.Number.

Based on pathes we can define the extended structure of a type $\mathcal{R} = (R, \Sigma)$.
The identification or the key of the type *House* is the set

{ *House!HInS.Street!SInT.Town.Name,   House!HInS.Street!SInT.Town.Area,*
   House!HInS.Street.Name,   Number } .

It should be noticed that modeling by weak entity types can be misleading.
For instance, we add owners of houses to the scheme in Figure 2 by inserting
a new entity type *Owner* and a relationship type *Owns = (House, Owner, ∅)*.
Then the type *Owns* uses the identification mechanism and is not only based on
the type *House*.

This identification mechanism is still too simple. If identifying relationship
types are not binary then the identification can be extended to trees. The example presented in Figure 3 has an identification mechanism which is more
complex.

A clan is a group of living and past relatives sharing one last name. The last
name can be received from the father at birth or from the husband at marriage.
The database to be designed contains the relations within a clan (by birth and
by marriage).

The identification mechanism which could be used is the complete unfolding
for a person's first name. The identification mechanism used in [SSW92, ScT93] is
partially usable. The depth-restricted unfolding or the unfolding by rational trees
does not give the right result. The finiteness condition is a sufficient condition
for the existence of an identification condition. For each person we generate the
complete tree of all ancestors and successors.

However, we can use potentially infinite trees for identification which are
defined by 'walking' through the structure. Finite subtrees are used as identi-

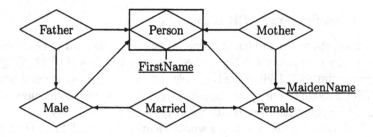

Fig. 3. The Clan Example

fication tree. For example, a person is identified by his/her first name and the names of the father and the mother. Then the identification tree is displayed in Figure 4.

The identification of a person is given by the set of pathes in the tree, i.e.
{ *Person. FirstName, Person! Mother. Female . MaidenName,*
    Person! Mother. Female. Person. FirstName,
    Person! Father. Male. Person. FirstName }
or using abbreviation techniques and shortest paths as a selection criterion for restoring the original path
{ *FirstName, Mother. MaidenName, Mother. FirstName, Father. FirstName* }.
The identification by trees is more expressive than the identification by a set of pathes. For example, requiring that if a person has a mother and a father which are objects in the database then both a married can be displayed in the graph 4. Further, we can require that a person is identified either by its first name or his/her first name and the names of his/her father and his/her mother. This is represented by a set of of trees as shown in Figure 4. Further, the second tree is not covered by the first. Persons which parents are not married are distinguished from those which parents are married. Different persons which parents are not married are distinguished by their first names.

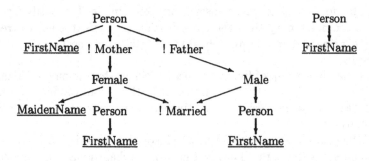

Fig. 4. Or-Identification Trees of a Person

Thus, we can use equations defined on the identification tree for expressing more complex identification mechanism. In general, an identification is defined by the strong identification tree, existence conditions for components and a set of equalities on nodes of the tree.

The key concept can be extended to relations permitting null values. Therefore, the identification concept can be also based on weak trees. The tree construction can be used for the definition of semantics. Instead of strong trees weak trees can be used. In this case we obtain another possibility to distinguish objects: missing values. In this case, existence of values for an object can be used for distinction as well. Further, or-trees can be used for restricting the structures with missing values. This approach is similar to key sets defined in relational databases which allows missing values.

The second new construct of the entity-relationship model extends the identification concept as well. Let us consider the two examples in Figure 5.

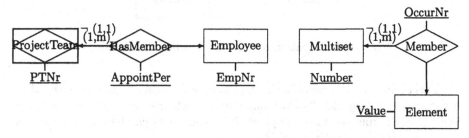

Fig. 5. Complex Identification through Relationship Types

In both examples the types can be identified. Project teams can be identified by their members and the appointment period. Multisets are identical if they have the same elements with the same occurrence number.

These conditions can be expressed by generalizing the notion of key dependencies. A key dependency is a functional dependency
$$R' \longrightarrow R$$
for a type $\mathcal{R} = (R, \Sigma)$ and a substructure R' of R.
This dependency can be expressed also by a first-order predicate formula
$$\forall v, v' \, (P_{\mathcal{R}}(v) \wedge P_{\mathcal{R}}(v') \wedge v \overset{R'}{=} v' \longrightarrow v \overset{R}{=} v) \quad .$$
In the relational model at the external level keys are used to represent identification and existence. This idea directs to another formula which is equivalent to the above key constraint:
$$\forall v_1 \mid_{R''}, v_2 \mid_{R''} \, (\forall v \mid_{R'} \, (P_{\mathcal{R}}(v \mid_{R'} \bowtie v_1 \mid_{R''})$$
$$\longleftrightarrow P_{\mathcal{R}}(v \mid_{R'} \bowtie v_1 \mid_{R''})) \longrightarrow v_1 \overset{R''}{=} v_2)$$
where R'' is the "difference" of R and R'.

Based on this re-definition we express now the key constraints for multisets by the formula
$$\forall m, m' \, ((\, \forall e, o \, (P_{Member}(m, e, o) \longleftrightarrow P_{Member}(m', e, o)) \longrightarrow m = m') \quad .$$
The project example can use the same approach :
$$\forall p, p' \, ((\, \forall e, a \, (P_{HasMember}(p, e, a) \longleftrightarrow P_{HasMember}(p', e, a))$$
$$\longrightarrow p = p') \quad .$$

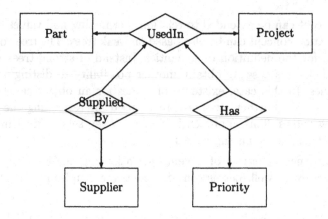

Fig. 6. Identification defined for Algebraic Expressions

This approach can generalized. The example in Figure 6 can be restricted by a constraint stating that "no two different projects use the same part with the same priority from the same supplier". This constraint can be expressed by the key constraint on *SuppliedBy* ⋈ *Has*:

{ *UsedIn.Part, SuppliedBy.Supplier, Has.Priority* } ⟶ *SuppliedBy* ⋈ *Has*   .

These constraints can be now generalized for the HERM algebra [Tha92, Tha97]. Using this algebra we can generate the set of queries which are expressible through this algebra. A T-query q generates sets of a type T. We denote the result of a query q applied to a database D^t by $q(D^t)$.

We introduce now the generalization of key constraints in extended ER models.
Given an extended entity-relationship scheme S, a type $\mathcal{R} = (R, \Sigma)$ of this scheme and an instance S^t database with an instance R^t for $\mathcal{R}$.
A set Q of $\mathcal{R}$-queries defined on a scheme S is called **general key** of R^t if the following formula is valid:

$$\forall m, m' \in R^t \ (\ \forall q \in Q \ (\ m \in q(S^t) \ \longleftrightarrow \ m' \in q(S^t) \ )$$
$$\longrightarrow \quad m = m' \ ) \quad .$$

2.3 Behavioral Extensions

Because of the hierarchical structure of HERM, the function type system is definable through structural recursion:
Given types T, T', a collection type C^T on T , the typical set operations (generalized union $\cup_{C^T}$, generalized intersection $\cap_{C^T}$), and generalized empty elements $\emptyset_{C^T}$ on C^T. Further let element h_0 be an element on T'.
Further we are given two functions:

$$h_1 \ : \ T \to T' \qquad \text{and} \qquad h_2 \ : \ T' \times T' \to T' \qquad .$$

Structural recursion on the basis of the insert operation is inductively defined on the basis of the following system:

$$srec_{h_0,h_1,h_2}(\emptyset_{C^T}) = h_0$$
$$srec_{h_0,h_1,h_2}(\{\!|s|\!\}) = h_1(s) \qquad \text{for singleton } \{\!|s|\!\}$$
$$srec_{h_0,h_1,h_2}(\{\!|s|\!\} \cup_{C^T} R^t) = h_2(h_1(s), srec_{h_0,h_1,h_2}(R^t))$$
$$\text{if } \{\!|s|\!\} \cap_{C^T} R^t = \emptyset_{C^T} .$$

The classes of types R are denoted by R^t.

Structural recursion on the basis of the union operation is inductively defined on the basis of the following system:

$$srec_{h_0,h_1,h_2}(\emptyset_{C^T}) = h_0$$
$$srec_{h_0,h_1,h_2}(\{\!|s|\!\}) = h_1(s) \qquad \text{for singleton } \{\!|s|\!\}$$
$$srec_{h_0,h_1,h_2}(R_1^t \cup_{C^T} R_2^t) = h_2(srec_{h_0,h_1,h_2}(R_1^t), srec_{h_0,h_1,h_2}(R_2^t))$$
$$\text{if } R_1^t \cap_{C^T} R_2^t = \emptyset_{C^T} .$$

For example $ext(h_1)(R^t) = srec_{\perp,h_1,\cup_{T'}}(R^t)$ is equivalent to *comprehensions*.

We can use now structural recursion in order to define the usual database operations like *insert*, *delete* and *update*. Based on this definition we can define a generalized predicate logic which is still a first-order language. Therefore, database dynamics can be based on predicate logics.

Dynamic and static constaints can be defined also on the basis of query languages. In [GLL93] QBE has been extended to ERQBE. We extend this approach to HERM/QBE. In HERM/QBE the relationship or entity name is written above the components. The identification query sets for the example in Figure 5 are given as follows. Given a query q_c for each $c \in dom(PTNr)$ by the HERM/QBE table:

$q_c = HasMember$

Project Team		Employee		AppointPer
PTNr	...	EmpNr	...	
P.c		P..x		P..y

The query q_c generates all triples which are associated with the project number. Then the set $Q = \{q_c | c \in dom(PTNr)\}$ of queries expresses the key constraint

$$\forall p, p' ((\forall e, a (P_{HasMember}(p, e, a) \longleftrightarrow P_{HasMember}(p', e, a))$$
$$\longrightarrow p = p') .$$

Uniqueness constraints are a special subcase of set generating constraints. They express identification concepts which are based on trees of depth 1. The following HERM/QBE tables define the identification discussed for the schema in Figure 6.

$q_{v,x,y}^1 = SuppliedBy$

Supplier		UsedIn	
Nr	...	Part	Project
		Nr	...	Nr	...
P..v		P..x	P..y	...

$q_{z,x,y}^2 = Has$

Priority		UsedIn	
Nr	...	Part	Project
		Nr	...	Nr	...
P..z		P..x	P..y	...

Let $q_{v,z,x,y} = q^1_{v,x,y} \bowtie q^2_{z,x,y}$ and
$$Q = \{q_{v,z,x,y} \mid v \in dom(Supplier.Nr),$$
$$x \in dom(Part.Nr),$$
$$z \in dom(Priority.Nr)\}.$$
The set of queries is equivalent to the constraint
$$\{ \; UsedIn.Part, \; SuppliedBy.Supplier, \; Has.Priority \; \} \; \longrightarrow \; SuppliedBy \bowtie Has \qquad .$$

2.4   Modeling Strategies

The discrepancy between the well-based techniques and theories for structural database design on the one hand and the poorly developed approaches to the design of the corresponding behavior on the other hand led us to ask the question which fundamental differences actually exist between structure design and behaviour design. Most of the approaches can be extended to behavioral design [ClT97].

Our starting point is to intuitively apply characteristics of the relation between database schema and database views to the behaviour component. The overall system behaviour, corresponding to the global database schema, can be projected on particular local *behaviour 'views'* that we want to refer to as *dialogs* in the following.

After illustrating the general dependencies between (database) schema, (database) views, behaviour and dialogs from such an intuitive point of view, we want to present a theoretical framework for transfering meta-characteristics of the schema/views relation to the behaviour/dialogs relation. We then will expose an approach to the practical consequences, especially for the *design and management of dialogs*.

There are four sides to database design: whereas schema definition and views characterise the system's statics, behaviour and dialogs capture its dynamics. On the other hand do schema and behaviour convey the aspect of globality, while views and dialogs represent local realisations.

Statics.   A schema can be understood as a type definition with a collection of static integrity constraints. The database schema captures the *global* view on a database's statics.

The application of view definitions to a type creates database views that *locally* present specific parts to the user. Views may also be defined over views, thus building more complex combinations of parts of the underlying database.

Dynamics.   The definition of all possible functionality within a database system with the collection of all dynamic integrity constraints is the system's behaviour. Those functions actually being performed then represent an instantiation of this behaviour. In correspondence to the (static) database schema, this part of a system's dynamics stands for the *global* aspect.

In order to support certain activities, however, parts of this global behaviour have to be selected and structured which is achieved by dialog definitions. The specific execution and 'staging' of dialog definitions are the eventual dialogs (dialog instances) that serve as a *local* representation of the system's behaviour in a specific context to the user. Again, dialogs can be defined over dialogs which corresponds to the definition of *dialog flows* as illustrations of underlying business processes.

Finally, it has to be pointed out that the specification of a system's dynamics necessarily includes its statics just as, e.g., function specifications incorporate information on input and output parameters since dynamic integrity includes static integrity.

It is well known that database design cannot be performed in one shot. Instead of that, in practice database schemata are developed using refinement and specialization. We can distinguish different abstraction layers:

Motivation layer for the specification of intention, motivation and ideas.

Business process layer for the specification of business data, business processes and the applications story.

Action layer for the specification of main data strctures, actions and scenarios.

Conceptual layer for the specification of the conceptual schema, processes and the applications script.

Implementation layer for the information obtained during logical and physical design.

The associations in this abstraction layer model are displayed in Figure 7.

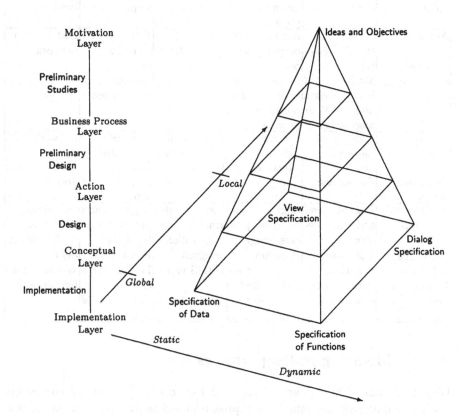

Fig. 7. The abstraction layer model of the database design process

The abstraction layer model is a model which can be used for *codesign* of *data structures*, *processes*, *views* and *dialoges*. We could add another othogonal dimension: *distribution*. We can distribute data, processes, control and presentation. The codesign process integrates the pieces developed so far. In [Tha97'] a complete integrated codesign methodology has been developed. The methodology is a step-wise procedure which is completed layer by layer. The integration of the codesign steps is based on type theory and approaches known in mathematical logic[CIT97]. The following table displays the different topics to be addressed in different layers whereas the distribution dimension has been linearized:

	Data	Process	View	Dialog	Distribution
Motivation layer	Ideas, motivation	Motivation, tasks	Ideas, motivations	Motives, ideas	Locations
Business scope	List of important things	List of important processes	Main views	Raw workflow Actors	
Business process layer	Business entities, thier interrelationships	Business processes Flows between business processes	Sketch of views	Story, sketches of scenes Actors and their main steps	Communication links between business locations
Business model					
Action layer	Predesign, HERM skeleton	Architecture design, actions	Predesign, view skeleton	Predesign, scenarios, raw scenes	Distribution network
Information systems model	Model of business data and their associations	Flows between application processes		Intensions of actors steps	
Conceptual layer	Conceptual database design	System design Processes	Conceptual view design ER views	Conceptual dialog design Script	Network design Configuration design
Technology model	ER schema			Steps of actors, roles	
Implementation layer	Logical and physical design	Logical and physical process design	View integration and cooperation	Logical and physical dialog design	Distribution definition, configuration definition,
Technology definition, information system	Database defintion, data storage structure	Program code, control blocks, executable code	Integrated DBMS views	Production Logical steps of actors Decoration of scenes	system configuration

3   OO Modeling in Deep Waters

Object-orientation is a powerful and useful concept which can be succesfully applied in database modeling. The approach should be applied with care as it is to be shown on the next two pages. In contrast to the safety of the ER approach, the oo approach is not safe in general. The results below are mainly based on the articles [BeT95, ScT93] and further on [SSW92, ScT98, Tha97].

3.1 Identification

Object-oriented databases use the concept of the object identifier (OID) which is still not well understood. The OID can be used also for computing complex queries which are not expressible by first-order predicate logics. The OID should be invisible to the user. OID's should not carry any meaning to the user. Otherwise it is a surrogate value. During design of an object-oriented database, OID's have to be modeled with highest care. The OID concept is so powerful that the computation of identification cannot be based on query languages as it is often claimed. We call an object algebraic identifiable iff the orbit (for the automorphism group) is trivial. An object is query identifiable iff there exist a query distinguishing this object from all other objects in the database. It can be proven that query identifiable objects are algebraic identifiable but not vice versa.

Identifiability has not necessarily to be based on values. In this case, identifiability of objects depends on the complete database which is not very useful. In [ScT93] we introduced the concepts of value-identifiability (existence of a uniqueness constraint), value-representability (existence of a value representation) and weak-value-representability (existence of an extended value representation).

The above discussed unfolding can be used for generating the reference graphs of objects. This technique can be used for proving the following results:

- The existence of a reference graph is a sufficient condition for value-representability.
- Value-representability is decidable for acyclic object graphs.
- If there exist an identification graph and uniqueness constraints and each component types are occuring as a label in the identification graph, then the type is value-identifiable.
- If there exists an acyclic identification graph the value-identifiability is decidable.
- If all explicit constraints are uniqueness constraints then value-identifiability and value-representability are decidable.
- All objects in each class are identifiable iff all classes in the schema are weak value-representable.

These results can be used during database design in the following way: Whenever we need an identification of objects then we should base this identification on the above discussed ER identification mechanisms.

3.2 Genericity

The existence of canonical update operations is one of the strongest properties of value-based database models. In this case, there is no need to program update operations for each type. This genericity is not maintained in object-oriented database models. It can be shown that generic update operations do not exist in object-oriented databases in general, more specifically:

- Let C be a class in a schema S. Then there exist unique canonical update operations on C iff C and all its superclasses are value-representable.

3.3   Consistency and Semantics

There exist several approaches to consistency maintenance in databases:

The classical transaction approach is used to reject any operation or transaction which leads to an inconsistent state from consistent states. The consistency maintenance for complex operations is the user's responsibility. Although this approach does not lead to inconsistency in databases if the the database has been consistent this approach is far too complex.

The active database approach uses production rules for repairing inconsistencies. Rules systems should be confluent and terminating. The rules can be generated in compile time. The conflict management is run-time. Rule triggering is not powerful enough. It could lead to strange results especially for cyclic classes.

For instance given three classes C_1, C_2, C_3 and integrity constraints $C_1 \subseteq C_2$, $C_1 \subseteq C_3$, $C_2 \| C_3$. Applying rule triggering leads to three different results in dependence from the execution order:

$$insert_{C_1} \rightarrow^* delete_{C_3} delete_{C_2} delete_{C_1}$$

$$insert_{C_1} \rightarrow^* insert_{C_3} delete_{C_2} delete_{C_1}$$

$$insert_{C_1} \rightarrow^* insert_{C_2} delete_{C_3} delete_{C_1}$$

None of the results is correct. Inserting into an empty class should fail.
Thus, rule triggering is unsafe. It can be shown[ScT98] that in hierarchical schemes and only in those rule triggering is safe.

The strongest and a safe approach is the generation of consistent specializations. Given a database scheme (S, O, Σ). Then based on the constraints specializations of operations can be generated which maintain consistency, i.e. we obtain another equivalent scheme (S, O', Σ). This approach allows compile-time generation of operations. In the example above, the results is $FAIL$.

Object-oriented models are defined on arbitrary type concepts and allow cyclic structures. It has been shown[Sch94] that in this case semantics cannot be based on set semantics but on topos semantics. Set semantics is understandable to most of the database users. Topos semantics is far too complex for database users.

In general, we have five different kinds of semantics which can be used to base database technology:

Set semantics is defined set-based types. Hierarchical models like HERM or some other extended ER models can use set semantics.

Pointer semantics is built on reference-based types. This semantics is safe for identifier-based models since these databases allow value-representability.

Topos semantics is founded on category-based types. Whenever the type system allows powerful constructors then we need this approach.

Nonclassical semantics on the basis of default logics, CWA, GCWA or epistemic logics is an alternative approach.

Dynamic semantics could be an option for the definition of semantics. However, there are very few results on this approach.

3.4   Translations

In [Sch94, Tha97] further negative results are obtained:

- Cyclic types without finiteness condition cannot be translated into types of commercial DBMS.
- There are exponentially many normalized schemata.
- Conceptual optimization with static and dynamic constraints, with operations is defined for hierachical structures but not for cyclic structures.
- Object-oriented types are category-based types. Thus, semantics of object-oriented databases can be defined using topos semantics. Set semantics can be used if the type system is strongly hierarchical. Whenever the type system allows powerful constructors then the semantics cannot be based on set semantics.

The last results show that object-orientation should be based on extended ER models.

References

[AbV95] S. Abiteboul, J. Van der Bussche, Deep equality revised. Proc. DOOD'95 (eds. T.W. Ling, A.O. Mendelzon, L. Vielle), LNCS 1013, 213 - 228.

[Alt96] S. Alter, Information systems. Benjamin/Cummings, Menlo Park, 1996.

[Bal96] H. Balzert, Lehrbuch der Software-Technik. Spektrum-Verlag, Heidelberg, 1996.

[Bee89] C. Beeri. Formal Models for Object Oriented Databases. Proc. DOOD 89, Kyoto 1989, 370 - 395.

[Bee93] C. Beeri, Some thoughts on the future evolution of object-oriented database concepts. Proc. BTW 93 (ed. W. Stucky), Springer, 1993, 18 -32.

[BeT95] C. Beeri, B. Thalheim, Can I see your identification, please? - Identification is well-founded in object-oriented databases. Manuscript, Cottbus-Jerusalem, 1995.

[Boo93] G. Booch, Object-oriented analysis and design. Benjamin-Cummings, Redwood, 1993.

[Bru92] T. Bruce, Designing quality databases with IDEF1X information models. Dorset House Publ., New York, 1992.

[Che76] P. P. S. Chen. The Entity-Relationship Model: Toward a unified view of data. ACM TODS 1,1, 1976, 9–36.

[ClT97] W. Clauß, B. Thalheim, Abstraction layered structure-process codesign. CO-MAD'97, Chennai (Madras), India 1997.

[Dat86] C.J. Date, An iontroduction to database systems. Addison-Wesley, Reading, 1986.

[Fin89] C. Finkelstein, An introduction to information engineering. Addison-Wesley, Sydney, 1989.

[GLL93] J. Grant, T.W. Ling, and M. L. Lee, ERL: Logic for entity-relationship databases. Journal of Intelligent Information Systems, 1993, 2, 115 – 147.

[Gog95] M. Gogolla, A declarative query approach to object identification. Proc. OO-ER95 (ed. M. Papazoglou), LNCS 1021, 65 - 76.

[KlR96] H.-J. Klein, J. Rasch. Value based identification and functional dependencies for object databases. Proc. 3rd Basque Int. Workshop on Information Technology, IEEE Comp. Sci. Press, 1997, 22-34.

[LaL97] K.C. Laudon, J.P. Laudon, Essentials of management information systems. Prentice Hall, Upper Sale River, 1997.

[Mar89] J. Martin, Information engineering. Prentice Hall, Englewood Cliffs, 1989.

[MaR92] H. Mannila and K.-J. Räihä, The design of relational databases. Addison-Wesley, Amsterdam, 1992.

[Rei94] M. Reigruber, W.W. Gregory, The data modeling handbook. John Wiley, New York, 1994.

[Sch94] K.-D. Schewe, The specification of data-intensive application systems. Advanced PhD, TU Cottbus, 1994.

[ScT93] K.-D. Schewe, B. Thalheim, Fundamental Conceps of Object Oriented Concepts. Acta Cybernetica, 11, No. 4, 1993, 49 – 81

[ScT98] K.-D. Schewe, B. Thalheim, On the strength of rule triggering systems for integrity maintenance. Proc. Australian Database Conference, ADC'98, 1998.

[SeT88] O.Selesnjew and B. Thalheim. On the number of minimal keys in relational databases on nonuniform domains. Acta Cybernetica, 8, 3, 1988, 267 - 271.

[SSW92] K.-D. Schewe, J.W. Schmidt, and I. Wetzel, Identification, Genericity and Consistency in Object-Oriented Databases. In J. Biskup, R. Hull (eds.), Proc. 3rd International Conference on Database Theory, ICDT '92, Berlin (Germany), Lecture Notes in Computer Science 14–16, 1992, Springer LNCS

[TeH93] A.H.M. Ter Hofstede, Information modelling in data intensive domains. PhD, University of Nijmegen, 1993.

[Tha92] B. Thalheim, Foundations of entity-relationship modeling. Annals of Mathematics and Artificial Intelligence, 7, 197 – 256, 1992.

[Tha92'] B. Thalheim, Semantics in entity-relationship models. Proc. Workshop "Semantics of Programming Languages and Model Theory" (eds. E. Börger, M. Droste, J. Gurevich), Morgan Kaufman, 1992.

[Tha97] B. Thalheim, Fundamentals of the entity-relationship model. Springer Publ., Heidelberg, 1998.

[Tha97'] B. Thalheim, Codesign of structures, functions and interfaces in database applications. Preprint I-05-1997, 22. 2. 1997, Institut für Informatik, Brandenburgische Technische Universität Cottbus, Cottbus, 1997, 80p.

[Vos91] G. Vossen, Data models, database languages, database management systems. Thompson Publ., Bonn, 1991.

Interaction as a Framework for Modeling

Peter Wegner[1] and Dina Goldin[2]

[1] Brown University
Providence, RI
pw@cs.brown.edu
[2] U.Mass - Boston
Boston, MA
dqg@cs.umb.edu

Abstract. The irreducibility of interactive to algorithmic computing requires fundamental questions concerning models of computation to be reexamined. This paper reviews single-stream and multiple-stream interaction machines, extensions of set theory and algebra for models of sequential interaction, and interactive extensions of the Turing test. It motivates the use of interactive models as a basis for applications to computer architecture, software engineering, and artificial intelligence.

1 Concepts of Modeling

Interactive models of computation provide a unifying conceptual framework that captures changes in computer architecture, software engineering, and AI in the last quarter of the 20th century [We1]. The evolution of computer architecture from mainframes to personal computers and networks, of software engineering from procedure-oriented to object-oriented and component-based systems, and of AI from logic-based to agent-oriented and distributed systems has followed parallel paths. The evolution of programming can, as a first approximation, be described as follows:

1950s: machine language programming, assemblers, hardware-defined action sequences
1960s: procedure-oriented programming, compilers, programmer-defined action sequences
1970s: structured programming, composition of action sequences, algorithm architecture
1980s: object-based programming, personal computers, sequential interaction architecture
1990s: structured object-based programming, networks, distributed interaction architecture

Whereas the shift from machine to procedure-oriented programming involves a quantitative change in the granularity of actions, the shift from procedure-oriented to object-based programming is more fundamental, involving a qualitative paradigm shift from algorithms to interactive computing. The shift from

P.P. Chen et al. (Eds.): Conceptual Modeling, LNCS 1565, pp. 243–257, 1999.

sequential interaction with a single agent to distributed interaction among multiple agents is a further fundamental paradigm shift in underlying models of computation. Turing machines (TMs) provide a robust model of computation for algorithmic (action-oriented) programming. Our goal is to develop interactive models of computation whose role is comparable to that of TMs for algorithms.

Database models have evolved separately from programming models, from hierarchical to relational and entity-relation models. Conceptual modeling [Ch] is rooted in the database tradition, flowered in the decade 1975-1985, and led to the development of object-oriented databases [ZM]. But this area failed to develop underlying models of computation comparable to those of Turing machines for automatic computing. It could not shake off the notion that database modeling should be rooted in algorithmic modeling, so that even books published in the mid 1990s [KR] appeal primarily to the tradition of Turing and Dijkstra in establishing a conceptual foundation for information modeling.

Turing's proof that algorithms, TMs, and the lambda calculus are equally expressive [Tu1], suggested that the question of expressiveness of computing had been settled once and for all, and channeled research to questions of design, performance, and complexity for a fixed notion of computability. Church's thesis that computable functions capture the intuitive notion of computability contributed to the belief that computing could be identified with algorithmic computation. The claim that interactive computation is more expressive than algorithms opens up a research area that had been considered closed, requiring fundamental questions concerning models of computation to be reexamined.

Our work over the last five years has shown that interactive models are not reducible to or expressible by algorithmic models. This paper reviews concepts and models of interactive computation discussed in [We1, We2, We3, We4, We5, WG]. Readers interested in an introduction to this work should read [We1], which is easily accessible and written for a general audience. The fundamental model is described in depth in [WG], which builds on recent extensions to set theory and algebra [Ac, BM, Ru1] in developing a model for interactive computing.

The irreducibility of interactive systems to algorithms was noticed by [MP] for reactive systems, by [Mi] in the context of process models, and by many other researchers. Our approach differs from related work in focusing on models of interaction and notions of expressiveness that are language-independent as well as domain-independent. A unifying language-independent model of computation for a variety of levels of expressiveness is developed, and is related to mathematical models of set theory and algebra [Ac, BM, Ru1]. This work has led to the development of persistent Turing machines (PTMs) as a canonical model of sequential computation, of an expressiveness hierarchy for sequential computation, and of the result that multi-stream interaction machines (MIMs) are more expressive than sequential interaction machines (SIMs).

Turing's seminal paper [Tu1] was not intended to establish TMs as a comprehensive model for computing but on the contrary to show undecidability and other limitations of TMs. Turing actually mentions irreducibility to TMs of interactive choice machines (c-machines) as a presumably well-known fact [Tu1].

TMs model "automatic" computation, while IMs extend the notion of what is computable to nonautomatic (interactive) computation. IMs can model TMs with oracles, which Turing showed to be more powerful than TMs in his Ph.D. thesis [Tu2].

The robustness of TMs as a model of computation led to Church's thesis that the intuitive notion of computability corresponded to TM computation of computable functions. Interactive computation has a richer notion of computability corresponding to computation of sequences and patterns of functions (algorithms). The richer notion of computation is captured mathematically by extending the input domain of functions from predetermined strings to interactively generated steams that cannot be represented as functions from integers to integers. Greater computation power is due not to greater transformation power but to richer domains of transformable inputs, that can be specified by non-well-founded sets.

The idea that interaction is not expressible by or reducible to algorithms was first proposed in 1992 at the closing conference of the fifth-generation computing project in the context of logic programming [We4]. Reactiveness of logic programs, realized by commitment to a course of action, was shown to be incompatible with logical completeness, realized by backtracking. The 5th-generation project's failure of achieving its maximal objective of reducing computation to first-order logic was attributed to theoretical impossibility rather than to lack of cleverness of researchers. The implication that success could not have been achieved by a twenty year extension or substantial further research shows that impossibility results may have practical impact in justifying strategic research decisions.

The irreducibility of interaction to algorithms and of computation to first-order logic implies that tools of algorithm analysis and formal methods cannot, by themselves, solve the software crisis. Software tools for design patterns, lifecycle models, embedded systems, and collaborative planning are not modeled by algorithms and their behavior cannot inherently be expressed by first-order logic. Fred Brooks' claim that there is no silver bullet for systems can be proved if we define "silver bullet" to mean "formal or algorithmic specification". New classes of models are needed to express the technology of interaction, since software technology has outstripped algorithm-based models of computation.

2 Models of Interactive Computing

Finite agents that perform actions, transforming inputs into outputs, are modeled by Turing machines (TMs), while finite agents that provide services over time, like objects, components, and databases, are modeled by interaction machines (IMs). TMs transform predetermined input strings into output strings, shutting out the world during the process of computation, while interaction machines (IMs) are transducers of interactively generated streams, solving a larger class of problems that TMs by interaction during the process of computation.

The shift from algorithms to interaction may be described as a shift from models of string transformation to models of stream transduction.

Expressiveness of finite computing agents is captured by the notion of observation equivalence, that measures the ability to make observational distinctions. Expressiveness depends both on the inherent computation power of observed systems and on the power of observers to observe or cause system behavior. The observed expressiveness of systems cannot be greater than that of observers who interact with them. When observers (testers) are limited to TMs that perform single interactions (ask single questions) then observed behavior is limited to TM behavior even for systems capable of interactive behavior [WG].

TMs are limited to single interactions that transform inputs to outputs, while IMs permit a greater range of interactive behavior, thereby extending the range of behavior of finite agents. Two distinct levels of interactive expressiveness corresponding to single-stream sequential interaction and multi-stream distributed interaction are identified:

> *single-stream (sequential) interaction*: realized by sequential interaction machines (SIMs)
>
> *multi-stream (distributed) interaction*: realized by multi-stream interaction machines (MIMs)

SIMs define a domain-independent model of sequential interaction that expresses sequential interaction between two objects in question-answering and control applications and more generally the interaction of sequential object-oriented languages and databases. MIMs provide a more expressive model for multi-stream (distributed) interaction that allows finite agents to interact with multiple autonomous agents, like an airline reservation systems that interacts with multiple travel agents or a distributed database that provides services to multiple autonomous clients. The greater expressiveness of MIMs over SIMs captures the greater problem-solving power of senior managers and CEOs over workers (finite agents) that perform sequences of interactively assigned tasks. Collaboration and coordination is shown to be more expressive than and not reducible to sequential interaction, contrasting with the fact that multitape TMs are no more expressive than single-tape TMs.

Adding autonomous streams (observation channels) to a finite agent increases expressiveness, while adding noninteractive tapes simply increases the structural complexity of predetermined inputs, and does not increase expressive power. Finite agents with autonomous multiple streams model distributed inputs by a form of interactive concurrency that is dual to algorithmic concurrency of process execution. MIMs support the behavior of nonserializable transactions and true concurrency [Pr], while SIMs support only serializable transactions and interleaving concurrency.

Sequential interaction is modeled mathematically by non-well-founded set theory [WG] and is captured by PTMs, which provide a canonical model for SIMs by a minimal extension of TMs to multitape machines with persistence. We show that PTMs with k+1 interactions are more expressive than PTMs with k interactions for all k, and that TMs have the expressiveness of PTMs with k=1. This hierarchy of expressiveness implies that interactive questioners can elicit more information about a questioned subject by k+1 sequences of follow-up questions than by k questions.

Observed behavior of finite agents can be meaningfully specified only relative to an observer, both for physical and computational systems. TM observers can observe only behavior for single I/O pairs, while SIM observers can observe the behavior of interactively supplied sequences of inputs that can depend on dynamically occurring events in the environment. For MIMs, finite agents can observe only sequential behavior of single streams. Complete behavior at all interfaces of a distributed system, such as an airline reservation system or nuclear reactor, cannot be observed by finite agents, though it could possibly be observed by physically unrealizable distributed observers (God). Since there are forms of behavior that can be specified but not observed, there is a distinction between specifiable behavior and observable behavior; in particular, the complete behavior of MIMs is specifiable but not observable.

The impact of models of observation on observed behavior has a simple form for SIMs, where stronger distinguishing power yields more expressive behavior, and has a subtler form for MIMs, where limitations of sequential observers in observing complete system behavior is related to quantum nondeterminism. Parallels between computational and physical models explored in [We3, WG] establish substantive connections between empirical computer science and models of observation in relativity and quantum theory. In particular, interactive models provide a stronger formulation of Einstein's argument that nondeterminism is due to incomplete observability, based on hidden interfaces rather than hidden variables. Einstein's intuition that God does not play dice and that observed nondeterminism is due to weaknesses of our model of observation rather than inherent in nature is modeled by primary observers who have no control over "random noise" due to secondary observers.

Interactive Models	Algorithmic Models
object-oriented programming	procedure-oriented programming
structured object-oriented prog.	structured programming
programming in the large	programming in the small
agent-oriented (distributed) AI	logic and search in AI
simulation, planning, control	rule-based reasoning
open systems	closed systems
empirical computer science	algorithmic computer science
nonenumerable (coinductive) sets	enumerable (inductive) sets

Fig. 1. Parallel Robustness of Interactive and Algorithmic Models of Computation

The parallelism between algorithmic concepts and corresponding interactive concepts is shown in Figure 1. Each algorithmic concept in the right-hand column is paralleled by a more expressive interactive concept in the left hand column. Object-oriented programs are more expressive than procedure-oriented programs in providing clients with continuing services over time: they are specified by marriage contracts that cannot be expressed by procedure-oriented sales contracts [We1]. Structured programming for actions (verbs) can be formally defined by compositional function specifications, while structured object-oriented programming is not compositional: composite structures of interactive components (nouns) have emergent behavior, such that the whole is greater than the sum of its parts. Programming in the large (PIL) is not determined by size, since a program with a million addition instruction is not PIL while an embedded system with only hundreds of lines of code is PIL. PIL can plausibly be defined as interactive programming and differs qualitatively from programming in the small (PIS) in the same way that interactive programs differ from algorithms.

Agent-oriented and distributed AI differs from logic-based AI in the same way that PIL differs from PIS. Simulation, planning, and control for interactive applications are not expressible by rule-based reasoning. Open systems cannot be expressed by closed algorithms that compute outputs noninteractively from their inputs. Interaction distinguishes robustly and precisely between empirical computer science and algorithmic models of computation. Each of the entries on the left hand column of Figure 1 has both sequential applications modeled by SIMs and more expressive distributed applications modeled by MIMs.

These parallel extensions from algorithms to interaction are captured by a mathematical paradigm shift that provides a foundation for sequential models of interaction, and requires new modes of mathematical thinking that will play an increasingly important role in undergraduate and graduate education. A key element in this paradigm shift is the extension from inductive definition and reasoning about enumerable sets to coinductive definition and reasoning about nonenumerable sets.

3   Mathematics of Interactive Modeling

Though impossibility results are useful in avoiding resource expenditures on unsolvable problems and in explaining the low profile of formal and algorithmic techniques in software engineering, they are not a sufficient basis for developing a technology of interactive computing. The impossibility of modeling interaction by mathematical models of first-order logic, recursive function theory, or traditional set theory at first suggested a sharp limitation of mathematics in modeling interaction and a tradeoff between formal algorithmic models and unformalizable interactive models. Fortunately a mathematical framework for interactive modeling has emerged [Ac, BM] that makes such a choice unnecessary.

The paradigm shift from algorithms to interaction is captured by a mathematical paradigm shift from inductive principles of definition and reasoning to stronger coinductive principles. Zermelo-Frankel set theory is extended by replacing the inductive *foundation axiom* by the coinductive *anti-foundation axiom*, which asserts that set equations of a certain form have a unique solution and provides a basis for non-well-founded set theory. This method of augmenting classes of mathematical objects is similar to algebraic methods of introducing rationals as solutions of linear equations with integer coefficients. Non-well-founded sets provide a consistent formal model for sequential interaction by formalizing stream behavior, and a denotational semantics for interactive models of sequential computation. Coalgebras provide a coinductive operational semantics for non-well-founded set theory [Ru1].

Induction is a technique for definition and reasoning over enumerable linear or partially ordered structures such as strings and trees. Coinduction is a technique for definition and reasoning over nonenumerable circular structures such as graphs and streams. TMs are inductively defined string processing machines that specify enumerable computations, while interaction machines are coinductively defined stream processing machines that specify nonenumerable computations. Inductively defined well-founded sets have enumerable elements, while coinductively defined non-well-founded sets may have nonenumerable elements.

Induction is specified by an *initiality condition*, an *iteration condition* that allows new elements to be derived from initial elements, and a *minimality condition* that only elements so derived can be considered. Coinduction eliminates initiality and is specified by an *iteration condition* and a *maximality condition* that models observers who consider all "possible worlds" not ruled out by observation.

Inductive definition: initiality condition, iteration condition, minimality condition.
Coinductive definition: iteration condition (circularity condition), maximality condition.

Initiality is a closed-system requirement whose elimination makes it possible to model open systems. There is a close relation between elimination of inductive initiality in mathematical models and shedding of the initial-state requirement of TMs for SIMs and PTMs. Initiality embodies preconceptions about the modeled world, and its elimination allows modeling of systems without preconceptions about the nature of their environments. In particular, predetermined static environments required by initiality can be generalized to incrementally supplied dynamic environments.

The minimality condition "everything is forbidden that is not allowed" specifies a smaller class of things than the more permissive maximality condition "everything is allowed that is not forbidden". Minimality is a property of constructive paradigms for definition and reasoning that characterize both algorithmic computation and constructive mathematics, while maximality is a property of empirical observation paradigms for describing observed behavior in an already constructed (existing) world. Minimality is modeled by least fixed points while maximality is modeled by greatest fixed points.

The distinction between minimality and maximality is a ubiquitous principle of system organization that extends from mathematical to social and political systems:

totalitarianism embodies the minimality principle: everything is forbidden that is not allowed
democracy supports the maximality principle: everything is allowed that is not forbidden

This association of algorithms with rule-governed restrictive forms of organization and of interactive models with permissive flexible forms of organization is a central theme in philosophy and the history of ideas, expressed by Isaiah Berlin in his parable of the hedgehog (who knows one big thing) and the fox (who knows many little things) [Be]. Hedgehogs embody minimalist depth at the expense of flexibility, while foxes are maximalist opportunists. Algorithmic models are hedgehog-like, focusing on functional correctness, while interactive models are fox-like, allowing dynamic flexibility of goals and forms of behavior that are to be modeled. Maximality and elimination of initiality extend mathematics so it can model fox-like systems that arise in computing, physics, and social organization.

Minimality of behavior is associated with maximality of constraints on behavior, while maximality of behavior is associated with minimality of constraints. This contravariance of constraints and behavior is illustrated by Berlin's essay "Two Concepts of Liberty" [Be], that contrasts negative freedom from interference by others with positive freedom to determine one's course of action. Berlin advocates negative freedom associated with minimal constraints on behavior and maximal fixed points, and is deeply suspicious of positive freedoms advocated by socialism or even liberalism, because they are realized by constraints designed to improve social conditions by constraining the freedom of indiviuals.

Maximal fixed points provide a mathematical framework for the empirical paradigm that any behavior (possible world) consistent with observation is admissible. Specifications that admit any possible world consistent with a specification are maximal fixed points. The reluctance of mathematicians to consider coinductive maximal fixed-point models stems in part from an inadequate analysis of the notion of circular reasoning [BM]. Russell and others failed to distinguish between inconsistent forms of circular reasoning that led to the paradoxes of set theory and consistent forms of circular reasoning.

However, a deeper reason was the strong influence on logic of Brouwer's intuitionism and Hilbert's formalism, which caused logicians to focus on properties of formalisms (proof theory) and to exclude consideration of independent concepts that formalisms aim to model. Constructive mathematics accords existence only to things that can be constructed, and even nonconstructive formalists restrict existence to finitely formalizable enumerable specifications. Both exclude concepts like the real numbers or the real world specified by nonenumerable elements or situations, which are unformalizable by enumerable inductive models, but can be formalized by coinductive (circular reasoning) models.

Godel's incompleteness result showed the impossibility of Hilbert's program of reducing mathematics to logic and by implication the impossibility of reducing computing to logic. In spite of this, Turing's model of computation is in the formalist tradition, implicitly accepting the Godel's limitation of incompleteness.

We show in section 5.2 that interactive models are formally incomplete in the sense of Godel.

Finsler's remarkable work on set theory in the 1920s [Fi] showed the consistency of non-well-founded set theory and anticipated Godel's incompleteness result. His work was largely ignored because it did not conform to the prevailing formalist tradition of Russell, Hilbert, and Tarski, resting instead on the Platonic tradition (espoused by Cantor) that concepts existed independently of the formalism in which they were expressed. Whereas formalist accepted "existence implies consistency", Finsler accepted the stronger ontological commitment "consistency implies existence". Finsler argued that since non-well-founded set theory was consistent it existed conceptually, independently of whether it had any useful models.

The discovery sixty years later that non-well-founded set theory models interactive computing provides an incentive for reevaluating Finsler's work, and validates the Platonic approach of according existence to conceptually consistent possible worlds independently of their formalizability or constructibility. Tensor analysis is another example of an abstract mathematical technique that found uses in relativity theory and a variety of other areas of applied mathematics many years after it was initially developed.

Godel's constructive demonstration of incompleteness of first-order logic by arithmetization of metamathematics (Godel numbering) was hailed as a seminal result by formalist logicians, while Finsler's prior result that formalisms are incomplete in expressing concepts, because we can conceive nonenumerable sets while formalisms express only enumerable sets, were not considered significant. Interactive models show the limitations of formalist inductive mathematics and have contributed to a mathematical paradigm shift that reestablishes the importance of independently given conceptual domains in mathematical modeling. Though philosophical questions concerning the foundations of mathematics are outside the scope of this paper, they are relevant to understanding the relation between formally specified finite interactive agents and their nonformalized environment.

4   Behaviorist Conceptual Modeling

The Turing test, which aims to express cognitive and conceptual inner properties of systems by their behavior, was criticized by Searle [Se] on the grounds that behavior cannot capture intentionality, and by Penrose [Pen] on the grounds that TM behavior is too weak to model the extensional behavior of humans or physical systems:

> **intentional skepticism**: TMs cannot model inner (intentional) qualities of thinking
> **extensional skepticism**: TM behavior is extensionally too weak to model thinking

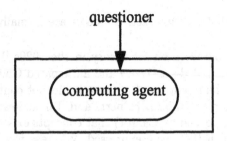

Fig. 2. Interactive Turing Test

We show [We1, WG] that replacing TMs by IMs in the Turing test (Figure 2) allows us to model not only stronger extensional behavior but also stronger intentional behavior. Turing not unnaturally assumed that the computing agent with which a questioner communicated was a TM, and his examples of Turing-test dialogs assumed that sequences of questions were unrelated, following a non-interactive, predetermined script [Tu3]. The interactive Turing test preserves Turing's behaviorist assumption that thinking is specifiable by behavior, but extends modes of questioning and responding to be interactive. Analysis of interactive question answering yields behaviorist models of "thinking" that are qualitatively different from the traditional Turing test model.

algorithmic thinking: TMs that answer single questions by algorithmic computation
algorithmic Turing test: single questions with algorithmically computable answers

sequential thinking: PTMs (SIMs) that answer sequences of history-dependent questions
sequential Turing test: dialog where questioner can ask sequences of follow-up questions

distributed thinking: MIMs that react to multiple autonomous streams of requests
multi-agent Turing test: coordination and collaboration for multiple autonomous streams

Algorithmic, sequential, and distributed thinking are progressively stronger forms of behavioral approximation to human thinking, defined by progressively more stringent empirical tests of behavior. Sequential thinking is realized by SIMs and observed by observers that ask follow-up questions (make sequential observations). Distributed thinking is realized by MIMs and requires multi-agent observers that can observe how the system responds to multiple potentially conflicting asynchronous requests.

Testing for multi-agent behavior extends the Turing test beyond SIMs to interaction with external resources like the Library of Congress, the Web, or human experts. Resources accessible to an IM are hidden from the questioner, who cannot distinguish whether the tested agent is an IM or a TM. The interactive Turing test extends machines without changing the form of the Turing test. Turing would certainly have accepted the sequential and multi-agent Turing tests as legitimate, and would have approved of the behaviorist notions of sequential and distributed thinking as conforming to the spirit of his notion of thinking.

Current IQ tests that focus on algorithmic intelligence by asking single questions have been shown to be poor predictors of later human success because they measure only limited forms of human problem solving. Sequential thinking can be tested by comparing the response of systems to sequences of related questions with human responses. Distributed thinking is tested by comparing system responses to autonomous streams with human responses. Sequential and distributed thinking require radical revision of methods of intelligence testing. Devising "intelligence" tests for sequential and distributed thinking is a challenging task that raises interesting research issues and could correlate significantly better than current IQ tests with later human success. Studies have shown that tests that measure human ability to delay gratification, such as the marshmallow test [Go], are better predictors of later success than IQ tests.

The arguments of both intentional and extensional skeptics lose much of their force when the algorithmic Turing test is replaced by the sequential and multi-agent Turing tests. The weak extensional behavior of TMs causes them to be ineffective in modeling intensional behavior. SIMs and MIMs can express stronger forms of intentionality because of their stronger extensional behavior. Searle's argument that machines cannot express intensional behavior is partly neutralized by SIMs that express intentionality through history dependence, and further weakened by MIMs that express the strong intentionality of multi-agent collaboration. The translators of Chinese stories in Searle's Chinese-room experiment must do more than follow transliteration rules in responding to interactive questions of sequential or multi-agent Turing tests. SIMs and MIMs have many, though not all, the properties that Searle calls intensional.

Penrose's arguments that computers cannot express extensional behaviors of physical object [Pen] are valid for TMs and possibly for SIMs but certainly not for MIMs [We3]. We agree with Penrose that TM models of computation are extensionally too weak to model physics. However, physics is computable according to the broader notion of MIM computability: Penrose's arguments about the noncomputability of physics by TMs become inapplicable when computing is broadened to include interaction.

Though Searle and Penrose are right that TMs are too weak to model thinking, the generalization that thinking cannot be modeled by behavior is an erroneous overreaction. The Turing test is deficient because TMs are too weak as a model of behavior, not because, as claimed by Searle and Penrose, computational behavior is an inadequate model of thought. Searle and Penrose were right about the inadequacy of the Turing test, but for the wrong reasons. By contrast, Turing had the right experimental design but applied it to the wrong model of computation. The interactive Turing test not only augments the extensional behavior that machines can exhibit, but also their ability to express intentional qualities.

Penrose argues in [Pen] that the nondeterminism of physics may be illusory because physical phenomena may be deterministic but noncomputable. He suggest that nondeterminism arises because we limit our physical model to being computable and that a noncomputable model of physics could potentially resolve nondeterminism. Though this argument is wrong in rhe sense that physical phenomena are computable by MIMs, it is nearly right. If Penrose's term "noncomputable" is replaced by the term "not-TM-computable", MIMs can be viewed as the "not-TM-computable" models that Penrose needs.

A MIM is a tool for studying the interaction of k+1 entities, where one plays a special role as an observed system and the remaining entities are observers, modeled by streams. For interacting SIMs, k = 1 and the observer with the observed system form a closed system. When the observed system is a MIM, k is greater than 1 and a primary observer representing the experimenter is distinguished from k-1 secondary observers. MIMs appear nondeterministic from the viewpoint of a primary observer who cannot predict or control the effects of secondary observers and may be unaware of their presence. Primary observer perceive MIMs as subjectively nondeterministic even when, viewed by an omniscient multi-agent observer (God), they are objectively deterministic (Figure 3).

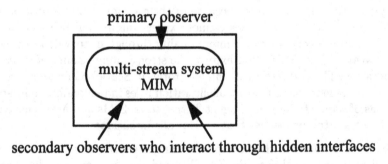

Fig. 3. Interactive Turing Test

In retrospect, Penrose's insight that nondeterminism of physics is due to a weakness of the model rather than an inherent feature of the physical world may turn out to be remarkably close to the truth. His mistake was to accept TM computability as the most powerful form of computing when in fact there are stronger models. By reformulating Penrose's argument in terms of non-TM computability and introducing MIMs as a stronger form of computation, we not only validate Penrose's argument but also demystify it by providing a concrete mechanism and model for the stronger form of computation. Whereas Penrose's hypothesis is not testable, we expect that the hypothesis that MIMs provide a model for quantum theory can be tested.

Penrose's view that computers cannot model physics is based on a misconception of the nature of computing shared by Church and Turing that has its historical roots in the rationalism of Plato and Descartes [We3]. Penrose's identification of computation with Turing computability and Turing's identification of thinking with Turing computability are based on rationalist presuppositions remarkably similar to Plato's model of observation in his parable of the cave [We3].

Plato's cave metaphor, which compares humans to cave dwellers who can observe only shadows (projections) of reality on the walls of their cave and not actual objects in the outside world, is a model of relationships between observers and observed systems that has played an important historical role and is still relevant today. We extend Plato's cave metaphor to cave dwellers who interact with the external world, and show that such interactive observers have the power of IMs and express Platonic empiricism.

Empiricists accept Plato's argument that people perceive incomplete projections $P(W)$ of an external world W on their sensory perceptors. However, they disagree with Plato's conclusion that empirical objects are therefore not worth modeling and that ideal (Platonic) tables are more real than empirically observable tables. Plato's belief that incompletely specifiable objects are not worthy of study, based on a faulty analysis of the notion of abstraction, contributed to a 2000-year delay in the emergence of empirical science. Empiricism repudiates the requirement of completeness, accepting that complete knowledge is unnecessary because the goals of prediction and control can be achieved entirely through incomplete observable shadows (projections) that are observational abstractions of inherently unobservable reality. The mathematical incompleteness of interactive models parallels the descriptive incompleteness of observed physical objects, while completely specifiable algorithms are the computational analog of Platonic objects.

Empirical computer science provides a concrete framework for studying observational abstractions in a context where "inner reality" can be specified and systematically varied. Computational abstractions provide insight into realist models of physics, where inner reality is unobservable and uncontrollable [We3].

Plato understates the information that can be gained by shadows on the walls of a cave. Humans can obtain a variety of different images of their environment through multiple senses (vision, sound, touch). They can obtain multiple simultaneous spatial images through two eyes and two ears to obtain a stereo effect. Multiple temporal images can be obtained by sampling the environment at multiple points of time, creating stereo-spatio temporal images that provide richer cues for image reconstruction than geometric two-dimensional images on the walls of a Platonic cave. The richness of images created in this way has been recognized by caves in virtual reality.

We not only can select the images we wish to perceive, but can act to modify the external world and observe the effect of our actions. The process of observing how shadows that represent the state of the world change as a result of our actions can be thought of as shadow boxing: you can observe, predict, and control the way shadows change when you punch them. Shadow boxing may be interpreted as interaction, and occupants of Platonic caves who can shadow-box correspond to full-fledged empiricists.

By showing that interaction machines express empirical computer science, we show that arguments of Penrose, along with those of Church, Turing, and Descartes, are rooted in a common rationalist fallacy concerning the role of non-interactive algorithms in modeling the real world. Penrose's instinct that Turing machines cannot model physics is correct, but his belief that noncomputable models are the key to a unified theory of physical and mental phenomena rests on a limited definition of computability.

Though Searle's and Penrose's criticisms of algorithmic thinking become much weaker when applied to sequential and distributed thinking, the anti-behaviorist argument that inner processes cannot be unambiguously described by behavior remains valid, since behavior is an abstraction of system structure. Since behavior specifications have nonenumerable system implementations, behavior is a weak determinant of system structure. However, the status of behaviorist models is completely changed when thought is modeled by interactive behavior that is extensionally and intentionally richer than algorithmic behavior.

References

[Ac] Peter Aczel, *Non Well-Founded Sets*, CSLI Lecture Notes #14, Stanford, 1988.

[Be] Isiah Berlin, *The Proper Study of Mankind*, anthology edited by Henry Hardy and Roger Hausheer, Farrar, Straus, and Giroux, 1997.

[BM] Jon Barwise and Lawrence Moss, *Vicious Circles*, CSLI Lecture Notes #60, Cambridge University Press, 1996.

[Ch] Peter Chen, The Entity Relationship Model: Towards a Unified View of Data, *Transactions on Database Systems*, 1976.

[Fi] Paul Finsler, *Finsler Set Theory: Platonism and Circularity*, Ed David Booth and Renatus Ziegler, Birkhauser, 1996.

[Go] Daniel Goleman, *Emotional Intelligence*, Bantam paperback, 1997.

[KR] Haim Kilov and James Ross, *Information Modeling: An Object-Oriented Approach*, Prentice Hall, 1994.

[Mi] Robin Milner, Operational and Algebraic Semantics of Concurrent Processes, *Handbook of Theoretical Computer Science*, J. van Leeuwen, editor, Elsevier, 1990.

[MP] Zohar Manna and Amir Pnueli, *The Temporal Logic of Reactive and Concurrent Systems*, Springer Verlag, 1992.

[Pen] Roger Penrose, *The Emperor's New Mind*, Oxford, 1989.

[Pr] Vaughan Pratt, Chu Spaces and their Interpretation as Concurrent Objects, in *Computer Science Today: Recent Trends and Developments*, Ed. Jan van Leeuwen, LNCS #1000, 1995.

[Ru1] Jan Rutten, A Tutorial on Coalgebras and Coinduction, *EATCS Bulletin 62*, 1997.

[Se] John Searle, *Minds, Brains, and Programs*, The Behavioral and Brain Sciences, 1980.

[Tu1] Alan Turing, On Computable Numbers with an Application to the Entscheidungsproblem, *Proc. London Math Soc.*, 2:42, pp. 230-265, 1936.

[Tu2] Alan Turing, Systems of Logic Based on Ordinals, *Proc. London Math. Soc.*, 1939.

[Tu3] Alan Turing, Computing Machinery and Intelligence, *Mind*, 1950.

[We1] Peter Wegner, Why Interaction is More Powerful Than Algorithms, *CACM*, May 1997.

[We2] Peter Wegner, Interactive Foundations of Computing, *Theoretical Computer Science*, Feb. 1998

[We3] Peter Wegner, Towards Empirical Computer Science, *The Monist*, Issue on the Philosophy of Computation, Spring 1999, available at `www.cs.brown.edu/people/pw`.

[We4] Peter Wegner, Interactive Software Technology, *Handbook of Computer Science and Engineering*, CRC Press, December 1996.

[We5] Peter Wegner, Tradeoffs Between Reasoning and Modeling, in *Research Directions in Concurrent Object-Oriented Programming*, Eds. Agha, Wegner, Yonezawa, MIT Press 1993.

[WG] Peter Wegner and Dina Goldin, Mathematical Models of Interactive Computing, `www.cs.brown.edu/people/pw`, December 1998.

[ZM] Stanley Zdonik and David Maier, *Readings in Object-Oriented Database Systems*, Morgan Kaufmann, 1990

A Summary of the ER'97 Workshop
on Behavioral Modeling

*Stephen W. Liddle, †Stephen W. Clyde, and ‡Scott N. Woodfield

*School of Accountancy and Information Systems, Brigham Young University
†Department of Computer Science, Utah State University
‡Department of Computer Science, Brigham Young University

Abstract. The ER'97 Workshop on Behavioral Modeling was held to consider the questions of what constitutes a "good" behavioral model, and assuming we have such a "good" behavioral model, what issues related to design transformations we should explore. This very international workshop included interesting and high-quality papers on both of these topics. The proceedings are available electronically through the World-Wide Web [10]. This paper summarizes the contributions of the Behavioral Modeling workshop and suggests directions for future research in behavioral modeling.

Introduction

Conceptual models are not just for databases any more. From its genesis in data modeling, the field of conceptual modeling has broadened to include behavioral constructs. The advent of technologies such as object orientation, active databases, triggers in relational databases, workflow systems, and so forth has placed greater emphasis on the need to model behavioral aspects of systems in addition to structural aspects. The literature reflects an increasing interest in conceptual models that cover both system structure and system behavior.

The problem of how to design a database system based on a semantic data model is well understood. The focus of traditional design is on issues such as constraint satisfaction, information redundancy, access times, etc. We apply well-studied information-preserving transformations (such as normalization or denormalization) to arrive at a database with the characteristics we desire. However, when we add behavior to the conceptual model, we introduce additional design challenges that are less well understood, such as controlling the amount of concurrency, optimizing communications between active components, ensuring correct synchronization of active components, satisfying real-time constraints, etc.

Researchers are devoting increasingly more energy to the problems of behavioral modeling in conjunction with traditional conceptual data modeling. Behavioral modeling is not new, but its tighter integration with traditional conceptual modeling has opened new questions and opportunities. ER'97 provided an ideal forum for gathering interested researchers to discuss challenges and progress, and to share ideas in this area.

On November 6 and 7, 1997, we held the *ER'97 Workshop on Behavioral Models and Design Transformations: Issues and Opportunities in Conceptual Modeling*, on

P.P. Chen et al. (Eds.): Conceptual Modeling, LNCS 1565, pp. 258-271, 1999.
© Springer-Verlag Berlin Heidelberg 1999

UCLA campus in Los Angeles, California [10]. In the present paper we summarize the context and contributions of this workshop and point to directions for further useful research in the area of behavioral modeling.

The goal of the Behavioral Modeling workshop was to better understand theoretical aspects of behavioral models and use that understanding to suggest transformations that would be helpful in the design of active systems. We issues two major questions in our call for participation:

1. What constitutes a "good" behavioral model?
2. Given a "good" behavioral model, what issues related to design transformations should we explore so that our understanding of behavioral design will be as good as our understanding of more traditional structural design?

In our call for participation, we suggested the following topics related to the first question:

- What are the essential characteristics of a behavioral model?
  - How close to the "real world" must a behavioral model be?
  - Is intra-object concurrency necessary or desirable?
  - Should the basic unit of behavioral transition be instantaneous?
- How do we formally compare different behavioral models?
  - How do we measure power in a behavioral model?
  - Is computational completeness adequate?
  - When does one model subsume another?
  - Is a formal definition necessary or desirable?
  - Are there issues of notational expressiveness we should consider?

And we suggested the following topics related to question 2:

- What are the desirable properties of a behavioral model design?
- Are there useful canonical/normal forms for behavioral models?
- Can we identify any meaningful behavior patterns that seem to recur frequently?
- How do we measure quality in a behavioral model?
- How do interface definitions impact the quality of a behavioral model?
- What design transformations are necessary or desirable?
- How do we guarantee information preservation in our transformations?
- Should behavioral design be independent of the implementation platform?
  - Are there useful design transformations that are platform independent?
  - Are there useful design transformations that are platform dependent?
  - Should design assume complete independence from the eventual implementation platform, should it be totally dependent on the platform, or should we use something in between?
- How does the inclusion of behavior in the conceptual model impact structural aspects of the model?
  - Are there subtle interactions between structural and behavioral constructs that we need to consider?

- Are the transformations used in the absence of behavioral constructs still information preserving and otherwise effective in the presence of behavioral constructs?

- How do designers know when a particular design is "done"? Can this question only be answered on a project-by-project basis, or even worse, must it be answered on a module-by-module basis?

We determined that issues related to actual implementation and specific methodology was well beyond the scope of our workshop. We would only address issues tied directly to conceptual modeling and conceptual design. This is the context in which the Behavioral Modeling workshop was created.

It turned out that the majority of our focus was on question 1, as the workshop participants felt we were not entirely ready to answer the second question. However, we made progress in both areas.

We now summarize the workshop papers in the order they were presented. We conclude with a section on research questions that merit further study.

A Framework for Assessing Database Quality

John Hoxmeier presented a framework for assessing database quality [6]. This paper addressed aspects of both of the workshop topics. In order to agree on what constitutes a good behavioral model, we first need to understand the parameters that allow us to compare behavioral models.

Hoxmeier proposes that the application of a quality process does not necessarily ensure that a quality system will result. That is, a system could have high "data quality" without also exhibiting good "semantic or cognitive fidelity." A truly effective system would exhibit good characteristics along this added dimension. In this context, Hoxmeier's contribution is to extend a previous hierarchical framework for database quality measurement with behavioral considerations. He builds on the work of a number of groups who are interested in database quality assessment.

Hoxmeier's four primary dimensions of database quality include the already well accepted dimensions of data and process quality, and the newly proposed dimensions of semantics and behavior quality. In his paper he presents a description of each of these four quality dimensions.

Hoxmeier concludes that database quality assessment is critical to modern information-heavy organizations, and that we need a combination of quantitative and qualitative measurements to effectively assess database quality. Moreover, the inclusion of behavioral aspects in database quality assessment is imperative to forming an accurate assessment.

Behavioral Model Quality and Transformation

In his position statement, Martin Gogolla outlined a proposal for understanding and assessing the quality of design transformations [5]. He assumed that design would be done in successive steps (transformations) where the degree of detail and closeness to an actual implementation would increase with each transformation. With each transformation, relevant properties of the conceptual model should be preserved.

Gogolla advocates using an object specification language that is formal and hence clear enough for measured comparison of behavioral and structural aspects of a conceptual model. His research group has developed TrollLight as an illustration of such a language.

Gogolla analyzed the characteristics of TrollLight with respect to the two questions of this workshop, namely, what constitutes quality in a behavioral model, and what design transformations should we explore.

There was a high degree of group participation and discussion during Gogolla's presentation. Several proposals were discussed:

- two-way transformations are superior to one-way transformations
- quality could be measured in terms of the amount of implementation detail introduced by a transformation
- transformations should be relatively uniform in scope

Dynamic Dialog Management

Bernhard Thalheim presented ongoing work (with W. Clauss and J. Lewerenz) that involves a new way of modeling and developing database systems for relatively naïve users based on the idea of dialog design [2]. Their research context is data warehousing. Thalheim proposed that instead of "behavioral" modeling we should be considering "dialog" modeling. Dialogs constitute a possible foundation for integrating database development along several dimensions, including static/dynamic, global/local, and architectural layers (or steps in the system lifecycle).

Many of the ideas developed in structural database design can be transferred to behavioral database design. The relationship between a "schema" and a "view instance" is analogous to the relationship between a "behavior definition" and a "dialog instance." Intuitively, a "dialog" is a "behavioral view." A dialog is the specification of how actors use database views to perform various activities within a system. In this sense, a dialog is much like a "use case" [7].

Thalheim et. al. take the point of view that whereas schema is the definition of possible database states, behavior is the definition of possible update operations that can transform one state into another. Dialogs integrate both of these ideas by showing how views (representing schema) are applied within the context of actual processes (representing system behavior).

When taking a dialog approach, it is no longer sufficient to focus merely on schema design. Instead, a structure-process codesign approach is more appropriate. That is, dialogs must be designed in conjunction with processes and views, because they present the end-user with access both to data and functions of the system. In analogy with theatrical production, the abstraction layers for dialog specification include idea (motivation), story, scenario, script, and production. Thalheim proposes that dialogs are appropriate for use at each of these layers, unifying the conceptual model used in specification, design, and implementation.

The dialog approach was demonstrated in the development of an information service based on a 25-line by 60-character display that is as easy to use as a television. This system is used to perform services such as buying theater tickets and reserving tables at restaurants. Open problems include the creation of a suitable dialog cooperation model (how do/should dialogs interact with one another) and the development of adequate dialog management tools.

Thalheim also identified a number of impedance mismatches in conceptual modeling and database design that relate to the topics of this workshop. In various ways, the dialog approach addresses these mismatches.

- abstraction level
- structure/process
- structure/semantics
- function/behavior
- interface/DB schema
- process/workflow
- CASE tool (lack of interoperability)
  - different specification languages
  - different treatment of semantics & meaning
  - user needs aren't being satisfied

On the Quality of Conceptual Models

Harmen van den Berg presented a paper in which he and W.B. Teeuw propose general quality criteria for conceptual models, and based on those general criteria propose more specific criteria for evaluating behavior models [14]. Their work is done within the framework of the "Testbed" project in the context of telecommunications applications.

Others have proposed three kinds of conceptual model quality:

- Semantic quality — degree of correspondence between a conceptual model and the real world.
- Syntactic quality — degree of correspondence between a conceptual model and its representation.
- Pragmatic quality — degree of correspondence between a conceptual model and its interpretation (degree to which model is understood).

Van den Berg proposes six general quality criteria:

- Completeness — constructs are sufficient to capture essential aspects of the real world.
- Inherence or propriety — constructs do not model derived features, only essential features.
- Clarity — the conceptual model is understandable by designers.
- Consistency — constructs do not conflict, are not ambiguous, and are parsimonious (a special case of inherence).
- Orthogonality or modularity — the independence/dependence of model constructs is the same as the independence/dependence of corresponding real-world aspects.

- Generality — model constructs are independent from applications and application domains.

The first three criteria correspond to external quality, and the last three to internal quality. Based on these criteria, van den Berg proposes a four-dimensional framework for evaluating models and tools for business process reengineering (BPR). These dimensions are functionality (expressiveness, abstractions, compositions, formal/methodological support, relevance of concepts, etc.), ease of use (accessibility, usability, adaptability, openness, etc.), BPR trajectory (which BPR phases are supported), and general (e.g., tool price, customer support).

Finally, van den Berg presented an example within the Testbed environment, illustrating how Testbed fits within the specified quality framework. He indicated that a bit more than half a dozen cases per year are being tested in actual practice with Testbed.

Behavioral Design Issues in a Distributed Environment

Stephen Clyde presented a position paper on problems that need to be addressed when designing the behavior of distributed systems [3]. Real-world distributed systems exhibit several important characteristics that distinguish them from centralized solutions:

- Concurrency — real objects act simultaneously, but centralized systems only simulate concurrency.
- Partial failure — independent objects can fail independently without causing system-wide failure, but centralized systems usually treat failure as an all-or-nothing condition.
- Dynamic, incremental change — real-world systems are not completely shut down to accommodate change; instead, they are modified dynamically.

In spite of the correspondence between the characteristics of real-world systems and distributed systems, it is not true that a good conceptual model of a real-world system translates directly into a good design for a distributed system. As a principle, it is a good idea to minimize conceptual distances between steps in the system development lifecycle. However, numerous issues work to increase conceptual distance:

- Complex mappings — analysis and design concepts are not one-to-one.
- Fragmented behavior — a software object may only represent a portion of the behavior of a corresponding analysis object. Many fragments may correspond to portions of an analysis object.
- Object distribution — physical distribution in the real world may not correspond to the best distribution of software objects.
- Emergent communications — software objects need to communicate for reasons different than those defined in the analysis model (e.g., for replica management, transaction synchronization, name resolution).
- Emergent resource sharing — software objects may share resources for convenience of implementation, not because those resources are actually shared in the analysis model.

- Transparency — attempts to shield users from issues of actual object/service location, replication, migration, etc. further transform the software design so it is less like the analysis model.

Clyde concludes that distributed systems design is unnecessarily complex because current conceptual models do not support the right abstractions, and that if we work on defining correct abstractions, we can minimize conceptual distances and hence also design complexity. He proposes that we develop the following abstractions for

- mapping software objects to analysis objects,
- describing object fragmentation, especially for behavior,
- specializing objects and object fragments without violating inherited semantics,
- specifying and constraining object distribution, replication, and migration,
- dealing with emergent communications and resource sharing,
- and for patterns/idioms that help achieve transparency and other desirable properties.

Integration of Behavior Models

Heinz Frank presented a paper (written with J. Eder) describing algorithms for view integration when the conceptual model includes behavior [4]. View integration is a very effective approach for developing conceptual models of a universe of discourse — start with views from many different users and then integrate them. However, traditional view integration techniques deal only with structural views. We need new approaches for views that include behavior. Object-oriented models typically use Harel statecharts (or something similar) to describe behavior. In their paper, Frank and Eder describe an integration method for models that use statecharts. This integration method has two phases: static-model integration and dynamic-model integration.

Static-model integration deals with structural elements (e.g., types, attributes, and their relationships to other types). The aim of this phase is to identify and resolve conflicts (naming conflicts or structural conflicts) among the types of the various views. The result of this integration phase is a static conceptual model of the universe of discourse, as one would expect with existing view-integration methods. The main topic of Frank's presentation is the second phase: dynamic-model integration.

Dynamic-model integration is divided into three steps. First, we formalize the dynamic model by describing ranges of all states in all statechart views together with constraints or conditions on the corresponding static type. For example, given a library, a book might be in the "available" state. If so, we require that the book's "status" attribute represent "in the library" and that its "reserved" attribute be "false". The range of a statechart is thus defined as a subspace of the object space spanned by the definition of the type. After formalizing the views, we analyze relationships between different views based on their marginal (or initial and final) states. Relationship classes include disjoint, consecutive, alternative, parallel, and mixed. For each relationship class, Frank and Eder have defined an integration operator to combine views related within that class.

The second step is integration-in-the-large, where we develop an integration plan whose goal is to minimize integration effort. An integration plan is a sequence of integration operators for the different relationships between statecharts. For mixed relationships (where fragments of both behavior models must be combined in the integrated type), we must further analyze all states and events, but for other relationships the integration operators only rely on marginal states. Mixed relationships are integrated as early as possible in the integration plan.

The third and final step is integration-in-the-small, where we perform the actual integration by executing the integration plan. Significantly, development of the integration plan is separated from execution of that plan. Relationships between views can be analyzed and explored without actually performing the integration, saving some effort during integration-in-the-large.

Dynamic-model integration will become ever more important as behavior becomes increasingly common in conceptual models. This behavior integration method is a useful contribution. And more particularly, this method is useful because it is automated.

A Comparison of Workflow Metamodels

Munindar Singh presented a paper (written with Y. Lei) comparing different metamodels for workflow modeling [8]. Singh and Lei's goal is to improve the level of conceptual modeling applied to workflow problems. As a fairly young field, much effort has been invested in improving tools and techniques for workflow, but less effort has been spent on conceptual modeling concepts. This paper presents metamodels for five common workflow approaches, defines evaluation criteria for workflow conceptual models, and uses these criteria to compare different approaches based on the metamodels.

The workshop participants observed that in a state-transition diagram (like that presented in Frank's work), work (or behavior) is accomplished in transitions. In contrast, in a workflow situation, work is accomplished in states. Thus, there is still a need for discussion on how best to model behavior (or if there is no "best", at least how to model behavior canonically).

Singh demonstrated how to study and understand existing workflow approaches. Using his metamodels, he is able to compare the salient features of different approaches. Having a basis for comparison, we can now improve our models formally and systematically. Singh believes that we will see more formal methodologies and also greater integration with database systems as workflow technology evolves. He also sees naturally decentralized models as a consequence of developing these metamodels. Finally, he predicts that the agent metaphor will be increasingly important in workflow. It was apparent to the workshop participants that workflow modeling is a significant area where behavioral issues arise. Future conceptual models need to support workflow techniques.

An Infological Perspective on Expressiveness

Björn Lundell presented a paper (written with B. Lings) on how the expressiveness of diagramming techniques can impact the use of conceptual models of behavior within an organization [11]. To do so, Lundell first places conceptual behavior modeling within the broader context of IS development, and then he describes how an "infological perspective" helps us improve the utility of behavioral conceptual models.

Lundell identifies two main problems. (1) An enhanced ER model extended to support behavior usually does so at the cost of significant added complexity in the resulting diagrams. This complexity is a barrier to use. (2) Instead of enhancing a conceptual model, we may use distinct models at the conceptual level to capture behavior. But when we do so, the number of interrelationships that must be maintained between related concepts in different models increases exponentially with the number of models used.

Traceability between behavioral models and other high-level conceptual models is very important, and Lundell observes that a repository should be used to capture this complex information. Once a model is in such a repository, the problem becomes one of extracting the information in appropriate views that are sufficiently expressive for the purpose at hand. Given a repository, then, we next need to develop appropriately expressive graphical view notations. What is expressive for designers, is not necessarily expressive for end-users, and vice versa. So, what constitutes appropriate expressiveness for different requirements and how do we measure it?

The "infological equation" states that information (I) is a function not only of data (D), but also an individual's existing (or pre-) knowledge (S) and time (t) available for interpretation (that is, $I = i(D, S, t)$). Lundell proposes that expressiveness be measured in terms of the infological I. This implies that we cannot merely take a quantitative approach to measuring expressiveness — we must also use qualitative techniques to account for the all factors present in the infological equation. Lundell concludes with the observation that we need to consider systems development as a social process that involves various levels of participants. As such, Lundell proposes that we should apply techniques from the social sciences to our conceptual modeling methodologies.

Modeling Temporal Behavior Conceptually

Chiyaba Njovu presented a paper (written with T.W. Lawson) on modeling temporal behavior in the context of the object-oriented (OO) paradigm common to OMT, Syntropy, and similar OO approaches [13]. Typically, these OO models do not directly support temporal relationships, which are vital in real-world situations. Njovu's contribution is to propose extensions (specifically, to the Syntropy model) that support temporal relationships, memories of event occurrences, and object histories.

This workshop was particularly interested in extensions to Syntropy's dynamic model. Behavioral models are fundamentally interested in temporal aspects of a system, addressing the issue of how a system changes over time.

Njovu presented three temporal concepts: time points, durations, and intervals. Further, he showed how these concepts can be combined as elements in a timeline (a temporal aggregate). Finally, he distinguished between the notions of "valid time" (when an event occurs in the real world), and "transaction time" (when the corresponding event is recorded in the automated system). Njovu's extensions to Syntropy are based on these elements.

Syntropy uses the statechart abstraction to represent object behavior. However, statecharts fail to represent (1) the difference between events and "memories of events", and (2) the fact that some object types need memories of all its states (Njovu used the example of a loan system to illustrate this). The element that is missing from typical models is a timeline of what has occurred during an objects lifetime.

Njovu proposes that we support temporality by adding "temporal qualification" to the associations linking object types and state types. Temporal information (such as the time point, duration, or interval) about associations thus qualified can be maintained automatically by the system, thus relieving developers of the burden of working around the system to capture such information.

Events as Information Objects and Change Agents

Lars Bækgaard presented a paper describing how behavior can be modeled as events that are both "information objects" and "change agents" [1]. An event modeled as an information object is like a traditional entity that has attributes and can be queried. An event modeled as a change agent is comparable to an executable transaction schema.

Bækgaard first described how events can be modeled as information objects, augmenting a typical semantic data model with the concept "event set", which is like an entity set that contains event entities. A primary difference between entities and events is that events exist at a point in time, while entities exist over a time interval. Each event entity is always associated with a time attribute to represent the event execution time. Events as information objects can profitably be used for constraint specification, for example to constrain possible state transitions in which an entity may participate.

As change agents, events can be used to specify how a system behaves when events occur. Event specifications have the form EVENT <event signal> DO <command list>. Bækgaard described two possible commands that can be used in a command list, including TELL and UNTELL (for inserting and removing information from the database, respectively). Both commands have a WHERE clause describing the set of data to be inserted or removed.

Bækgaard next described how to specify event patterns, and he concluded with a discussion of how this compares with object oriented techniques. He identified several problems with traditional OO when applied to databases. For example, strong encapsulation forces the distribution of behavioral specifications associated with an event that is modeled as a change agent. Bækgaard concluded with the observation that traditional OO is not well suited for symmetric modeling of events as both information objects and change agents.

Mismatches between Models and Implementation Environments

Scott Woodfield described problems with the relationship between conceptual models and implementation environments [15]. To minimize expensive, early errors in software development, we use conceptual models that are moving increasingly closer to reality and farther from computer implementation environments. But as we move closer to natural forms, we introduce conceptual mismatches (often called "impedance mismatches") between analysis models and implementation languages. In this paper, Woodfield describes eight specific problems associated with transforming an object-oriented conceptual analysis model into an implementation:

- Persistence — OO conceptual models assume persistence, but OO programming languages do not.
- Classes — in a conceptual model, classes usually have an extent that can be queried, and objects can migrate from class to class. In an implementation environment this is usually not the case.
- Relations — implementation environments usually do not have relations, only attributes.
- Generalization/Specialization — conceptual models use "is-a" semantics, while OO languages use inheritance. There are major differences between these two ideas, and we lose a great deal of the meaning of generalization/specialization when we restrict ourselves to inheritance.
- Active Objects — OO conceptual models assume that objects can be active, but OO languages assume passive, invocation-driven behavior with an assumption of uniform service availability.
- Concurrency — both inter- and intra-object concurrency is assumed at the conceptual level, but implementation environments generally support a much more limited version of concurrency.
- Complex Interactions and Communication — again, conceptual models provide more general forms of communication than are directly supported in typical OO languages.
- Declarative Information — constraints and derivation descriptions are common to conceptual models, but OO languages generally rely on applicative expressions.

Woodfield suggests numerous techniques for addressing these impedance mismatches, including the use of design patterns, generic packages, and pattern languages and tools. Ultimately, the best approach would be to evolve our implementation languages so that they support all the concepts found in our models directly, but before we can do this efficiently, we need to gain more experience with how these ideas can be effectively implemented in practice.

Behavioral Design through Seamless Modeling

Steve Liddle presented a position paper describing a seamless approach to behavioral design [9]. According to this approach, the conceptual model and the implementation language used to propose, design, and implement a system should be fully equivalent. Furthermore, the development environment for information systems projects should include several layers that are thoroughly integrated:

- Metamodel — metaschema that describes features of the model
- Model instance — "schema" layer that contains structural and behavioral descriptions of a particular system
- Data instance — actual objects and relationships that are interacting to carry out the behavior of a system and that reflect the current system state

Liddle suggested that underlying such a layered system should be standard mathematical model theory. Given such a well-understood basis, behavioral design transformations can be expressed formally, and thus studied and compared precisely in a model-theoretic framework.

Furthermore, Liddle took the position that the conceptual model should be close to the "real world" as opposed to being close to the "software development world". He views most popular conceptual models as being oriented too much towards developers and not enough towards end users. Pushing a model towards the real world means leaving techniques that are easy to implement efficiently on actual computers with modern programming languages and databases. Overcoming inefficiencies is the biggest challenge of implementing systems in the seamless modeling paradigm.

Liddle also proposed a number of characteristics that he believes should be desirable for conceptual behavior models, such as supporting a mixture of active and passive objects with intra-object concurrency and non-uniform service availability. He then described desirable behavioral design properties, such as maximizing reuse and robustness with respect to possible failure modes. We refer the interested reader to his paper for the complete lists. Liddle concluded with proposals for design transformation patterns and canonical forms of behavior.

Research Directions

At the conclusion of the workshop, we attempted to identify proposed design transformations that could be further studied. However, we agreed that before we can do a thorough job of such identification, we first need better definition of the term "design transformation." Nevertheless, here is the (certainly incomplete) list of transformations we generated.

- Reduce concurrency
- Increase concurrency (note that depending on the design characteristics we seek, concurrency might need to be reduced under one set of circumstances, but increased under another)
- Add transaction specifications
- Reduce interaction/communication

- Transform non-uniform service availability to uniform service availability (see [12] for definitions of "service availability").
- Reduce recursion
- Integrate views (in the sense of Heinz Frank)
- Introduce temporal specification
- Remove temporality (again, whether the presence or absence of temporality is desirable may depend on the particular circumstances, so we should develop both kinds of transformations)
- Map event-based model to implementation

These and other transformations could be studied profitably as we seek to improve our understanding of behavioral model design.

We also discussed open research issues, and the following directions of investigation with respect to behavioral modeling were suggested:

- We need better tool support at various conceptual levels (e.g., understanding, design, and implementation).
- We need to develop appropriate methodologies for the evaluation of CASE tool support for behavioral modeling.
- We need to find an integrated way to move from high-level design or specification to implementation
- We're missing mappings.
- Look at specific domains — try our theoretical ideas in practice.
- Work on different categories of transformations: specification to design, design to implementation, etc.
- Increase our capability to generate code.
- We need improved metrics for better formal comparison.
- What is the impact of the use of ERP's like SAP, Bonn, PeopleSoft, Oracle, etc.?
- Behavioral modeling is not adequately understood — continue dialog on this before we work on transformations.
- As much as possible, transformations should be two-way, because one-way transformations lose the tie between implementation and conceptual model.

Acknowledgements

We thank all the participants from around the world who attended and contributed to this international workshop. Attendees included:

- Lars Bækgaard, Aarhus School of Business, Denmark
- Alcides Calsavara, Pontificia Universidade Catolica Do Parana, Brazil
- Stephen Clyde, Utah State University, USA
- Cesar Ferreira de Matos, IRS/Finance Ministry, Brazil
- Heinz Frank, Universität Klagenfurt, Austria
- Martin Gogolla, University of Bremen, Germany
- John Hoxmeier, Colorado State University, USA
- Nick Knowles, OTI, UK

- Steve Liddle, Brigham Young University, USA
- Björn Lundell, University of Skövde, Sweden
- Chiyaba Njovu, University of Wales, UK
- Katia Regina de Souza, IRS/Finance Ministry, Brazil
- Carlos Silberman, SERPRO, Brazil
- Munindar Singh, North Carolina State University, USA
- Markus Stumptner, Technische Universität Wien, Austria
- Bernhard Thalheim, Brandenburg Technical University of Cottbus, Germany
- Harmen van den Berg, Telematics Research Centre, the Netherlands
- Scott Woodfield, Brigham Young University, USA

References

1. L. Bækgaard, Conceptual Modeling of Events as Information Objects and Change Agents, in *ER'97 Workshop 4 Proceedings*, 1997.
2. W. Clauss, J. Lewerenz, and B. Thalheim, Dynamic Dialog Management, in *ER'97 Workshop 4 Proceedings*, 1997.
3. S.W. Clyde, Design Issues in Modeling Object Behavior for Distributed Systems (Position Statement), in *ER'97 Workshop 4 Proceedings*, 1997.
4. H. Frank and J. Eder, Integration of Behavior Models, in *ER'97 Workshop 4 Proceedings*, 1997.
5. M. Gogolla, On Behavioral Model Quality and Transformation (Position Statement), in *ER'97 Workshop 4 Proceedings*, 1997.
6. J.A. Hoxmeier, A Framework for Assessing Database Quality, in *ER'97 Workshop 4 Proceedings*, 1997.
7. I. Jacobson, M. Christerson, P. Jonsson, and G. Overgaard, *Object-Oriented Software Engineering: A Use Case Driven Approach*, Addison-Wesley, Reading, Massachusetts, 1992.
8. Y. Lei and M.P. Singh, A Comparison of Workflow Metamodels, in *ER'97 Workshop 4 Proceedings*, 1997.
9. S.W. Liddle, Behavioral Design through Seamless Modeling (Position Statement), in *ER'97 Workshop 4 Proceedings*, 1997.
10. S.W. Liddle (ed.), *Proceedings of the ER'97 Workshop on Behavioral Models and Design Transformations: Issues and Opportunities in Conceptual Modeling*, 6-7 November 1997, UCLA, Los Angeles, California. Available electronically at URL http://osm7.cs.byu.edu/ER97/workshop4.
11. B. Lundell and B. Lings, Expressiveness within Enhanced Models: An Infological Perspective (Position Statement), in *ER'97 Workshop 4 Proceedings*, 1997.
12. O. Nierstrasz, Regular Types for Active Objects, in *OOPSLA '93 Conference Proceedings*, pp. 1-15, Washington, D.C., October 1993.
13. C. Njovu and T.W. Lawson, Modeling Temporal Behavior at the Conceptual Level, in *ER'97 Workshop 4 Proceedings*, 1997.
14. W.B. Teeuw and H. van den Berg, On the Quality of Conceptual Models, in *ER'97 Workshop 4 Proceedings*, 1997.
15. S.N. Woodfield, The Impedance Mismatch Between Conceptual Models and Implementation Environments, in *ER'97 Workshop 4 Proceedings*, 1997.

What Is the Role of Cognition in Conceptual Modeling? A Report on the First Workshop on Cognition and Conceptual Modeling

Venkataraman Ramesh[1], Jeffrey Parsons[2], and Glenn J. Browne[3]

[1]Department of Accounting and Information Systems,
Indiana University,
venkat@indiana.edu

[2]Faculty of Business Administration,
Memorial University of Newfoundland,
jeffreyp@plato.ucs.mun.ca

[3]Department of Information Systems and Quantitative Analysis,
Texas Tech. University,
gbrowne@coba2.ttu.edu

Abstract. Conceptual modeling has been advocated as an approach for representing the subject matter of an information system in a way that better reflects the way users think about that subject matter. Therefore, conceptual modeling appears to have a natural cognitive basis. However, there has been a surprising lack of attention in conceptual modeling research to cognitive issues and the role of cognition in both the development and evaluation of conceptual modeling techniques. The objective of the First Workshop on Cognition and Conceptual Modeling was to bring together researchers studying a wide range of questions relevant to the conference theme. This paper summarizes the motivation for the workshop, the presentations made, and outlines the workshop's contribution to furthering our understanding of the role of cognition in conceptual modeling.

1   Introduction

The Entity-Relationship (ER) model was developed around 20 years ago [5] to serve as mechanism for modeling the data that needs to be stored in a database independent of the underlying database technology. Therefore, the ER model is rightly viewed as a conceptual model. Since its introduction a large number of new conceptual models, many based on the original ER model, have been proposed. These are broadly classified under the name of semantic data models [15]. One of the main objectives of these semantic models was to make conceptual schemas richer by embedding more semantics in them, which in turn (arguably) made them more comprehensible by users. The advent of models with more semantic capabilities also meant that conceptual schemas created using these models were more just "blueprints" for the logical design of the database. Conceptual schemas created using these models began

P.P. Chen et al. (Eds.): Conceptual Modeling, LNCS 1565, pp. 272-280, 1999.

to be used for a variety of purposes, including, serving as a mechanism for representing user requirements and serving as a communication mechanism between users and analysts. Such models were also used by analysts' to verify their understanding of users' knowledge of an application domain before proceeding with database design and implementation [12].

However, the growth in the number of conceptual modeling techniques, as well as in the ways in which they are used, seems to have outstripped the rate of research aimed at understanding the foundations of these techniques and their range of appropriate uses.   In particular, research on conceptual modeling has paid surprisingly little attention to developing representation formalisms that are based on the structure of knowledge. Cognition is the branch of cognitive psychology that seeks to understand thought processes and the structure of knowledge. Better understanding of these processes and structures can inform the conceptual modeling techniques that are used to develop such representations.

The purpose of the First Workshop on Conceptual Modeling, held in conjunction with ER'97 in Los Angeles, was to focus on using the "science of knowledge", or cognition, to understand existing conceptual modeling techniques, to guide the design of new techniques, and provide criteria for evaluating techniques and methods. The workshop provided a forum to present the state-of-the-art in applying research on human cognition to problems and issues in conceptual modeling.

The papers presented at the workshop addressed two main issues:

a)   How can research on cognition enable us to enhance the expressiveness of conceptual models so that they better capture and represent user requirements?

b)   How can research in cognitive psychology help us develop better diagrammatic representations of conceptual models that can serve as an improved medium of communication between analysts and users?

The rest of this paper presents a brief summary of the issues raised during paper presentations and panel sessions at the workshop [26].

2   Enhancing the Expressiveness of Conceptual Models

A conceptual schema constitutes a model of users' knowledge about some subject matter and also serves as a (semi-)formal specification of the requirements for a database. Hence, it is critical that schemas reflect user perceptions of the structure of the problem domain as completely and unambiguously as possible. The semantic richness of a conceptual model is in part determined by the expressiveness of the relationship constructs that it can support [14]. Most models used to create conceptual schemas (i.e., semantic models) can represent three kinds of relationships explicitly: association, generalization/specialization and aggregation. However, these relationships represent only a subset of the relationships that are likely to be used by people in describing an application environment. Thus, using existing semantic models for conceptual modeling may result in abstractions of the real world in which some important information from the requirements is either not represented or is represented inappropriately [19].

2.1   Causation

The paper by Ramesh and Browne [20] attempts to demonstrate the need for new relationship types in semantic models. Specifically, it studies the effects of the lack of a *causation* construct in semantic models on analysts' ability to express causal relationships mentioned in a requirements document. The paper focuses on causal relationships since causation is a fundamental aspect of cognition, and is the most common type of relationship revealed in studies of human reasoning [6, 23]. Hence, it is likely that such relationships will be found in requirements specifications.

Two groups of subjects were used in the study, one familiar with semantic data modeling techniques and the other one unfamiliar with any modeling techniques. Both groups of users were asked to develop a representation (note that neither group was asked to develop an ER type model) of a fictitious requirements document. The description contained embedded causal relationships (as well as other relationships such as, association and generalization) in it. The rationale for the two groups was as follows. Since causation is a natural relationship used by people, subjects unfamiliar with database modeling should use causal relationships as naturally appropriate in developing a representation of the requirements. However, since current data models do not support the representation of causal relationships, subjects familiar with data modeling will not use such relationships in their representation. Rather they will force causal relationships into types supported in current conceptual modeling methods or not express them at all.

The results of the study showed that subjects unfamiliar with data modeling expressed causal relationships better in their representations than did subjects who had some prior exposure to data modeling. This seems to indicate that the lack of constructs for capturing causation in semantic models hinders the ability of people trained in data modeling techniques to recognize and express causal relationships in conceptual schemas. This in turn suggests that there is a need for developing semantic models that provide constructs for capturing causation and other cognitive relationships.

Interestingly, another paper (summarized in the next section) presented at the workshop [11] independently identified the need for supplementing ER models with causal relationships.

2.2   The Structure of Concepts

In the paper by Kashyap and Gale [11], the authors speculate that one of the reasons users find current conceptual models non-intuitive may be because it is difficult for them to relate to the "things" defined in a conceptual model. They suggest that this problem may be addressed by reconsidering how concepts (or things) are specified in a conceptual model. Current conceptual models define concepts, (typically, entity types or object classes) by specifying the properties that define them. However, it is well known from research in cognitive psychology that people have difficulty specifying the necessary and sufficient properties that define a particular concept, e.g., an elephant [18]. The authors note that adopting an alternative viewpoint which suggests that it may be more useful to define a concept in terms of its similarity to prototypes [21] might be more intuitive to users. For example, people easily identify a robin as a typical bird while a penguin is usually not. In particular, the authors suggest that typicality-based categorization might be useful for defining "natural-kind" concepts. They note that conceptual models for new application domains such as, multimedia information retrieval and knowledge mining, are likely to need this broad definition of concepts.

Conceptual models that use this broader definition of concepts are also likely to require representations for more "natural" relationships, specifically, causal relationships. In the paper the authors show how a model that represents causal relationships present in a (healthcare) knowledge mining application can be integrated with ER models describing the data to generate a conceptual model that is more understandable and easier for people to interact with.

The paper by Kangassalo [9] also questions the means by which current conceptual models define concepts and presents a mechanism for defining a conceptual schema that departs from the usual classification of concepts into entities, attributes and relationships. They suggest that a concept can be defined to be an independently identified construct composed of knowledge primitives and other concepts. A knowledge primitive is the smallest structural unit of knowledge, each having a corresponding cognitive capability in human mental processes, e.g., a semantic rule explaining the concept. Concepts are, of course, based on the point of view of an individual (or a small group of people). A concept is also connected to a set of rules of application, which specify the context within which a defined concept can be used. The paper describes how a concept can be defined using an **intensional containment** relationship between these knowledge primitives and other concepts. The definition of concepts using this technique results in the generation of a concept structure. The authors note that such a definition of concept hides the implementation-oriented details from the user and thus makes it easier for them to relate to the conceptual model. The structure of a conceptual schema created using such concepts is also inherently different from ER type schemas and empirical tests describing the benefits of such a representation can be found in [10].

2.3 Classes as Artifacts

The presentation by Parsons and Wand [17] challenged a basic, but arguably naÔve, assumption about cognition that is implicit in the use of classification (e.g., entity types, object classes) in conceptual modeling techniques: namely, the *assumption of inherent classification*, which holds that individual things in a problem domain can be referred to only as instances of one or more classes. Intuitively, this assumption is appealing, because we regularly refer to things such as "this student" or "that car," thereby tagging the object we are referring to as an instance of some class.

Parsons and Wand argue that the assumption of inherent classification, though pervasive in conceptual modeling and database design, is incompatible with recent research in cognition and linguistics. In particular, research indicates that classes, rather than having some Platonic existence independent of human perception, are artifacts constructed by humans to serve some useful purpose [13]. Consequently, instances can be seen as existing independent of any classification, but can also be classified in many different ways (by the same person or different people) depending on what is useful in a given context.

Using this cognitive perspective, the authors argue that a variety of schema design problems are rooted in the assumption of inherent classification in conceptual modeling. Specifically, the problems of: showing that an instance can simultaneously belong to more than one class; integrating local schemas to produce a global schema; maintaining an evolving schema as the structure of a domain changes over time; and supporting interoperability (at the class level) among independent information systems – either disappear or are significantly reduced if the assumption of inherent classification is dropped.

Finally, the authors describe an "instance-based" approach to conceptual modeling, in which the representation of instances and properties is separated from the representation of information about how instances are classified. In addition to being free of the problems listed above, the conceptual model provides a framework for a new database model that offers greater flexibility than current class-based models, such as the relational and object data models.

It can speculated that a conceptual model that addresses one or more of the issues identified above can potentially be better at supporting the user-analyst communication, since the conceptual schemas will be easier for the user to understand and interpret correctly. Another important, yet mostly overlooked, component that can facilitate the user-analyst communication is the representational scheme used by a conceptual model. The papers summarized in the next section describe how research in cognition can help in this regard.

3   Enhancing Diagrammatic Representations of Conceptual Models

Almost all conceptual models have a graphical notation associated with them. A conceptual schema defined using a given model is represented using this graphical notation. These diagrams are the external representations of users' knowledge. Basic principles of perceptual and cognitive psychology play a role in how well users can comprehend a model represented using a given representational scheme, especially for large and complex schemas. For example, people in western cultures read diagrams from left to right and from top to bottom, just as they read text. Empirical evidence has shown that when diagrams are not arranged following these principles, significant biases in the interpretation of the diagrams emerge [7, 25]. The workshop papers by both Rossi [22] and Browne [3] argue that very little consideration has been given to basic cognitive and perceptual guidelines when developing representational schemes for conceptual models. They both point to the need for research into incorporating perceptual and cognitive guidelines into representations of conceptual models and suggest that this is one mechanism by which conceptual schemas could be interpreted more accurately and comprehensively. It should be noted that the authors' are not suggesting that none of the current models incorporate these guidelines. However, they are pointing out the fact that even when these guidelines are being incorporated they are being done so in an ad hoc fashion and that a more systematic examination of these issues is warranted.

Browne also points to a variety of empirical evidence [25] that suggests that how people search for information in diagrams should be taken into account when developing a representational scheme for conceptual models. It has been shown that perceptual processes such as, discrimination of objects and grouping of symbols guide users in their initial understanding of diagrams [24]. Hence, for example, the clarity and differentiation of symbols would be an important factor in determining how well users understand diagrams [8]. The choice of symbols and the level of familiarity of users with such symbols, is another important cognitive characteristic of the representational scheme that affects the how well people understand models. For instance, hierarchies, flow diagrams, and matrices have been shown to be symbol systems that people generally understand and are able to follow in predictable ways [25]. Browne suggests that further research into developing models based on cognitive guidelines, such as, limitations of working memory, knowledge organization and reasoning and judgement is necessary.

4   Improving Understanding of Analyst/Designer Behavior

The papers described below relate to conceptual modeling in a somewhat indirect fashion since they do not address limitations in conceptual models, per se. However, they are related to the theme of workshop in that they both employ cognitive techniques to better understand analyst/designer behavior, which in turn should lead to the generation of better conceptual schemas.

The paper by Pitts [16] focuses on the process of information requirements determination (IRD). IRD is an important phase in the development of any information system, including a database system. The completeness and comprehensiveness of the requirements elicited have a direct impact on the quality of conceptual model that can be constructed. The analyst is usually in control of assessing the sufficiency of the information acquired during IRD. The paper attempts to identify the cognitive rules employed by analysts to decide when to stop gathering requirements for system development. The paper postulates that the cognitive limitations of analysts will result in flawed application and evaluation of stopping rules, producing premature termination of the IRD process, which in turn will lead to incomplete schemas.

The paper proposes a two part study. The first study attempts to identify and categorize the stopping rules used by analysts during IRD. The second part of the study investigates the possible benefits of using a strategic prompting tool specifically designed to reduce the risk of premature stopping by the analyst. Such a prompting tool would allow the analyst to use context-independent prompts based on argument types such as, causation, analogy and generalization, and argument strategies, such as, scenario building, elaboration and to elicit information from users.   The author speculates that these prompts, which are designed to overcome cognitive obstacles faced by the analyst, such as, limitations of short-term and long term memory, confirmation bias etc., represent strategies that can be used to supplement existing stopping rules used by analysts and should result in a more efficient, higher quality requirements determination process.

The paper by Altus [2] investigates the role of cognitive plausibility and beliefs during conceptual schema creation. Unlike the paper by Pitts [16] this paper investigates the issue of how the cognitive process used by a database **designer** can be improved. From a cognitive perspective, database designers also face the same cognitive limitations such as, short-term memory (72 chunks of information) as well as long-term memory recall, as analysts. The author proposes that these limitations can be overcome by viewing the process of conceptual schema design as the process of achieving a series of goals. Examples of goals in the context of conceptual schema design are, generate an entity type, modify an attribute type etc. The authors contend that designing a conceptual schema requires that designers assess the plausibility of attaining each of these goals within the context of a given application domain. They argue that the existence of well-defined goals and the fact these goals can be achieved using one or more design primitives helps overcome some of the cognitive limitations faced by the designer (by presenting them with meaningful chunks of information). This in turn can result in faster learning of the semantics of the design primitives that underlies the conceptual model and result in better schemas [1].

5   Conclusions

This paper summarized the main issues discussed during the First Workshop on Cognition and Conceptual Modeling. The three main themes that emerged from the workshop were, a) the need to rethink the way concepts are represented by current conceptual models, b) the need to support additional, more natural, relationship types such as, causation, in conceptual models and c) the need to base the choice of (diagrammatic) representational schemes on perceptual and cognitive guidelines. The papers and panel discussions clearly showed that research from cognition can be effectively applied to find theoretically grounded solutions to address these (and other) limitations of existing conceptual models. However, it was also clear that most projects addressing cognitive issues in conceptual modeling were relatively new and small in scope. Given the vast amount and maturity of existing research in cognition and the relative immaturity of research on the appropriate application of these concepts to conceptual modeling, it is the authors' contention that investigating the role of cognition in conceptual modeling represents a ripe area for further research.

References

1. Albrecht, M., M. Altus, E. Buchholz, A. Dusterhoft, and B. Thalheim, "The Rapid Application and Database Development (RADD) workbench – A comfortable database design tool," in Proceedings of the 7th International Conference on Advanced Information Systems Engineering – CaiSE'95, Jyavaskyla, Finland (1995).

2. Altus, M., "Cognitive Plausibility in Conceptual Database Design," in *First Workshop on Cognition and Conceptual Modeling*, Los Angeles, CA (1997).

3. Browne, G.J., "Cognition and Conceptual Modeling: Communicating Information Requirements for Conceptual Models," Panel Presentation at *First Workshop on Cognition and Conceptual Modeling*, Los Angeles, CA (1997).

4. Browne, G.J., V. Ramesh, Mitzi G. Pitts and Michael Rogich, "Representing User Requirements: An Empirical Investigation of Formality in Modeling Tools", *3rd Annual Americas Conference on Information Systems*, Indianapolis, Indiana, (1997) 89-91.

5. Chen, P. P. "The Entity-Relationship Model: Toward a Unified View of Data." *ACM Transactions on Database Systems*, Vol.1, No.1, (1976) 9-36.

6. Curley S.P, G.J. Browne, G.F. Smith, and P.G. Benson. "Arguments in the Practical Reasoning Underlying Constructed Probability Responses." *Journal of Behavioral Decision Making*, 8 (1995) 1-20.

7. Guri-Rozenblit, S. "Effects of a Tree Diagram on Students' Comprehension of Main Ideas in an Expository Text with Multiple Themes." *Reading Research Quarterly*, 26, (1989) 236-247.

8. Jarvenpaa, S.L. and J.J. Machesky. "Data Analysis and Learning: An Experimental Study of Data Modeling Tools." *International Journal of Man-Machine Studies*, 31, 1989, pp. 367-391.

9. Kangassalo, H., "Conceptual Description for Information Modelling Based on Intensional Containment Relation," in *First Workshop on Cognition and Conceptual Modeling*, Los Angeles, CA (1997).

10. Kangassalo, H. and P. Aalto, "Experiences on User Participation in the Development of a Conceptual Schema by Using a Concept Structure Interface," in B. Shackel (Ed.), *Human-Computer Interaction – INTERACT'84*, North-Holland (1985).

11. Kashyap, V. and M. Gale, "Knowledge Mining Applications in InfoSleuth: An approach based on incorporating cognitive constructs in E-R models," in *First Workshop on Cognition and Conceptual Modeling*, Los Angeles, CA (1997).

12. Kung, C. and A. Solvberg, "Activity Modelling and Behaviour Modelling," in T. Olle, H. Sol and A. Verrijn-Stuart (Eds.), *Information Systems Design Methodologies: Improving the Practice*, Amsterdam, North-Holland, (1986) 145-171.

13. Lakoff, G., Women, Fire, and Dangerous Things: What Categories Reveal about the Mind, Chicago: University of Chicago Press (1987).

14. Navathe, S.B. "Evolution of Data Modeling Formalisms." *Communications of the ACM*, 35 (1992) 112-123.

15. Peckham, J. and F. Maryanski, "Semantic Data Models", *ACM Computing Surveys*, 20(3), (1988) 153-189.

16. Pitts, M., "The use of Evaluative Stopping Rules in Information Requirements Determination: An Empirical Investigation of Systems Analyst Behavior," in *First Workshop on Cognition and Conceptual Modeling*, Los Angeles, CA (1997).

17. Parsons, J. and Y. Wand, "Emancipating Instances from Class Tyranny," Presentation at *First Workshop on Cognition and Conceptual Modeling*, Los Angeles, CA (1997).

18. Medin, D. and E. Smith, "Concepts and Concept Formation," *Annual Review of Psychology*, 35 (1984) 113-138.

19. Ram, S., "What is the Role of Cognition in Conceptual Modeling," Panel Presentation at *First Workshop on Cognition and Conceptual Modeling*, Los Angeles, CA (1997).

20. Ramesh, V. and G.J. Browne, "An Empirical Investigation of Causality in Conceptual Modeling," Paper Presentation at *First Workshop on Cognition and Conceptual Modeling*, Los Angeles, CA (1997).

21. Rosch, E., "On the Internal Structure of Perceptual and Semantic Categories," in T. Moore (Ed.), *Cognitive Development and the Acquisition of Language*, New York: Academic Press, (1973) 111-144.

22. Rossi, M., "Visual Properties of Conceptual Modelling Methods," *First Workshop on Cognition and Conceptual Modeling*, Los Angeles, CA (1997).

23. Schustack, M.W. "Thinking About Causality." In R.J. Sternberg and E.E. Smith (eds.), *The Psychology of Human Thought*. Cambridge: Cambridge University Press (1988) 92-115.

24. Treisman, A. "Perceptual Grouping and Attention in Visual Search for Features and for Objects." *Journal of Experimental Psychology: Human Perception and Performance*, 8, (1982) 194-214.

25. Winn, W. "An Account of How Readers Search for Information in Diagrams." *Contemporary Educational Psychology*, 18 (1993) 162-185.

26. 1st Workshop on Cognition and Conceptual Modeling, (Eds.) Jeffrey Parsons and Ramesh Venkataraman, *Electronic Proceedings available at* .

Conceptual Modeling in Multimedia Information Seeking

Carlo Meghini and Fabrizio Sebastiani

Consiglio Nazionale delle Ricerche
Istituto di Elaborazione dell'Informazione
Via S. Maria 46 - 56126 Pisa, Italy
{meghini,fabrizio}@iei.pi.cnr.it

1 Motivation

Information retrieval, once considered "the Cinderella of computer science" (in the words of one of its main advocates), is now witnessing a booming interest in the light of the ever-growing amount of information repositories available on both local and, especially, distributed platforms, including the Web and the Internet at large. Other relatively new paradigms of information seeking, such as browsing, information gathering and information filtering, are just other tiles in this generalised search for tools and techniques capable of reducing information overload and of selecting the right information at the right time in very large, dynamically evolving sets of documents.

The availability of non-textual ("multimedia") documents has given a new twist to information retrieval research, unfortunately setting even farther in the future the time in which generalized, completely automatic indexing methods will be available that allow the answering of content-based queries. If a system really capable of fully automatic recognition of "Authoritative sources on the social impact of nuclear waste disposal" seem currently out of reach, even more so for needs of "piano sonatas in styles influenced by art nouveau", "cubist paintings representing violins" or "scenes on sieges from war movies".

Complex queries such as the above mentioned only reflect the complexity of the information needs of many sophisticated information seekers of today; and it is only apparently that the queries of less sophisticated users have a smaller intrinsic complexity. While in a few decades these information needs might be satisfied by fully automatic systems, for today and tomorrow we will have to make do with systems relying on a mixture of automatic, semi-automatic and manual indexing methods, as it is only through manual intervention that it is possible to inform a retrieval system of the ins and outs of a (non-textual) document.

In this respect, an important contribution to multimedia information seeking may come from the more content-minded conceptual modelling and knowledge representation communities, as these have been developing formal and semi-formal languages and methodologies for the representation of information and for the conceptualization of an application domain. It is expected that, in the

P.P. Chen et al. (Eds.): Conceptual Modeling, LNCS 1565, pp. 281–286, 1999.
© Springer-Verlag Berlin Heidelberg 1999

mid to long term, successful information seeking systems will have to be based on the close interplay of manually (or semi-automatically) created representations of document content based on conceptual modelling technology, and the automatically created representations of document form of the information retrieval tradition.

2   Topics Addressed at the Workshop

The papers presented at the Workshop address several related aspects of the information seeking problem. In the following, we have categorized them in three broad classes: modeling Web documents, modeling multimedia documents, and browsing. While the last class is clearly disjoint from the previous ones, the other two classes only overlap in the abstract sense. Concretely, the papers thay containg emphasize different aspects and thus interact only to a negligible extent.

The first category has attracted most attention, due to the importance of the Web as a repository of information. Indeed, the success of the Web is due to the total freedom it leaves to information publishers with respect to document formats and content. However, the price that everybody pays everyday for this freedom is the lack of effective access to information. The papers falling under this category address the problem of providing access facilities to the Web based on a predefined model for its documents.

The section on multimedia is devoted to models for video data or for complex documents, comprised of time-dependent basic media. The papers greatly differ in style: one is entirely informal, whilst the other is (almost) entirely formal. They both make valuable proposals, taking the notion of multimedia at heart.

Finally, effective browsing is an open problem for the users of multimedia digital collections. Due to either the limited effectiveness of the underlying retrieval services, or to the imprecision and vagueness of user queries (if not both), these users often face the problem of exploring large answer sets to find out what they are looking for. The first paper presented in this section introduces generic tools for supporting effective browsing, while the second one discusses the problem of browsing through a special class of documents, namely videoconferencing records.

3   Modeling Web Documents

In "Formal model for integration of data in complex structure", Y. Kambayashi and S. Meki discuss the problem, of particular relevance to the field of Data Warehousing, of recognising structure in heterogeneous data obtained from distributed and heterogeneous platforms, such as the Web, and of identifying commonalities and differences in structure among different data items, which ultimately allow the classification of these items into a common scheme. Extracting structure is seen here as preliminary, but ultimately conducive, to the extraction of content, and to the recognition of common content features.

The authors develop a model of structure for these heterogeneous types of data. The basic assumption is that structure reflects semantic constraints that the data items comply with, and that structure identification may thus be conducive to inferring these constraints. The approach exposed in the paper is articulated in three main steps: (a) extracting semantic constraints from the data obtained from a given source, (b) identifying the commonalities among semantic constraints pertaining to the different sources, and (c) providing a structure that accommodates the data that complies with the constraints so identified.

Issues dealing with the visualization of structures are tackled by distinguisishing abstract structure (here called form, and represented by regular expressions) from the possible ways of visualizing it (called frames). Abstract structure is the main focus of the paper, which developes a set of rules for the translation between equivalent abstract forms and the detection of commonalities between non-equivalent ones.

In "Web document modelling and clustering" W. Song discusses the need for a formal model for the description and characterisation of Web documents, a model that would allow to represent the bewildering variety of Web-based information chunks under a common scheme. The benefits of this proposed scheme would consist in greater ease of Web-based document searching, grouping, classification and filtering. Song argues that keyword-based searching, as performed by many well-known search engines, yields too low precision and recall to meet the need of sophisticated information searchers, and that these needs can be met only if adequate ways of describing Web documents are introduced that allow search engines to exploit the descriptions built along these guidelines. The paper goes on to propose a model, called WDM, which has the objective of being sufficiently general to accommodate existing structures of Web documents, and to be easily applicable for a variety of document management tasks, such as classification or clustering. The model is based on the hypothesis that Web browsers should become capable of interpreting metadata labels from a label taxonomy; these labels describe documents under a variety of facets, e.g. access rights or content, and may be provided either by the authors themselves or by third-party rating services. As different authors or sites may exploit different labels, a WDM schema integration method is proposed that closely resembles the well-known methodologies for subschema integration in conceptual database design. The paper also proposes that a number of previously proposed similarity measures for documents described in WDM should be used for document clustering, or categorisation, so that related documents may be either stored or browsed together.

"A new approach to query the Web: Integrating Retrieval and Browsing", by Z. Lacroix, A. Sahuguet, R. Chandrasekar and B. Srinivas presents AKIRA, a system for accessing the Web via queries expressed in the PIQL language, an extension of the OQL query language with object identity and generalized path expressions. To this end, AKIRA views the Web as an object oriented database, which can be queried in the standard way, with additional predicates for matching text expressions. The result of a query is then a view of the whole database, whose structure is defined by the original query. This view, which current Web crawlers store in an apposite cache, is handled by AKIRA through an object-oriented DBMS, where the view is accumulated by Web crawling agents and accessed by the user through PIQL. Essentially, the view creation process is based on information retrieval techniques, applied to the candidate Web pages by the AKIRA agents; once a view is obtained, it is filtered and structured as specified in the user query, by relying on database techniques. The main merit of this work is its attempt to provide a more sophisticate interaction with the Web than current Web search engines. This goal is pursued from within a database perspective, by employing information retrieval techniques as well as by relying on advanced software technology, such as agent-based system engineering. Despite the fact that several aspects of AKIRA deserve a higher attention, the system is a step in the right direction, that is the development of systems that permit to study the problem of accessing the Web from a pragmatical point of view.

In "Multimodal Integration of Disparate Information Sources with Attribution", T. Lee and S. Bressan present COIN, a system providing access to a number of diverse information sources, including flat files, databases and, of course, the Web, through a relational database interface. The novelty of COIN over the many systems that offer the same, or a more general, service, is the explicit handling of attribution, that is information about the source where the data retrieved to the user come from. The authors argue in favor of attribution as a way of (a) ensuring the protection of intellectual property, (b) giving a mean to test the quality of the retrieved data, and (c) monitoring updates and revisions of data in, e.g. data warehousing. At the formal level, the authors rely on an extension of relational algebra to treat attribution information. At the implementation level, a key role in the COIN system is played by COIN Web Wrappers, that is software modules extending the typical functionality of wrappers to handle Web pages and attribution information.

4   Modeling Multimedia Data

In "A Multiple-Interpretation Framework for Modeling Video Semantics", C. Lindley attacks the problem of identifying a rich semantic model for the retrieval, browsing and synthesis of video data. The paper starts out with a wide review of current approaches, pointing out their various limitations in providing a satisfactory account of video content. The author observes that the kind of representations considered, while successfull from a purey computational viewpoint, performs poorly in terms of effectiveness, as judged from a user perspective. In order to overcome these limitations, the author argues in favour of a semantically richer model, able to capture aspects of a video that directly relate to the cultural context in which the video is meant to perform its information purpose. As a necessary step in this direction, the notion of interpretation paradigm is introduced. An interpretation paradigm is a set of fundamental assumptions about the world to be modelled, along with a set of beliefs following from those assumptions. The meaning of a phenomenon is then to be understood as the interpretation of that phenomenon within the selected interpretation paradigm, while modelling semantics reduces to identifying the interpretation paradigms that are suitable to the phenomenon at hand. For video data, four paradigms are identified by the author. The diegetic level deals with the narrative elements of a video. These include the video narration, fictional time and space dimensions, the characters, landscape, and events, all giving raise to a four-dimensional spatio-temporal world. The connotative level is the level of metaphorical, analogical and associative meaning that the diegetic level may have. The subtext level deals with the hermeneutics of video, that is the hidden and suppressed meanings, extending the immediacy of intuitive consciousness. Finally, the cinematic level is concerned with how formal and video techniques are used to express the meanings of a video. The author shows how typical content-based queries relate to the four levels of his framework, and discusses the implications of his model for system infrastructure. The tight links with semiotic analysis make this work really valuable; the discussion on the state of the art in the field is pregnant.

In "Modelling Multimedia and Hypermedia Applications using an E-LOTOS/ MHEG-5 Approach", P. Maia Sampaio and W. Lopes de Souza apply formal models techniques to support a crucial phase of multimedia/hypermedia document authoring, namely the specification of the temporal and logical synchronization of the various components making up a document. The basic motivation underlying this work is the development of a concise, well-understood and well-founded notation to describe multimedia/hypermedia documents, thus favouring the interoperability over heterogeneous platforms of applications handling such documents. The approach followed by the authors is to combine the international standard MHEG-5 Multimedia and Hypermedia InformationCoding Expert Group) with E-LOTOS, an extension of LOTOS (Language Of Temporal Ordering Specification). In particular, the building blocks of the notation are E-LOTOS processes, which may be instantiated and composed to define a specification. There are two libraries of such processes: the presentation library, constituted by basic media objects (video, image or audio sequence), and the constraint library, containing objects for expressing non-trivial logical and temporal synchronization constraints among media objects. The paper discusses how these blocks can be modelled in MHEG-5, deriving a complete mapping of the considered primitives. The resulting model is a contribution to the retrieval of multimedia documents on the basis of their structure. In fact, the model can be understood as a formal specification of the strucutre of dynamic multimedia documents, from which a suitable representation and an associated query language may be derived.

5   Browsing

In "Browsing navigator for efficient multimedia information retrieval" T. Kakimoto and Y. Kambayashi tackle the problem of providing users of information retrieval systems with friendlier tools for the browsing of retrieved documents.

The problem is of special importance in the non-textual case, as, due to the still low effectiveness of current multimedia retrieval systems, following a user request many documents may have to be visualised before the user has satisfied his information need, and this visualisation process may be too time-consuming for the user. A set of tools is proposed aimed at making browsing the retrieved documents easier and more intuitive. One of these tools is a clustering facility, that allows the set of retrieved documents to be partitioned into clusters of documents having a strong intra-cluster similarity; a variety of similarity measurements may be used, including system-generated or user-tailored similarity functions. Clusters are also automatically analysed in order to find, based on the above-mentioned similarity measures, documents that may be used as cluster representatives in order to spare the user the cognitive load of visualizing too many documents. Users may also give feedback to the system by marking documents relevant, and the system is able to exploit this "relevance feedback" information by individuating the documents that are similar to the documents marked relevant by at least a pre-specified threshold, thus displaying them to the user as "strong candidates" for relevance. The problem of visualising the retrieval results is also tackled, and a solution involving Kohonen's "Self-Organizing Maps" is proposed; the separate visualization of clustering results obtained through different similarity functions may thus help the user to select the similarity function that gives the results most appropriate for his needs.

In "Index generation and advanced search functions for multimedia presentation material" Y. Kambayashi, K. Katayama, Y. Kamiya and O. Kagawa tackle the problem of providing sophisticated facilities for browsing recordings of presentations, possibly produced by videoconferencing software. Presentation records are usually stored as a video of the presentation complemented by the set of overhead slides that were used by the speaker; the video and the slide sequence are synchronised. This record can be searched, e.g. by people who were not able to attend the presentation, by the standard functions defined either on the video component, including "playback", "fast forward" and "fast rewind", or on the slide component, such as "go to the next slide", etc. One of the main problems of video retrieval is the location of relevant portions of a video, because current scene analysis technology is not yet ready to provide automated content-based indexing of videos, and because manual content-based indexing is impractical. The authors suggest that the slides component of a video recording of a presentation may be useful for this, as portions of the video may be located by using standard textual information retrieval techniques against this component, thus allowing to locate sections of the presentation in which the speaker was discussing a given topic of interest to the searcher. The authors present a sophisticaded method for exploiting this idea that can not only search slides by direct location, or by content, but that can also use as searching aids the recordings of important actions by the speaker, such as manually underlining (or using the pointer to locate) portions of a slide, meaning that those portions are of particular relevance to the presentation section synchronised with these actions.

Future Directions of Conceptual Modeling

Peter P. Chen[1], Bernhard Thalheim[2], and Leah Y. Wong[3,4]

[1]Computer Science Department
Louisiana State University, Baton Rouge, LA 70803, USA,
Chen@bit.csc.lsu.edu

[2]Computer Science Department
Technical University, Cottbus, Germany
thalheim@Informatik.TU-Cottbus.DE

[3]SPAWAR Systems Center, D44208
San Diego, CA 92152-7151, USA
Wong@spawar.navy.mil

Abstract. This paper discusses several important future research directions in conceptual modeling. Since this field is very broad, the list of topics discussed here is not an exhaustive list but rather the "partial" composite views of the co-authors on the important issues from their own perspectives. Some of the important issues are omitted because they were covered extensively in [1], and the readers should also read the papers in that volume to get a more comprehensive view of where the field is going. Also, the selection of research topics is independent of their difficulties. Some of the research problems discussed here could be solved in the next decades while the others may take much longer to develop a reasonable solution.

Introduction

In the past decades, information technology has become an important part of our daily life, and it will be the cornerstone for technology infrastructure of our society in the next century. Central to such a cornerstone is the process of conceptual modeling.

What will be the active research areas in the future? Or, where should we focus our attention and efforts in the years to come? Nobody can foresee the future, but we will try to share our visions with you. We believe that the following areas are very important research areas in conceptual modeling:

- Active Modeling
- Relationship between Natural Languages and Conceptual Modeling
- Conceptual Framework for Sharable Information Services
- Relationships between the Real World and the Software World
- Conceptual Model as the Basis for Interoperability

---

[4] Co-author Leah Y. Wong's contribution is the work of a U.S. Government employee prepared as part of the employee's official duties and therefore is not protected by U.S. copyright, see 17 U.S.C. 105.

P.P. Chen et al. (Eds.): Conceptual Modeling, LNCS 1565, pp. 287-301, 1999.

- Conceptual Modeling as First Step for Application Engineering
- Global Communication
- Human Knowledge Integration

In this paper, we suggest an agenda for future R&D directions in these areas.

Review of Strength and Pragmatics of Conceptual Modeling

Before discussing the research and development directions let us restate the strength of the theory and pragmatics developed so far in the field of conceptual modeling.

Conceptual modeling has been primarily based on different dialects of the entity relationship (ER) model. The ER model has reached maturity such that it can be used for modeling of very complex applications. The basic constructs of the model (entity type, relationship type) are defined on the basis of set semantics, which can be understood intuitively by designers and users. It has been shown that the model can be mapped to an extended variant of first-order predicate logic, which is well understood and a common framework for computer science. Semantic properties of applications are modeled by constraints in the ER model. Since these constraints can be mapped to formulas of the first-order predicate logic, the properties of applications can be expressed by first-order predicate logic. At the same time the database itself can be represented by a set of formulas. Thus, the static part of an application can be based on predicate logic. For this reason, the static part in conceptual modeling is well founded. Database dynamics can also be expressed in logic. Actions such as update operations or retrieval operations are representable in an extended predicate logic as well as semantic restrictions of such operations. For this reason we can claim that the dynamic part in conceptual modeling is also well founded.

Conceptual modeling is a very important and powerful step in relational database design. It overcomes several restrictions of the relational model. The orientation of current relational technology has led to several problems of database modeling and design. For instance, the following restrictions and problems can be solved [6] if conceptual modeling approaches are used:

- Normalization is mainly an optimization of structures. Given a set of integrity constraints, the enforcement or maintenance of these constraints has to be programmed. For instance, functional dependencies cannot be represented by constraints defined in relational DBMS. Such constraints are also the reason for anomalous behavior of update functions. Normalization aims now in restructuring database relations through decomposition in such a way that the only constraints, which have to be added to the structure, are those which are based on the DBMS. However, normalization does not take into account the behavior of the database itself. For instance, if operations, which are used often in the application, require the consideration of several relations and for this reason the performance of the DBMS for such operations is too low, then the solution is to compose those relations again into one relation. This process is called denormalization. Denormalization can also be required after restructuring or extending the database. Since the normalization process is an optimization process independent of the DBMS and since the process is supported by algorithms, the normalization of conceptual models of the reality can be incorporated into the translation process. From the other side, normalization can be performed already on the conceptual level. Therefore, structural optimization and behavioral optimization can be treated consistently during conceptual modeling if a powerful proof method is used during optimization.

- The same application can be modeled by different models. These models can be equivalent. Since the ER model has a powerful theory behind it, we can consider different models at the same time for different user groups and map these models to each other. The other model can be considered to be a view of the first. The same observation can be made for multidimensional databases and OLAP applications. The star and the snowflake schemata are views on the conceptual schema. Whether views are materialized as it is the case in multidimensional databases depends on the application and on the complexity of the view generation.

- Conceptual modeling has been understood for a long period as modeling of structures and static integrity constraints. Because some powerful structural constructs have been developed and used in practice, a belief has been developed in the community that semantics can be completely represented by structures. Based on this belief it has been assumed that application programming can do the rest and that triggers can be used without problems. Later, it has been discovered that triggering is only safe under certain hierarchy conditions. Therefore, the current thinking is that conceptual modeling should integrate modeling of structures and behavior at the same time.

- During the search for powerful modeling constructs, different proposals have been made. Each of these proposals had its advantages. Some of them have been very influential and have radically changed the research direction. At the final end these proposals led to extensions of the basic ER model, which can be still considered to be the "father" of all these models. Putting together parts and pieces of an extended ER model covers other models such as object-oriented models, rule-based models and object-role models. Therefore, conceptual modeling is currently a "composition" of many such developments, which have previously been considered to be independent.

Based on these observations, we can claim that conceptual modeling will be one of the major approaches for describing reality and the basis for human-database-interfaces. The research and development directions discussed below indicate many potential applications and extensions of conceptual modeling

Future Directions

Active Modeling

Active modeling is a continual process of describing the important and relevant aspects of the real world including the activities and changes under different perspectives based on our knowledge and understanding. At any given time, the model is viewed as a multilevel and multi-perspective abstraction of reality.

Conventional conceptual modeling focuses primarily on "static" relationships of entities. Constructs for modeling changes of the entity behaviors and the dynamic and time-varying relationships among them are very inadequate. Furthermore, it is very difficult to use the existing constructs to model a wide spectrum of situations based on different perspectives of the real world.

There are several limitations on the design and use of databases due to the natural limitations of the current focus on "static modeling." The database implemented in today's DBMS only reflects the static characteristics of the intended Universe-of-Disclosure (UoD) captured by the conceptual model as distinct snapshots of the reality. It provides us with the "almost recent" information only. It does not provide us with the historical information on causal-effect relationships. It also cannot easily simulate situations we try to project. The notion of time, which is not directly supported, makes the modeling of the temporal relationships between the entity behaviors difficult. Therefore, data changes, schema changes, and historical information cannot be collectively supported or managed.

What are the benefits of active modeling? Why do we need to do active modeling? One of the benefits of traditional conceptual modeling is to help us better understand a specific real-world domain and enhance communication among ourselves. A potential main benefit of active modeling is to provide a closer conceptualization of reality for global understanding and communication. Later on in this paper, we will discuss more on the subject of global communication.

We mentioned the needs for different perspectives in active modeling. What are the important perspectives that should be considered in performing active modeling? We believe that at least three perspectives are needed: personal, organizational, and global perspectives. For the personal perspective, a conceptual mental model could be used for specifying the personal information requirement. For the organizational perspective, a conceptual model that captures the organizational functional requirements will be used to create the corporate database with changeable data structures that support flexible query processing and complex application development (e.g. educational, medical, entertainment, economical, political, etc.). For the global perspective, a conceptual metamodel will be required for information abstraction to support information exchange from multiple lower-level perspectives and multiple domains. Each of the conceptual models can be implemented as an information base from which related information can be derived.

The active modeling can be realized through assimilation and integration of several related technologies such as computer technology, software technology, software engineering, artificial intelligence, communication, and others. The existing methodologies and techniques in conceptual modeling can be used as the starting point. However, modeling techniques will need to be integrated to model different characteristics of the world (e.g., temporal, multimedia, distributed, spatial, cognitive, philosophical, historical, etc.) in a visualized manner. Specific issues that need to be further explored include:

- Capturing human intelligence
- Integration of conceptual-modeling aspects
- Visual conceptual modeling
- Data, information and knowledge integration
- Self modeling
- Executable active Entity-Relationship model
- Ontology generation and exchange
- Uncertainty modeling

- Temporal conceptual modeling
- Multi-perspective modeling
- Interactive modeling and computing
- Conceptual modeling for multi-agent systems
- Dynamic reverse modeling

Relationship between Natural Languages and Conceptual Modeling

It is now understood that that conceptual models have their root in the phrasal form of natural languages. The Chinese and Ancient Egyptian character construction techniques are very similar to the modeling techniques of ER diagrams. The same observation has been made for the sentence construction of the English language as well as for the more complex constructions used, for example, in the German language. It has been shown that the basic primitives in the sentence construction and the grammar of the English language are very similar to the primitives in ER diagram technique. Because of this similarity, it is conjectured that conceptual modeling could be as powerful as natural languages as a tool for modeling the reality. Current research shows that approaches such as ellipses, ambiguity, changes in semantic meaning can be expressed through constructs developed for conceptual modeling. As a result of this type of research activities, conceptual models now can describe the reality more formally and with a well-defined semantics specifications made on the basis of natural languages.

Linguists treat semiotics as consisting of three parts: syntax, semantics and pragmatics. Syntax defines the rules for forming sentences. Semantics is concerned with the meaning of words and sentences. Pragmatics deals with practical results, reasons and values. Computer scientists are often mainly concerned with syntax, only partially concerned with semantics and very seldom concerned with pragmatics. Conceptual modeling is based on a certain syntax, which has to have a well-specified meaning. It also has to deal with pragmatics. For this reason, a well-founded theory of conceptual modeling has be extended by methodologies for modeling [5]. These methodologies should be integrated into the framework of the conceptual modeling in a consistent fashion.

Research topics in this direction include:
- What modeling primitives and principles can be extract from natural languages? Can we use these primitives and principles to improve the conceptual modeling methodologies and techniques?
- Identify the differences in modeling the same concept in different languages. Can we use these differences to identify the social, historical, and environmental impacts on language and cultural developments. For example, why are the characters for "water" and "sun," very similar in both Chinese characters and the Ancient Egyptian characters? Why are the characters for "king" and "queen" quite different in Chinese characters and in Egyptian characters? Similarly, why do some of the grammar rules in English differ from those in German? Perhaps, there are reasons for these differences?
- After identifying the underlying reasons for these similarities and differences in different natural languages, how can we utilize this information in the design of

algorithms for understanding semantics and translations of different natural languages?

- Based on the trace of social, historical, and environmental impacts on the natural language grammars and character developments, would it be useful to customize the software development and conceptual modeling methodologies for each country or culture so that they will be more natural to the people in that environment?
- Ancient Egyptian characters and Chinese characters have ideogram-based components. Can we use the same principles in constructing the ideograms in the design of graphics icons for computer user interfaces?

Conceptual Framework for Shareable Information Services

Humans interact with the underlying database or information system via a set of services. In this section, we will discuss the evolution of information services from a stand-alone local service to a system of sharable services. In this transition, we need a solid conceptual framework to guide us through this complicated growth process.

There are some obvious limitations in existing systems. Current systems provide utilities for storing limited types of data and manipulating data through basic commands (e.g., Read, Update, Delete, etc.), which are insufficient for supporting complex applications. It is evident that DBMSs are changing their roles from being stand-alone systems for supporting application development, to becoming parts of a larger system and to being embedded systems.

Information services are viewed as behaviors of the information system. Different services are needed depending on the application complexity. Although databases are still being used to support daily operations in most organizations, they are gradually becoming the foundation of electronic commerce. In a recent issue of *Communications of ACM* [2], an information explosion was predicted as a result of low-cost computing and Internet accesses. Future information environments will face the challenge of storing large volumes of dissimilar information and efficiently manipulating information to satisfy personal and organizational needs. New services for efficient retrieving, merging, fusing, filtering, monitoring, and disseminating information will be required. As data and information can be made available on-line, we can create testbeds in parallel via the web, thus allowing simulation (viewed as high level proactive query) to become a service in the information environment. The concepts of transaction, security, privacy, concurrency control, and integrity need to be re-examined in the combined context of the conventional DBMS and Internet information base. Basic services provided by the conventional DBMS (e.g., loading, backup, file organization, performance monitoring, etc.) will be supported in a different way.

Current DBMSs are monolithic, i.e., the DBMS software system is a black box. The functionality offered is generally fixed and non-extensible. This rigid assumption has motivated researchers to look into an extensible architecture for rapid development of DBMSs. As can be found in Elmasri and Navathe [3], the GENESIS and EXODUS projects were developed based on this approach. The idea of plug-compatible software modules was further exemplified by the PROBE and STARBURST (also in [3]). The underlying motivation was to provide a set of software building blocks for the users to compose tailored DBMSs by selecting the required functionality.

Development of the proposed services relies on implementing the active model to provide information sharing and processing-services sharing. Future information systems will behave like an assistant (e.g., an agent, a complex active entity) to humans in relieving the burden of complex task handling. Behaviors of the information system will be modeled as a set of well-defined operations to be implemented as „intelligent" services to provide cooperation between users, applications, and the information system environment. Customized DBMSs will be available as a lightweight kernel with shareable information services in a mobile environment.

Results from research on aspects of information technology (e.g., distributed, multimedia, heterogeneous, temporal, spatial, deductive, real-time, active, etc.) and their relationships need to be examined from an integrative perspective. The cognitive processes (e.g., acquire, recognize, analyze, deduct, infer, etc.) used for information management by the human mind will be the new information service candidates, possibly implemented as intelligent agents. Communication among intelligent agents need to be realized using primitives higher than those provided by Knowledge Query Manipulation Language (KQML) or Foundation for Intelligent Physical Agents (FIPA). To provide efficient use of these services, structured Application Programming Interface (API) design based on a conceptual model with well-defined inputs and outputs will be required. Simulation and information visualization will need to be included for projecting future world states during the active modeling process.

Conceptual modeling and its derived software implementation of sharable information services in a global information architecture will be a major challenge. Relationships among these services with respect to the information system kernel need to be further examined. A consortium of the state-of-practice of conceptual modeling tools can be used as a case study for evaluating the theoretical results and state-of-art of different approaches. Issues that need attention include:

- Usability modeling of information services
- Conceptual modeling for API design
- Extensible architecture for composable services
- Software composition
- Combined black-box, white-box, and software behavior testing

Conceptual Model as the Basis for Interoperability

There is an increasing need to link all systems and databases together. However, many hardware and software platforms are not compatible with each other. It has been a challenging job to integrate all the systems and databases running on incompatible hardware and software platforms in a consistent and seamless manner. Many attempts to solve this problem either have failed or have only limited successes. We believe that most of the failures are caused by not using conceptual modeling. Many such projects (or even some interoperability standards) are based on the bottom-up approach (the so-called "let us glue pieces together" approach) instead of the top-down approach based on conceptual modeling. It is very important to have a clean conceptual model of major components and services to guide us in this integration process. It should work like a multi-level "map," starting from a high-level map, which can be expanded into low-level maps in a hierarchical way. Each new software module constructed should follow this conceptual "guidance" model (map) and provides a self-description on details of the components and interfaces specified by the conceptual guidance map. These self-descriptions will greatly increase the interoperability of the software modules.

In the past two decades, conceptual models have been proposed as the standard formats for data interchange for different file and database systems. It is a theoretically sound approach and should gain more popularity in practice due to the increasing needs to link heterogeneous systems together instead of the homogeneous systems together, which has been the norm until recently. We believe the conceptual models are not only useful as the standard data formats but also as "guidance" map for software module interoperability as discussed in the previous paragraph.

Research issues in this direction include:

- Specification of a conceptual guidance model (map) for software and data interoperability
- Construct a template for self-description of new software modules and data
- Construct a template for self-description of legacy software modules and data
- Specification of the dynamic interaction process of system and data integration
- Prototypes to test the effectiveness of this approach.

Relationships between the Real World and the Software World

While a computer system consists of two major components: hardware and software, the software component becomes the dominant one that the user interfaces with. Each new generation of computer systems provide a user interface which hides more hardware details from the users. In other words, the user view of a computer system is primarily the view provided by its software. Therefore, we can say that the world of computer system has been transmuted into a world of software.

Software, which symbolizes the products of our ideas, appears to be free and flexible. Yet, its implementation relies on formal theories, a set of engineering principles and well-defined languages. Software products either serve as tools for human task automation, problem solving, or abstractions of human activities. The software world can be viewed as a mapping of the real world. In mapping real-world requirements to the software world, its implementation needs to satisfy the constraints of the real-world domain and the constraints derived from the computer world. It is important for us to apply appropriate constraint management at each phase of the development process to provide software and system integrity.

Humans, who created the software universe, need to be in control of it. Realization of the software world requires an explicit model for implementation, communication, and control. Better management of the software world will be required for balanced technology advancement. In today's software enterprise, we lack a model of the software world and its activities, as well as methods to actively monitor the evolving process for acquisition, development, and utilization. This software-world model could serve as a conceptual infrastructure for the development of an active repository of software, to be used for technology assessment and transfer.

The dynamic and interactive relationships between the two worlds can be implemented as a set of interfaces to support human-system interaction based on an interactive conceptual model. For example, the user interfaces provided by current DBMSs for accessing data include menu-based, graphical, form-based query, natural language, etc. Humans communicate with the underlying system through these interfaces based on a single modality. As most human communication takes place in more than one modality at the same time, we need to explore how information and its meaning can be conveyed via multiple modalities (e.g., visual, auditory, olfactory, touch, speech, etc.) in an integrated manner. Future information systems will most likely be multimedia (video, text, handwriting, graphics, images, animation, etc.). High-level interfaces will be required to support the multimedia, multiple-modal information environment. A simple graphical user interface (e.g. ERD) created by dynamic reserve engineering/modeling from the underlying database system and applications would be a starting point for exploring such dynamic relationships between the two worlds. The Internet has already provided the setting for exploring such interfaces.

While information is produced by software, computerized information can be viewed as software products. Software and information system developments seemingly share a similar conceptual realm. In examining how software and information technologies may benefit each other, we need to further investigate, in an open architecture, the technical issues common to these two technologies. To develop a new conceptual framework for their cross infusion, a closer look at results from various aspects of the two technologies and their synthesis will be necessary. Specific issues that need to be examined include:

- Software world modeling
- Software systems communication
- Knowledge discovery from the software world
- Software understanding
- Real-world and software-world ontology generation and translation
- Software and information quality
- Human-system interface management

Conceptual Modeling as the First Step for Application Engineering

Conceptual modeling is currently understood as modeling of structures, processes and interaction. This codesign of structural, operational and interface requirements provides a better means for a wholly integrated modeling. Structural metadata and static integrity constraints can be formally described by conceptual models. Since optimal behavior of systems also depends on functionality, which is used by actors, processes and dynamic integrity constraints should be modeled as well. Processes are internal processes or communication processes. Workflow modeling aims in formalizing activities involving the coordinated execution of multiple tasks performed by different processing actors or software system. A task defines some work to be done. Actors performing tasks interact with the system through interfaces. Interfaces can be based itself on rather complex processes. For this reason, their complexity needs to be considered as well if an optimal behavior is required.

If the system has to satisfy the needs of different users who are not familiar with the system, then these users need to know which data they can expect, which restrictions are applied to the data, how data are processed, how to retrieve data etc. Some metainformation on the structures, processes and interaction is usually available to the system but not to the user. Consistent behavior of actors requires the knowledge of the complete metadata. Therefore, metadata on the meaning of data and structures should be captured during modeling, together with the information on the structures and processes itself.

Databases and information systems are becoming an integral part of the infrastructure of enterprises. The infrastructure is usually supporting the enterprise in order to reach its aims under consideration of its politics, standards, management decisions, chances, obligations, responsibilities, rights, privileges etc. The database system should properly fit into the infrastructure. The infrastructure is constantly changing. Therefore, the software system should accommodate change as well.

Software systems and database systems evolve over the time. Database operations and transactions provide point-in-time snapshots. The structures and the processes modeled by the database designer change over time. Thus, a challenging task for conceptual modeling is to anticipate changes and to accommodate possible changes. Since older processes are not thrown away, database operating is also based on keeping track on different versions of the database schema. Distributed databases have already developed approaches to versioning. These approaches can be extended to evolution of database systems.

Database technology is mainly based on relational DBMS. Whenever the database schema is becoming larger it is not comprehensible to casual users. Views are simpler to comprehend for a user. The current approach is to develop possible views in advance. Whenever a user needs another view on the database the new view should be defined. At the same time, users need to understand the data provided by the database. Aggregated data can be such data. In this case the user may want to know the data which have been the basis for the aggregated data. Therefore, views should be extended by functions made available to the user. This approach has been used for the development of decision support systems and database warehouses on the basis of multidimensional or OLAP databases. However, this approach is not powerful enough for databases which have to satisfy the needs of casual users. There are already known approaches which can be used for attaching functionality to views.

Legacy database systems are systems that significantly resist modification and evolution to meet new and constantly changing business requirements. Several approaches have been worked out such as reverse engineering, reengineering and data reuse. The best approach against the legacy problem is to consider possible changes already during conceptual modeling. The anticipation of all possible changes is, however, in most cases unfeasible. Conceptual modeling might be understood as a continuous engineering task. Any change of structures, processes and interactions is made through conceptual modeling This approach enables the enterprise to keep the system running with new and old applications at the same time.

In summary, conceptual modeling is the first step and one of the most important steps for application engineering, which includes management of change, extension of scope and utilization as well as integration into existing infrastructure. Specific research issues that need a deeper treatment include:

- Development of approaches to codesign of structures, processes and interaction
- Intuitive understandable structures and simple to use processes
- Metadata dictionaries for the database or the information base
- Versioning of databases over time
- Deriving functionality together with view specification
- Coping with aging of database systems
- Continuous conceptual modeling

Global Communication

The purpose of information is for communication. Similar to using human languages to express and communicate among ourselves, computer languages are used to communicate among software entities. While striving for a common ground among different languages, we are trying to accomplish a generalized computer language (e.g., Java) for mobile computing that is platform- and language- independent.

With the advent of the Internet and World Wide Web (www), conceptual modeling is shifting to the proposed active paradigm. The www can be viewed as a natural, evolving, distributed, heterogeneous, multimedia information base reflecting a snapshot of the real-world domain at a given time. This self-composed information repository (e.g., web pages and their linkages) allows us to create, obtain, disseminate, and exchange information, giving us the potential for global communication.

Information management, which has a new meaning in the context of the Internet and www, calls for new modeling techniques. For example, after entering the www, we generally specify our information requirements and then task search engine(s) to collect the related information. The search specification and returned results can be viewed as two related models. The specification model describes our mental model of the world view represented by the subject(s) of interest. The result model describes the available entities and relationships that satisfy the view definition. New conceptual modeling techniques need to be explored for creating and presenting such models as an alternative to the current search facility.

Information cannot be fully utilized unless communication takes place between the source of the information/knowledge and the potential user of that information/knowledge. While the Internet offers an opportunity for global communication, shareable knowledge remains a key concern. Today's information systems, which are developed based on data flow and linguistic representations, need to be enhanced to include aspects of knowledge management (e.g., acquisition, generation, representation, exchange, dissemination, etc.). The future information environment may include intelligent software agents that collectively perform well-defined human tasks. Communication among human, software agents, and the Internet open source will need to be further explored. In addition to information exchange, we will be facing the challenge of information understanding (e.g., message meaning, etc.). Support for multiple languages (e.g., human and computer) allowing for semantics exchange and integration at the semantic level rather than the syntactic level will be essential.

Information, as processed by humans, is data perceived or noticed, selected and organized by its receiver, because of his subjective human interests, originating from his instincts, feelings, experience, intuition, common sense, values, beliefs, personal knowledge, or wisdom simultaneously processed by his cognitive and mental processes, and seamlessly integrated in his recallable knowledge. Users of an information system need a certain information. Information need is the conceptual incongruity in which a person's cognitive structure is not adequate to a task; when a person recognizes that something wrong in their state of knowledge and desires to resolve the anomaly; when the current state of possessed knowledge is less than is needed; when internal sense runs out; and when there is insufficient knowledge to cope with voids, uncertainty or conflict in a knowledge area. Within this complex framework users and their information needs have to be modeled explicitly. Therefore, conceptual modeling of information services incorporates modeling of the information need of users as well as modeling of their behavior.

Global information systems are based on a large variety of data structures such as text data, complex data, image data, graphical data, analog video data, digital video data, and digital audio data. These data differ not only in their intention and storage techniques but have quite different functionality attached to them and very different characteristics. In order to be used consistently a new conceptual modeling approach is necessary which can handle the integration of different media and their data together with the variety of functionality.

The www enables users of a database system to interact with other databases. Such database systems could be able to automatically discover and interact with other database systems available and accessible on the network. In this case database systems have to provide substantially more metadata that describes the structure, functionality and meaning of the data and information they manage. In order to communicate the DBMS must be able to cast data from other databases. Database systems communicating over a network can be based on federations of database systems with or without a trader and contracts. The collection of different databases can be understood as a farm of databases. Conceptual modeling of database farms together with modeling of supporting infrastructure is still an open issue. Modeling includes in this case also characterization of quality, accuracy and preciseness of the data from other and own sources.

Recent development of communication technologies, which include satellites, mobile, and personal communicators, offers high potential for information exchange at the universal level. Modeling of communication mechanisms and systems will be essential in order to provide the required exchanged information. Communication technology not only provides the freedom of information transportation, it is causing us to re-examine the boundaries of countries as well as the social, cultural, economic, and political systems in the information world. The question of „Are global understanding, communication, and information management in information systems possible?" (as discussed in some of the papers in [1]) remains as a challenge. Specific issues that need to be addressed include:

- Common model supporting multiple languages
- Information understanding
- Development of simple-to-comprehend information sources
- Semantic representation and exchange
- Communication technology integration

- Coping with federations and farms of databases
- Coping with a variety of different data types
- Internet integrity and policies establishment and enforcement
- Law and Internet law

Human Knowledge Integration

Information comes from our interactions as we associate with a specific domain. Data, knowledge, and information are viewed as three interrelated entities. Data, knowledge, or both may produce information. Data are generally presented to us through our senses. From that data, we infer the presence of objects or the existence of a state of affairs. The effect of this inference, which may involve reasoning, results in information. Knowledge is having information with understanding about something (e.g., an item, a specific domain, etc.). To understand X means forming some relationship(s) with X that may be direct or indirect. Direct relationship means having some experience with X. Indirect relationship means having facts about someone else's experience with X. As part of the world, human beings are among the facts to be learned. We know ourselves by knowing the world.

One of the purposes of information technology development is to produce tools for deriving information about different aspects of the world. As information needs to be discovered, understood, and described through various disciplines (e.g., history, science, philosophy, cognitive science, metaphysics, etc.), each discipline produces partial human knowledge about the world under a specific perspective.

Human knowledge can be understood from three perspectives as depicted in Figure 1, which is our modification of the figure originally proposed in [4]: (1) Normative: as knowledge of the laws and norms, (2) Situational: as knowledge of the world situation, and (3) Existential: as knowledge of ourselves. Each represents a perspective of the whole of human knowledge. Information collected from each perspective need to be integrated to achieve human knowledge understanding. Although the integrity and validity of the knowledge obtained from the Internet is not guaranteed, the Internet provides a new way for learning and knowledge integration. Fragments of human knowledge based on these three perspectives are in place.

Human knowledge integration is the ultimate goal for information technology development. The future Internet and www could be used as a tool for describing world history, beyond the vision of global digital libraries where people can find out the state-of-art and ongoing progress about each discipline (e.g., science, history, technology, philosophy, etc.). Information technology advancement will allow us to collectively experience the growth of the world, analyze its maturity, and learn from each other to establish a better human race.

The active modeling paradigm discussed early in this paper is a starting point for integrating human knowledge by focusing on methods for obtaining human knowledge. The active paradigm calls for collaborations among science and non-science research (i.e., use of language, logic, history, science and technology, philosophy, etc.) where further investigation of the following will be necessary:

- Perspective integration
- Summary information modeling and presentation
- Information quality

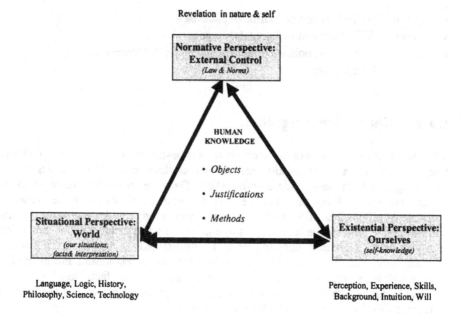

Fig.1. Human knowledge from different perspectives

- Integration science
- Coordination science

Concluding Remarks

In this paper, we have outlined several important areas for future research in conceptual modeling. Conceptual model has reached a high maturity due to the availability of a sound and complete theory. The active paradigm is used as an alternative for providing a closer conceptualization of the world to be implemented as a global information architecture. The active model allows for continual learning about the world and provides a constant challenge for technological inventions. Further studies of the relationships between natural languages and conceptual modeling will give us insights on developing better techniques on conceptual modeling and on better ways to represent and to translate semantics in different natural languages. New information services provided by the architecture will better support complex domains. Conceptual modeling is currently becoming the important foundation of interoperability and application engineering. The advent of the Internet and www presents a great motivation for further exploration of conceptual modeling, which directly impacts the information technology development. From manual file systems to electronic shareable documents, history seems to have repeated itself, albeit in a different manner. While the current focus is primarily on the syntactic aspects (e.g., language) of information management, we are entering an era where information content is a key concern. Through the software world, we are in a better position to pursue global understanding and communication via the integration of human knowledge from science and technology and from non-science disciplines, in order to build a better world for the future.

References

[1] Chen, P., Akoka, J., Kangassalo, A., and Thalheim, B. (eds.), *Conceptual Modeling: Current Issues and Future Directions*, LNCS 1565, Springer-Verlag, Heidelberg, 1998.

[2] *Communications of ACM. Vol. 40*, no. 2, February, 1997.

[3] Elmasri, R. and Navathe, S., *Fundamentals of Database Systems (second edition)*, The Benjamin/Cummings Publishing Company, Inc., 1994.

[4] Frame, J., *The Doctrine of the Knowledge of God*. Presbyterian and Reformed Publishing Co., Philipsburg, NJ, 1987.

[5] Mannila, H. and Räihä, K.-J., *The Design of Relational Databases*. Addison-Wesley, Reading, MD, 1992.

[6] Thalheim, B., *Fundamentals of Entity-Relationship Modeling*. Springer-Verlag, Heidelberg, 1999.

Author Index

Springer
and the
environment

At Springer we firmly believe that an
international science publisher has a
special obligation to the environment,
and our corporate policies consistently
reflect this conviction.
We also expect our business partners –
paper mills, printers, packaging
manufacturers, etc. – to commit
themselves to using materials and
production processes that do not harm
the environment. The paper in this
book is made from low- or no-chlorine
pulp and is acid free, in conformance
with international standards for paper
permanency.

Springer

Lecture Notes in Computer Science

For information about Vols. 1–1513
please contact your bookseller or Springer-Verlag